INTERNATIONAL JUSTICE

International Justice

Edited by
TONY COATES
Department of Politics
The University of Reading

Routledge
Taylor & Francis Group
LONDON AND NEW YORK

First published 2000 by Ashgate Publishing

Reissued 2018 by Routledge
2 Park Square, Milton Park, Abingdon, Oxon OX14 4RN
711 Third Avenue, New York, NY 10017, USA

Routledge is an imprint of the Taylor & Francis Group, an informa business

A Library of Congress record exists under LC control number: 99085922

ISBN 13: 978-1-138-70327-8 (hbk)
ISBN 13: 978-1-138-70326-1 (pbk)
ISBN 13: 978-1-315-20323-2 (ebk)

Contents

Acknowledgments vii
UK Association for Legal and Social Philosophy viii

Introduction 1
Tony Coates

SECTION 1: THE AUSTIN LECTURE 7

1 Is There a Right to Development? 9
Brian Barry

SECTION 2: TRADITIONS OF THOUGHT AND INTERNATIONAL JUSTICE 25

2 Justice and International Order 27
Chris Brown

3 International Justice and Just War Theory 46
Tony Coates

SECTION 3: PRINCIPLES AND CONCEPTS OF INTERNATIONAL JUSTICE 63

4 Universalism, Particularism and Cosmopolitan Justice 65
Michael Freeman

5 Cosmopolitan Communities 89
Lukas H. Meyer

6 International Justice – Amongst Whom? 111
Peter Jones

7 Global Equality of Opportunity and the Sovereignty of States 130
Simon Caney

8 Global Justice as Impartiality: Whither Claims to Equal Shares? 150
Andreas Føllesdal

9 Contractualism and the Moral Significance of Human Well-being 167
Matt Matravers

SECTION 4: SOME ISSUES AND PROBLEMS OF INTERNATIONAL JUSTICE 193

10 International Social Justice, Global Warming and Global Democracy 195
Barry Holden

11 Slaughtering a Few Sacred Cows: Do We Really Oppose International Intervention? 213
Avner de-Shalit

12 Justice and Fairness in the Battle Against Acid Rain 230
Cecilia Albin

13 Restoring Justice in the Aftermath of Conflict: Bridging the Gap between Theory and Practice 264
Rama Mani

List of Contributors 300

Acknowledgments

Most of the papers on which these chapters are based were first presented at the 25th Annual Conference of the UK Association for Legal and Social Philosophy, held at the University of Reading in April 1998. The editor is most grateful to the officers of the Association, particularly Pat FitzGerald and Sandra Marshall, and to Richard Bellamy and Pat Hicks, his colleagues at Reading, for their help in organizing the conference. He is also greatly indebted to Pat FitzGerald for her preparation of the manuscript for publication in camera-ready form.

UK Association for Legal and Social Philosophy

The UK Association for Legal and Social Philosophy (ALSP) is open to everyone interested in the interaction between theory and practice in the areas of legal, social and political thought; the interplay between these areas; and the applications and outcomes arising out of the inter-disciplinary nature of such debate. In seeking to extend debate beyond the traditional academy, it is especially concerned to include students and practitioners in its activities, as well as to promote discussion with, among and beyond full-time academics.

Membership is currently £35 (waged) or £17.50 (unwaged) per annum, and includes a subscription to *Res Publica: A Journal of Social and Legal Philosophy* and the Association's newsletter. For details, please write to the Treasurer, Henry Miller, 14 Southampton Street, Brighton, BN2 2UT or visit the Association's website at http://www.law.ed.ac.uk/alsp/ukalsp.htm.

Introduction

TONY COATES

This book is based on the proceedings of the 25th Annual Conference of the UK Association of Legal and Social Philosophy held in 1998 at the University of Reading. Most of the chapters originated as papers delivered at the conference. Naturally, the book reflects the interests and approaches of the conference participants. It is not intended to – nor does it – provide either a representative sample of contemporary thinking about international justice or a comprehensive survey of its subject matter. As it happens, most of the contributions belong to a liberal-cosmopolitan tradition of thought, though a tradition that is broadly enough defined to leave ample room for disagreement and argument.

In Section 1 the 1998 Austin Lecturer, Brian Barry, poses the question, 'is there a right to development?'. That the keynote address at the conference should have been given by Barry seems fitting, given his prominence in the contemporary debate about international justice, and the number of contributions to this volume that engage with Barry's work is evidence of his widespread influence. In the lecture Barry examines the idea of a right to development contained in the UN Declaration. He argues that the main deficiency of the Declaration is its statist bias (its understanding of the right to development as a *collective* right) and its neglect of the key issue of sustainability. He concludes that what is required is the adoption and working out of a cosmopolitan and intergenerational perspective that addresses the needs of *individuals* rather than those of states and collectivities.

In Section 2 Chris Brown and Tony Coates examine the idea of international justice in relation to different traditions of political and international theory. Chris Brown charts the emergence of international justice as a topic of international relations theory, an emergence that he attributes as much to political events as to theoretical developments. Brown argues that in its earlier manifestations, international relations theory was uniformly hostile to considerations of justice, at least in any substantive sense. The root cause of this hostility was the dominance of realism in the thinking of the discipline's founding fathers. Brown sees the increasing prominence given to international justice as vindication of a more idealistic, openly critical (even utopian) and constructivist approach to international relations.

Coates explores the just war concept of international justice. He argues that, by virtue of its classical natural law principles, the just war tradition is well placed to overcome the divide between realism and cosmopolitanism that is seen to mar discussion about international justice. The argument defends the claim that just war theory avoids the characteristic and damaging one-sidedness of other positions by giving due weight to *both* particularity and universality.

The chapters that make up Section 3 explore the principles and key concepts that inform the contemporary debate about international justice. Freeman and Meyer focus on the tension between particular and universal ties and obligations that activates most discussions. Michael Freeman's argument starts from the premise that '[i]f the concept of international justice is to be viable, ethical universalism must be vindicated'. At the same time, he acknowledges the ethical as well as the psychological force of particular attachments. The problem is seen to be one of reconciling the two, apparently conflicting, claims. His argument proceeds via a comparison of David Miller's ethical defence of nationalism with Brian Barry's argument for ethical universalism. Finding neither position entirely satisfactory, Freeman concludes by proposing the idea of 'cosmopolitan realism' – of an integrative and cosmopolitan form of nationalism that the adoption of a more complex, dispersed and multilayered, system of political authority might be expected to promote.

Lukas Meyer also focuses on the tension between 'loyalist' particularism and cosmopolitan universalism. While acknowledging that in some of its more abstract formulations liberal cosmopolitanism can appear indifferent to the particular attachments so dear to loyalists, Meyer argues that there is nothing inconsistent or incoherent about a cosmopolitan defence of particular values and loyalties – as long as it remains critical and discriminating. There, of course, lies the rub so far as international justice is concerned. Both Meyer and Freeman make it clear that cosmopolitan support for particular attachments is dependent upon acceptance of liberal values. In neither case, therefore, does universalism take a form that appears designed to respect the integrity and the worth of non-liberal societies and cultures.

Peter Jones' chapter, in which he examines the crucial issue of the bearer of rights, relates closely to the argument of Brian Barry's lecture. While sharing much of Barry's scepticism and concern about the status and role of states in the matter of international justice, Jones argues that if there *is* a right to development, then it must be a group right not an individual one. However, this emphasis on the group is not seen as prejudicial to liberal individualism, since 'the crucial matter is how we conceive political communities as bearers of rights and duties'. Distinguishing between 'corporate' (strong) and 'collective' (weak) conceptions of groups as moral claimants, Jones argues that we should regard the parties to international distributive justice as political communities in the collective sense. The chief merit of this approach, Jones suggests, is that it enables us 'to insist that the ultimate units of morality must be individual persons while recognizing fully the collective nature of human existence'.

Simon Caney defends global or cosmopolitan principles of distributive justice against particularists or those who oppose universalist norms in the name of the sovereign state. His defence involves the repudiation of some commonly voiced criticisms: that the promotion of international justice requires a repressive world government; that it undermines the freedom and independence of rich states; that it impairs the self-determination of recipient states; and, that it interferes with the state's fulfilment of its responsibilities towards its citizens. Caney argues that none of these claims is well founded, each being seen to rest on exaggerated or one-sided notions of what both state sovereignty and international justice entail.

Like other contributions to this volume Caney's essay can be seen as an attempt to unite the particularist and universalist poles of the argument about justice. While highly critical of some versions of the state sovereignty position, Caney is at pains to demonstrate the commitment of cosmopolitanism to at least some of the values associated with the advocacy of state sovereignty. Whether he does enough to satisfy external critics of liberal cosmopolitanism is another matter. As with Freeman and Meyer, his acceptance of state sovereignty appears conditional upon the state's acceptance of liberal values, principles and institutions. Such highly qualified acceptance leaves non-liberal states in a position of some vulnerability.

Among liberal cosmopolitan accounts of international justice the idea of justice as impartiality is widespread. Part of its attraction for liberals is its perceived capacity to uphold considerations of justice while respecting that plurality of values that is seen to exist both domestically (at least in the West) and internationally. In the idea of justice as impartiality the universal claims of justice appear reconcilable with the diverse conceptions of the good that define the present condition of humanity.

Several contributions adopt an impartialist approach but two in particular consider the nature and the merits of the impartialist argument itself. Andreas

Føllesdal argues that the contractualist or impartialist account of justice can uphold the normative and distributive significance of state borders (as Rawls originally argued). Such an account is not seen to entail a global as well as a domestic difference principle. In a states-system, giving moderate priority to compatriots on the basis of shared social institutions (*not* on the basis of shared values) is seen to be justified provided that economic and financial regimes secure basic human needs and prevent domination by rich states. With the perceived breakdown of the states-system, however, and with increasing global participation in shared institutions, the case for the moderate priority of compatriots is seen to weaken.

Matt Matravers' criticism of the impartialist theory of justice is sympathetic yet fundamental. Its focus is that distinction between the *right* (which defines the public sphere – the sphere of justice) and the *good* (which defines the private and the moral sphere) on which the entire impartialist project is often seen to turn. Matravers argues that this key distinction is radically unstable and that a satisfactory account of justice cannot remain neutral between competing conceptions of the good (as the impartialist theory requires). He proposes 'an alternative liberal theory' that is based explicitly on a concept of the good or of human well-being, a suitably thin concept, formed in the light of liberal principles and values and designed to secure the interests of individuals.

One of the merits of Matravers' criticism is that it makes explicit what remains implicit or covert in impartialist accounts of justice, namely, that they are not in fact impartial or neutral between conceptions of the good. The rational and autonomous individual (with a commitment to 'reasonableness' and a detachment from, or independence of, concrete social norms and institutions) that the impartialist project presupposes is, as communitarian critics have often argued, itself a liberal construct and an expression of liberal values.

The question is what impact does this unmasking have on the issue of international justice? Does an explicitly liberal concept of the human good hold 'the promise of universality' that any satisfactory theory of international justice requires? It seems not. The 'thin' concept of the good is deceptively intrusive. The moral primacy that such a concept of the good gives to individual autonomy seems inherently at odds with those cultures and societies that take a more traditional and collective form.

Section 4 of the book addresses more specific issues and concerns. Writing from a cosmopolitan standpoint, Barry Holden argues that the current form of international governance is fundamentally inadequate. It does little to advance the cause of international justice and impedes the solution of such urgent problems as global warming. Its principal defect is seen to be its failure to generate a sense of global community, a deficiency that a new democratic form of global governance is expected to rectify. Here is a functional argument for global democracy. Its key role and chief merit would lie in its promotion of a cosmopolitan consciousness and global citizenry. The gravity and urgency of the specific issue is used to lend momentum to the moral and institutional project of cosmopolitanism.

Avner de-Shalit takes up the issue of intervention. Though defending the principle of international intervention and dismissing arguments against it based on state sovereignty and autonomy, de-Shalit is as much concerned to make a humanitarian case *against* intervention as he is to make a case *for* it. By adopting a broad ('socialist') concept of intervention that focuses on its diverse forms (economic, ideological or cultural, and military), he identifies an array of existing and, arguably, unjust forms of intervention. Whatever form international intervention takes, from the ethical, humanitarian and 'socialist' standpoint adopted by de-Shalit, the fundamental question is 'whether it is exploitative or not'. Is it designed to secure the autonomy and well-being of the state subject to intervention, or is it simply a way, more or less covert, of protecting and promoting the interests of the intervening state or states?

A radical scepticism about the practicality and utility of international ethics in general, and of justice in particular, has been a fundamental theme of the realist tradition. However laudable as moral aspirations, or as guides to personal conduct, such ways of thinking are seen to be out of place in the imperfect and hostile world of international relations. Inefficacy is compounded by the very real threat that these moral aspirations are seen to pose to the fragile peace that, at best, characterizes international relations. Cecilia Albin and Rama Mani meet this criticism head-on by arguing that justice is an essential part of any realistic or effective process of peacemaking or conflict-resolution.

Albin examines the part played by considerations of justice and fairness in the European acid rain talks that commenced in the mid-1970s and that culminated in the 1994 Oslo Protocol. While acknowledging the central role of power and interests, Albin argues that the appeal to ethics in those negotiations was more than merely ideological or rhetorical, and that the progress of negotiations depended crucially on the creative interplay of ethical principle and national interest. Perhaps there is an important lesson here for both realists and moralists.

In her study of peacemaking Rama Mani argues that, far from being a luxury that we can ill afford, justice is indispensable. There can be no real peace without it. The resolution of conflict – its real overcoming as distinct from its temporary cessation – is seen to be impossible without addressing the demands of justice. In the ensuing argument Mani explores the varied nature of those demands: 'rectificatory', 'distributive' and 'restorative' justice are all seen to play their part in the complex and arduous process of peacemaking.

Mani's emphasis on justice as an essential part of the strategy of peacemaking appears well founded. At the same time, here as elsewhere, realist concerns must never be ignored. In the realm of international relations a surfeit of morality can be as dangerous as a deficit. Considerations of justice need to be balanced by considerations of order. Nowhere is this more urgent than in the case of war, where an unbridled concern for justice may generate a moral enthusiasm that threatens to sweep aside all moral inhibitions over the use of force. To fulfil its promise of a safer and a better world the idea of international justice needs to be applied with restraint. A 'militant humanitarianism' can be at least as dangerous as some more obvious expression of militarism. How to avoid such excess without surrendering to moral complacency and the passive acceptance of the international status quo is, perhaps, the fundamental problem to which the achievement of international justice requires a solution.

SECTION 1
THE AUSTIN LECTURE

1 Is There a Right to Development?

BRIAN BARRY

The Status of International Law

John Austin notoriously claimed that there was no such thing as international law because it failed to satisfy his criterion for a law that it should be a command issued by a sovereign and backed by sanctions. However, as Herbert Hart reminded us in *The Concept of Law*, his master, 'Bentham, the inventor of the expression "international law", defended it simply by saying that it was "sufficiently analogous" to municipal law' (Hart, 1994, p. 237). To the dismay of some of my audience – and the relief of others, no doubt – I shall assume that the anti-Austinians have the best of it. This still leaves all the usual questions about the sources of international law. Since I intend to focus on the United Nations Declaration on the Right to Development, adopted by the General Assembly in 1986, I need to say a little about this, if only to motivate further discussion of this right.[1]

Writing in 1961, Hart argued that, although international law had enough in common with municipal law to count as law, it lacked the crucial feature of being a union of primary and secondary rules, and was simply a set of primary rules. However, he concluded by saying that international law was 'perhaps' in a 'stage of transition' towards 'a basic rule of recognition', and that this would 'bring it nearer in structure to a municipal system' (Hart, 1994, p. 236). Almost 40 years later, it seems that a good case can be made for saying that the transition has occurred and that the United Nations itself constitutes, at any rate under some conditions, an authoritative source of international law, binding on states without their having to sign up to some relevant Covenant. If this is so, the United Nations has come to occupy a position analogous to that of the state in a municipal system.

One fairly straightforward move here is to say that the Charter of the United Nations is subscribed to by all states as a condition of membership, and that the General Assembly can articulate its implications. 'Surprising as it may seem', Oscar Schachter (quoted in Steiner and Alston, 1996, pp. 134–5) has written,

> the authority of the General Assembly to issue such declaratory resolutions was accepted from the beginning. At its first session, in 1946, the Assembly considered the Nuremberg Principles and they 'affirmed' them in a unanimous resolution. In another resolution adopted at the same session, genocide was declared a crime under international law. This, too, was unanimous .... The Assembly also interpreted and applied the Charter in particular cases, characterizing certain conduct as illegal. The resolutions condemning South Africa for apartheid and for its administration of South West Africa fall into this category. The competence of the Assembly to do this ... was not questioned.

Does the Declaration on the Right to Development fall within the ambit of the Charter? The Preamble cites 'the purposes and principles of the Charter' but does not make any very precise connection. Perhaps the best case would be to follow the line taken by many supporters of the Right to Development, that it is a necessary means to the realization of the right of peoples to self-determination, and that claim is in fact made in Article 1 (2) of the Declaration. Article 1 (2) of the Charter refers to 'the principle of ... self-determination of peoples', so the connection is secure as long as the claim that the Right to Development is accepted as following from it. Leaving aside the notorious issues involved in the interpretation of the principle of self-determination by the United Nations (about which I shall say a little later), it seems plausible to me to argue that this further step is a step too far.

However, that is not decisive because we may be prepared to give credence to 'a declaratory resolution that purports to state the law independently of any Charter rule'. Schachter suggests:

> When all the States in the United Nations declare that a ... norm is legally binding, it is difficult to dismiss that determination as ultra vires – or reduce it to a recommendation because it was made in the General Assembly. The fact is that the declaration purports to express the *opinio juris communis*, not a recommendation ... (ibid., p. 135).

This is not, however, a lot of help to the Declaration on the Right to Development because it was not adopted unanimously: the USA voted against, and eight countries abstained, including Britain, West Germany (as it was then) and Japan (see Carty, 1992, pp. 43–60, 59). Moreover, the Working Group set up by the Commission on Human Rights in 1993 'to clarify the concept and make it operational' has failed to get anywhere, reflecting the underlying lack of consensus (Steiner and Alston, 1996, p. 112). If we add to this the absence of decisions in international fora based on the Declaration, it seems fairly safe to say that there is, as a matter of international law, no Right to Development.

This is not, however, my primary concern here. As a political philosopher rather than a student of international law, I am more interested in the question of whether or not there should be a right to development. Quite apart from interest, I certainly feel more competent to address that question. To that end, I shall proceed as follows. First, I shall say something about the part played by the concept of rights in United Nations discourse. I shall then respond to the recent criticism of rights in general, but go on to argue that for several reasons rights are not a useful or plausible way in which to frame whatever claims poor countries have on rich ones. I shall instead suggest that what is needed is a cosmopolitan conception of intergenerational global justice.

Individual and Group Rights

Rights are the *lingua franca* of the United Nations. Virtually all the Declarations and Covenants of the United Nations fall into the pattern of enunciating rights – rights, it may be added, of very heterogeneous kinds. There are a lot of proposed ways of dividing them up, but for my purposes the most useful line of division is between individual rights and group rights. In order to make progress, however, I shall have to take a rather dogmatic line on issues that much ink has been spilt on. In my defence, I shall remark that a good deal of the debate strikes me as pretty barren.

Individual rights, then, are rights that can be claimed by individuals, typically against governments – the rights not to be 'disappeared', tortured or convicted without a fair trial, for example. Some individual rights may require association with others to be effective – for example, most religious faiths make at any rate some acts of worship collective acts, but the right to freedom of worship is still an individual right. The contrast here is with irreducibly collective rights, that is to say rights that cannot intelligibly be predicated on anything except a group. Thus, obviously, the right of a state that has been duly recognized to be represented in the United Nations is uncontroversially a right that can be attributed only to states. Similarly, if we say that states have a right not to be subject to aggressive warfare conducted by other states, that is also a right that is necessarily predicated of states.

There are also rights that are ascribed to 'peoples' and these too are necessarily held collectively. That is not to deny that an objection to some practice may be made by or on behalf of an individual. The point is simply that the practice objected to must be one that affects the individual in his or her capacity of group member. Thus, the crime of genocide is defined as 'acts committed with an intent to destroy – in whole or in part – a national, ethnical, racial or religious group, as such'. One of these acts is, of course, 'killing members of the group', but only when it forms part of a genocidal plan: 'the murder of a single individual may be characterized as genocide if it constitutes a part of a series of acts designed to attain the destruction of the group to which the victim belonged'.[2]

Another necessarily collective right is the right to self-determination. This is supposed to be a right of 'peoples' but it is familiar ground that 'peoples' have been interpreted in a highly statist fashion, so that they are inhabitants of some preexisting political entity, such as (especially such as) colonies. Even where the United Nations has become involved in the dismemberment of a state, as it did in the former Yugoslavia, it has insisted on sub-state statism, ruling out the possibility of changes in their territorial boundaries without the consent of the governments involved, for example, Serbia and Croatia. There is obviously much to be said against this, and the sub-state extension is especially obnoxious because of the way in which it faces states with perverse incentives. (Would an Italian legislature be as willing as it was to carve out an autonomous province of Alto Adige for its predominantly German-speaking population if it had realized it was creating a prima facie basis for secession?) Suppose, however, that 'peoples' were to be read more along the lines of the groups that have been declared to be potential victims of genocide. It would still have to be true that self-determination is a collective right if it is a right at all. For the 'self' in 'self-determination' cannot be a single individual. Any claims that an individual can make must be simply for the 'people' to whom he or she belongs to be able to exercise the right to self-determination.

The right to development is, I suggest, of this irreducibly collective nature. The wording of the declaration of the Right to Development attempts to fudge this, so as to relate it to the discourse of human rights, conceived of in individual terms. Thus, Article 1 (1) runs as follows:

> The right to development is an inalienable human right by virtue of which every human person and all peoples are entitled to participate in, contribute to, and enjoy economic, social, cultural and political development, in which all human rights and fundamental freedoms can be fully realized.

But the notion of an individual right to development is surely paper-thin here. Just as killing one person amounts to an act of genocide only in a larger context, so an individual could complain of a violation of the right to development only by pointing to disadvantages shared with others. Article 2 (2) characterizes the right more perspicuously by saying that everybody has a responsibility to 'promote and protect an appropriate political, social and economic order for development'.

Another way of reaching the same conclusion is to go back to the point already made about the connection with the right to self-determination. Article 1(2) reads as follows:

> The human right to development also implies the full realization of the right of peoples to self-determination, which includes, subject to the relevant provisions of both International Covenants on Human Rights, the exercise of their inalienable right to full sovereignty over all their natural wealth and resources.

Whatever we think of these claims, they are undeniably collective in nature: they are the rights of 'peoples' (in practice, of course, states) to self-determination in some form stronger than formal sovereignty, and to collective control over the exploitation of natural resources. Indeed, the statist content of the right to development is made explicit in Article 3, which says: 'States have the primary responsibility for the creation of national and international conditions favourable to the realization of the right to development.'

I should add, for the sake of heading off legitimate criticism, that not all rights fall neatly into the individual or collective category. There are undeniably borderline cases, of which the most important appears to me to be that of the rights of minorities. However, I do not believe that it is a matter of indifference how such rights are expressed. It is not that the same content emerges from both ways of setting up the rights. Rather, there are competing conceptions of what the point of such rights is, and the difference has potentially important implications.

Thus, the title of the Declaration concerned with minorities is individualistic: it is 'on the Rights of persons Belonging to National or Ethnic, Religious and Linguistic Minorities'. And most of the text is in terms of the rights of 'persons belonging to' these minorities. However, the document as a whole straddles individual and collective versions, in that Article 1 (1) reads as follows: 'States shall protect the existence and the national or ethnic, cultural, religious and linguistic identity of minorities within their respective territories, and shall encourage conditions for the promotion of that identity' (Phillips and Rosas, 1995, pp. 159–64). It is interesting that this odd-clause-out came into being only in the last round of drafting: the text adopted by the Working Group on first reading had the option, as did the remaining articles, of either referring to minorities or individuals belonging to minorities (ibid., p. 190).

Does it make a difference? I think it does. Consider one of the best-known cases brought under Article 27 of the International Covenant on Civil and Political Rights. This Article is set out in individualistic terms, saying that 'persons belonging to ... minorities shall not be denied the right, in community with the other members of their group, to enjoy their own culture, to profess and practice their own religion, or to use their own language' (ibid.). Sandra Lovelace was 'born and registered as a Maliseet Indian' in Canada, and lost her membership in the band when she married a non-Indian (ibid., p. 238). At the time of her submission to the Human Rights Committee, she had 'returned to the Reserve with her children' but was able to remain 'only because dissident members of the tribe who support[ed] her [had] threatened to resort to physical violence in her defence should the authorities attempt to remove her' (ibid., p. 243). Sandra Lovelace won her case, but had the relevant rights been set out in collective terms, it seems to me that the outcome would have been far more in doubt. As it was, she was able to claim against the Band Council that she was being denied the right to enjoy her culture as a Maliseet Indian. But if the right had been stated on the lines of Article 1(1) of the Declaration, the Canadian government would surely have had a much stronger case for saying that, in supporting the Band Council, it was carrying out the duty laid on states by the Declaration to 'protect the existence and the ... identity of minorities ... and ... encourage conditions for the promotion of that identity'.

In Defence of Rights

As far as I can tell, when the centenary of the French Revolution came round in 1879, the general view was that, although (of course) there were some regrettable excesses, it was on the whole, in the terms of *1066 and All That*, a Good Thing. By 1979, the verdict seemed to be a good deal more mixed, and in the following two decades the backlash against liberty, equality and secular rationality has accelerated. This naturally goes with a profound scepticism about the value of rights in general and universal human rights in particular.

In Britain, the fag-end of American so-called communitarianism *à la* Etzioni forms an unholy (or, unfortunately, holy) alliance with a form of Christian socialism in which the socialist element has been discarded. As Ian

Bell wrote in the *Observer* (1998, p. 26),

> The whiff of the Sunday School is everywhere. It radiates from Harriet Harman as she strokes the wash'n'work hair of all those lovely industrious 'mums' (no more Listen with Non-Working Mother for you, children). It informs the muscular Christian platitudes in Mr Field's Green Paper. It is the phlogiston in Tony Blair's burning ambition to make us decent and pleasant at last.... We should not misunderstand the moral dimension of the Blairite project. It has a particular nature, a conservative cast. A taste for a little safe-but-groovy music aside, it shares the Tory distaste for the Sixties, for their sexual liberties, for the personal freedoms which ensnared even the son of the impeccably moral Jack Straw. There is a specific spooky moral imperative to government now.

The code for all this is that rights have got out of hand and need to be balanced by responsibilities. In fact, all the rights that are being complained of have correlative duties: they are not what are usually called liberty-rights. The real complaint about many social and economic rights is that the correlative duties lie with governments and through them with the rich and powerful. Thus, if we suppose there to be a right to a decent standard of living (say half the average income), then this imposes quite stringent duties on those with high incomes to pay taxes to provide the wherewithal. Similarly, if we think that there is a right to employment, this directs attention away from so-called 'employability' (which makes the duty of getting employed fall on the potential employee) and instead on the duties of employers to make it possible for people (e.g. the disabled or those with young children to care for) to work, puts the onus on shareholders to accept that they will have to put up with smaller profits in the public interest, and probably casts the state in the role of employer of last resort.

I would argue that instead of talking about the balance of rights and responsibilities – which is essentially to deny that there are any social and economic rights of citizens – we should talk about the balance of *advantages* and responsibilities. In other words, those who do do especially well under the prevailing rules – those with inherited wealth, those with high earnings, shareholders and so on – should make up for their good fortune (which they enjoy only because the state enforces the rules) by accepting greater responsibilities towards the rest of the society.

On the international scene, there is an equally if not more sinister development in the form of a proposal that, parallel to the Universal Declaration of Human Rights, there should be a Universal Declaration of Duties. There is a project on this which is being run by the Philosophy and Ethics Division of

UNESCO. Having joined the group for its most recent meeting (in December 1997), I am delighted to be able to say that this appears to be going nowhere, and I certainly did my bit to help that outcome along. However, Hans Küng has proved utterly tireless in promoting the draft declaration. Having drawn a blank with our group (he stormed off, muttering imprecations), he is still hoping to get it before the United Nations via a rather rum body consisting of ex-prime ministers and presidents. (Jim Callaghan is our representative, incidentally, and is reputed to be hanging on for grim death so as to keep Baroness Thatcher out.) This bunch of has-beens, which includes Lee Kuan Yew, has endorsed Küng's draft, and I am given to understand that this will help it on its way towards the United Nations General Assembly.

It strikes me as a good general principle that anything supported by Lee Kuan Yew should be opposed. Whether this generalization is correct or not, it is definitely valid in this case. As with the Blairite agenda, the duties tend to be those of the citizens and states are invited to enforce them. Thus, there is a deeply unpleasant Article about the responsibilities of journalists, which manifestly plays into the hands of authoritarian regimes such as those in Singapore, Malaysia and Indonesia, in which journalists guilty of 'irresponsible' reporting (as defined by the state) are jailed. The reason for having a Declaration of Rights and not a Declaration of Duties is that governments need no encouragement to impose duties: their metier is to do that anyway. What they are reluctant to do is concede rights, and that is why international pressure is needed to enforce human rights.

The Basis of Rights

Where do rights come from? There is a legal, if disputed, answer to this question: that an internationally recognized right exists if it forms part of customary law, and customary law can (perhaps rather curiously) be added to by declarations of the United Nations (especially if unanimous) and maybe also by Covenants (if they have so many signatories as to create normative pressure even on non-signatories), so long as enough judicial or quasi-judicial bodies salute them. But that still leaves a philosophical question: what lies behind them? How do we argue for rights?

From a philosophical point of view, declaring a right is a form of justification that has all the advantages of theft over honest toil. Peter Jones (1994, p. 5) has summed up this objection to rights as follows:

> People have a way of just 'declaring' rights as if nothing need be said in justification of what they declare. Disputes phrased in terms of rights often present us with little more than assertions and counter-assertions .... The rhetoric of rights can seem to do more to impede than aid our understanding of moral and political issues.

Rights are a conclusion, not a premise. But that does not mean that the premises are necessarily elusive. Rosalyn Higgins, an ex-colleague at the LSE who is now a judge on the International Court of Justice, has put the case for human rights eloquently, and I can do no better than quote her. She points out that the cultural relativist argument against universality (quoted in Steiner and Alston, 1996, pp. 219–20)

> is rarely advanced by the oppressed, who are only too anxious to benefit from perceived universal standards. The non-universal relativist view of human rights is in fact a very state-centred view and loses sight of the fact that *human* rights are human rights and not dependent on the fact that states, or groupings of states, may behave differently from each other so far as their politics, economic policy and culture are concerned. I believe, profoundly, in the universality of the human spirit. Individuals everywhere want the same essential things: to have sufficient food and shelter; to be able to speak freely; to practice their own religion or to abstain from religious belief; to feel that their person is not threatened by the state; to know that they will not be tortured, or detained without charge, and that, if charged, they will have a fair trial. I believe there is nothing in these aspirations that is dependent upon culture, or religion or stage of development. They are as keenly felt by the African tribesman as by the European city-dweller, by the inhabitant of a Latin American shanty-town as by the resident of a Manhattan apartment.

The case for human rights is, in essence, that their observance is necessary to secure the minimal conditions for a decent life. But Higgins's emphasis on these rights as necessary to individuals raises in an especially acute form the question of the rationale, if any, for intrinsically collective rights. I am going to assume without argument that collectivities have no value as such. That is to say, whatever value collectivities have is reducible without remainder to the value they contribute to the lives of individual human beings. This does not, of course, make it impossible to justify universal collective rights. But it does mean that any justification has to jump a high hurdle – and quite right too.

I do not wish to rule out the possibility that there might be justifiable rights of this intrinsically collective kind. However, I do not believe, on reflection, that it is in fact possible to justify any. If we start from the premise that the only justification for a collective right is that it serves the interests of individuals, we shall not find any collective right that invariably has this property. A collective right is a right for a collectivity – a state or a 'people', however we construe that – to do what it likes within a certain sphere. But whether or not the possession of that right actually serves individual interests depends entirely on what use is made of it. I am unable to think of any collective right whose contribution to human well-being is not contingent in this way on what is done with it. If this is so, there are no unconditional collective rights, in other words no universal collective rights.

The right of a state not to be invaded by another is one of the most firmly established in the postwar scheme of international law. And most of the time it is no doubt beneficial, compared to the alternative. But it is trumped by the crime of genocide, so India's war with Pakistan to get that state out of the half of its territory that became Bangladesh was laudable. That it served India's interests by dismembering its regional rival does not make that any less the case. The NATO attack on Serbian forces in Kosovo in 1999 is another example.

An example of a collective right whose value is far more deeply contingent than that one is the right of self-determination. There is simply no *a priori* expectation that any given act of self-determination would on balance be beneficial for all the individuals affected. These include, needless to say, all those within the territory of the proposed state but also those outside its borders, including, but not limited to, those in the larger state or states in which the territory of the proposed new state lies. Where a group with sufficiently nation-like features is being oppressed, self-determination may well be better than the alternatives, even if one has no illusions about the likely course of politics in the new state. The Tibetans, the Kurds, the Kosovans and the Palestinians are obvious current candidates under this head.

Conversely, some 'peoples' want self-determination primarily in order the settle accounts with minorities in the territory they claim as their homeland. The entire grisly Yugoslav unravelling was set off when the (at first *de facto* then *de jure*) independent Croatian state set about eliminating Serbs from the police force, the civil administration and even ordinary jobs (see Glenny, 1992). Similarly, the creation of a separate Slovak republic has put in power a government marked by particularly virulent cultural nationalism, which has immediately engaged in harsh measures aimed at the 20 per cent of ethnic Hungarians, including the attempt to suppress Hungarian as a medium of instruction in schools, a refusal to require officials to respond to Hungarian, and the gerrymandering of local government boundaries so that there will be no sub-units within which ethnic Hungarians form a majority.

The Right to Development

What of the Right to Development? Many of the articles that make up the Declaration are totally unexceptionable, but this is because they have nothing to do with the notion of a collective right at all. Thus, Article 6 (1) says that 'All States should cooperate with a view to promoting, encouraging and strengthening universal respect for and observance of all human rights and fundamental freedoms for all without any distinction as to race, sex, language or religion', and the rest of the Article continues in the same vein. Aside from its imparting a high-minded tone to the whole Declaration, it is hard to see what this kind of thing is doing in it at all, since it adds absolutely nothing to existing, and well-established, documents.

However, anybody who was not born yesterday knows perfectly well that this is not what it is all about. The Declaration on the Right to Development is a recycling at a higher level of abstraction of the New International Economic Order promoted by the so-called 'Group of 77' and its organ within the United Nations, the UN Conference on Trade and Development (UNCTAD). Inspired by the misleading success of OPEC, the leaders of a number of 'Third World' countries came up with the idea that the rich countries should cooperate in establishing an international commodity regime aimed at regulating the prices of raw materials. Although officially presented as a way of ironing out fluctuations, it would have been regarded as a flop if it had not in fact driven up prices, leaving a worldwide analogue of the Common Agricultural Policy in which the only alternatives were indefinite stockpiling or the enforcement of production quotas on a country-by-country basis.

Needless to say, the industrialized countries declined to cooperate and the whole idea collapsed. But its attraction to the Third World elites who sponsored it is easy enough to see. It would, if it had worked, have provided countries that were large exporters of raw materials with unconditional incomes above the pre-existing level. The governments of relatively poor countries (though not the poorest countries, which would on balance have lost) would thus have gained greater autonomy, since they would have become less dependent on either borrowing or official aid.

That the Declaration is the lineal descendant of the new international economic order (NIEO) is shown especially by Article 2. Thus, the first part of it makes the connection with self-determination. In terms of the familiar distinction between first-generation rights (civil and political) and second-generation rights (social and economic), the Right to Development is presented as the second-generation analogue of the first-generation right to political self-determination. This, however, highlights its limitations. Whether or not more power for governments is good for individuals depends on what they do with that power. Many Third World governments are pure kleptocracies, intent only on looting the country and transferring as much of its national income as they can get their hands on into Swiss bank accounts. Even the rest are for the most unprepared to undertake serious land reform or tackle huge disparities between the standard of living of the elite and the majority. To the extent that the effect of the Declaration would be to give these governments more elbow room it would clearly be either irrelevant or positively inimical to the objective of securing to everybody in the world conditions for a decent life – adequate diet, shelter, pure water and sanitation, health care and education, for example.

The second part of Article 2 is a straight holdover from the era of the NIEO in declaring the right to state sovereignty over all natural resources within the state's territorial boundaries (including, of course, its offshore boundary). It is clearly related to the notion of economic self-determination in that it again enables at any rate those states endowed with valuable natural resources to gain a certain degree of autonomy. I believe that this claim to a collective right over the natural resources within a state's territory is wholly misconceived. It is a last gasp of the discredited notion of state sovereignty and should be replaced with the idea of natural resources as the heritage of mankind as a whole.

The implication of that idea is that the value realized from the exploitation of natural resources should be subject to an international levy and divided in a way that attributes to each person in the world an equal share. However, precisely because most states are such inadequate guardians of the majority of their populations, there would be no point in doing this unless the money were distributed to states conditionally upon its getting to everybody (or the poor especially) either in the form of a basic income or public goods specifically benefiting the poor either exclusively or at least proportionally. It need hardly be said that this focus on the internal distribution of resources is the last thing that most third world governments want, so it is not a practical proposal. If, some day, a clear majority of governments were genuinely concerned with the well-being of their citizens, however, a measure such as this could be an effective instrument for pulling the rest into line, since they would have to clean up their act to get the money while being subject to economic sanctions if they did not pay their contributions to the fund.

Article 4 (2) of the Declaration reads as follows:

> Sustained action is required to promote more rapid development of developing countries. As a complement to the efforts of developing countries, effective international cooperation is essential in providing these countries with appropriate means and facilities to foster their comprehensive development.

This is fine as far as it goes, but it conceals two major issues raised by the idea of a Right to Development. The first is: who has the right? The entire Declaration is highly state-centric: Article 3 (1) says that 'States have the primary responsibility of the creation of national and international conditions favourable to the realization of the right to development'. But what if the main obstacle to development is the state itself – its corruption and incompetence? Then it seems that the right to development subsists in the inhabitants against the government, and the most useful thing other states can do is to help them to overthrow it.

Moreover, this may be almost the only thing that other states can do. It is by now plain that, in the absence of effective public administration and a rule of law that secures property and other rights, external aid is of no avail. Even if we say that the proper claimants of a 'right to development' are 'peoples' rather than states, the right can be claimed only by 'peoples' who want development enough to give up competing aspirations. Hobbes postulated that the fear of violent death was the supreme motive among human beings. As a universal statement, this was clearly wrong. Many millions of people have proved that they would sooner pursue religious or national collective goals than live in peace and prosperity.

It is a hard but unavoidable truth that people cannot make any claims on others for economic assistance if they themselves rank prosperity below settling scores with other ethnic groups, forcibly imposing a particular interpretation of a religion on a whole society, fighting with other countries over boundaries, and so on. There are, in other words, a variety of institutions and motivations that are basic to economic development and in their absence there can be no economic development and therefore no right to it. There may still be a case for humanitarian aid, but this should be sharply distinguished from development aid, since it does nothing for economic self-sufficiency and if anything tends to undermine it. Even then, there is no obligation to give aid unless the conditions exist in which it can be effective. I read a couple of years ago of an international aid worker in Rwanda complaining of 'compassion fatigue' and saying 'Whenever we build a school they burn it down.' Assuming this to be true, refusing to rebuild the school under existing circumstances is not 'compassion fatigue' but elementary rationality.

The final nail in the coffin of the Right to Development is that the entire Declaration does not contain the word 'sustainability'. Surely, whatever we think is the basis of the claim of all contemporary human beings to the resources necessary for a decent life, it must entail that people in the future have exactly the same claim. Therefore, whatever economic development occurs in the present must be compatible with the demands of intergenerational justice. I take the key demand of intergenerational justice to be a sort of intertemporal version of the Golden Rule: the current generation should not collectively have a higher material standard of living than can be maintained indefinitely into the future.

If we call this condition 'sustainability', then it is clear that sustainability can be defined only over the world as a whole: 'sustainability in one country' is a manifest absurdity. It follows from this that there can be no unconditional right to development, any more than the already rich countries can have a right to produce any amount they like in any way they like. All development must therefore take place within the constraints that are required to maintain biodiversity, reduce 'greenhouse gas' emissions, prevent the pollution of the marine environment, and so on.

Although many third world countries are grievous offenders against sustainability (Brazil and Indonesia are two especially prominent examples), the rich countries must accept most of the responsibility. Japan provides the markets for the timber cut so destructively in Indonesia and Americans eat the hamburgers made from the cattle reared on the fragile soil of cleared Brazilian rain forest. And the rich countries contribute the great bulk of the 'greenhouse gas' emissions. What this means is that it makes no sense at all to isolate a 'right to development' for certain countries when what is needed is a global strategy for a move towards justice among contemporaries and between generations. But what is justice? You will be relieved to hear that I do not propose to offer an answer to that question here. If I may end this chapter with a plug, however, may I refer you to a book recently published by Princeton University Press and edited by David Mapel and Terry Nardin. It is entitled *International Society* and contains an essay by me on 'International Society from a Cosmopolitan Perspective', which lays out some ideas on the requirements of justice in this context.

Notes

1 *Declaration on the Right to Development*, General Assembly Res. 41 /128 (1996). Abbreviated text on pp. 1124–6 of Steiner and Alston, 1996.
2 All quotes from p. 1028 of Distein, 1996.

References

Bell, I. (1988), *The Observer*, 29 March.
Carty, A. (1992), 'The Third World Claim to Economic Self-Determination: Economic Rights of Peoples: Theoretical Aspects' in S.R. Chowdhury, E.M.G. Denters and P.J.I.M. de Waart (eds), *The Right to Development in International Law*, Martinus Nijhoff, Dordrecht.
Distein, Y. (1996) 'International Criminal Law' in H.J. Steiner and P. Alston (eds), *International Human Rights in Context: Law, Politics, Morals*, Clarendon Press, Oxford.
Glenny, M. (199), *The Death of Yugoslavia: The Third Balkan War*, Penguin Books, London.
Hart, H.L.A. (1995) [1961], *The Concept of Law*, Clarendon Press, Oxford.
Jones, P. (1994), *Rights*, Macmillan, London.
Phillips, A. and Rosas, A. (1995), *Universal Minority Rights*, Abo Akademie University Institute for Human Rights, Turku/Abo and London.
Steiner, H.J and Alston, P. (eds) (1996), *International Human Rights in Context: Law, Politics, Morals*, Clarendon Press, Oxford.

SECTION 2
TRADITIONS OF THOUGHT AND INTERNATIONAL JUSTICE

2 Justice and International Order

CHRIS BROWN

Introduction

In recent years 'international justice' has become a recognized focus for academic study, with an already sizeable, and growing, literature of its own (Brown, 1997). Contributions to this literature have come from a number of different starting points, most particularly from the 'justice industry' revived by Rawls in 1971 and now a multinational enterprise with global reach, and from the, not-unrelated, 'Kantian' revival in the philosophy of international law (Rawls, 1971: Tesón, 1998). What is, however, noticeable is that the contribution of scholars of international relations (IR) to discourse on international justice has been comparatively minor. There seems to be something about the professional formation of IR that makes its practitioners reluctant to engage with the subject in its full sense, that is to say as encompassing both formal and distributive conceptions of justice. Some IR scholars have no truck with the notion at all, others take on formal or procedural conceptions quite readily but very few are prepared to think seriously about international social justice.

As someone whose own background is in IR but who *is* interested in international social justice, I find this interesting, and a little worrying. What I want to do in this essay is to examine how and why most of my professional colleagues in international relations theory approach things rather differently from the way I do! First, I will, quite briefly, outline the characteristic ways in which IR scholars approached issues of justice in the formative, post-World War II years of the discipline; I will then examine the debates of the 1970s in which issues of international distributive justice were, indeed, addressed but where a shift in this direction was largely rejected, before moving on to the openings in IR theory which took place in the late 1980s and 1990s, openings which have brought some IR scholars quite close to the discourses of contemporary political philosophy – which have led, in other words, to the emergence of 'international political theory' as a possible valid alternative to 'international relations theory'. This sounds like a rather dry disciplinary history, but – at the risk of giving away the plot of the essay, if not its ending – what makes it interesting is the persistence throughout of one crucial issue, the matter of institutional design, and the sceptical attitude of international relations theorists towards the possibility of international institutional reform. This scepticism was built into the discourse of international relations at its foundation and has informed – perhaps 'disabled' would be a better word – IR theory ever since. At the end of the essay I address this matter directly, asking why such scepticism has not similarly afflicted the discourse of international political theory, and, more specifically, asking whether the moves made by the latter discourse to counter this scepticism have constituted legitimate avoidance, or illegitimate evasion. Finally, in order to keep this essay to a reasonable length, I will take as read the work of political philosophers such as John Rawls, Charles Beitz, Thomas Pogge, David Richards and Brian Barry and discuss the reaction of international relations to these writers rather than their work as such.

Justice and Conventional International Relations Theory

International relations as taught in the English-speaking world is a post-1945 academic discipline (or sub-discipline, field, or whatever – the appropriate description for the discourse is not an issue here). The first Chairs of International Relations were established in the aftermath of the First World War in Britain and the USA by philanthropists (David Davies in Wales, Montague Burton at LSE and Oxford) who were concerned to promote the cause of peace, but, for the most part, the quite prominent individuals who held these posts before 1939 did not consider themselves to be founding an academic discipline. They were classics scholars, international lawyers or historians whose duties were defined in terms of an obligation to speak to the wider world rather than to train graduate students, much less teach undergraduates. Figures such as Alfred Zimmern and E.H. Carr rarely visited their University College in Aberystwyth – admittedly not somewhere it is possible simply to drop in on – and were not expected to actually teach students as opposed to giving the occasional formal lecture. Arguably, only the philosopher of international law. C.A.W. Manning, Montague Burton Professor at LSE from 1930 to 1962, saw himself as forming a distinct discourse and his conception of the subject was sufficiently eccentric for this commitment to be of doubtful utility in the development of the discipline.[1] After 1945, on the other hand, many scholars did aspire to create a discipline of IR, in Britain, but perhaps especially in the USA where the growth of American power during the war had created both a need for the previously domestically-oriented political elite to be informed of international affairs and a foreign affairs bureaucracy which needed to be staffed – moreover, the rise of Nazism had endowed American universities with a number of exiles eminently qualified to create this new discipline, most especially, of course, Hans J. Morgenthau who brought his 1920s training in the philosophy of law in Germany to bear on the study of international relations at the University of Chicago.

The discipline these scholars created had as its dominant theory, 'realism'[2] – the theory that state action is to be understood as the pursuit of interest defined in terms of power, and that international outcomes reflect the struggle for power, international order being based, rather shakily, on power counteracting power, the 'balance of power' (Morgenthau, 1948). The classical American realists – Morgenthau, George Kennan, Reinhold Niebuhr – were mentally and spiritually a long way away from 'blood and iron' figures such as the late nineteenth century German political theorist Heinrich Treitschke, but clearly their account of international relations created little room for the emergence of a theory of international justice. They started out from an Augustinian pessimism about the human condition, combined, rather uneasily, with a Weberian account of the diplomatist's ethic of responsibility; each state was understood as responsible for the welfare of its citizens – duties towards compatriots were taken by these writers to trump duties towards foreigners. Rosenthal (1991) and Murray (1997) argue convincingly that the classical realists did possess a conception of the interests of humanity, but it is clear that this conception was too limited to allow the development of an elaborate account of international justice. Morgenthau was certainly prepared to defend the proposition that international law existed as law, but as a decentralized system, weak and ineffective.

The most important mainstream counter to American realism was provided by theorists of international society, scholars often know as the 'English School' not because they were necessarily English (or even British) but because many of them worked in England, at LSE, Oxford or Chatham House, and the approach was dominant in the UK.[3] As the term international *society* indicates, these scholars envisaged relations between states as, in some sense social, which they took to mean norm-governed (although none of them denied the importance of the contingencies of power). Unlike realists, they regarded international law as one of the two key practices of international society (along with diplomacy), and in this sense at least were prepared to think in terms of a form of international justice, but the account they produced was of justice as adherence to a set of rules, that is, of justice as formal and procedural, and of justice in the context of a world of states. The conception of international law with which they worked was traditional with little of the radicalism displayed later by Myres McDougal and the Yale School, or by modern neo-Kantians.

It is a moot point whether these theorists were as different from American realists as they liked to think. Martin Wight's very influential 1946 Chatham House Pamphlet was actually entitled *Power Politics*; he makes it clear that by this term he does *not* mean the 'sinister' doctrine of *Machtpolitik* – but then Morgenthau would have made the same claim for his account of power politics (Wight, 1946/79, p. 29). Hedley Bull probably got things about right when he remarked that American realists were providing for the new American political elite 'a crib to the European diplomatic tradition' – the implication being that the English School were providing a more advanced version of the same basic doctrines (Bull, 1972, p. 39). Certainly when Wight in *Power Politics* wants to stress the extent to which norms can influence state conduct, the comment he offers bears out Bull's point.

> Powers will continue to seek security without reference to justice, and to pursue their vital interests irrespective of common interests, but in the fraction that they may be deflected lies the difference between the jungle and the traditions of Europe (Wight, 1946/79, p. 297).

American realists such as Morgenthau might have been a little more sceptical about the 'traditions of Europe' than Wight, but their general stance was much the same.

Thus, the two main theories which underpinned the post-1945 emergence of IR as a discrete field of study were both characterized by, at best, a minimalist account of justice in international relations, and a predisposition to assume that states will 'seek security at the expense of justice' and 'pursue vital interests irrespective of common interests'. The reason for this common commitment to the essentials of 'realism' lies in the, pre-disciplinary, foundational experience of IR, the collapse of international order in the 1930s – and here we can see taking shape the great obstacle that IR theorists believe to lie across the path of attempts to develop notions of international justice, the alleged impossibility of international institutional reform.

In the interwar period, institutional reform was at the heart of the thinking about international relations promoted by the aforementioned philanthropists and scholars, the *Thinkers of the 'Twenty Years Crisis'* (Long and Wilson, 1995). A vast amount of effort in the form of public lectures, books, pamphlets, tracts, committees of scholars and officials, domestic and international was poured into defending and improving the League of Nations and its offshoots in the interests of a more just world order. Much of this reformism (or 'liberal internationalism') was directed towards closing the alleged 'gaps' in the Covenant of the League in order to make interstate war unambiguously illegal, but, in response to the Depression of the 1930s there were many committees investigating 'peaceful change', 'economic nationalism' and the like; the drive towards a just world order was not confined to the political realm – economic justice was involved as well, although since colonial matters could only be raised obliquely the scope of the latter was somewhat restricted. The assumption underlying this activity was that in order for a just world order to be created, just institutions would have to be created. The scholars involved in this activity saw themselves as building upon past work – in the words of the preface of one of the best surveys of international thought produced during the period, F. Melian Stawell's *The Growth of International Thought* (1929):

> ... a sane nationalism, when it understands itself, points the way to internationalism as its completion. The principle that builds the single State cannot end with the single State. This has been felt, sometimes clearly, more often dimly, by all the best thinkers of Europe.

Far from marginalizing issues of international justice, this reformist tradition placed such issues at the heart of the discourse.

International relations as an organized academic discipline was founded upon the destruction of this reformist discourse. The rise of the dictators – in particular of Hitler and Nazism – placed in power national leaders who regarded war and violence not as occasional, regrettable, necessities but as positively desirable in their own terms. Moreover, the dictators generally had some claim to popular mandates, unlike the pre-1914 militarists who could more plausibly be fitted into a liberal view of the world as anachronistic survivors of a pre-modern era. Reformists whose slogan had been 'law not war' were now faced with the probability that only war could preserve law. The value of schemes of institutional reform seemed nonexistent in a world in which those condemned by the League of Nations were able to leave that body with apparent impunity. The theory of 'collective security' – one for all and all for one – was put to its first serious test in Abyssinia in 1935, and failed miserably. Indeed, it could well be argued that the situation in Abyssinia, and later in Spain, was actually made worse by the ineffective legalism of the League which ruled out the kind of power political deals which might have salvaged something for Haile Selassie and the Spanish Republic, without putting in its place an effective alternative defence for the victims of aggression.

Such, at least, was the charge of the realist critics of liberal internationalism – which they renamed 'idealism' or 'utopianism'. E.H. Carr's *The Twenty Years Crisis* of 1939 is exemplary here. Although Carr insists that utopian impulses must be preserved alongside realism, the burden of his book is the need to demolish the pretensions of the reformers, who he compares to alchemists and vendors of anti-earthquake pills – because, when challenged as to the effectiveness of their remedies they reply, like the latter, 'but what would you put in their place?' (ibid., p. 8). Since Carr's response to the reformers was a qualified support for appeasement, he is vulnerable to counterattack on this point – but his more general critique of the liberal notion of a harmony of interest applied internationally, and of the inappropriateness of employing 'domestic' notions of justice and community at the international level pose a more serious challenge to reformist thinking.

The impact of Carr and his American equivalents in the 1930s and 1940s on the discipline of IR cannot be overestimated. It is not simply the cogency of Carr's arguments that is crucial (although *The Twenty Years Crisis* is a very tightly argued book) it is also the apparent endorsement of his position by the course of events in the 1930s and 1940s. Of course, 'history' cannot endorse one side or the other of an argument of this kind, and for all his claim to science Carr did not produce the kind of hypotheses that could be tested to the satisfaction of Gary King and his colleagues, but there is a sense in which the bleakness of this era does speak for itself, and it is hardly surprising that reformist aspirations should have been so widely talked down (King, Keohane and Verba, 1994). When the Second World War segued into the Cold War in the late 1940s, it was hardly to be expected that the new discipline of IR would manage to maintain the enthusiasm and optimism of its interwar forebears. Indeed, one of the roles of the new discipline was actually to *lower* expectations – writers such as Morgenthau and Kennan in the USA saw it as part of their duties to explain to the American public why the aims of Wilsonian liberalism could not be attained; in Britain, researchers such as Denis Healey played the same role within the British Labour Party.

I have written above of 'mainstream' IR, the dominant voices within the subject; before moving on, it may be helpful to examine some dissident voices. Put briefly, neither of the two main areas where dissidence was to be located in 1940s IR was particularly receptive to thinking about international justice in the full sense of the term. Marxism in this period meant Marxism-Leninism-Stalinism and a very deterministic account of the world; E.H. Carr himself had quasi-Marxist leanings and his materialist account of the role of the haves and have-nots in world politics, along with his critique of morality as class-based was echoed by most Marxists of the period (Brown, 1992). More promising was the continued existence – albeit rather submerged in the Anglo-Saxon world – of a Catholic Natural Law tradition, which had a 'take' on international relations as it had a take on everything else. Natural lawyers had had a clear sense of what constituted justice between communities since the time of Aquinas if not Augustine, predating interwar IR as they will, no doubt, outlast postwar IR. However, the 1940s and 1950s were not a period in which Catholic thinking on international economic justice – or indeed on the 'just war' – was encouraged; the necessity to prosecute the Cold War with vigour was felt as strongly in the Vatican as it was in the White House. The significance of these two non-mainstream approaches to IR for debates on justice was only to become apparent somewhat later, with the emergence of a new agenda in the 1970s.

Vietnam, the New International Economic Order and International Justice: An Opportunity Declined?

By the late 1960s and 1970s, mainstream IR was in crisis, under challenge from a number of directions. The 'behaviouralist revolution' in the social sciences hit international relations hard, its ur-disciplines of history, philosophy and law being rather further away from the behavioural science model of a discipline even than political science. Shifts in the course of the Cold War had challenged certainties about the virtues and unity of the West, while the rise of new international economic actors seemed in the process of undermining the state-centricity of the discipline, a process still continuing in the late 1990s. Two sets of events in the real world challenged postwar IR in ways that were particularly relevant to our concerns in this paper – the Vietnam War, which revived thinking about the 'just war', and by extension, political justice between communities more generally, and the rise of the south and its demand for a new international economic order, which raised directly the issue of international distributive justice. Both challenges and the response to them will be examined below; what is of particular interest here is why neither challenge actually produced a positive response from the mainstream of the discipline, in particular, why, when international distributive justice did emerge as a focus in the late 1980s, it did so more in response to works of political philosophy than to any real world events.

The Vietnam story is relatively simple and uncomplicated. Postwar IR's approach to war rested uneasily on two propositions. In principle, war was to be seen as an act of state policy in the national interest, regrettable, no doubt, but sometimes necessary; but the general understanding was that Western liberal democracies did not wage aggressive war and therefore the liberal conscience need not be troubled too much by IR's apparent endorsement of the practice.[4] However, America's war in Vietnam was seen by many to be a war of aggression, which called into question realism's approach to the subject. One response might have been – and was – to adopt pacifism, but many opponents of US involvement in Vietnam did not want to take this step, partly, perhaps, because their support for Israel in the Six-Days War of 1967 would have been incompatible with such a position. Instead, these thinkers looked to discriminate, to find principles which would distinguish legitimate from illegitimate use of force in international relations. The best source of such principles available was the natural law tradition and the notion of 'just war', and the 1970s saw a number of studies by political theorists and activists which attempted to revise, adapt and update 'just war' thinking, most notably by Thomas Nagel and Michael Walzer as well as works by theologians and Catholic moral philosophers such as Paul Ramsey and E.B. Midgely (Nagel, 1972; Walzer, 1977; Ramsey, 1968; Midgely, 1975).

Meanwhile, throughout the 1960s, the largely poor, newly decolonized states of Africa and Asia joined with many of the equally deprived Latin American states to form a voting bloc in the UN which was held together by its concentration on economic issues. The UN Conference on Trade and Development (UNCTAD) was formed in 1964 and during the late 1960s and early 1970s it, and other southern groups, pressured for the establishment of a new international economic order (NIEO). A series of UN resolutions set out what was called for in the early 1970s – more investment on favourable terms in the south, cancellation of existing debt, increased foreign aid, preference for industrial products from the south, a stabilization fund for commodities paid for by the north, control of multinational corporation activities in the south. This amounted to a new political as well as a new economic order. The theories that underlay the NIEO were neo-Marxist, by no means orthodox, but drawing upon the tradition, especially as interpreted by the Argentinian economist Raul Prebisch (1950) whose work at the UN Commission for Latin America had set the scene for centre-periphery, *dependencia* theories in the early 1950s. However, in spite of the Marxist origins of this thinking, the demand for an NIEO was specifically cast in terms of justice – supporters of the NIEO in the south and the north presented their case not simply as the product of an alternative form of economic analysis, but as a demand for a just distribution of the world's resources and of life-chances. In this respect, this development can be aligned with the emerging debate on distributive justice in the 1970s, stimulated by the publication of John Rawls' *A Theory of Justice* (1971), although, on the whole, NIEO activists did not refer to this literature.

Here, then, were two quite forceful invitations to international relations scholars to pick up the agenda of international justice either in the form of just relations between states – call this 'justice in a world of states' – in the context of war, or in a wider sense in the form of international distributive justice – call this 'international social justice'. Individual citizens and diplomatists were inviting the discipline of IR to take on board this agenda; this was not simply a matter of social philosophers causing problems – although, as intimated above political philosophers are certainly involved in the debates. The invitation was, for the most part, declined. The 1970s were, as suggested above, a period of turmoil for the discipline of IR with challenges to the dominant realist paradigm from theorists of interdependence and from behaviouralist social scientists. These challenges were resolved for the mainstream of the discipline in the USA at the end of the 1970s by the rise of 'neorealism' with its rational choice methodology, the main challenge to which came from 'neoliberal institutionalists' employing similar tools (Waltz, 1979; Gilpin, 1981; Keohane, 1989). The main theoretical issues in the discipline came to revolve around the behaviour of 'egoists' under conditions of 'anarchy', focusing on the terms (if any) under which stable cooperation between states would be achievable (Baldwin, 1993). The Hobbesian presuppositions of this work took considerations of issues of justice under anarchy out of mainstream analysis – it became a matter for 'normative' theory as opposed to the more highly valued explanatory variety. The insistence that states were 'like' units, differentiated in terms of power but not functionally, made the dependency theorists account of centre-periphery relations impossible to translate accurately into neo-realist terms – the weakness of peripheral, poor, southern, states cannot be distinguished from the weakness of small, rich, northern states.

The unwillingness of the new IR theory to take on board issues of international justice is not particularly surprising; what is rather more surprising – and interesting – is the reaction of IR theorists who were very decidedly unsympathetic to the new modes of analysis. Two writers here can be taken as central: the then leading figure of the 'English School', the Oxford-based Australian Hedley Bull; and the Francophile follower of Raymond Aron, the Harvard-based American Stanley Hoffmann. Both produced major works on international ethics and morality in this period, but both, interestingly, produced far less radical accounts of international justice than one might think the situation demanded.

Bull addresses the subject of international justice twice, in his major work *The Anarchical Society* (1977) and in the later Hagey Lectures on *Justice in International Relations* (1984). His general approach to international justice is caught well by the title of chapter 4 of *The Anarchical Society*, 'Order versus Justice in World Politics', in which Bull distinguishes between moral rules establishing 'international or interstate justice' (the rights and duties of states), 'individual or human justice' (the rights and duties of individuals) and 'cosmopolitan or world justice' ('what is right and good for the world as a whole, for an imagined *civitas maxima* or cosmopolitan society to which all individuals belong and to which their interests should be subordinate' (p. 81)). International society is not basically unfriendly to international justice, so defined, insofar as moral rules are based on reciprocity and emerge out of an ethics of coexistence – although his criticism of Walzer as excessively idealistic in the demands he makes of states does not instil confidence that international justice is going to take us very far. International society is not very hospitable to human justice (unless issues of human justice are pressed by *states*) and is wholly inhospitable to cosmopolitan justice, a revolutionary doctrine that would transform the states system – '... to pursue world justice in the context of the system and society of states is to enter into conflict with the devices through which order is at present maintained' (ibid., p. 85). Order is crucial even at the expense of international justice. We should note that 'international order is preserved by means which systematically affront the most basic and widely agreed principles of international justice' (ibid., p. 87); institutions such as the balance of power and war mandate behaviour which violates the requirements of international justice. Order is not always under all circumstances to be given priority to justice, but in general terms it is a more basic value. In his Hagey Lectures Bull shows somewhat more sympathy for the demands of the south for justice, and, in any event, was never an unquestioning supporter of the rights of the great powers, but the basic message remains hostile to international distributive justice.

Hoffmann's major work, *Duties Beyond Borders* (1981), takes a similar line on justice as between states; on matters of war, for example, he describes his method as moving from the 'is' to the 'ought', as opposed to the idealism of Michael Walzer, who moves from the 'ought' to the 'is'.[5] His account of international distributive justice is more extensive than that of Bull, partly because he actually addresses the attempt to import Rawlsian ideas into international thought of writers such as Charles Beitz.[6] He is unsympathetic to these attempts, although he does acknowledge a national and international duty to reduce injustice and is sympathetic to the idea of at least minimal rights for all peoples, and will have no truck with the view that the inequality of nations is not a suitable topic for IR theory. His basic approach rests on a quite extensive account of the actual problems of the south, the relationship between these problems and capitalism more generally, and the prospects for anyone being able to do anything serious about these problems, which he regards as remote. It is the impracticality, as he sees it, of ideas of international distributive justice that he regards as central. We cannot accept obligations to the poor in the world at large that we are unable to deliver on, and – different kind of argument – which might conflict with our obligations to our own citizens.

Hoffman makes explicit in empirical terms what Bull approaches via generalities – an effective response to the demands for international distributive justice emanating from the south (and from social theorists such as Beitz) would require a revolutionary transformation of the international order, undermining the notion of sovereignty and the society of states. There are two reasons why we might not want to take this step; first, because we approve of the norms of sovereignty, which is likely to be the case if we are beneficiaries of these norms – and Bull in particular makes the point that the elites of southern states are indeed such beneficiaries, even if their peoples suffer the economic consequences of these norms, a similar point is made by the realist Steven Krasner, who identifies a demand to reduce their own vulnerability as lying behind the push for a NIEO from southern states (Krasner, 1985). Secondly – and here we return to an earlier theme – calls for a transformation of the international order need to be backed up with some account of how the international order is to be transformed and such an account is singularly lacking in both the writings of the social theorists and the demands of the south. The former mostly ignore the issue, the latter are positively unhelpful insofar as they press simultaneously for wholesale reform of the international system while insisting that the sovereignty of southern states and the norm of nonintervention must be preserved. The NIEO is a programme for action and reform within the UN system and resolutely state-centric – more so in fact than many of the proposals that were under discussion in the 1930s.

In effect Bull and Hoffmann remain within the framework established by the victors in the realist/utopian debate of the 1930s, in which calls for the transformation of IR are marginalized and de-legitimated. They can cope with discussions of international justice that stay within the existing institutional structure – justice within the society of states – but they reject demands that could only be effective if this structure was dramatically changed. They are helped in this latter rejection by the incoherence of many of the demands for international distributive justice which simultaneously call for wholesale change while endorsing key norms of the existing order. To take the argument any further, the underlying realist framework of thought on IR needed to be challenged and this was not happening in the 1970s.

International Justice in the 1990s: Ideal Theory and Moral Cosmopolitanism

If international justice did not take off as a focus for study in the 1970s, it most definitely has done in the late 1980s and 1990s. Political philosophers have turned their attentions in this direction in large numbers, partly driven by dissatisfaction with Rawls' handling of the issue in *A Theory of Justice*, but also from utilitarian and Kantian backgrounds that have been only marginally influenced by Rawls. International relations theorists such as Terry Nardin, Mervyn Frost and Andrew Linklater have also contributed in major ways to the new international political theory, as have some of the successors of Bull and Wight, who have identified and developed a 'solidarist' as well as a 'pluralist' dimension to the work of the English School (Nardin, 1983; Frost, 1996; Linklater 1990; Wheeler, 1992; Dunne and Wheeler, 1996). Indeed, such has been the nature of the change that the very distinction between a political theorist and an international relations theorist has been undermined, in many cases turned into a matter of biography rather than principle – especially the case when it comes to the youngest generation of IR theorists in Britain (and to a lesser extent in the USA). It would be a mistake to say that the mainstream discipline of IR has positively welcomed this change; the American discipline in particular still marginalizes normative concerns, although the emergence of an 'International Ethics' section of the International Studies Association holds out some hope for the future. However, there is no doubt that the study of international justice is a recognized activity now in a way that wasn't the case in the past. Why so?

To explain this change we certainly need to refer to the general climate of international relations in the post-Cold War era. The ending of the quasi-ideological tensions of that great power confrontation has liberated some conceptual space, and changes in the world economy – the alleged move towards 'globalization' – has also led to a willingness to re-examine some of the assumptions of the discipline. Partly because of these shifts, for the last few years, IR has been a kind of intellectual Salisbury Plain, a testing ground for a whole variety of new ideas and perspectives; given this receptiveness it is hardly surprising that the rather well established discourse on justice has been able to homestead in IR.[7] However, what has also contributed to the success of discourse on international justice has been the willingness of its practitioners to make a number of intellectual moves which have allowed it to avoid, or perhaps, evade the characteristic charge of utopianism directed against normative work in IR by the mainstream of the discipline.

To document these moves, I will employ the work of Charles R. Beitz, not because they are original to him, but because it is through Beitz's work that many of these issues entered the domain of IR – in particular, his pioneering study *Political Theory and International Relations* (1979) has been deeply influential on a generation of IR theorists. The first move – certainly not original to Beitz – is the production of overtly 'ideal' theory. In *Political Theory and International Relations* Beitz sets out a strong case for undermining the norm of sovereignty and for applying a version of Rawls's 'difference' principle to international economic arrangements. He acknowledges that some will criticize his position on the basis of the lack of global political institutions to bring about the changes he wants, and of the lack a sense of world community to underpin such institutions had they existed. But, he replies (1979, p. 156),

> [s]uch objections are not persuasive because they misunderstand the relation between ideal theory and the real world. Ideal theory provides standards that serve as goals for political change in the non-ideal world ... the ideal cannot be undermined simply by pointing out that it cannot be achieved at present.

Realists in the 1930s and 1940s accused the 'utopians' of taking their wishes for reality; Beitz cannot be charged in this way because he is quite explicitly making it clear that what he is doing is providing ideal theory not an account of how the world is.

What kind of political change do we want to encourage the emergence of a just world? Beitz (along with the majority of writers on international justice) is a cosmopolitan. What does this mean? In a later essay, Beitz draws an important distinction between 'institutional' and 'moral' cosmopolitanism (Beitz, 1994). Institutional cosmopolitanism is the doctrine that the world's political structure ought to be reorganized to create some kind of 'world government'; moral cosmopolitanism is concerned not with institutions but 'the basis on which institutions, practices, or courses of action should be justified or criticised' (Beitz, 1994, p. 124). Moral cosmopolitanism, which Beitz endorses as more basic, is a state of mind, an orientation towards the world, an aspiration to see things whole – to regard the world in some sense as one entity.

This approach to cosmopolitanism has much to be said for it. The original cosmopolitans – moral philosophers in the Hellenic world – were certainly not institutionalists. Their ideas were developed precisely because the political institutions of the Greek world let them down. More to the point, by being a moral cosmopolitan one can, once again, avoid the realism charge of utopianism, unlike the lost souls Beitz mentions in his text, the American international lawyers who spent the 1960s designing changes to the UN Charter which would never be adopted. The moral cosmopolitan, working in a world of ideal theory, is able to let his or her imagination run free; so long as the measures to achieve justice one propose are not actually physically impossible they can be set as ideals to stimulate political action, and one is not obliged to address questions of political plausibility or actual institutional reform.

There is no doubt that for many theorists of international relations this cast of mind has been liberating. Like the B movie hero of old, in one bound we were free. International relations, the new 'dismal science', the discipline whose role in the social sciences was to tell everyone else why it wasn't possible to do things became transformed into a potentially emancipatory discourse – so much so that, in my experience, old-style political philosophers and sociologists quite frequently become irritated with IR theorists for not being sufficiently interested in power any more. But does the move to ideal theory based on moral cosmopolitanism avoid the problems which beset past normative thinking in IR, or does it evade them – I use these terms here with their Inland Revenue definitions in mind?

There is no doubt in my mind that the interwar reformers would have regarded these moves as evasive. Many of them *were* institutional cosmopolitans, putting in endless hours on earnest committees dedicated to redesigning international institutions with a view to producing a more peaceful and just world. They did not see themselves as engaged in constructing ideal theory – or at least when they did posit ideals they also regarded it as part of their role to show how these ideals could be put in practice. As writers like Carr stressed, they certainly had a tendency to assume goodwill where none was present and to build institutional structures on insecure foundations in terms of global popular support; their response to this criticism would have been – and was – that as concerned global citizens they felt obliged to try to put their ideas into practice. Most of the 'utopians' bore the label with pride, and would have been rather surprised that later cosmopolitans would construct their ideas so as to be able to avoid being accused by realists of utopianism.

I suggest that today's international political theorists ought to be more willing to emulate the spirit of the old prewar reformers, more willing to engage with issues of international institutional design and, therefore, more willing to engage head-on with today's realists. It may well be important to develop the kinds of attitudes to the world encapsulated in the notion of 'moral cosmopolitanism' – although Stawell's earlier-noted proposition that internationalism develops naturally out of a sane nationalism draws attention to the fact that there are other routes to a concern for the common good of humanity – but when the cultivation of a state of mind is allowed to become a substitute for the less attractive but more demanding task of reform something has gone wrong.[8]

Happily, there is at least some evidence that opportunities are opening up for a more engaged, institutionally-oriented approach to international justice, and it may be helpful to end this paper by mentioning a few, quite disparate, examples of such opportunities – areas where international political theorists are making a contribution or where such a contribution might fit with existing work carried out under other auspices.

First, there is currently a great deal of interest in the reform of the central institutions of the UN, including the Security Council and the General Assembly. Most of the thinking in this area is coming out of the UN itself, or from institutional analysts (Roberts and Kingsbury, 1993). There are, I think, quite good reasons why we ought to be sceptical of any attempt to relocate Government House to UN Plaza, as the utilitarian Robert E. Goodin put it – the UN is a state-centric body which is most unlikely to agree to serious derogations from state-sovereignty – but it would certainly be good if more people who were interested in international justice were to be more deeply involved in these projects than is the case at the moment (Goodin, 1995). For example, while there is a great deal of work under way currently on the reform of UN very little is by individuals with a serious interest in international political theory – just one of the ways in which an undervaluing of institutional cosmopolitanism takes its toll. In the same vein, the issue of the establishment of an International Criminal Court is clearly much in the news but is similarly neglected by moral cosmopolitans.

Second, and more promising, there is a growing interest in finding an institutional base for the democratization of the current international order. David Held's work on cosmopolitan democracy comes to mind here, which ties in with Andrew Linklater's work on 'post-Westphalian citizenship (Held, 1995; Linklater, 1998). Held's conception of a kind of people's UN running in parallel with the state-centric version is clearly utopian in the old sense of the term but it does have some real-world echoes in the new international politics of global poverty (Thomas, 1997). The People's Global Alliance is a relatively new body whose claim to wide support in the south could easily be challenged but it is not too fanciful to see this body growing in significance over the years – in spite of its unfortunate acronym. The unofficial Women's Conference that shadowed the official intergovernmental Conference on Women in Beijing in 1995, and the raft of unofficial groups that surrounded UNCED in Rio in 1992 are more straws in this particular wind.

More generally, the growth of institutions that may eventually make up a genuine global civil society has received nowhere near the kind of academic attention it deserves from international political theorists, with some honourable exceptions (Frost, 1996; Walzer, 1995). Bodies such as Amnesty are widely recognized as potentially significant, but such phenomena as 'ethical' investment and consumerism have not received the kind of attention they deserve. Again, the number of serious books on the ethics of international business is pitifully small, let alone works on the ethical implications of international markets; the work of Thomas Donaldson in this area is pioneering, yet little known (Donaldson, 1989) – and yet, whatever view we take of globalization, it is still clear that any account of a just world order is going to have to be at least as concerned with the behaviour of business enterprises as it is with the behaviour of states.

To summarize my argument: the record of international relations as an academic discourse has not been very distinguished when it comes to normative issues and the matter of international justice, however defined. The very founding act of the discipline – the destruction of 'utopianism' – made it difficult for IR to encompass the ethical concerns which ought to have been regarded as central. This state of affairs is now changing, but the terms under which the change has taken place have involved ignoring the issues of institutional design that once were thought to be central to serious thought about international justice. The need now is to pick up the story where the interwar reformers were forced to let it drop, preferably without making the kind of mistakes which left them so open to realist criticism. The challenge to the successors of these liberal internationalists is to develop ideas on international institutional design that both respond to the widespread demand for international justice, and keep contact with the realities of political action – in short, the challenge is to be 'utopian realists' rather than realists or utopians (Booth, 1991).

Notes

1 Manning's description of the discourse as 'social cosmology' is rather promisingly postmodern, but I think eccentric is an appropriate term for his single book length study of the field, the flavour of which is caught nicely by the index entry 'horse, pantomime, see pantomime horse' (Manning, 1973, p. 218).
2 The term 'realism' is unfortunate; it is not related to the philosophical understanding of that term – indeed, Martin Griffiths (1992) argues convincingly that the realists were actually in philosophical terms idealists – and is too often equated with 'realistic', as, no doubt, its originators intended.
3 Nowadays the 'Anglo-Welsh School' would be a rather more appropriate term given the number of high quality international society theorists working at University of Wales, Aberystwyth.
4 This latter proposition has now been refined in the 'democratic peace' thesis to read that 'democracies do not fight democracies', and in this form does seem to be well-founded. See Russett, 1993.
5 IR theorists seem to have a vision of Michael Walzer as a starry-eyed impractical idealist, which is not always how political philosophers approach his work.
6 Bull, in a footnote on theories of justice, rather loftily attributes all contemporary distinctions between kinds of justice to Aristotle, and, rather less plausibly, equates the work of John Rawls with that of Morris Ginsburg (Bull, 1979, p. 311).
7 I take the 'homesteading' metaphor from Christine Sylvester (1994).
8 A *mea culpa* should be recognized here; much of my own work has been in the realm of ideal theory.

References

Baldwin, D. (ed.) (1993), *Neorealism and Neoliberalism*, Columbia University Press, New York.

Beitz, C.R. (1979), *Political Theory and International Relations*, Princeton University Press, Princeton.

Beitz, C.R. (1994), 'Cosmopolitan liberalism and the states-system' in C. Brown (ed.), *Political Restructuring in Europe*, Routledge, London.

Booth, K. (1991), 'Security in Anarchy: Utopian Realism in Theory and Practice', *International Affairs*, 67, 4, pp. 527–45.

Brown, C. (1992), 'Marxism and International Ethics' in T. Nardin and D. Mapel (eds), *Traditions of International Ethics*, Cambridge University Press, Cambridge.

Brown, C. (1997), 'Theories of International Justice', *British Journal of Political Science*, 27, pp. 273–97.

Bull, H. (1972), 'The Theory of International Politics, 1919–1969' in B. Porter (ed.), *The Aberystwyth Papers*, Oxford University Press, London.

Bull, H. (1977), *The Anarchical Society*, Macmillan, London.

Bull H. (1984), 'Justice in International Relations', *The Hagey Lectures*, University of Waterloo, Waterloo, Ontario.
Carr, E.H. (1939), *The Twenty Years Crisis*, Macmillan, London.
Donaldson, T. (1989), *The Ethics of International Business*, Oxford University Press, New York.
Dunne, T. and Wheeler, N.J. (1996), 'Hedley Bull's Pluralism of the Intellect and Solidarism of the Will', *International Affairs*, 72, 1, pp. 97–107.
Frost, M. (1996), *Ethics in International Relations*, Cambridge University Press, Cambridge.
Gilpin, R (1981), *War and Change in World Politics*, Cambridge University Press, New York.
Goodin, R. (1995), 'Government house utilitarianism' in R. Goodin (ed.), *Utilitarianism as a Public Philosophy*, Cambridge University Press, Cambridge.
Griffiths, M. (1992), *Realism, Idealism and International Politics*, Routledge, London.
Held, D. (1995), *Democracy and the Global Order*, Polity Press, Cambridge.
Hoffmann, S. (1981), *Duties beyond Borders*, University of Syracuse Press, Syracuse, New York.
Keohane, R. (1989), *International Institutions and State Power*, Westview Press, Boulder, Colorado.
King, G., Keohane, R. and Verba, S. (1994), *Designing Social Inquiry*, Princeton University Press, Princeton.
Krasner, S. (1985), *Structural Conflict*, University of California Press, Berkeley, California.
Linklater, A. (1990), *Men and Citizens in the Theory of International Relations*, Macmillan, London.
Linklater, A. (1998), *The Transformation of Political Community*, Polity Press, Cambridge.
Long, D. and Wilson, P. (eds) (1995), *Thinkers of the 'Twenty Years Crisis'*, Oxford University Press, Oxford.
Manning, C.A.W. (1973), *The Nature of International Society*, second edn, Macmillan/LSE, London.
Midgely, E.B. (1975), *The Natural Law Tradition and the Theory of International Relation*, Paul Elek, London.
Morgenthau, H.J. (1948), *Politics Among Nations*, Alfred P. Knopf, New York.
Murray, A.J. (1997), *Reconstructing Realism*, University of Keele Press, Edinburgh.
Nagel, T. (1972), *Moral Questions*, Cambridge University Press, Cambridge.
Nardin, T. (1983), *Law, Morality and the Relations of States*, Princeton University Press, Princeton.
Prebisch, R. (1950), *The Economic Development of Latin America and its Principal Problems*, United Nations, New York.
Ramsey, P. (1968), *The Just War*, Charles Scribner's Sons, New York.
Rawls, J. (1971), *A Theory of Justice*, Oxford University Press, Oxford.

Roberts, A. and Kingsbury, B. (eds) (1993), *United Nations, Divided World*, Clarendon Press, Oxford.

Rosenthal, J. (1991), *Righteous Realists*, University of Louisiana Press, Baton Rouge, Louisiana.

Russett, B. (1993), *Grasping the Democratic Peace*, Princeton University Press, Princeton.

Stawell, F.M. (1929), *The Growth of International Thought*, Hutchinson, London.

Sylvester, C. (1994), *Feminist Theory and International Relations in a Post-Modern Era*, Cambridge University Press, Cambridge.

Tesón, F.R. (1998), *A Philosophy of International Law*, Westview Press, Boulder, Colorado.

Thomas, C. (1997), 'Poverty, Development and Hunger' in J. Baylis and S. Smith (eds), *The Globalisation of World Politics*, Oxford University Press, Oxford.

Walzer, M. (1977), *Just and Unjust Wars*, Penguin, Harmondsworth.

Walzer, M. (ed.) (1995), *Toward a Global Civil Society*, Berghahn Books, Providence, Rhode Island.

Waltz, K. (1979), *Theory of International Politics*, Addison Wesley, Reading, Massachusetts.

Wheeler, N.J. (1992), 'Pluralist and Solidarist Conceptions of International Society', *Millennium*, 21, 3, pp. 463–87.

Wight, M. (1946/78), *Power Politics*, second edn, Leicester University Press, Leicester.

3 International Justice and Just War Theory[1]

TONY COATES

Introduction

Deep divisions mark the contemporary debate about international justice. Realists are ranged against idealists, communitarians against cosmopolitans, particularists against universalists. The differences relate to methods or approaches as well as matters of substance. Realists and communitarians criticize idealists and cosmopolitans for their prescriptivism or utopianism; for their atomistic understanding of international relations with its exclusive and artificial focus on rational individuals abstracted from their social and historical situation; and for their ensuing neglect of real, particular and communal, identities and values. Conversely, cosmopolitans criticize realists and communitarians for their positivism and uncritical acceptance of the status quo; for their preoccupation with the state and the claims of particular moral and political communities; and for their consequent denial or neglect of universal or global values and needs.

Within the terms of the debate thus conceived international justice, in its fullest sense, comes to be regarded as the preserve of cosmopolitanism. In its pure or classical form realism is seen to dispense entirely with considerations of justice, regarding ethical concerns in general as essentially alien, even hostile, to the proper conduct of international relations. In a more moderate, or 'liberal', guise realism is able to admit justice but only in a narrow legalistic or corrective sense and mainly as a way of preserving state autonomy; the domain of distributive or substantive justice remains a purely domestic one.

By contrast, cosmopolitanism's uncompromising universalism makes imperative the application to international relations of substantive and distributive as well as formal and legal justice. From this cosmopolitan perspective the boundaries of particular states and societies, or the political and social identities of individual human beings, appear largely irrelevant to questions of justice comprehensively understood. What matters is whether or not the needs of individual human beings are being met and their rights upheld. For citizens of the cosmopolis rights and duties cannot be confined within state boundaries or restricted to formal principles that maintain the security and integrity of states without reference to their internal constitution or their impact on individuals. To suggest otherwise is to renounce any real notion of the universal community of humankind in favour of some form (more or less extreme) of moral particularism.

As often happens in a fiercely contested debate, where each side develops its own self-image largely in opposition to the other, the tendency is to concentrate on the points of difference rather than the points of contact or affinity. The result is a polarization of the argument in which universalism comes to be understood as the very antithesis of particularism (and vice versa), and in which the claims of the world community are seen to vie with the claims of particular states. Polarization, therefore, has a thoroughly distorting effect leading, inevitably, to one-sided and incomplete conceptions of international relations and, by extension, of international justice.[2]

By drawing on a just war tradition that is neither realist nor cosmopolitan the argument of this chapter attempts to construct more rounded concepts of international relations and international justice. In Section 1 the current polarity between realism and cosmopolitanism is examined in the light of the morality of states. The assimilation of the just war tradition to realism (in the guise of the morality of states) is noted in Section 1 and criticized in Section 2. While the universalist principles of just war theory are seen to belie its realist image (Section 2), in Section 3 the concrete or rooted universalism of just war theory is contrasted with the abstract universalism of cosmopolitanism. The conclusion reached is that the merit of the just war approach lies in its transcendence of the realist-cosmopolitan divide through its upholding of the claims of *both* particularity and universality.

The Current Polarity: Cosmopolitanism, Realism and the Morality of States

The polarized or dualistic way of thinking is evident in the accounts given of the range of conceptions (past and present) of international relations and, by implication, international justice. In his *Political Theory and International Relations* (a book that has exercised a considerable influence on contemporary cosmopolitan thought) Charles Beitz (1979, p. vii) positions cosmopolitanism in relation to what he considers to be the traditional and main alternatives:

> To assert the possibility of international political theory, one must first reexamine the traditional image of international relations as a state of nature and purge it of its skeptical elements. The traditional alternative to this view, which I call the morality of states, must be reconstructed to correct for the persistent misunderstanding of the notion of state autonomy. The result is a third view of international morality, which might be described as cosmopolitan.

This tripartite characterization of past and present thinking about international relations ('realism', 'morality of states', 'cosmopolitanism') is a commonly accepted one (see, for example, Vincent, 1986, ch. 7; Nye, 1997, pp. 19–24; Dower, 1998, pp. 17–20; Barry, 1999). Despite its more complex appearance it does little to undermine the dualistic opposition of realism and idealism, or of communitarianism (or statism) and cosmopolitanism. In fact it reinforces it since, from a cosmopolitan standpoint at least, the distinction between realism and the morality of states is of minor significance.

The morality of states is not seen to constitute a decisive enough break with realism. In fact it is thought to amount to a distinction within realism, being seen (perhaps correctly) as no more than a moderate or liberal form of realism that leaves the fundamentals of realism intact. Though, unlike pure or classical realism, it accepts the moral or ethical determination of international relations, the form of international ethics it upholds is limited in nature and scope. It is an ethic with a negative rather than a positive emphasis, in which order may be seen to dominate justice. Its object is to regulate the external relations of states with a view to curtailing (rather than resolving) conflict by safeguarding the integrity and autonomy of each state. Insofar as justice is seen to apply at all to the domain of international relations it applies in the restricted sense of corrective justice. The idea of distributive justice, with its universalist assumptions and intrusive implications, is seen to conflict with those key principles of the system of states, state sovereignty and nonintervention, that the morality of states is meant to uphold.

Understandably, cosmopolitans find the morality of states wholly inadequate. Like realism, it fails to articulate a community of interest or need, grounded in a common humanity and transcending particular states. It seems designed rather to allow states to go their own ways, in a state of mutual indifference, than to realize a common identity or to work out a common fate. This is not an alternative to realism but simply a more presentable form of realism, realism with a moral face. Some cosmopolitans are even inclined to doubt that: 'Is the morality of states a morality at all?', asks Brian Barry (1999, p. 16) – '[i]f universal egoism counts as a morality, then so does its statist analogue'.

The morality of states, therefore, does little to shake the duopoly of statism and cosmopolitanism or to produce a more balanced understanding of international relations. It is far too closely identified with one side of the argument for that. Inevitably, its defence of the state and the states-system is at the expense of those global and universalist considerations that are central to international justice. The morality of states is too narrow in its scope to embrace the agenda of international justice, of which regulative or corrective justice forms only a part (and a part that depends for its validity on its connection with the whole).

But does this trinity of realism, morality of states, and cosmopolitanism exhaust the possibilities so far as conceptions of international relations and international justice are concerned? It seems an unduly economical or abbreviated account of the potential, or actual, spectrum of thought. Even recent thinking about international relations is more varied and complex than that. Recognition of that variety and complexity seems a matter of some urgency given the polarized or dualistic state of the argument. The variety and complexity of thought suggest that the choice is not simply between realism and cosmopolitanism, or between the claims of particular polities and those of the universal or global community. The polarized nature of the debate has obscured those concepts of international relations that are not classifiable as either realist or cosmopolitan.

Chris Brown alludes to this variety in his review of postwar international theory. Even though international relations theory has been dominated throughout most of the twentieth century by the struggle for mastery between realists and idealists, statists and cosmopolitans, dissenting voices have been heard from time to time. One such voice (Brown suggests) is that of the just war tradition with its roots in natural law theory. In the context of the debate about international justice what is interesting about this tradition is its claim to transcend the conventional division between realism and cosmopolitanism through its reconciliation of particular and universal values.

It is a claim that is frequently denied or overlooked. The reason for this oversight is significant and points to the internal variety and ambiguity of the just war tradition itself as well as to partial and incomplete readings of that tradition. In its contemporary form just war theory is commonly regarded (especially, perhaps, by cosmopolitans) as a version of the morality of states, that is, not as a theory spanning the realist-cosmopolitan divide, but as a theory firmly planted on the realist side of that divide, a form of moral particularism. As such it appears incapable of grounding any concept of international distributive justice. Is this view of just war theory warranted?

Realism, Morality of States and Just War Theory

The view of just war theory as a form of realism owes much to the identification of contemporary just war theory with the work of Michael Walzer. More often than not the critique of just war theory amounts to little more than a critique of Walzer (see Holmes, 1989; Thompson, 1992; Campbell, 1993; Norman, 1995; Zolo, 1997). It is the assimilation of the tradition as a whole with the specific form or shape that Walzer has given it that largely accounts for its 'realist' or 'statist' reputation. Here, according to one critic, is 'a theory of justice based on the entitlements of sovereign states', an 'inherently conservative' theory that 'takes the entitlements of sovereignty for granted and [that] closes off attempts to criticise these entitlements' (Thompson ,1992, pp. 13 and 17). Another claims that 'in Michael Walzer's extended discussion of just-war theory, territorial integrity and political sovereignty are the absolute rights of nations in a world comprised of sovereign states'. As a result 'just-war theory is woefully inadequate as a concept for anything other than the rationalization of war' (Campbell, 1993, pp. 23 and 80). Yet another suggests that 'national survival, or more basically, national egoism is the governing norm' of Walzer's theory with the result that 'reason of state begins to show itself in the guise of the just war theory' (Holmes, 1989, p. 170).

The concept of international justice associated with such a statist version of just war theory cannot be other than minimal. 'It is an immediate implication of Walzer's particularism', writes Brian Barry (1995, p. 79), 'that there can be no such thing as international distributive justice'. At best, it yields a legalistic notion of international justice that 'consists in people recognising and respecting the sovereignty exercised by others unless there are very good reasons for intervention' (Thompson, 1992, p. 12). As a response to the pressing problems and urgent needs of the global community it appears wholly inadequate.

The attention paid to Walzer's work is neither surprising nor unjustified. He has done, perhaps, more than any other contemporary writer to breathe life into a tradition that, for a variety of reasons, had become somewhat moribund. That said it would be a mistake to regard Walzer's version of just war theory as definitive or exhaustive. In many fundamental respects Walzer's interpretation may be at odds with the classical tradition of just war thought (and with the pre-modern or pre-enlightenment tradition of natural law on which the classical version – but not, it seems, Walzer's – rests). Significantly, those points of conflict or tension often coincide with the points of criticism raised by those of a more universalist persuasion and critical disposition.

The charge levelled at just war theory – that by giving normative primacy to state sovereignty it lapses into moral particularism – *may* have some foundation in Walzer's work[3] but as a statement about the tradition as a whole it appears wide of the mark. It is true that within the tradition the 'state', or (more neutrally) the political community, is seen to play a key, even constitutive, role and to enjoy a certain moral entitlement (a role and an entitlement denied, or at any rate obscured, by the cosmopolitan tradition). To claim, however, that this theory of justice is *based* on the entitlement of sovereign states is a gross distortion of a tradition that, in its classical (and pre-Westphalian) form at least, grounds the rights of states or polities (including the right to war) in a conception of natural law and the moral community of mankind. It is this grounding that gives just war theory a critical edge and universalist orientation that are missing from realism and the morality of states. The fact is that in just war theory, at least in its classical version, the idea of the universal community of mankind is the basic norm that structures the entire theory. It is this universalist principle that underpins those concepts that make up the tradition's understanding of war and peace.[4]

The concept of legitimate authority, for example, that establishes the right to war or to the use of coercive force, is not to be confused with the 'weak' or realist version of conventional usage From the realist – even the moderate realist – standpoint this is a criterion that any state would find it easy to satisfy. The *competence de guerre* is, in realist terms, simply a formal accompaniment of state sovereignty that all states enjoy merely by being in effective control of their territory. Conversely, the resort to force by non-state or sub-state agents is automatically ruled out.[5]

This 'realist' understanding of legitimate authority or the right to war is frequently assumed in criticisms of just war theory. One criticism, for example, makes much of the fact that '[governments] tend to assume that they have an automatic right of military resistance to any violation of national sovereignty [yet] tend to regard armed resistance to internal oppression as much less justifiable' (Norman, 1995, p. 156). No doubt this is the case but it hardly seems relevant to the criticism of a tradition that accepts, in principle, the right of revolution (or at any rate of resistance), and that derives the state's right to war not from its *de facto* sovereignty but, proximately, from the political community on whose behalf power is exercised and force employed and, ultimately, from its membership of an international community to the law and common good of which it is seen to be subject. In the light of that framework of moral universalism the sovereignty of the state must be seen as relative and conditional, *not* as an absolute sovereignty. The view that Thompson attributes to cosmopolitanism, allegedly in contradistinction to just war theory, that 'the entitlement of states to exist and exercise sovereignty is a derivative and conditional right' (Thompson, 1992, p. 76), is as much a principle of just war reasoning as it is of cosmopolitan thinking (even though the specific grounding of the right may be understood differently).

A similar logic is discernible in reasoning about just cause. Conventional thinking about just cause is often dominated by the aggressor-defender distinction, a just war being equated simply and uncritically with a war of self-defence and an unjust war with a war of aggression. This way of thinking reflects the prevalent states system with its established principles of sovereignty and nonintervention. It fits much less comfortably with a tradition, like the just war tradition, that rests the assessment of war on the premise of the universal community of mankind.

The right of self-defence is an important part of just war reasoning but it does not monopolize that reasoning in the way that it has monopolized recent thinking about war. What is really at issue is the grounding or derivation of the right. Whereas in realist thought the state's right of self-defence is seen to follow automatically from its independent sovereignty, in the just war tradition it is seen as a vindication of the legal and moral community or whole of which states form a subordinate part. In upholding its own right the state is at the same time upholding the legal and moral system from which its right is derived. This different grounding gives just war reasoning a critical force that is missing in the case of realism. The right of self-defence can no longer be taken for granted. A state that habitually contravened the moral law could not plausibly be construed as upholding that law by exercising its 'right' of self-defence. Some states may, by virtue of their disordered internal constitution, lack the right of self-defence.

The universalist assumptions of just war theory cast further doubt on the moral adequacy of the aggressor-defender distinction. Not only is the justice of a defensive war questionable so too is the presumed injustice of offensive recourse. Traditionally, the vindication of the universal community included the use of war in an offensive role, the protection of the innocent being considered a duty that befell rulers even when the innocent in question were citizens of another state or political community. This duty of humanitarian intervention sprang from the notion of a universal moral community whose members enjoyed reciprocal rights and duties, precisely as members of that community and not just as citizens of particular states.

The moral primacy of the community of mankind is evident in the other criteria of just war theory. Proportionality, for example, is a central criterion of just recourse: do the potential benefits of war outweigh the potential costs? Just war theory in its traditional form brings to this principle too a universalist perspective. 'Since one nation is a part of the whole world', wrote Vitoria, 'if any war should be advantageous to one ... nation but injurious to the whole ... that war is unjust' (quoted in Fernández-Santamaria, 1977, p. 141). The proportionate worth of a war must be assessed in the light of the state's membership of a global community and of a global common good to which the good of the state is seen to be essentially related.

The same approach is evident in the moral treatment of the *conduct* of war. The just war category of *ius in bello* is informed by a sense of moral community. It is the recognition of an adversary's common humanity that dictates his just treatment (just as its suppression by some process of dehumanization leads in a contrary direction). The proportionate and discriminate conduct of war that just war theory stipulates assumes membership of a community transcending the warring states. As members of that universal moral community belligerents enjoy reciprocal rights and duties that are rooted in their common humanity and that remain in force even in the midst of war. The moral claims that belligerents rightly make upon each other are grounded in their membership of the universal community of mankind.

But what moral force or impact does the theory have as a whole? Critics of just war theory have argued that, whatever the specific merits or demerits of this theory of war, that is what it remains – a theory of *war* – and, therefore, a system of thought that is quite incapable of generating a comprehensive and at all adequate account of international justice. Geyer and Green, for example, voice a common criticism when they write of the just war tradition's 'essentially negative preoccupation with questions as to whether, or when, or how to resort to war'. As such this is 'an ethic of war' only – not 'a complete ethic of war and peace' that includes 'the positive imperatives and strategies of peacemaking' (Geyer and Green, 1992, p. 24).

This alleged preoccupation with war is seen as confirmation of the realist nature of just war theory. Like realism, it is argued, just war theory sees war as paradigmatic. The realm of international relations is understood as a natural state of war with the moderation of conflict defining the limit of moral ambition or aspiration. Both realism and just war theory are understood to be theories that regard international relations as intrinsically conflictual and that, therefore, put a premium on order rather than on justice. The 'peace' that both uphold is really a covert form of war, an interlude between hostilities, a cessation of conflict that does little to remove the causes of war or to secure a lasting peace. Both take war for granted and regard its abolition or supersession as a utopian and moralistic fancy that, if acted upon, seems likely to worsen the state of international relations.

It is true that for many realists the balance of power has often exhausted the concept and the strategy of peace – 'this approximate, tenuous equilibrium that provides whatever peace and order exists in the world of nation states' (Morgenthau and Thompson, 1985, p. 388) – but can the same be said of just war theorists? A partial recognition and acceptance of the utility of balance of power politics is not inconsistent with just war thinking. The tradition is worldly enough – realistic enough perhaps – to acknowledge the limits as well as the possibilities of a peaceful ordering of international relations, and modest enough to accept the instrumentality, if not of evil, then of impure or tainted means. Yet the balance of power remains something about which just war theory seems bound to harbour grave reservations.

In the first place the policy is open to abuse. Though it can be understood as a strategy consistent with a global concern and pacific purpose, the likelihood is that considerations of global peace and security will be sacrificed to the advancement of a national or imperial interest. Secondly, the policy itself seems intrinsically disordered or unethical, the logic of the balance of power appearing to dictate policies of dubious moral worth, more in tune with *raison d'etat* than with a strategy that serves a moral or ethical purpose. Operationally, the balance of power may dictate not merely the toleration of injustice but the collusion with, and even perpetration of, injustice. Thirdly, its pacific consequences, by which so much store is set, are themselves questionable. Far from preventing war the pursuit of this policy can become one of the principal causes of war.

For reasons such as these just war theory's acceptance of balance of power politics must remain strictly guarded or inhibited, even though the complexities and difficulties that beset the international realm in its present condition are seen to give those politics some limited and contingent justification. Fundamentally, the realist concept of peace is too conservative to comply with just war criteria. What realism lacks is that idea of peace that just war theory shares with more critical and more utopian ways of thinking and that springs from a deep dissatisfaction with the present state of international relations – the idea of the qualitative improvement of the international order, its radical transformation from something akin to a state of war to something akin to a state of genuine peace.

It is peace in this dynamic sense that structures just war theory, a theory that is not, despite what critics might say, a theory of war, primarily, but a theory of peace. The *ius ad bellum* is subordinate throughout to the *ius ad pacem*. What just war theory affirms, quite unequivocally, is the moral primacy of peace over war. This search for a more authentic peace corrects the realist imbalance between the values of order and justice. The idea of peace without justice is in just war terms a self-contradictory notion. That is why the work of peacemaking does not end with the cessation of war. The agenda of peace is not limited to the control of conflict but includes the positive and progressive removal of the causes of conflict.

The reason for realism's lack of ambition is that it is without a sense of international community. Being founded precisely on the reverse assumption of a natural or essential *dis*unity, it cannot see beyond the requirements of order, an order that is thought too fragile a construct to bear the weight of justice. By contrast, in just war theory, the paradigm of international relations is a state of peace not a state of war, a harmony or unity of parts not a conflict between sovereign and independent entities. Peace in this positive and radical sense *is* a kind of community and to be just war itself must constitute a vindication of that community, both actual and potential.

Cosmopolitanism and Just War Theory

What kind of international community does just war theory uphold? The question is a decisive one so far as peacemaking is concerned for not all concepts of unity (or community) promote peace. Some have quite the reverse effect, deepening divisions, multiplying grievances, exacerbating the state of war. Such is the case with an imperial unity where the claims of a particular polity, culture, religion or ideology are imposed upon the rest. By contrast the natural law tradition on which just war theory draws (an earlier Thomist and Aristotelian tradition very different from the modern natural law tradition out of which the morality of states and cosmopolitanism have developed[6]) conceives of the community of mankind as a plurality, a differentiated whole made up of parts that, in the interests of unity itself, are themselves to be considered wholes.

It is here, perhaps, that the essential difference between the just war approach and that of cosmopolitanism is to be located. Unlike realism, both just war theory and cosmopolitanism are forms of universalism but the concepts of universalism that they uphold seem worlds apart. Unlike cosmopolitan universalism, the universalism of just war theory remains open to the realm of the particular. There is here none of that hostility to particular societies commonly, and rightly, associated with cosmopolitanism. The universal is not regarded as the particular's polar opposite precisely because it is understood to be the particular's own internal principle (and *vice versa)*. The relation between particular and universal in just war thought is understood to be one of mutual reciprocity not, as in the cosmopolitan conception, one of mutual antagonism. As a result, while both just war theory and cosmopolitanism employ the idea of the universal community of mankind as a normative principle, they conceive of that community in radically different ways and to radically different effect.

The source of the difference lies, perhaps, in their contrasting conceptions of human nature. Unlike cosmopolitanism (and, in this respect at least, like communitarian thought), the just war tradition conceives of human nature in social and political terms. The atomistic conception of the rational, autonomous and self-constituted individual that structures the liberal cosmopolitan tradition vies with the Thomist-Aristotelian concept of 'man as social and political animal'. According to the latter, the social and political community with its complex of institutions is to be understood not contractually and instrumentally (and, therefore, purely derivatively), as a means to the advancement of autonomously chosen ends, but constitutively, as the real foundation and essential context of human growth and fulfilment. Viewed from within this tradition, the achievement of human well-being is as much a communal achievement as it is an individual one, an achievement crucially dependent upon the moral and not just the material resources of a society. Here is a way of thinking that is deeply sympathetic to social and political institutions by virtue of its understanding of human nature itself.

By contrast, the rational-individualist premise of liberal cosmopolitan thought (according to which 'human beings [are] ... only incidentally members of polities' (Barry, 1999, p. 35)) creates a natural antagonism to all inherited social institutions and historic communities. Those institutions (and communities) are seen to confront rational and autonomous individuals with the threat of heteronomy. The only form in which institutions appear at all acceptable is when they are seen to result from rational planning or construction and, in that way, are able to be construed entirely as the work of autonomous individuals.

The idea of the moral as well as material dependence of individuals on society that is so central to just war theory is here denied or suppressed. The contrary view that 'membership of a society does not have deep ethical significance' (Barry, 1998, p. 145) seems representative of the tradition as a whole. As a result, 'cosmopolitan liberalism [unlike just war theory] accords no ethical privilege to state-level societies' (Beitz, 1999a, p. 519). 'There would have to be something crazy', Barry writes (1999, p. 38), 'about giving value to states as such'.

The anti-communal and anti-statist sympathies of liberal cosmopolitanism are reinforced by the common cosmopolitan assumption that the advocacy of the particular community will invariably take a 'closed' form, one that is fundamentally hostile to universalist values. Cosmopolitan criticisms of 'statist' or 'communitarian' thought often assume a nationalist, even xenophobic and militarist, concept of the state or community (see Barry, 1999). There are good grounds for criticizing the nationalist concept of the state (not just in its extreme form) but that criticism is not the monopoly of cosmopolitans. As the case of just war theory exemplifies, acceptance of the claims of particular states or political communities does not entail support for nationalist politics (whether moderate or extreme), much less the denial of universalist values. In that theory the claims of particular communities are upheld but only in a form that is reconcilable with the moral community of mankind.

Cosmopolitans may argue, however, that although the *concept* of the state articulated by 'statist' theorists need not (and in some cases does not) take a 'closed' form, that is where, in practice, such advocacy leads. Brian Barry, for example, appears to argue along such consequential lines when he writes about 'the disjunction between what nationalists do and what their apologists among the political theorists defend';[7] or, when he suggests 'that those sympathetic to nationalism, while talking a different language, are in fact acting as a front for blood and soil nationalism' (ibid., pp. 25 and 41). Though a liberal form of nationalism (or statism) is conceivable, it is not the form that tends to prevail in the real world (or the form to which, for all its good intentions, liberal statism tends to give rise).

This practical or consequential criticism may be a double-edged sword as far as cosmopolitanism is concerned. The tendency of cosmopolitanism (and cosmopolitan politics) to devalue particular and historic social and political attachments in favour of a more abstract and rational-legal order might be expected to encourage those attachments, real as they are, to reassert themselves in a more virulent and aggressive form. Arguably, this is at least as likely a consequence of cosmopolitanism as it is of 'statism'. Cosmopolitanism's assumption of a 'closed' and particularist form of 'statism' simply makes things worse, reinforcing the opposition between particularist and universalist values and encouraging states to disown universalism in favour of a narrow and parochial particularism.

In contrast to its cosmopolitan counterpart, the just war concept of the community of mankind is built on the ethical recognition of particular communities. Like cosmopolitanism just war theory conceives that universal community in progressive terms. On this view, however, its development is seen as a social and historical process that is not impeded but strengthened and enriched by a plurality of cultures. It is the work of individual human beings but of culturally situated and culturally endowed individuals. It is the work, moreover, not of any one culture but of the many. Recognition of the integrity and the worth of those cultures is an essential requirement. The community of mankind is conceived as a unity but as a unity of particulars, a unity in which no one culture is allowed to lord it over the rest.

It is important not to conceive of international justice in material terms alone. The extreme poverty and physical degradation of life in the Third World encourages us to do so but this is a form of reductionism which perhaps says more about the values of the First World than it does about the values and consequent needs of the Third. International justice consists in more than dealing with the problems of material deprivation. It involves doing justice to the social, cultural and moral complexity of the particular communities that make up the community of mankind. It would be an injustice if the price that poor nations were forced to pay for the satisfaction of their material needs was the loss of cultural autonomy through their subjection to Western values and institutions. That loss would be of as much consequence to the universal community as it would to the particular communities themselves.

Does cosmopolitanism promote international justice in this inclusive sense? It seems not. Its rational-individualism precludes the kind of distributive recognition that international justice demands. The community, the social identity of individuals, is its traditional blind spot and one that leads to a distorted concept of what international justice entails. As one of its foremost contemporary advocates argues: 'cosmopolitan liberalism' consists in 'the application to the global level of the individualist moral egalitarianism of the Enlightenment' (Beitz, 1999a, p. 518).[8] In other words, a creed that is contentious even within its own Western cultural confines (partly because of its perceived corrosive effect on society) is to be used to determine the fate of the global community.[9]

The temptation to conceive the unity of mankind as an imperial unity is a long-standing one. Arguably, cosmopolitanism in its ancient and Stoic form succumbed to it (see Germino, 1982, ch. IV). It is to be hoped that cosmopolitanism in its modern form does not suffer the same fate.

'It is often', wrote Eliot (1962, pp. 91–2)

> the anti-imperialists who, being liberals, are the most complacent believers in

> the superiority of Western civilisation ... According to such enthusiasts, we do well to intrude ourselves upon another civilisation, equip the members of it with our mechanical contrivances, our systems of government, education, law, medicine and finance, inspire them with a contempt for their own customs and with an enlightened attitude towards religious superstition – and then leave them to stew in the broth which we have brewed for them.

Conclusion

Universalism in its abstract cosmopolitan form appears indifferent, or even hostile, to the particular, while a reverse preference is evident in realist particularism. What is precisely required is the avoidance of this polarization of the debate. Universalism need not take a cosmopolitan form, particularism need not take a realist form as the just war idea of a global or world community that recognizes the value and respects the integrity of particular states or polities suggests. Global unity is best conceived not as an imperial and uniform unity but as an ecumenical unity, one that not only tolerates cultural differences, grudgingly and patronizingly, but that recognizes the superiority and added strength of a unity based on diversity. What is needed (and what just war theory has traditionally upheld) is a unity conceived as a plurality.[10]

Notes

1 I am grateful to my colleague Richard Bellamy for the very helpful comments and suggestions that he made on an earlier version of this chapter.

2 The phenomenon is not new. Rousseau provides a good example of such thinking when he writes: 'The patriotic spirit is an exclusive spirit which makes us look on everyone but our fellow citizens as strangers, and almost as enemies ... The spirit of Christianity on the contrary makes us look on all men as brothers, as the children of God ... its ardent zeal embraces indifferently the whole human race. Thus it is true that Christianity is in its very sanctity contrary to the particular social spirit' (quoted in Colletti, 1974, p. 177).

3 The criticism even of Walzer's work often seems selective and tendentious, exaggerating its realist and positivist aspects and suppressing its moral or critical force. It is difficult, for example, to reconcile the charge that Walzer regards state entitlements uncritically with the claim advanced in *Just and Unjust Wars* that '[t]he moral standing of any particular state depends on the reality of the common life it protects and the extent to which the sacrifices required by that protection are willingly accepted and thought worthwhile', or with the view that '[i]f no common life exists, or if the state doesn't defend the common life that does exist, its own defense may have no moral justification' (Walzer, 1992, p. 54).

4 For a fuller discussion see Coates, 1997.

5 It is this positivist conception of legitimate authority that Brian Barry seems to have in mind when, in his criticism of statism, he contrasts the universal condemnation of insurgent terrorism by the 'trade union of states' with the self-indulgent condoning of much more destructive acts of violence by the states themselves (Barry, 1999, 37).

6 'The new natural law', wrote Rommen (1947, p. 75), 'differed in many respects from the traditional one. It represented a peculiar hypertrophy of the older conception'. A key feature of the modern version is 'the individualistic trait manifesting itself in the predominance of the doctrine of the state of nature [or 'original position']' (ibid., p. 93). In Rommen's view, 'Kant exhibits ... the individualistic natural law in its final, highest form' (ibid., p. 100). In similar vein, Midgley writes of Grotius's 'individualistic formulations [that] represent a grave emasculation of the traditional doctrine [of natural law]' (Midgley, 1975, p. 159. For a fuller discussion of the distinction's impact on the realist-cosmopolitan debate see Coates, 1999; see also Hayek, 1973, p. 21).

7 Among the apologists Barry identifies are Walzer, Taylor, Kymlicka, Miller and Elshtain.

8 Elsewhere Beitz (1999b, p. 296) writes: '[C]osmopolitan liberalism takes the interests of individuals as fundamental and as entitled to equal concern on a global scale, and it holds that the basic institutions of society, at both the global and sectional levels, should be justified in ways consistent with this fundamental commitment'.

9 According to Brian Barry (1999, pp. 32–3 and 57) 'the fundamental human right [is] to live in a liberal society'. 'There is,' he writes, 'a straightforward conflict between the values of group autonomy and liberalism here, and a cosmopolitan is bound to say that the latter should take precedence' ... 'Liberals are first and foremost people who want to see liberal institutions thrive'.

10 The argument is considered further in Coates, 1999.

References

Barry, B. (1995), 'Spherical Justice and Global Justice' in D. Miller and M. Walzer (eds), *Pluralism, Justice and Equality*, Oxford University Press, Oxford.

Barry, B. (1998), 'International Society from a Cosmopolitan Perspective' in D. Mapel and T. Nardin (eds), *International Society: Diverse Ethical Perspectives*, Princeton University Press, Princeton.

Barry, B. (1999), 'Statism and Nationalism: A Cosmopolitan Critique' in I. Shapiro and L. Brilmayer (eds), *Global Justice. NOMOS XLI*, New York University Press, New York, pp. 12–66.

Beitz, C.R. (1979), *Political Theory and International Relations*, Princeton University Press, Princeton.

Beitz, C.R. (1999a), 'Social and Cosmopolitan Liberalism', *International Affairs* ,75, 3, pp. 515–29.

Beitz, C.R. (1999b), 'International Liberalism and Distributive Justice', *World Politics*, 51, 1, pp. 269–96.

Campbell, D. (1993), *Politics Without Principle*, Lynne Rienner, Boulder and London.

Coates, A.J. (1997), *Ethics of War*, Manchester University Press, Manchester.

Coates, A.J. (1999), 'Neither Realism Nor Cosmopolitanism: A Response to Danilo Zolo' in B. Holden (ed.), *Global Democracy*, Routledge, London.
Colletti, L. (1974), *From Rousseau to Lenin,* Monthly Review Press, New York.
Dower, N. (1998), *World Ethics*, Edinburgh University Press, Edinburgh.
Eliot, T.S. (1962), *Notes Towards the Definition of Culture*, Faber & Faber, London.
Fernández-Santamaria, J.A. (19770, *The State, War and Peace*, Cambridge University Press, Cambridge.
Germino, D. (1982), *Political Philosophy and the Open Society*, Louisiana State University Press, Baton Rouge.
Geyer, A.F. and Green, B.G. (1992), *Lines in the Sand*, Westminster/John Knox Press, Louisville.
Hayek, F.A. (1973), *Law, Legislation and Liberty,* Vol. I, Routledge & Kegan Paul, London.
Holmes, R.L. (1989), *On War and Morality*, Princeton University Press, Princeton.
Midgely, E.B. (1975), *The Natural Law Tradition and the Theory of International Relation*, Paul Elek, London.
Morgenthau, H.J. and Thompson, K.W. (1985), *Politics Among Nations.* 6th edn, McGraw-Hill, New York.
Norman, R. (1995), *Ethics, Killing and War*, Cambridge University Press, Cambridge.
Nye, J.S. (199), *Understanding International Conflicts*, Longman, New York.
Rommen, H.A. (1947), *The Natural Law*, Herder, London.
Thompson, J. (1992), *Justice and World Order*, Routledge, London.
Vincent, R.J. (1986), *Human Rights and International Relations*, Cambridge University Press, Cambridge.
Walzer, M. (1992), *Just and Unjust Wars*, Basic Books, New York.
Zolo, D. (1997), *Cosmopolis*, Polity Press, Cambridge.

SECTION 3
PRINCIPLES AND CONCEPTS OF INTERNATIONAL JUSTICE

4 Universalism, Particularism and Cosmopolitan Justice

MICHAEL FREEMAN

Introduction

The idea of international justice presupposes the meta-theory of ethical universalism, which holds that there is a compelling ethical code applicable to humanity as such. Ethical universalism is deeply rooted in Western culture. It is a fundamental component of Christian doctrine; it was adopted by secular liberalism and socialism; it underpins the condemnation of such 'obvious' evils as xenophobia, anti-Semitism and racism, and provides an ethical perspective adapted to a 'globalized' world in which the values of universal human rights and international cooperation are widely shared. Thus, a doctrine that is 2,000 years old seems more plausible than ever.

Ethical universalism has, however, been challenged throughout its career, both in practice and in theory. Human history has contained more particularistic conflict than universalistic altruism. Universalism has been the ideology of intellectuals rather than the operational code of policy-makers. The realist tradition in international relations has argued that self-interested states constitute the principal agents of international affairs, and attempts to oppose this on universalist grounds would be either futile or dangerous: futile because policies motivated by ethical universalism would break on the rock of statist realism; dangerous because, in a Hobbesian world of interstate competition, ethical universalism would leave the relatively decent states vulnerable to the aggression of the most ruthless.

An alternative line of opposition to ethical universalism is associated with Hegel's critique of Kant and the opposition of *Sittlichkeit* to *Moralität*. Hegel's philosophy is itself universalist, but, within its universalist framework ethics is particularistic: obligations are local – to family, corporation and state – and not universal. Universalism and particularism were also combined by nineteenth century liberal nationalism, which affirmed both the value of the nation as the expression and protector of liberty and the moral unity of mankind.

A similar combination of universalism and particularism is written into the United Nations Charter, which proclaims, on the one hand, the values of world peace and universal human rights, and, on the other hand, the sovereignty of the state and the principle of the self-determination of peoples. Both the Kantian and the Hegelian traditions endorse, for different reasons, particular obligations on universalist grounds.

The tension between the ethical universalism of liberal cosmopolitanism and the ethical particularism implied by the principle of national self-determination has been introduced into contemporary political philosophy by the communitarian critique of liberalism. Communitarians reject the decontextualized self to which ethical universalism and liberal cosmopolitanism are supposed to be committed. Selves are said to be socialized 'all the way down'; communities are valued as ontologically prior, and necessary to the well-being of individuals; and natural, pervasive sentiments of affection, loyalty and solidarity towards family, friends and nation are accorded a high ethical status. Ethical universalism is called into question as vacuous, futile, or at best marginal, and at worst imperialistic. Postmodernist deconstructions of the idea of human nature have reinforced the critique of ethical universalism.

In this chapter I shall attempt to clarify the claims of ethical universalism and ethical particularism, and their implications for the idea of international justice. Strong forms of ethical particularism eliminate the concept of international justice altogether, and weaker forms marginalize its demands. If the concept of international justice is to be viable, ethical universalism must be vindicated. However, both ethical particularism and ethical universalism appeal to strong intuitions. Ethical universalism appeals to our humanity; ethical particularism to our special commitments. Both seem to carry ethical force. The problem is that they appear to give rise to mutually incompatible obligations. We can love our children and give money to Oxfam, but it is not clear that we can fulfil all our obligations to our children and also meet the requirements of international justice. A well-informed person with a sense of justice may well fear that the principles of international justice might impose insupportable moral burdens.

Ethical universalists and ethical particularists have often sought to reconcile the two sets of intuitions. I shall try to show that such reconciliations have not been successful. I shall do this by the analysis of two theories. The first is the defence of nationalism by David Miller on the basis of ethical particularism, which seeks to find a place for universal obligations. The second is Brian Barry's theory of justice as impartiality, which is explicitly universalist, but which seeks to find a place for particular obligations. These two theories have deservedly received considerable critical attention (O'Leary, 1996; *Political Studies*, 1996; Kelly, 1998). Each is an admirably well-articulated theory, but each fails, in different ways, to reconcile particularism and universalism convincingly. Both suffer from unresolved internal tensions. I shall argue, however, that Barry's theory of justice as impartiality provides a superior basis for the development of an ethically satisfactory theory of international justice. I shall conclude by indicating how such a theory might be developed by sketching an approach that I call 'cosmopolitan realism'.

The Ethics of Nationalism

David Miller defends ethical particularism as part of his defence of 'nationality'. A person who acknowledges a national identity, he maintains, thereby acknowledges special obligations to fellow nationals that are not owed to other human beings. This proposition, he admits, seems to contradict 'a powerful humanitarian sentiment' that affirms the moral equality of all human beings (Miller, 1995, p. 49).

Miller argues that, although ethical universalism and ethical particularism are competing accounts of ethics, the choice between them is not absolute. Universalists can accommodate particularist concerns to a considerable extent, and vice versa. The elements of ethical universalism are individuals with their generic capacities, considered prior to their relations to other individuals. Each person is a moral agent in a universe of similar agents, and the principles of ethics specify the obligations and rights of each of these agents. These principles are universal in form, and so only general facts about individuals can determine the obligations of others towards them. Facts about relations between particular individuals do not enter the fundamental level of ethics. Universalists may argue that such facts should enter into ethical judgements at a less fundamental level. However, the universalist must derive particular obligations from universal principles. Ethical particularism, by contrast, holds that relations between persons lie at the basic level of ethics, so that fundamental principles govern these relations directly. It constructs an ethical universe in which agents are encumbered with various commitments to particular other agents (ibid., pp. 49–51).

Both ethical universalism and ethical particularism seem to have strong arguments in their favour, Miller says. We do feel a sense of responsibility to other human beings as such. Yet our everyday obligations arise primarily from particular relations. It is, therefore, tempting to develop an ethical theory that would include both sorts of intuition. Miller proposes two lines of argument that the universalist might use to justify special obligations. The first says that the recognition by each agent of special obligations to particular others in close relations would produce *an efficient ethical division of labour*. According priority to obligations to particular others has two advantages from a universalist point of view: each can help those they are most able to help and those whose needs they know best. Miller cites as an example of an argument from the need for an ethical division of labour Goodin's suggestion that agents have a special responsibility to those particular others whose interests are *vulnerable to their actions* (ibid., pp. 51–2). However, Miller's reference to Goodin shows that the argument from the need for an ethical division of labour contains at least *three* more specific theses: 1) we have a special obligation to help those whom we are most able to help; 2) we have a special obligation to help those whose needs we know best; 3) we have a special obligation to help those whose interests are most vulnerable to our actions.

The second universalist argument for special obligations affirms that every agent has the right to establish a particular set of relations with associated rights and obligations. Special obligations derive, according to this argument, from *the universal right to freedom of association*. The right to freedom of association is a standard universalist principle, and the universalist might wish to argue that the general right entails certain particular rights and duties, for the failure to recognize these would render the general right nugatory (ibid., pp. 52–3).

The ethical particularist accords ethical priority to obligations to particular others, but can recognize obligations to human beings as such by virtue of their common humanity. The ethical particularist can give *some* moral weight to obligations based on common humanity, but has to decide how much, and, in particular, to what extent, if any, particular obligations, which are primary for the particularist, may or should be overridden by common-humanity obligations (ibid., p. 53).

Despite these possibilities of reconciling universal and particular obligations, Miller argues that there is a fundamental gulf between ethical universalism and ethical particularism. The gulf is *not*, however, he maintains, that between the universalists' commitment to ethical *impartiality* and the particularists' commitment to ethical *partiality*. The meaning of 'impartiality', he insists, is context-dependent. A mother may, for example, treat her children impartially, but not be impartial between her children and other children. The ethical particularist, he claims, does not advocate partiality. Ethical particularism requires impartiality but denies that impartiality entails universalism (ibid., pp. 53–4). This argument is unconvincing, because it rests on an unconventional use of the terms 'partiality' and 'impartiality'. Miller is correct to point out that the requirement of impartiality can be context-dependent: impartiality in one's relations with one's own children is consistent with partiality towards them in relation to other people's children. Nevertheless, ethical particularism *necessarily* entails partiality towards some people in relation to all those who are excluded from the scope of the particular obligation.

Universalists, according to Miller, object to the priority that they believe that particularists give to sentiment over reason. Universalists argue that particularists, by allowing actual relations to enter the basic level of ethics, fail to subject them to critical scrutiny. By contrast, universalists seek principles with universal scope that provide the criteria for evaluating more specific ethical intuitions. Particularists argue that universalism implausibly separates moral agency from *personal identity* and *personal motivation*. Universalist moral agents are rational beings as such, and as such lack all actual human particularity. They act only from rational ethical conviction. It seems unlikely, Miller suggests, that rational conviction carries sufficient motivational force for most people. Ethical motivation is generally based on Humean natural sentiments rather than Kantian reason (ibid., pp. 55–8). Miller's argument that ethical particularism motivates us to comply with the requirements of morality because we identify our own good with that of our community implies that ethical particularism is a form of enlarged selfishness. This is why it can be a powerful motivator, but also why it is ethically questionable. Miller's theory is partly based on the requirement that a plausible ethical theory provide the motivation for its realization. This is a reasonable requirement, but it is a poor reason to yield too quickly to natural sentiments. It is not difficult to motivate people to xenophobia, but this motivational fact is an inadequate basis for a theory of justice.

Nationalism is ethically valid, Miller asserts, only if ethical particularism is valid. Universalism rejects special obligations to fellow nationals at the basic level of ethics. However, the universalist might seek to derive the ethical validity of nationalism from basic, universal principles. Universalists might, for example, derive the value of nationalism from the need for an ethical division of labour. There is, however, no reason to suppose that nationalism provides the appropriate division of labour to implement universal principles. It is true, Miller says, that we may understand the needs of those with whom we share a culture better than the needs of those with whom we do not. This argument is, however, vulnerable to the objection that those we understand best may not be the neediest, so that according priority to those with whom we share a culture may be unjust from a universalist perspective (ibid., pp. 62–4). However, we have seen that the argument from the need for an ethical division of labour can appeal to at least three different lines of reasoning: 1) we should help those we *can* help (the ability argument); 2) we should help those whose needs we know (the knowledge argument); 3) we should help those who are vulnerable to our actions (the vulnerability argument). Miller considers only the knowledge argument, and opposes it with the counter-argument that this would not necessarily (or even probably) lead us to help the *neediest*. However, a universalist can give *some* weight to the knowledge principle, on the ground that there is an obligation to understand the needs of those whom one has an obligation to help, without ignoring the need principle. Miller has here, not *refuted* the universalist argument from the need for an ethical division of labour, but *proposed a fourth version of it: help the neediest*. This is not inconsistent with the other three division-of-labour principles, but has to be weighed in the balance with them. In other words, both knowledge and need are reasonable criteria for an obligation to aid, but neither is sufficient for such an obligation. This argument is universalist in form, and defends the division-of-labour principle against Miller's objection to it. Whether the universalist case for an ethical division of labour supports *nationalism* remains an open question.

Universalists might treat nations as voluntary associations with particular rights and obligations. These rights and obligations might accordingly be derived from a fundamental right to freedom of association. Miller rejects this argument on the ground that nations are not, for most people, voluntary associations. Individuals do not choose to 'join' nations; rather, nations constitute (in part) the identity of individuals. Individuals can, of course, choose to change their national allegiance, but this is relatively rare; national identity is normally a matter of inheritance and habit, and not of choice (ibid., pp. 59–62). To this it may be objected that, although it is indeed relatively rare that individuals choose to change their nationality, individuals can choose what attitude to adopt to the nationality that they have inherited. The universalist principle of freedom of association does not require that association be 'voluntary' in the sense of deliberately chosen, any more than the universalist right to family life presupposes that people choose their families. The universalist right to freedom of association protects associations based on inheritance and habit, provided that no universalist principle is thereby violated (for example, violations of human rights). Liberal universalists can endorse associations, membership of which is 'voluntary' in the sense of 'not coerced'. Thus, the universalist can endorse nationalism on the ground of freedom of association.

The combination of the universalist principles of the need for an ethical division of labour and of freedom of association may, therefore, allow universalists to endorse some forms of nationalism. Whether universalists *should* endorse nationalism on these grounds depends on the particular theory of international justice that they adopt and on complex empirical questions. Without a theory of international justice, universalists would at least require nationalism to be consistent with the implementation of universal human rights. Miller argues that universalists should regard nationality as a sentiment that may be useful in the short term, but which in the long term should be transcended in the name of humanity (ibid., p. 64). It is not clear, however, that universalist principles would be served in the long term by such a transcendence. The implementation of such principles must begin from our present situation, and it may be reasonable for universalists to take account of the fact of national sentiment as a condition of policy, and endorse altruistic nationalism as the best option for the foreseeable future.

Nationalists, on Miller's account, can recognize obligations to foreigners. There are generic conditions for living a decent life that can be expressed in terms of basic rights. We have obligations to respect these rights of others that derive from our common humanity. However, conflicts may arise between our obligations to fellow nationals and our obligations to respect the basic rights of foreigners. Universal obligations to respect the most fundamental rights of foreigners trump national obligations, 'provided the cost of protecting these rights is relatively small' (ibid., pp. 73–5).

Since shared identities generate obligations, Miller continues, local and national communities are the primary bearers of the obligation to protect the basic rights of their members. If these communities cannot fulfil their obligations, outsiders who can help may have the obligation to do so. If those with the primary obligation can fulfil it, but choose not to do so, the first obligation of others is to try to get those with the primary obligation to acknowledge it, by persuasion if possible, but, failing this, by such force as is commensurate with the right in question. If these measures fail, outsiders may incur the obligation to help the rights-holders directly. Miller maintains that the principle of national self-determination severely limits the obligation to protect the basic rights of foreigners. Ethical universalists, he believes, are committed to taking seriously the case for benevolent imperialism. That universalists normally do not endorse benevolent imperialism shows that they tacitly (and inconsistently) recognize the ethical value of nationalism (ibid., pp. 75–8). This argument begins with the contentious assumption that shared identities generate obligations. However, Miller not only fails to show this, but also fails to address the problem that some shared identities are evil, and presumably do not generate *ethical* obligations at all. The argument then moves on to a *non sequitur*. It does not follow from the claim that shared identities generate obligations that local and national communities are the *primary* bearers of obligations to protect basic rights. If need can generate obligation, then the *primary* obligation to meet need might fall on those with the greatest *ability* to do so. Miller's insistence that the principle of national self-determination severely limits the obligation to protect the basic rights of foreigners does not seem to be consistent with his own view of the obligations of outsiders. Finally, his suggestion that universalists are committed to taking seriously the case for benevolent imperialism is misleading, since it borrows some of its force from the historical record of imperialism, which clearly violated universalist principles. Well-designed external interventions to protect basic human rights are not ethically undermined by the charge of 'benevolent imperialism', whereas appeal to the principle of national self-determination to protect human rights violations is ethically objectionable. Miller holds that the obligations of nations to protect the human rights of foreigners is governed by a principle of limited sacrifice, which assigns a relatively small ethical weight to human rights when compared with national obligations, and which he never justifies.

Miller grounds his critique of universalism in the Humean meta-ethic of natural sentiments, which he deems to be superior to the Kantian meta-ethic of reason (ibid., p. 58). Yet this meta-ethic fails, on his own account, to support his particularistic nationalism completely, for he concedes that we have powerful humanitarian sentiments. It is true that he accords to humanitarian obligations a secondary role in his theory, but, if obligation depends on sentiment, the balance between national and universal obligation becomes contingent on the state of our sentiments. This would make our obligations vulnerable to the play of power and other ethically arbitrary forces. The distinction between good and bad sentiments requires ethical reasoning to which Miller is unwilling to give a primary role in his meta-ethic.

Miller does not attempt to undermine universalism completely, and admits that both universalism and particularism have some intuitive appeal. He claims, however, that nationality is ethically defensible, and defensible only on the ground of ethical particularism. There are nevertheless two universalist components of his theory. He recognizes the case for universal, basic rights, and that these rights sometimes entail obligations of nations to help foreigners. This concession is limited, however, because nations are not obliged to incur much cost in fulfilling these obligations, and it follows that the basic rights of the world's neediest and most oppressed people are relatively weak.

The second universal principle is that of nationality itself. Everyone has the right to the benefits of nationality. This raises at least three problems. The first is that Miller fails to show that his theory of human nature justifies giving such a strong priority to the universal right of national self-determination over other universal human rights. The second problem is that Miller's requirement that we generally give priority to the interests of our fellow nationals entails that our obligation to respect even the right to national self-determination of foreigners is limited. According to Miller's nationalism we could have an ethical obligation to promote the imperialist adventures of our own nation if, in doing so, we were promoting its interests. Miller can avoid this conclusion – which involves an incoherence in his theory since he both endorses and subverts the right to national self-determination – only by a more robust, universalist theory of human rights, which would ground the right of national self-determination in a more persuasive account of human interests. The third problem is that the weight that Miller gives to *national* obligations may be very subversive of the system of *states*. Miller could respond by saying so much the worse for states. This response could, however, be countered by arguing that, since Miller's conception of nationality is ethno-historical, it envisages a world of ethnic nation states, which is not clearly ethically superior to the world of multinational states.

Miller says that the ethics of nationality is plausible because it rests on 'well established facts about human identity and human motivation' (ibid., p. 80). The well established facts about identity and motivation are that they are complex, and include subnational and transnational, as well as national components. Making ethical inferences from facts about identity and motivation is also a complex task. It is not disputed that national identities can motivate great evils. Miller believes that universalists cannot easily motivate supranational ethical commitments. In this he is half right and half wrong. He is wrong in that he conflates the ethical problem of identifying right action with the psychological problem of motivating people to act justly. He is right to suggest that it is difficult to be good. The universalist, normative component of Miller's defence of 'nationality' suggests that the theory of international justice requires a meta-ethic that provides a stronger justification and a stronger motivation for the most powerful to help the neediest than Miller's Humean foundations can provide.

Impartial Justice

Brian Barry's theory of justice as impartiality appears to be precisely the kind of rationalistic, universalist theory that Miller calls into question. Barry holds that it is possible to construct a universally valid case for liberal egalitarian principles. The basis of justice as impartiality resides in our common humanity. Thus, whereas 'common humanity' was, for Miller, an ethical principle that supplemented 'nationality', it is basic for Barry. His theory of justice entails the robust defence of human rights in societies in which they are not supported by the national cultures. He criticizes political theories that claim to be rooted in particular cultures because they exaggerate the homogeneity of those cultures and implicitly rely on universal principles. They also exaggerate the incommensurability of different cultures, which can provide the basis for a universal conception of justice. Justice as impartiality appeals to the reason of each person, but a theory of justice must articulate with common-sense thinking about morality in order to be a theory of *justice* at all. Common-sense morality may, however, be challenged on the ground that it has been vitiated by unequal power relations. It should be tested by the criterion of what reasonable persons would agree to under conditions of equality and the absence of coercion (Barry, 1995, pp. 3–7, 10, 15–16, 68, 198, 209–10; 1998, p. 222).

Barry locates himself in the tradition that conceives of 'justice' as an idea that is intended to provide protection for the vulnerable. It would be widely acknowledged, he believes, that an arrangement was unjust if those who did badly under it could reasonably reject it. His theory of justice derives from the proposal of T.M. Scanlon, who invites us to consider a situation in which well-informed people with equal power seek to reach agreement with others who are similarly motivated on terms that cannot reasonably be rejected. The theory is 'impartial' in the sense that all those affected must be able to think that they have done as well as they could reasonably hope to. Agreements are not, however, rendered unjust by objections based on false beliefs or the self-interest of the objector. To qualify as 'reasonable' people must know the basic facts about their society, that other societies do things differently and that their own could feasibly be different. Barry admits that justice as impartiality is contentious in the sense that some people will reject it as incompatible with their beliefs. Such beliefs are not reasonable grounds for objection if it is not reasonable to expect others with different beliefs to be bound by them (Barry 1995, p. 7, 10, 15–17, 72, 107, 112–14, 122, 142–3, 163–4, 167–9, 208–9; 1998, p. 224).

Impartial justice, Barry claims, is neutral between different conceptions of the good. It assumes that there is an irreducible pluralism of such conceptions. Disputes about the good, he argues, are unresolvable, and there is thus no conception of the good that nobody could reasonably reject. He supports this thesis by appeal to the empirical fact that no conception of the good has been universally accepted. This is, he maintains, a reasonable ground for scepticism about the possibility that there is a conception that all reasonable people can be expected to accept. Justice as impartiality seeks a basis for social institutions and public policies that can in principle appeal to every member of society, whatever his or her conception of the good. The fairness of a rule of justice may be inconsistent with a particular conception of the good. However, the rules endorsed by impartial justice leave people with a considerable freedom to live according to their own moral ideas. Justice is a moral concept: it is wrong to behave unjustly because that is to breach the terms of fair agreement. But justice as impartiality differs from particular moral systems in that it sets the limits to the pursuit of the precepts that they endorse. It does not, therefore, constitute a comprehensive moral system. It does not give us a complete guide as to how we should live. Rather, it tells us how we should live *together*, given that we have different ideas about how to live. Justice as impartiality does not, therefore, have a substantive answer to every question: in many cases it endorses whatever outcome emerges from a fair procedure. There is a sense, however, in which impartial justice is *not* neutral between different conceptions of the good, for it will require more restrictions on the freedom of those whose conceptions of the good are relatively less compatible with the requirements of impartial justice than it will of those whose conceptions are more compatible (Barry, 1995, pp. ix, 13, 26, 72, 77, 82–3, 113, 139, 167, 169, 171, 174, 192, 197; 1998, p. 192–3).

Barry acknowledges that there must be moral inputs to any theory that has moral outputs. Thus, although the theory of justice of impartiality is neutral between conceptions of the good, it is based on the substantive moral idea of the equality of all human beings. It can also accommodate other moral ideas that are recognized within a wide variety of conceptions of the good. For example, Barry argues, the concept of 'harm' does not reflect a particular conception of the good. He supports this claim by empirical evidence that the range of punishments used around the world is very limited. The prevention of harm is required by justice as impartiality because what is harmful is deleterious to the furtherance of virtually any conception of the good. The neutrality of justice as impartiality also does not prevent people from pursuing their own conception of the good in public life as well as in private, but it requires them to do so only by means that are available to others on the same terms within a neutral constitutional framework. Thus, public policy on many matters will reflect some conception of the good (Barry, 1995, pp. 7–8, 12, 72, 88, 113, 141–3, 160–1, 175–6, 201).

The cogency of this theory depends, as Barry admits, on the meaning of 'reasonable'. Other theorists might argue that they could reasonably reject Barry's theory. Barry would argue that this would be unreasonable. Appeals to what is reasonable do not by themselves resolve such disagreements. Barry is also vulnerable to the argument that his theory implausibly rests on scepticism about conceptions of the good and the rejection of scepticism about theories of justice. It is further arguable that Barry's conception of the reasonable conceals an idea of 'overlapping consensus' (of reasonable persons) that the theory of justice of impartiality is supposed to dispense with (Hardin, 1998; Caney, 1998, pp. 91, 100; Bubeck, 1998, p. 172; Barry, 1998, pp. 189–91, 196, 208, 212, 237). Barry's 'neutrality' between 'conceptions of the good' is, therefore, consistent with some fundamental assumptions about what is good, with the use of conceptions of what is good (or bad) that are common to most 'conceptions of the good', and with public policies that embody particular conceptions of the good if those policies have been adopted by fair means.

Miller maintained that ethical particularism was superior to ethical universalism in supplying motivation for imperfect altruists. Barry identifies the motive to comply with the requirements of impartial justice as the desire to act in ways that can be defended to others, which, he claims, has force with almost all of us to some degree. Justice as impartiality appeals to the motive of people's desire to behave fairly. The theory assumes the existence of the desire to live in a society whose members all freely accept its rules of justice and its major institutions (Barry, 1995, pp. 10, 51, 164). Miller may have the superior theory of motivation, for there is no doubt that national identity can be a strong motivator (though not necessarily, or even typically, for justice). Barry's account of motivation for justice has two weaknesses. Firstly, we may doubt whether the desire to behave fairly and justify one's actions to others is strong transnationally (Hardin, 1998, p. 146). Secondly, in discussing the desire to behave fairly, Barry seems to be thinking primarily of justice *within* national societies, since he speaks of the desire 'to live in a society' whose members commit themselves to justice. Barry has said, in response to scepticism about the motivational component of his theory, that it is enough if the desire to behave justly 'has some efficacy' (1998, p. 236). Clearly, it has that. What is questionable, however, is whether it has anything like enough efficacy to motivate conformity with Barry's demanding conception of justice.

The issues raised by Miller's distinction between *ethical universalism* and *ethical particularism* are treated by Barry by the distinction between *second-order impartiality* and *first-order impartiality*. Second-order impartiality governs the search for the principles and rules of justice: it is a test to be applied to the moral and legal rules of a society. First-order impartiality is a maxim of behaviour in everyday life that excludes preferential treatment for persons with whom one has special relations. Second-order impartiality does *not* entail universal first-order impartiality, but requires only that the rules of first-order impartiality should be consistent with the principles of second-order impartiality. It conforms, for example, with the principles of common-sense morality that require parents to be impartial among their children, but does not require them to be impartial between their children and those of other people. It also recognizes the ethical significance of personal and institutional obligations (Barry, 1995, pp. 11–15, 23–5, 194, 246–7).

The theory of justice as impartiality is, therefore, favourable to the sustenance of personal relationships. We all have only a finite amount of time and affection to devote to other people, and life would not normally be worth living if we could not decide for ourselves, once we had met our general social obligations, on whom these should be bestowed. Universal first-order impartiality would make demands that ran counter to sentiments 'whose long-term survival value no doubt means that they have a basis in human biology'. There is, Barry insists, a 'natural inclination' to make special efforts on one's own behalf and on behalf of those about whom one cares. Universal first-order impartiality would, therefore, impose insupportable burdens. It is the role of rules of justice to set bounds to the working of particularistic inclinations by ruling out actions that injure others and prohibiting unfair partiality (ibid., pp. 84, 121, 201, 205–6). Barry relies here on a doctrine of natural sentiments that are rooted in biology. The theory thereby partly converges with Miller's particularism, although, for Barry, first-order natural sentiments are allowed free play subject to the requirements of justice and second-order impartiality. Barry emphasizes the constraints on first-order partiality more strongly than Miller does in order to rule out particularistic aggression and unfair discrimination (ibid., pp. 18, 253–5).

Barry concedes that, up to a certain point, increasing the stringency of first-order impartiality works to the advantage of the least advantaged groups in a society. But he denies that a regime of universal first-order impartiality would be the most advantageous to the worst-off. Justice as impartiality rules out practices and institutions involving social relations within and between societies with an unequal impact that cannot be defended against reasonable rejection on the part of those who lose from the inequality. Thus, freedom of association can work to the disadvantage of those excluded from the association. Barry suggests that associations which control widely-valued social goods should have less freedom to be partial, especially if their partiality is part of a wider pattern of discrimination, than one has in the choice of friends (ibid., pp. 15–17, 211–13). His discussion of limits to freedom of association refers implicitly to intra-societal justice, but it has implications for limits to the right of national self-determination that suggest that Barry would be more willing to sacrifice this principle for the sake of international justice than Miller would.

There can be, Barry concedes, situations in which impartial justice would require great sacrifice of personal relations. He treats these, however, as exceptional (ibid., pp. 223–4). Yet justice entails 'large-scale' international redistribution (ibid., p. 115). Miller, it will be recalled, imposed on nations the obligation to protect the basic rights of members of other nations if the fellow-nationals of the rights-holders could or would not do so, and such action involved little sacrifice. Barry mentions large-scale international redistribution separately from the problem of the sacrifice of personal relations, so that it is not clear how much sacrifice of such relations would be demanded by international obligations. He had previously made a distinction between particularistic nationalism and universal nationalism. The relation between the former and the latter, he said, was the same as that between selfishness and individualism: selfishness being the pursuit of one's own interests without regard to the interests of others, individualism being the doctrine that it is legitimate to pursue one's own interests on the same terms as those on which others are free to pursue theirs. He distinguished both types of nationalism from 'cosmopolitanism', which holds that the interests of all human beings have in principle an equal claim on all of us. It is obvious, he said, that cosmopolitanism is a denial of nationalism (Barry, 1991, p. 354). This formulation does not clearly differentiate the obligations of nations according to Barry's 'universal nationalism' from those generated by Miller's particularistic nationalism. Barry appears to have changed his position, for he now endorses both civic nationalism and cosmopolitanism (Barry, 1997). The consistency of his views may be saved, at the expense of the consistency of his terminology, if the 'cosmopolitanism' that is the denial of nationalism is equated with universal first-order impartiality. Second-order impartiality may endorse a form of cosmopolitanism that can in turn endorse 'universal', civic nationalism. This still leaves the obligations of nations to foreigners very indeterminate. Clearly, large-scale international redistribution could potentially require considerable limitations of personal freedom, including freedom to benefit one's nearest and dearest, and Barry does not explore this area of conflict between first-order freedom and the constraints of second-order justice and impartiality. He does say that justice as impartiality asks what rules people placed in an original position of equality would choose. Preference for family, friends or nations are *sometimes* permitted by second-order impartiality, but it remains unclear what rules of international justice would be chosen in an original position of equality (Barry, 1995, pp. 226–7).

To the problem of how we ought to balance our particular with our universal obligations Barry proposes the Goldilocks solution. Justice as impartiality calls for neither too much first-order impartiality nor too little, but just the right amount, or, more precisely, an amount within a range whose limits would be established by the parties to a Scanlonian original position. This requires a set of rules of justice that provides everyone with a fair opportunity of living a good life, while leaving room for the kind of freedom in shaping one's life that is an essential constituent in every conception of the good life (ibid., pp. 206–7, 230). The first part of this requirement would indeed entail large-scale international redistribution, but it is unclear to what extent this would restrict the second part. The problem unresolved by Barry is that the provision of a fair opportunity for everyone in the world to live a good life, starting with the actual status quo as a baseline, would require a redistribution of resources on such a large scale that the freedom essential to every conception of the good life would be impossible. How much individual freedom for those who are now relatively rich by global standards would be compatible with fair opportunity for those who are now worst-off is very uncertain. Justice as impartiality remains rather indeterminate on the question as to how we should balance our legitimate first-order interests with our second-order obligations. Barry may retort that 'if something is not easy to determine then it is not easy to determine, and any theory that makes it look easy must be some sort of fraud' (Barry, 1998, p. 213). It is certainly unreasonable to require much determinacy in a theory of international justice, but Barry should say enough to show that, faced with the dilemma of particular and universal obligations, he is not evading it, but, rather, clarifying, as precisely as possible, how it should be resolved.

One interpretation of the Goldilocks solution is the Rotherham principle. Universal morality, Barry says, consists largely in general prescriptions that generate specific obligations in the circumstances of everyday life, including the obligation 'to play our part in the social practices of our society'. My obligation to contribute to the pension of someone who lives in Rotherham, but not to the pension of someone who lives in Rennes, derives from the fact that I belong the same scheme of social insurance as the former but not the latter (Barry, 1997, pp. 66–7). Insofar as second-order impartiality permits and may require first-order partiality the Rotherham principle is *prima facie* sound. However, Barry obscures the problem by comparing Rotherham with Rennes rather than with, say, Rwanda. Thus, he begs the question as to whether we are obliged, or even ethically permitted, to support our national scheme of social insurance in the face of global poverty.

For both Barry and Miller, natural sentiments justify giving priority to those with whom we have particular relations over those with whom we have no such relations. For Barry, these priorities are constrained by the principle of second-order impartiality, which means that they must be justifiable to reasonable others. For Miller, particular obligations are not so much constrained by principles of impartial justice as qualified by duties of humanity, which are themselves constrained both by the priority of particular obligations and the principle of national self-determination. Barry appears to attach little significance to national boundaries as such – and thus fits Miller's definition of a universalist – but would not object to national commitments *provided that they could be justified to reasonable foreigners*. Barry's nationalism appears to be weaker than Miller's, but the contractualist test of reasonableness is highly indeterminate. It would rule out direct human rights violations against foreigners (which Miller also rules out) and support for human rights violating regimes. Whereas Miller objects to 'benevolent imperialist' violations of national self-determination for the sake of human rights protection in principle, Barry would probably accept only pragmatic objections to such interventions, although he concedes that such objections can be very cogent. Barry offers, therefore, a stronger basis for an ethical theory of international justice, but a weaker account of motivation, since the desire to justify our actions to others probably gets weaker as we move from particular to universal relations. The desire of nations and states to justify their actions at the bar of universal justice as impartiality is not nonexistent, but it is limited.

The implication of Barry's theory of justice as impartiality is that national sentiment ought to be much weaker than it is. This is ethically appealing – because, if implemented, it would relieve millions of human beings from undeserved suffering – but psychologically unconvincing. Barry can make his theory motivationally convincing only by weakening his commitment to natural sentiment. This would require some revision of his division of ethical labour between first-order partiality and second-order impartiality, between our commitment to particular others and our obligations to strangers.

Barry has, in a recent paper, closed the gap somewhat between his universalism and Miller's nationalism. He agrees that nations can legitimately take pride in their cultural achievements. He departs from Miller, however, in holding that a common sense of history is not necessary for national pride. He concedes that *civic* nationalism is essential for the successful operation of a liberal-democratic polity. Liberal democracy is, for him, the domestic aspect of cosmopolitanism, and liberal-democratic nationalism is required by cosmopolitan morality. The principles of this form of nationalism, he claims, support cosmopolitan redistribution and intervention. The transfer of resources from rich countries to poor ones does nothing to injure civic nationalism in the rich ones, and offers a chance to the poor countries of creating civic nations of their own (Barry, 1997, pp. 58, 61–2, 65–7). It is clear that cosmopolitanism endorses transfers of this kind, but we have seen that Barry begs the question as to how, given limited resources, we can conform with the obligations generated by the Rotherham principle and help poor countries become civic nations. If the licence that second-order impartiality gives to first-order partiality is rather expensive, it is not clear how we can fulfil our obligations of impartial justice to the large number of severely deprived human beings who may (reasonably?) object to the Rotherham principle (Arneson, 1998, p. 85; Barry, 1998, p. 231).

Finally, Barry argues that the idea of a national purpose is a danger to the integrity of a liberal democracy (Barry, 1997, p. 66). Here, again, Barry's cosmopolitanism risks ceding ground to liberal-democratic nationalism, for surely cosmopolitan principles require that liberal-democratic, civic nation states should have cosmopolitan national purposes. Arguably, therefore, Barry still gives too much weight to our obligations to our fellow-citizens from a cosmopolitan point of view, and misses the opportunity to endorse *cosmopolitan nationalism*, which might combine the motivational power of nationalism with the ethical ends of international justice.

Conclusion: Cosmopolitan Realism

Miller's particularistic defence of nationalism and relatively weak support for universal human rights rest on a Humean meta-ethic of natural sentiments that accords considerable ethical importance to identity and motivation. This meta-ethic is vulnerable to the objection that, although any plausible ethical theory must take identity and motivation into account, these elements of human nature can lead to evil as well as good, and therefore should not be regarded as constituting the fundamental level of ethics. Barry's theory, by contrast, is universalist in the sense that it claims to generate universally valid principles of justice which transcend the boundaries of nation-states, override conflicting national cultures, and offer their benefits to everyone in the world on the same terms. However, it differs from the ethical universalism characterized by Miller in that it does not apply to pre-social individuals with only general features. Real individuals with their particular natures and special commitments are subject to the rule of impartial justice. Barry's distinction between second-order and first-order impartiality allows him to derive from his universalist theory similar particular obligations to those which Miller treats as fundamental. It seems that Barry would allow some particular obligations to be fundamental, since he believes them to be rooted in human biology, and he holds that impartial justice endorses civic nationalism and special obligations to fellow-citizens. His universalist egalitarianism implies a much stronger internationalism than Miller's theory allows, but the extent to which personal relations and the obligations of citizenship should be sacrificed for the sake of international justice remains unclear.

Miller's particularistic ethic is unattractive because it endorses only a weak, low-cost humanitarianism, and thereby endorses a great deal of collective selfishness and is indifferent to a great deal of human suffering. Barry's universalism is potentially more demanding, and thus raises motivational problems. He also fails to prove his claim that it is possible to construct a universally valid case for liberal egalitarian principles. He implies that no-one can reasonably reject liberal egalitarianism. Sceptics may argue that, since he bases his conception of justice on a hypothetical agreement among free and equal persons, the liberal-egalitarian policies and institutions that appear in his conclusions may be derived tautologically (Bubeck, 1998, pp. 166, 170–1). Barry appears to concede this, but defends the derivation on the ground that it is required by the laws of logic (Barry, 1998, p. 193). However, he is clear that logic is not enough for a political theory. Its conclusions must not be 'manifestly outrageous' (ibid., p. 218). Barry's theory may be defended, therefore, as ethically attractive, on the ground that, unlike Miller's nationalism, it takes the basic needs and rights of all human beings seriously.

Barry leaves our particular and our universal obligations in a potentially strong and unresolved tension. Miller's particularism recognizes universalist sentiments and obligations, only to weaken them for the sake of national obligations, leading to a less than wholly consistent approach to national self-determination and intervention. Thus, *both Miller's particularism and Barry's universalism fail to give a satisfactory account of the obligations that we have for the sake of international justice.* This is a striking conclusion, since Miller proposes one of the best ethical defences of nationalism that we have, and Barry offers one of the most powerful contemporary arguments for ethical universalism. Since Miller and Barry converge on there being a case to be made for international justice, their failure to spell out the supporting theory adequately suggests that some kind of new approach is required.

Miller tries to show that universalists cannot derive the value of nationalism from their fundamental principles. I have argued that Miller cannot derive the ethical value of nationalism from the meta-ethic of particularism, but has to employ implicit universalist premises about the value of national identity. He values national identity, for example, in part because he believes that economic globalization is likely to distribute the benefits of global culture unequally and unjustly (Miller, 1995, pp. 186–7). But this is a universalist argument for nationalism. Barry has shown that universalists can attribute considerable ethical weight to special relations, and they may hold that such relations and their associated obligations can have instrumental value for impartial ends (McMahan, 1997, pp. 114–5). Lawrence Blum (1996) has plausibly argued that communities can be the source of actions that are virtuous by universalist standards. Charles Beitz has argued that one may, from an impartial point of view, respect the sovereignty of states (and, by implication, the right to self-determination of nations) because, all things considered, universal values (such as those of human rights) would be better served by doing so (Beitz, 1991, pp. 248–9). Universalists can, therefore, take account of the realities of nationalism, and treat them as having some value as instruments for the pursuit of universalist goals. This is the position of cosmopolitan nationalism. Thomas Pogge has defended a form of cosmopolitanism that involves a diversity of institutions regulated by liberal and democratic principles that does not exclude a role for nation-states (Pogge, 1992). Nationalism takes many forms and has many consequences, and universalists can take account of these facts and accordingly construct a rather complex set of attitudes to nationalism.

As second-order impartiality permits and regulates first-order commitments in Barry's theory of justice, so cosmopolitanism can permit and regulate nationalism. This approach I call 'cosmopolitan realism'. This is Kantian in inspiration, and seeks to adapt to contemporary conditions both Kant's cosmopolitanism and his realism. Cosmopolitan realism endorses the principle of universal equality that Barry's theory of impartial justice requires, but treats national identities and loyalties both as *intrinsically ambivalent*, like all particular relations capable of good and evil, and as *potentially instrumentally valuable* to the end of promoting universalist principles. The cosmopolitan realist must reject Miller's Humean meta-ethic, and can treat Barry's Scanlonian contractualism as a more or less useful 'device of representation' (as Rawls called his 'original position'), while endorsing his underlying neo-Kantian universalistic egalitarianism. This form of cosmopolitanism has nothing to do with that shallow, cultural eclecticism that Miller calls 'cosmopolitanism'. It is precisely an attempt to think about what the concept of 'international justice' entails. Cosmopolitanism should also have nothing to do with the various forms of futile or dangerous utopianism that are sometimes attributed to it. Barry has shown that cosmopolitans can enjoy as 'thick' a culture as any communitarian, while tolerating or celebrating a rich diversity of cultures worldwide, subject only to the constraints of international justice, which would at least guarantee basic rights, fair opportunities and protection from preventable harm to everyone. Cosmopolitanism can be unapologetically rather indeterminate about such questions as the value of nationalism, the right to self-determination and the justification of benevolent intervention, for this indeterminacy is not a weakness of cosmopolitan realism, but a problem inherent in the relation between systematic political philosophy and the complex and ever-changing world in which practical political policies must be formulated and implemented.

The meta-ethical basis of cosmopolitan realism is Kantian. Kant held that human beings were less good than they could be, a proposition that Miller should not wish to deny. Kant believed it to follow that they had an obligation to be better than they were. In the absence of empirical evidence that no moral progress is possible, there is a moral duty to believe that it is possible, and to endeavour to bring it about. Duty must therefore struggle against disheartening facts. Ought implies can, and no-one can therefore have an obligation to do what is impossible. Moral ideals, however, so long as it is not demonstrably impossible to fulfil them, entail moral duties to strive to realize them (Apel, 1997, pp. 98, 106). This does not require us to accept the idea of the unity of the ideal: that, ideally, all rational persons would reach agreement on all ethical questions. We may subscribe to moral pluralism, and hold that legitimate values can conflict, and that therefore conflicting values cannot be reconciled without some ethical loss. The values endorsed by ethical particularism, including those of nationalism, may not be wholly reconcilable with universalist values without some loss on one side or the other, or on both (Baynes, 1997, pp. 230–1). Thus, there may be no determinate solution to the problem of reconciling particular and universal obligations that Barry left unresolved, but we may say that, *pace* Miller, the actually existing balance is weighted far too much in favour of particular, and especially national commitments.

Barry has said that cosmopolitanism is a moral outlook, not an institutional prescription. It leaves much space for dispute about the institutions that would best promote cosmopolitan justice. It has no principled position on national or state boundaries. It refuses, however, to *assume* that existing institutions are the best possible. For the cosmopolitan, the value of an institution derives from its contribution to human well-being. However, given the dire record of both states and nations with respect to human well-being, cosmopolitans tend to be favourably disposed towards international regimes designed to protect human rights and promote peace and international justice (Barry, 1997, pp. 34–40, 44, 50, 62–3). Pogge distinguishes between moral cosmopolitanism and legal cosmopolitanism. The former is concerned with moral relations between persons and the moral obligations that persons have to each other, including the obligations to establish and support appropriate institutions. It may or may not support sovereign states and/or autonomous nations. Legal cosmopolitanism is concerned with a political ideal of a global order that would embody cosmopolitan principles. Moral cosmopolitanism assigns moral obligations to individual and collective agents, whereas legal cosmopolitanism assigns such responsibilities to institutional schemes. On the latter view the responsibility of persons is indirect. It is a shared responsibility for the justice of institutions that one supports, not to participate in an unjust institutional scheme without making reasonable efforts to aid its victims, and to promote institutional reform for the sake of justice. Pogge favours a scheme that would disperse political authority in a multilayered system of nested territorial units, in which the geographical shape of political units is determined by the autonomous preferences of situated individuals. Such a scheme would give political recognition to the multiple identities that people actually have. It would therefore offer political protection to cultural diversity. *It could endorse certain forms of nationalism*. It would also provide many checks and balances to prevent excesses of power and thereby defend human rights. Its emphasis on the dispersion of political power would encourage active democracy. The idea of a multilayered system allows decision-making to be placed at a supra-national level, if this is required by justice, and thereby offers the prospect for *more* autonomy for the world's poorest people than do conventional notions of state sovereignty and national self-determination, which tend to reproduce the existing global order, and thus the unjust privileges of rich and powerful nations (Pogge, 1992, pp. 48–9, 58, 60, 63–6).

Cosmopolitanism, far from being, as Miller suggests, recent and shallow, has deep historical roots in Western culture, stretching back to the Stoics (Nussbaum, 1997). It also informs the UN Universal Declaration of Human

Rights, which was reaffirmed by the 'international community' at the Vienna World Conference on Human Rights in 1993. Cosmopolitanism is an ethical and political theory that has empirical foundations in the existence of global institutions. Miller claims that there is no world community that can in itself generate obligations of justice for the rich to help the poor. He concedes, however, that if the rich nations were *causally responsible* for the violation of the basic rights of the poor, they would have an obligation to help them. Pogge finds the link between causal and moral responsibility in unjust, global institutions, in which rich nations participate. Since Miller appears to accept that there are such unjust institutions, his view of the obligation of rich nations should be closer to Pogge's (Miller, 1995, pp. 191–2; Pogge, 1992, pp. 50–2). One great merit of Pogge's institutional approach is that it helps to resolve the tension between particular and universal obligations, which Barry left unresolved. Individuals should support institutions, including national institutions, with goals endorsed by the principle of international justice. Miller's nationalism rests, in part, on the Humean axiom of limited altruism. This axiom, however, although it may be psychologically plausible, is not a plausible basis for *nationalism*, for limited altruism can be mobilized for national obligations only by means of mediating institutions, and limited altruism could be mobilized for international obligations similarly. Miller is sceptical about this, employing the weakness of commitment to the European Union as supporting empirical evidence. But it may be argued against Miller on this point that: a) not much effort (at least in the United Kingdom) has been made to mobilize a sense of European obligation; and b) despite relatively weak official mobilization of cosmopolitan sentiment, there is considerable public support for international humanitarian aid when the mass media choose to mobilize it. The mobilization of cosmopolitan sentiment is, therefore, a tough, but not an unrealistic project. Cosmopolitanism is neither superficial nor utopian; it is serious, and it is here, now. Freedom of association and the ethical division of labour are already helping some people to address the enormous problems of international justice in the form of non-governmental, governmental and intergovernmental organizations and institutions. If their achievement has so far been disappointing, the task of political analysis (normative and empirical) is to identify the blockages to progress, not to show that such progress is either impossible or undesirable.

References

Apel, K.-O. (1997), 'Kant's "Toward Perpetual Peace" as Historical Prognosis from the Point of View of Moral Duty' in J. Bohman and M. Lutz-Bachmann (eds), *Perpetual Peace: Essays on Kant's Cosmopolitan Ideal*, The MIT Press, Cambridge, Massachusetts.

Arneson, R. (1998), 'The Priority of the Right Over the Good Rides Again' in P. Kelly (ed.), *Impartiality, Neutrality and Justice: Re-Reading Brian Barry's Justice as Impartiality*, Edinburgh University Press, Edinburgh.

Barry, B. (1991), 'Nationalism' in D. Miller (ed.), *The Blackwell Encyclopaedia of Political Thought*, Blackwell, Oxford.

Barry, B. (1995), *Justice as Impartiality*, Clarendon Press, Oxford.

Barry, B. (1998), 'Something in the Disputation not Unpleasant' in P. Kelly (ed.), *Impartiality, Neutrality and Justice: Re-Reading Brian Barry's Justice as Impartiality*, Edinburgh University Press, Edinburgh.

Barry, B. (1999),'Statism and Nationalism: A Cosmopolitan Critique' in I. Shapiro and L. Brilmayer (eds), *Global Justice. NOMOS XLI*, New York University Press, New York, pp. 12–66.

Baynes, K. (1997), 'Communitarian and Cosmopolitan Challenges to Kant's Conception of World Peace' in J. Bohman and M. Lutz-Bachmann (eds), *Perpetual Peace: Essays on Kant's Cosmopolitan Ideal*, The MIT Press, Cambridge, Massachusetts.

Beitz, C.R. (1991), 'Sovereignty and Morality in International Affairs' in D. Held (ed.), *Political Theory Today*, Polity Press, Cambridge.

Blum, L.A. (1996), 'Community and Virtue' in R. Crisp (ed.), *How Should One Live? Essays on the Virtues*, Clarendon Press, Oxford.

Bubeck, D. (1998), 'Care, Justice and the Good' in P. Kelly (ed.), *Impartiality, Neutrality and Justice: Re-Reading Brian Barry's Justice as Impartiality*, Edinburgh University Press, Edinburgh.

Caney, S. (1998), 'Impartiality and Liberal Neutrality' in P. Kelly (ed.), *Impartiality, Neutrality and Justice: Re-Reading Brian Barry's Justice as Impartiality*, Edinburgh University Press, Edinburgh.

Hardin, R. (1998), 'Reasonable Agreement: Political not Normative' in P. Kelly (ed.), *Impartiality, Neutrality and Justice: Re-Reading Brian Barry's Justice as Impartiality*, Edinburgh University Press, Edinburgh.

Kelly, P. (ed.) (1998), *Impartiality, Neutrality and Justice: Re-Reading Brian Barry's Justice as Impartiality*, Edinburgh University Press, Edinburgh.

McMahan, J. (1997), 'The Limits of National Partiality' in R. McKim and J. McMahan (eds), *The Morality of Nationalism*, Oxford University Press, Oxford.

Miller, D. (1995), *On Nationality*, Clarendon Press, Oxford.

Nussbaum, M. (1997) 'Kant and Stoic Cosmopolitanism', *The Journal of Political Philosophy*, 5, pp. 1–25.

O'Leary, B. (ed.) (1996), 'Symposium on David Miller's On Nationality', *Nations and Nationalism*, 2, 3, pp. 407–51.
Political Studies (1996), 'Brian Barry's Justice as Impartiality: A Symposium', *Political Studies*, 44, 2, pp. 303–42.
Pogge, T. (1992), 'Cosmopolitanism and Sovereignty', *Ethics*, 103, pp. 48–75.

5 Cosmopolitan Communities[1]

LUKAS H. MEYER

Introducing Liberal Cosmopolitanism

Cosmopolitanism,[2] as I understand it here, is, first of all, broadly consequentialist in character. Wherever they may live, all cosmopolitans share one communal goal, as Christoph Martin Wieland suggested in 1788:

> It is intrinsically the simplest, purest, and most beneficent goal that one can imagine, for it is neither more nor less than the following formula entails: 'To reduce, as much as possible without wreaking havoc, the sum total of evil oppressing mankind, and to increase as much as possible the sum total of good in the world.'[3]

Even though the wording is antiquated, the idea expressed – that everyone should do his or her best to promote the well-being of all people, whoever they may be – is characteristic of the cosmopolitan position. It is worth stressing, however, that cosmopolitanism, as I understand it, is not strictly consequentialist in character.[4] Rather, it is broadly consequentialist in character. Cosmopolitans acknowledge that the consequences of one's action often have normative significance. At the same time, they will argue that performing an action can be intrinsically valuable. Indeed, I believe, that the plausibility of cosmopolitanism turns in part on its capacity to attribute intrinsic value to certain forms of human interaction.

Second, proponents of this view endorse the position of value-individualism. They assess a current or imagined state of (international) society by looking to the quality of the lives that this state tends to produce and sustain. What counts is the quality of the life of the individual human being. Cultural, or religious communities, nations, or states are units of concern in so far as individuals realize values as members of these groups.

Third, the (liberal) cosmopolitan typically believes that value-individualism holds universally: the status of being ultimate units of concern ought to be attributed to all human beings equally. In addition to being a human being, you may have some properties that qualify you for membership in some group or other, say, to the Caucasians, Roman Catholics, or women, but your status of being an ultimate unit of concern does not depend on membership in any such group. According to the strand of Greek thought associated with the Sophists, the idea that we all enjoy moral status in virtue of being human rather than by means of membership in some exclusive group was expressed by contrasting man-made law and custom with the order of things as provided by Nature (*physis*). Accordingly, Antiphon criticizes attributing value to people depending on their origin:

> We respect and honour those who are descendents of noble fathers while not respecting and honouring those who are not from a noble house. In doing so, we relate to each other as do Barbarians, for by Nature, we are created equal in all respects, whether we be Barbarians or Hellenes. This emerges clearly once we stop to consider those things that by Nature all people need. All will acquire them in the same way and where those things are concerned we are different neither from the Barbarians nor the Hellenes. We all, each and every one of us, breathe out of our mouths and noses, and we eat by using our hands.[5]

Next, the proponent of (liberal) cosmopolitanism thus specifies an agent-neutral criterion for right action. The comparable assessment of the moral quality of any two states of affairs does not vary from person to person with an eye to what one's particular situation is.[6] Your membership in a specific group may not matter where the question of how you proceed in assessing states of affairs is concerned. It is right for every moral agent to do what is in the best interest of all those entities that deserve moral respect – namely, all human beings.

Having characterized the cosmopolitan position solely by means of these four features, it is important to note that there are as many variants of this position as there are theories of value compatible with the four features mentioned. In other words, what it is that proponents of a moral theory – characterized by the four features mentioned above – believe a moral agent ought to do, all things considered, will depend largely on the account of the good in human life that they endorse. The good in question can be explained in subjective terms. In this case we are supposed to be concerned about, for example, human happiness or the fulfilment of desires or the satisfaction of preferences or the avoidance of pain.[7] Alternatively, the good in question can be explained in more objective terms. A cosmopolitan may argue that we should be concerned about whether people's needs are fulfilled or whether they have the capabilities to achieve well-being (see Sen, 1984, pp. 325–45; Raz, 1994, pp. 3–38). Also, cosmopolitans may be concerned about whether people have sufficient resources (see Dworkin, 1981, and his more recent restatement, 1993) or primary goods[8] at their disposal. Other cosmopolitans prefer an account in terms of human rights: we should be concerned that no-one's basic rights are violated or that no-one lacks protection (see Shue, 1980). Having agreed upon the relevant notion of the good for individuals, cosmopolitans may still disagree on how the good is to be measured. Are we to rank states of affairs by the total sum of the good realized or by the per capita average? Alternatively, cosmopolitans might think that what really matters is how people fare relative to others. For example, we might believe that no-one should be worse off than anyone has to be or that no-one should find herself below the mean.

It will be obvious that this is not a full list of the possible variants of liberal cosmopolitanism as characterized by the four features I have mentioned. I do not believe that all the variants are equally plausible. Still, for the purpose of my present discussion, it will not be necessary to argue that one of the options is to be preferred over all others. Whatever account of the value of the life of individual human beings by liberal cosmopolitans is endorsed and however the relevant good is measured, the proponents of these widely differing accounts of liberal cosmopolitanism will, I believe, most likely converge in a substantive normative judgment. To be plausible at all, I suggest, any variant of liberal cosmopolitanism has to specify as the most urgent agent-neutral reasons for action the curbing or preventing of severe human deprivations where that is possible. Thus, when people are starving to death or facing the threat of starvation that can be prevented by others, the latter will have the most urgent agent-neutral reasons for taking action to prevent this suffering and these deaths. Also, when (large numbers of) future people can be expected to be deprived of subsistence, say, of uncontaminated water or nutritious food, without their having had the chance to provide these goods for themselves, and this state of affairs can be prevented by people living today, the latter will have the most urgent reasons for doing so. In both cases our reasons for providing aid arise from the interests of the needy and the helpless.

None can reasonably doubt that under the current dire conditions of international society, severe human deprivations are prevalent and that they must be expected to be so in the future (see e.g. World Commission on Environment and Development, 1987, pp. 27–41).[9] At the same time, one has to be extremely sceptical about the prospects for reform of the international system in order to believe that the (current and expected) degree of human suffering under the prevailing order is to be understood as 'unavoidable costs' for the flourishing of human life in some regions of the world today. Though doubts remain, particularly when it comes to the long-term consequences of proposed political strategies of reforming the international system,[10] a further claim seems equally valid. Given the current state of international society, to follow the most urgent agent-neutral reasons for action would imply rather dramatic changes in the communal way of life of, *inter alia*, Western societies.[11] I take this claim to be characteristic of the cosmopolitan position.[12]

The Loyalists' Objection to Cosmopolitanism

Thus, we can assume that the proponents of the moral theory under consideration will criticize the prevailing conditions of international society and will lend their support to an effort to change these conditions.[13] Some of those who fundamentally object to liberal cosmopolitanism, the loyalists as I will call them, suspect cosmopolitans of wanting not simply to change things but positively to reject certain characteristics constitutive of individual and collective ways of life that may be particularly valuable to us. As the objection goes: The cosmopolitan approach attributes only instrumental value to attachments that are constitutive of the ways of life of most, if not all, people. In doing so, cosmopolitans seriously misinterpret the values realized in relationships as these are understood by the people who are involved in them.

Indeed, liberal cosmopolitans have often been accused of being unable to explain the moral significance of our particular attachments to our commitments and projects as well as to the (national) community to which we belong.[14] This complaint seems to be rooted in the conviction that people can refer to their particular attachments and, on the basis of an evaluation of these attachments, can resist the cosmopolitans' often radical proposals for changing the institutions of international and national societies. In other words, loyalists suggest that the particular attachments people have adopted give them reasons for action that outweigh the reasons for action to which the liberal cosmopolitans appeal in arguing that morality demands dramatic changes in the communal (national) way of life of, *inter alia*, Western societies.[15] The cosmopolitans tend to reply by accusing their opponents of defending a status quo that is parochial (and nationalistic) in its outlook and that cannot be defended in the court of morality. After all, they are likely to hold that dramatic changes are required in response to what they acknowledge as the most urgent agent-neutral reasons for action.

In this chapter I shall ask what account of the value of communities may give rise to reasons for individually or collectively resisting dramatic changes in the communal way of life where such changes seem to be required by the most urgent agent-neutral reasons for action.[16] I suggest that we would be able to resist demands for changes in the communal way of life based on the most urgent agent-neutral reasons for action only if we succeeded in defending an account of the value of communal life that might be characterized as follows: first, the value of a particular society can be understood (accounted for) only by appeal to the features that it alone possesses. Second, the value of our particular communal way of life, thus understood, gives us reasons for action that override the most urgent agent-neutral reasons for action where the latter would have us (dramatically) changing our communal way of life. To give the defender of such an account of the value of communal life a name, I will dub her a 'parochial collectivist' (or 'collectivist').

Parochial collectivism is not, I believe, a defensible view. My argument here has two steps, and I will set out the latter of these alone. Both collectivists and liberal cosmopolitans, I assume, will find it plausible to attribute instrumental value both to state organizations and to citizens' affiliations with them. Neither liberal cosmopolitans nor collectivists are committed to any particular legal structure of international society. In particular, cosmopolitans are not committed to any form of world government.[17] Moral cosmopolitanism and legal cosmopolitanism should be distinguished.[18] Indeed, given that we have good reasons to believe that a world state could not fulfil basic minimal functions that we would like to be able to attribute to states before granting them some measure of legitimacy,[19] the dispute between the cosmopolitan and the collectivist does not concern the existence of a plurality of basic political units as such.[20] Thus, it would be a mistake to understand the dispute between collectivists and cosmopolitans primarily in terms of the nature of the legal structure of international society that we should strive for.[21]

Rather – and this is the second step of the argument – the dispute between the two positions under consideration comes to the fore when we ask whether existing communal ways of life should continue to exist. To put it bluntly, the cosmopolitan will often require change, whereas the parochial collectivist will as often defend the existing ways of life as legitimate. Within their broadly consequentialist and agent-neutral framework liberal cosmopolitans attribute (individual and collective) instrumental as well as intrinsic value to the communal way of life that people share. The liberal cosmopolitan will want to attribute intrinsic value to a communal way of life *in part* for the particular features that this way of life alone possesses. However, we can resist demands for changes in the communal way of life based on the most urgent agent-neutral reasons for action only if we follow the collectivist in attributing intrinsic value to a society *solely* on the basis of the particular features that it alone possesses, and only if we hold that the value of society so understood gives rise to reasons for action that take priority over the most urgent agent-neutral reasons for action. Those views of the value of communal life are mistaken.

Attributing Instrumental Value to Society

Obviously, where dramatic changes in the communal way of life seem to be required by the most urgent agent-neutral reasons for action, we are not going to acquire reasons for individually or collectively resisting such changes by attributing only instrumental value to the organization of people in basic political units that contain particular communal ways of life. Indeed, many cosmopolitans have put forward an argument for such units that is indirectly consequentialist in type (see, e.g., Goodin, 1988, esp. p. 685).[22] The value of such units is understood to be a function of their positive contribution to the realization of cosmopolitan, that is, value-individualistic, universal, and agent-neutral values.

For example, people may value their society simply as an environment in which they can pursue their private ends. Such people value their society purely in terms of what it contributes to the realization of their private pursuits. Those private pursuits themselves are not thought to be dependent on the society in question in any further way. In particular, for such people participation in their society is not a constituent component of their ends in life; rather, participation is simply a means for furthering their private ends.

However, persons' pursuance of their private aims is not in itself valuable. A cosmopolitan who endorses the indirect consequentialist argument will judge persons' participation in the *modus vivendi* offered by such a society to be of value only in so far as it contributes to the realization of the cosmopolitan values she endorses. Change in such societies and in the communal ways of life they reflect is indicated whenever it can be shown that the communal way of life after the change will better contribute to the realization of the cosmopolitan values.

When we attribute value to membership in communities in which we participate only in so far as this is conducive to the realization of our private aims, then given that the pursuance of our private aims is not valuable as such, we cannot resist changes in the way of life of those communities on that basis when the change in question is required by the most urgent agent-neutral reasons for action. Within a consequentialist framework, the most urgent agent-neutral reasons for action are those that have outcomes of extreme importance to the realization of the values endorsed. As long as we accept that there are these agent-neutral reasons for action and that some of them normally have overriding force, we cannot simply point to any private aim we are pursuing in order thereby to resist undertaking the action required by an urgent agent-neutral reason. If, for example, it could be shown that a redistribution of the means for the promoting of one's private ends is required by urgent agent-neutral reasons, one could not plausibly resist such a change for the reason that it diminished one's chances of succeeding in one's own private aims. I conclude that an instrumental account of the value of communities does not give rise to reasons for resisting dramatic changes in our communal way of life when such changes seem to be required by the most urgent agent-neutral reasons for action.

Attributing Intrinsic Value to Societies of a Certain Quality

Clearly, the collectivist rejects the idea of attributing only instrumental value to communal life. Rather, she will claim that the good of a community is an intrinsic good for its individual members as well as an intrinsic collective good. However, in attributing intrinsic value to communal life, the collectivist does not differ from the liberal. Liberals attribute intrinsic (individual and collective) value to societies of certain qualities, say, to tolerant or just societies (Raz, 1986, esp. pp. 199–20; Raz, 1989, pp. 1225–9; Rawls, 1993b, pp. 201–4). Thus, the dispute between the collectivist and the liberal cosmopolitan does not turn on the attribution of intrinsic value to communities itself.[23] Rather, as I will show, it turns on the reasons for attributing such value to society.

People may value their membership in a community as an end, on the grounds that living under, say, just institutions counts as a goal in its own right. A just political society can be thought to be an intrinsic good for persons taken individually, since living in a just political society is 'among citizens' most basic aims by reference to which they express the kind of person they very much want to be' (Rawls, 1993b, p. 202). In other words, living in a society of a certain quality is constitutive of the well-being of individuals living in the society. Attributing intrinsic value to living in a society of a certain quality does not preclude attributing instrumental value to such a society. For example, people may value living in, say, a just society as being intrinsically good and, at the same time, they may hold that under modern conditions the justice of a society is highly conducive to its stability, which might be thought to be of instrumental value for securing values like safety of life and protection from deliberately inflicted harm.

Living in, say, a tolerant society is not just an individual intrinsic good. The end of living in such a society can only be achieved through the collective activity of the members of that society. We will be able to achieve the end of living in a tolerant society only if we share that end. Thus, living in a tolerant society is a collective good in the sense that members of a society mutually depend on one another to undertake actions that are appropriate for establishing and successfully conducting a society of this quality.[24]

Can we resist changes in the way of life of these communities on the basis of such an account of the intrinsic value of society, when the change itself is required by the most urgent agent-neutral reasons for action? When the members of a community value their association as an end, dramatic changes in their communal way of life can affect what they consider to be constitutive of their well-being. They may be affected not merely in that they suffer a diminution of the means necessary to the pursuit of their private ends, but also in the very pursuit of what they regard as an individual and collective intrinsic good. Thus, it appears that members of such a society have good reasons to resist change.

The liberal cosmopolitan will respond, first, by acknowledging the intrinsic values in question. However, she will give an account of those values that fits her value-individualistic, agent-neutral and universal framework. We do not attribute intrinsic value to just any society, but only to societies of a certain quality, namely those societies that allow their members to realize certain values – for example, living in a just or tolerant society. Living in such a society is valuable, first, because it serves the interests of individuals who are members of the society in allowing them to realize a good that is intrinsically valuable for them. Living in such a society is valuable, second, because it serves the interests of individuals as members of the society taken together in allowing them to realize the collective intrinsic good by undertaking the appropriate actions for establishing and successfully conducting a society of this quality in mutual dependence on each other. Our assessment of the value of living in a just or tolerant society does not depend on our being members of such a society. Furthermore, the values in question can be realized by more than one society. Ideally speaking, they should be realized by all societies.

So the cosmopolitan can acknowledge the intrinsic value of societies of certain qualities within her broadly consequentialist framework. Second, when she assesses the impact of changes on the communal way of life of a society, she will take into account what effect the changes have upon the chances of the members of the society to realize the intrinsic goods in question. But many changes, including those that many will often regard as radical, do not reduce their chances of realizing the value of living in a just or tolerant society.

Relying on a capability approach, the cosmopolitan might argue that, under the current conditions of international society, we have the most urgent agent-neutral reasons to provide helpless people with the basic capacities that are required for them to be able to choose and carry out projects as participating members of their societies in the first place. To provide this help, people living in other societies will not only have to give up some material goods, but, I am assuming, will have to change their communal way of life as well, with dramatic effects for the prospects of at least some of their members' success in projects to which they have been committed. But, even though these costs to individuals are considerable, the cosmopolitan can often plausibly claim that, after the transition has been completed, more people will be able to participate in realizing the values of a society of certain qualities. People who have no chance today of participating in the realization of societal values will be in a position to do so, while those who helped them develop the capacities to do so will still be able to realize the intrinsic goods in question, albeit under different conditions. This suggests that when the most urgent agent-neutral reasons for action demand changes in communal life, it is unlikely that the costs to those concerned – even when they are considerable – will outweigh the benefits expected.

More generally, I want to suggest that when people follow a cosmopolitan policy as backed by the most urgent agent-neutral reasons, their opportunity to participate in the realization of the values of society will often be left undiminished. Following cosmopolitan reasons for action will not necessarily undermine the enjoyment of those goods. Thus, we might plausibly endorse the intrinsic values of society within a value-pluralist account of the cosmopolitan position while at the same time holding that we have the most urgent, overriding agent-neutral reasons for curbing and preventing severe human deprivations. The question whether following these reasons for action can ever require us to give up our capability to participate in the good of society of a certain quality can be left unanswered here.[25]

Attributing Intrinsic Value to a Society on the Basis of Its Particular Features

To be in a position to insist that we can resist changes in our communal ways of life on the basis of an account of their intrinsic value, the collectivist will have to show that the above discussion misses the true meaning of attributing value to communities. She will claim that we attribute intrinsic value to society on the basis of its particular features alone, and that the value of participating in the good of society, thus understood, yields reasons for action that are stronger than the most urgent reasons for action as specified by the cosmopolitan.

People may value their membership in a community as an end owing to the unique opportunities which that community offers to them. They understand that the options open to them depend largely on the practices established in the society to which they belong. Those options are, so to speak, products of the culture of their society, and that culture is unique. It has developed under specific climatic and geographic conditions; the goods that are available on a public basis – such as educational opportunities, access to arts, social and medical insurance – can only be understood in terms of that society's particular history.

The collectivist will suggest that people intrinsically value their community for its particular features. Furthermore, she will suggest that a society qua society with particular features is collectively valuable. People then understand that the range of opportunities open to them in their society has been brought about by and can only be preserved through the collective activity of the members of that society. Living in that particular society is a collective good in the sense that the members of the society are mutually dependent on one another for the undertaking of the appropriate actions for establishing and sustaining a society with these particular features. Can people resist dramatic changes in their society on the basis of attributing intrinsic value to that society's particular features when the changes are required by the most urgent agent-neutral reasons for action?[26]

The consequentialist cosmopolitan can clearly acknowledge that being a member of a society is of intrinsic value *in part* because of the society's particular features. Indeed, she can acknowledge that, for you and for me, being a member of a society is of intrinsic value in part because of our membership in this particular society. It is a matter of how people normally become members of basic political and cultural units and how they then tend to relate to themselves as members of such units. Our membership in these groups is normally not determined by our choosing to belong to such groups on the basis of, say, a comparative assessment of the relative value of our possible membership in them. Rather, we belong to them because, say, we were born into them. We normally do not first ponder the question of which basic units we care to join and then develop the talents, capacities, tastes, and the like that are typical for members of this society and that make it possible for them to pursue valuable projects within the social framework provided by this particular society. Nor is our membership normally determined by others' judgments about our qualifications for becoming members of such a group. Rather, we simply find ourselves there, as members of a society whose influences on us have been pervasive owing to the fact that we have been brought up in that particular society. In short, that we are members of a particular society normally cannot be numbered among our accomplishments.[27] This fact, however, does not necessarily undermine the value, for its members, of being a member of this society. On the contrary, for many people the fact that

> these are groups, membership of which is a matter of belonging and not of accomplishment, makes them suitable for their role as primary foci of identification. Identification is more secure, less liable to be threatened, if it does not depend on accomplishment. Although accomplishments play their role in people's sense of their own identity, it would seem that at the most fundamental level our sense of our own identity depends on criteria of belonging rather than on those of accomplishment (Margalit and Raz, 1994, p. 117).

Indeed, for many people their membership in a community is of intrinsic value partly because of the way they have involuntarily become members of a particular community, and on the basis of that genesis they can relate to themselves as members of that particular community. This is to say that for them the intrinsic value of being a member of a community depends in part on the particular features of the community whose members they are.

An illustration of this is provided by the way the South African writer Breyten Breytenbach relates to himself *vis-à-vis* his country. Born and raised an Afrikaaner in South Africa's Cape Province, he left the country for Europe in 1959 at the age of 20. After having married a Vietnamese woman, he was forbidden by the apartheid state's anti-miscegenation laws from going home. Travelling on behalf of a shadowy resistance group, Breytenbach made a clandestine visit to his native country in 1975, and was arrested and sentenced to nine years imprisonment for 'terrorism'.[28] He served seven years, two in solitary confinement. Since his release from prison he has lived the life of a nomad. In November 1993, after the overthrow of the apartheid regime, Breytenbach was asked whether he would ever return to live in South Africa.[29] He replied, *inter alia*:

> We have an expression there: The bird sings the way it is beaked. There are resonances there, rhythms there, sounds, smells, spaces there, the way in which you see the world and perceive yourself and others, that are learned in a nonverbal way in the place where you grew up. It is perhaps the only place that I could allow myself to be blind in and I would not be lost (*New York Times Book Review*, 28 November 1993, p. 3 (interviewed by Lynn Karpen)).

So Breytenbach clearly acknowledges that for him the value of being a member of South African society depends partly on the way in which he relates to its particular features after having been born and raised there. The cosmopolitan can approve of this account, for it is fully compatible with his agent-neutral framework. Everyone can acknowledge that for most people this account of the intrinsic value of being a member of a society is valid.

The collectivist will respond that I have still missed the point. Her resistance to changes in the society to which she belongs can, she claims, be based on an account of the intrinsic value of society where intrinsic value is attributed to a society solely on the basis of its particular features. In so far as change is not itself a particular feature of the society in question, every change will conflict with the intrinsic value of being a member of this particular society. Given that the collectivist also holds that the intrinsic value of society so understood is never to be diminished or infringed, she will have put forward a position according to which we should resist (dramatic) changes in society even if they appear to be required by the most urgent agent-neutral reasons for action as specified by liberal cosmopolitanism.

This position, however, is indefensible. As the cosmopolitan acknowledges, the intrinsic value of our being a member of a society will depend in part on the ways in which we relate to its particular features, yet we clearly do not attribute intrinsic value to just any society. Rather, for a society to have intrinsic value it will have to fulfil certain minimal requirements. Let me illustrate this again by turning, again, to the way in which Breytenbach relates to his South Africa. Had he been asked as a bachelor and young arts student in Paris in the 1960s whether he wanted to return to live in South Africa, and had he answered this question then in the way in which he in fact answered it in 1993, most of us would have felt that he had given, at best, an incomplete answer. Why so? Because we believe that the value of being a member of a particular society does not solely depend on our relating ourselves in a special way to some of its particular features. Rather, where membership in a society can be of intrinsic value to its members, such membership has to fulfil minimal requirements concerning its internal as well as its external relations. The cosmopolitan allows for a plurality of basic political units with each of them manifesting particular ways of communal life. At the same time, she demands that people as individuals and as representatives of groups follow the most urgent agent-neutral reasons for action. These reasons for action also help to specify what the cosmopolitan takes to be minimal constraints on communities' internal and external relations. The minimal constraints correspond to the most urgent agent-neutral reasons for action and are understood to be universally valid. What these minimal constraints come to will depend on the account of the good of human life endorsed by the cosmopolitan. Whatever account the cosmopolitan endorses, it seems very likely that she will judge the former apartheid regime of South Africa to have violated the most obvious and objective constraints on how a society is to be internally organized and how it is to relate to non-members. Thus, if there was any value in belonging to it, the value of belonging to the South African society under the apartheid regime was clearly diminished for everyone. To fail to recognize this counts, I believe, as a moral mistake.

Notes

1 For valuable comments on and criticism directed to a longer version of this paper I am grateful to Joseph Raz, Stanley L. Paulson, Bonnie Litschewski Paulson, Barbara Reiter, Catherine Framm and Timothy Macklem.

2 The modern liberal proponents of the version of cosmopolitanism I am characterizing here include importantly Barry, 1989; Beitz, 1979; Pogge, 1989. In the characterization of this type of liberal cosmopolitanism I partly follow Pogge, 1992, pp. 48 f.

3 A translation of Wieland, 1788, p. 453: 'Dieser Zweck ist an sich der einfachste, unschuldigste und wohltätigste der sich denken läßt; denn er ist weder mehr noch weniger als was in folgender Formel enthalten ist: "Die Summe der Uebel, welche die Menschheit drücken, so viel ihnen ohne selbst Unheil anzurichten möglich ist, zu vermindern, und die Summe des Guten in der Welt, nach ihrem besten Vermögen zu vermehren."'.

4 Cosmopolitanism does not claim that '[t]he only reasons for or against the performance of any action are the consequences that its performance or non-performance will or may have'. This characterization of strict consequentialism is found in Raz, 1986, p. 268.

5 My translation of Antiphon [480–411 BC], B. Fr. 44 b, Cols. 1–2 (as partly reconstructed by Diels and Kranz, 1959, Vol. II, pp. 352 f).

6 See Scheffler, 1982, p. 1; for an important discussion, see Korsgaard, 1993.

7 For a variant of liberal cosmopolitanism that endorses a subjectivist, averaging account, see Birnbacher, 1988.

8 Beitz was the first to present a fully developed argument in favour of applying the Rawlsian difference principle to international society. See Beitz, 1979, Part III.

9 To invite the reader's attention to the magnitude of the problem, I quote one paragraph of the report on poverty: 'There are more hungry people in the world today than ever before in human history, and their numbers are growing. In 1980, there were 340 million people in 87 developing countries not getting enough calories to prevent stunted growth and serious health risks. This total was slightly below the figure for 1970 in terms of share of the world population, but in terms of sheer numbers, it represented a 14 per cent increase. The World Bank predicts that these numbers are likely to go on growing' (World Commission on Environment and Development, 1987, p. 29).

10 As Jon Elster (1991, p. 122) writes, we do not have a theory that 'can help us predict the long-term steady-state consequences of global policy changes'. We do not have a theory of 'general social and economic equilibrium' that could form a basis for prediction (see Lipset and Lancaster, 1956–7; see also Margalit, 1983). This is, of course, not new; see Popper, 1945 and 1957, Vol. I, pp. 161 f.: '[W]e do not possess anything like the factual knowledge which would be necessary to make good [the ambitious claim that we are able rationally to plan the reconstruction of society as a whole]. We cannot possess such knowledge since we have insufficient practical experience in this kind of planning, and knowledge of facts must be based upon experience. At present, the sociological knowledge necessary for large-scale engineering is simply non-existent.' Popper (ibid., Vol. I, p. 157) introduces the notion of piecemeal engineering as opposed to utopian engineering that attempts to reconstruct a society as a whole in accordance with a blueprint of an ideal society. For a critical discussion of Popper's original presentation of these two models of planning as being mutually exclusive, see Höffe, 1985, pp. 255–63; Etzioni, 1968, pp. 249–309, esp. pp. 268–73; see also Elster, 1984, ch. 1.

Elster suggests that, historically speaking, long-term and large-scale reforms have been anchored in a conception of justice. Having been perceived as fundamentally just, these reforms have generated sufficient support so that people are willing to put up with the costs of transition and of experimenting with different modes of implementing it (Elster, 1991, pp. 135–42). F.W. Scharpf (1988) supports such an interpretation.

11 For empirically informed arguments to this effect see, e.g., World Commission on Environment and Development, 1987, esp. pp. 67–9 (arguing that the Western model of welfare is not universalizable on the ground that it depends in part on an international economy that systematically disadvantages people living in other regions of the world; long-term sustainable development requires that Western countries change their way of life rather dramatically). See Weizsäcker, 1989, esp. pp. 215–18 (arguing that the Western countries have to change their model of welfare and support a new economic world order in order to gain any credibility in their environmental policies towards the so-called Third World). For a critical and comparative review of these and other studies see Marmora, 1990.

12 This is not to dispute the costs, emotional and otherwise, that may arise for us when we are disrupted in the pursuance of our projects and have to adopt new ones or when we adjust our projects to the demands of morality. Enduring these costs can, however, be worthwhile, morally speaking.

13 Brian Barry writes (1995, p. 115): '[J]ustice calls for radical changes. In many ways, these run against contemporary tendencies. ... [J]ustice entails large-scale international redistribution and also much more equality within countries.'

14 It comes as no surprise to learn that cosmopolitans have always discussed these issues. In the late eighteenth century, positions as diverse as the following were advanced in Germany

with respect to the issue of whether cosmopolitan convictions and our particular attachments to the (national) communities are compatible: First, patriotism and cosmopolitanism are synonymous; second, they are incompatible; and, third, they are mutually dependent. The first position was popular among German and Italian republicans in their struggle for national self-determination and unification (see Coulmas, 1990, pp. 354–6, 372–5). Christoph Martin Wieland argues for the second position in his *Das Geheimnis des Kosmopoliter-Ordens* (1788), pp. 455 f. Friedrich Bouterwek, a student of Immanuel Kant, argues for the third position in his *Fünf kosmopolitische Briefe*, published as an appendix to Bouterwek, 1794, pp. 1–148, 11, 19, 61. My argument in this chapter can be understood as supporting a highly qualified version of this third position.

15 I am quite deliberately constructing the loyalist position in opposition to the cosmopolitan one as characterized, above. I do not claim that anyone has actually defended the position I am attributing to the loyalist, but the following authors come close to a defence of the loyalist position as I understand it in the text: Oldenquist, 1982; Cottingham, 1986; Fletcher, 1993.

16 Alternatively the loyalist might want to rely on Bernard Williams' claim to the effect that 'ground projects' give rise to agent-relative reasons that, in some situations, take priority over even the most urgent agent-neutral reasons for action (Williams, 1981, pp. 1–19). Alasdair MacIntyre has suggested (1983 and see also 1984) that one can utilize Williams' notion of ground projects to defend what Henry Shue has called 'the priority thesis' – namely, broadly speaking, that when human interests are being considered, one's compatriots should take priority (Shue, 1980, pp. 131 f.). As I understand it, this argument is unworkable.

17 We owe most of the arguments for and against the idea of world government to Kant, who presents his arguments in a discussion of whether a world state provides an adequate response to the problem of war. The most relevant of Kant's texts are *Perpetual Peace* (1795), *Idea of a Universal History with a Cosmopolitan Purpose* (1784), *On the Common Saying: 'This May be True in Theory but it does not Apply in Practice'* (1793), *The Metaphysics of Morals* (1797), *The Contest of the Faculties* (1798) (all in Kant, 1970; German texts in Kant, 1968, Vols vii, xi).

The so-called Clark-Sohn proposal is the best-known post-World War II proposal for the establishment of a world government. See Clark and Sohn, 1954 (and the revised 1984 edition; see further, Suganami, 1989 (systematizes and discusses alternative proposals for restructuring international society in accordance with its domestic counterpart).

18 Further, one should distinguish between legal and political sovereignty. Whereas legal sovereignty does not admit of degrees, political sovereignty is characterized in precisely these terms, namely, particular degrees of sovereignty. For a general discussion of the functions of attributing sovereignty to political units, see Krasner, 1988–9. The legal concept of sovereignty is highly important in the processes of state-building. The revival of the idea of legal sovereignty in Eastern Europe (and Germany) is a matter of addressing problems created by the destruction of the post-World War II order, comparable to the high value sovereignty acquired in the post-colonial so-called Third World. But, as this experience makes abundantly clear, having 'full' legal sovereignty does not necessarily imply having political sovereignty in any meaningful sense. See Jackson, 1990; see also Simma, 1977 (arguing that the idea of observing human rights as a minimal requirement for the legitimacy of political action is compatible with the *legal* sovereignty of states).

19 This is also the assessment of John Rawls (1989, p. 10): '[A] world government would be either an oppressive global despotism or a fragile empire torn by frequent civil wars as

separate regions and cultures try to win their political autonomy'. See also Rawls, 1993a, pp. 41–82, 220–30, 54 f. and the accompanying n. 12, p. 222. Thomas Nagel provides strong arguments in support of this conclusion; see Nagel, 1991, pp. 170, 174–8, and he trenchantly makes the point: 'It would be close to the truth to say that if a legitimate world government were possible, it would not be necessary' (ibid., p. 174 f.). Of course, even if one accepts the tyrannical nature of a world state, one could argue that an effective world state, i.e., a global tyranny, is nevertheless the best among the attainable alternatives for its establishment, say, is the only effective way of abolishing war or preventing an environmental catastrophe. This would mean giving up on the project of liberal politics altogether. For such a position *qua* response to the expected global ecological catastrophe, see Bahro, 1987, Part IV, 'Der Fürst der ökologischen Wende' ['The Prince of the Ecological Turn'], pp. 325–42.

20 The cosmopolitan strategy for the legitimacy of a plurality of basic political units has traditionally been, first, to refute the idea of a world government and then, second, to specify the conditions under which a plural system of basic political units can be legitimate. The classical texts presenting this strategy – though in different versions – are Bentham, 'Principles of International Law, Essay IV: A Plan for a Universal and Perpetual Peace', 1843, pp. 535–60; Kant, 1970; John Stuart Mill adopts this strategy in 'A Few Words on Non-Intervention' (1867); see Miller, 1961, pp. 493–514, esp. 504–10; but see Michael Walzer's interpretation of Mill's position in ch. 6, 'Interventions' of his *Just and Unjust Wars* (1977).

Modern proponents of different versions of the strategy include Lichtenberg, 1981, pp. 79–100, esp. 92 f.; Birnbacher, 1988, pp. 16–23, 173–96, in particular, 219 f.; Goodin, 1988, esp. 679, 682, 685; Nathanson, 1989, esp. 542; Gewirth, 1988, esp. 291 f., 298–301; O'Neill, 1991.

For critical discussion of this strategy see Beitz, 1991, esp. 246–54; Kymlicka, 1989; Miller, 1988, esp. pp 651–53; Miller, 1989, ch. 9, esp. pp. 235–41; Miller, 1995. For a discussion of Miller's non-cosmopolitan position, see Barry, 1996; Gans, 1997; and Michael Freeman's contribution to this volume.

21 Indeed, when it comes to describing the political impetus of cosmopolitanism historically one might want to distinguish between two types. One is directed mainly against illegitimate restrictions of the freedom of individuals. Here, the motive is often that of achieving or defending the right of the individual to be free to withdraw from the politics of his particular time and place. It is, so to speak, an individualistic motive. The other type is directed at reorganizing the way in which political power is exercised on the level of world society. Here the motive is social or political.

Arguments put forward by the sophists exemplify the first type. In defending the classical ideal of a community of free and equal human beings as citizens of a *polis*, they argued that the laws of a polis ought to be understood as man-made, rather than imposed by the gods. '[L]aw [*nomos*] is only a convention, "a surety to one another of justice", as the sophist Lycophron says' (Aristotle, 1984, p. 2032). The local despots, the sophists contend, cannot legitimize their oppressive regimes as somehow willed by the gods. Rather, the validity of the conventions and laws, merely imposed on human beings by others, are to be tested by the laws of nature (*physis*), which *qua* laws of nature can truly claim to be universally valid. The political freedom the sophists often argued for was a freedom tied to the *polis*, i.e., the freedom of its citizens. But see Jaeger, 1936, pp. 412–18 (showing that some of the sophists' arguments already appeal to the idea of world citizenship and its accompanying rights). For Greek poets and thinkers, predating the classical period, who endorsed cosmopolitan ideas, see Harris, 1927, esp. pp. 2f., 5.

The second type of political impetus, sometimes thought to be essential to cosmopolitanism, is directed at a political reorganization of mankind by establishing something like a world government or world state. It was first exemplified by the endeavours of Alexander the Great. Alexander might be said either to have made an attempt at globalizing the benefits of the life in an idealized *polis* or to have been the first imperialist masquerading as an idealist. In any case, his activities do not simply reflect the cosmopolitan idea of everyone's having obligations towards everyone else whether he happens to be a member of one's particular *polis* or not. Rather, Alexander's endeavours amounted to an attempt politically to reorganize humankind by establishing something like a world government. Such a political impetus is not, however, characteristic for cosmopolitans. Although they have been firmly committed to the abolition of practices most obviously in conflict with their value-individualistic convictions – such as slavery, torture, the death penalty, and war – very few can be cited as arguing for the establishment of a world government. When cosmopolitan ideas were rediscovered in the eighteenth century, it was only Baron Cloots who proposed something akin to the establishment of a world state (see Coulmas, 1990, p. 366). Typically, cosmopolitans have worked on reconciling people's universal obligations with those among their special obligations that arise from their being members of particular, historically formed societies and from their individual attachments.

While not arguing for a world state, contemporary cosmopolitans often argue for supra-state institutions as they are thought to be necessary to advance cosmopolitan ideals. Competing cosmopolitan accounts of the value of supra-state institutions can be distinguished. Barry (1998, esp. pp. 153–56), Beitz (1994, esp. pp. 129, 135), O'Neill (1996, esp. pp. 172–4) and Pogge (1992, esp. pp. 52–5) have provided instrumental reasons for supra-state institutions. Held (1995, esp. pp. 145–56 and chs 5 and 6) and Linklater (1996, esp. pp. 294–6; 1998, esp. pp. 7, 101) argue for democratic supra-state institutions on the grounds that people have a right to govern the forces that shape their lives.

22 For a characterization of this type of argument, see Raz, 1986, pp. 280 f.

23 In the following I will call societies that qualify for being attributed intrinsic value 'communities'.

24 See Meyer, 1997, pp. 141–5, where I analyse living in a society that is open to the future as a public good.

25 See Ackerman, 1980, pp. 93–5, endorsing the view that it is only for securing the value of living in a liberal community – in his terms, for protecting 'the ongoing process of liberal conversation itself' (p. 95) – that we may restrict immigration to our liberal community under conditions in which adopting an immigration policy is thought to be the only feasible way of helping needy people who happen not to be citizens of a liberal state.

26 An example of how the conflict may arise might help to bring to the fore the type of conflict that I have in mind.

In a country *A* farmers have produced over many generations a variety of foodstuffs in their crops by using specific methods of cultivation. The farmers are dedicated to their work. For many of them, their work is an important life project, whose success weighs heavily in the determination of their self-esteem and self-respect as well as their relative wealth. For many of today's families of farmers, this has been the case for generations. The ways in which the farmers go about their work inform and reflect the customs, traditions and institutions of country *A*. For example, no other method produces the kinds of food that most of the farmers' fellow citizens tend to like and their way of farming shapes the landscape of country *A*. The size of the farms reflects the rules of inheritance that have been in force in country *A*. The citizens of country *A* acknowledge the farmers' contribution to their flourishing community life as important. Without any doubt, their work has been genuinely appreciated by their fellow citizens.

Over a short period of time, the population outside country *A* grows enormously. The size of the population of country *A* remains stable. Many people living outside country *A* are starving to death. In response, scientists propose that the methods of farming in country *A* should be changed. If a new method of cultivation were employed, significantly more food could be produced in country *A*, and all or most of its own people as well as those of the foreign population could be fed. Indeed, as things stand, the only effective way to prevent those foreigners from starving to death is to adopt the new method and to establish an institutional scheme for the distribution of food to the needy non-compatriots. Still, whereas to do nothing to improve the lot of the foreigners would have no consequences whatsoever for the people living in country *A*, to employ the new methods of cultivation would have a good number of undesirable consequences for country *A*'s people, including:

a. Using the new methods requires the labour of fewer farmers. Thus, if the new methods were introduced, a good number of farmers would be made redundant, would have to give up being a farmer. Furthermore, the new methods would radically change the character of farming, so that after the introduction of the new methods of cultivation and the like, it would mean something quite different to be a farmer than had been the case earlier.

b. Although the modern methods produce more foodstuffs that are from a nutritional standpoint fully satisfactory, they do not contribute to the production of those kinds of food people of country *A* are used to and like. If the new methods were introduced, people would then have to give up their acquired tastes and adapt themselves to new varieties of food. Furthermore, something that had been regarded as a particular feature of the culture of country *A* and that had been highly valued as such by many, namely its cuisine, would be lost.

c. Introducing the modern methods would, then, amount to a dramatic change in the landscape of country *A*. Although no negative medical or biological consequences are to be expected, if the new method were introduced, the cultural landscape of country *A* would be transformed, a particular feature of country *A* that has been formed and developed over generations and has been highly valued by many.

If people intrinsically value their membership owing to that society's historically unique features, the introduction of the new methods of cultivation might well conflict with what they take to be constitutive of the intrinsic value of their society: the specific ways in which farming has been done, the particular cuisine that depends in part on the particular foodstuffs provided by the farmers of that country, the cultural landscape of the country that has been formed over generations, and so on. The change will radically and predictably bring to an end the farmers' chances of succeeding in a project to which they have been profoundly committed, namely, being a farmer in the traditional sense of country *A*, and for many of them it will, indeed, bring their very life as farmers to an end. Other citizens of country *A* also have reasons to resist the change proposed. They will point out that familiarity and appreciation of the cultural landscape of their country as well as its traditional cuisine is central to their attachment to their particular culture, traditions and institutions.

27 Of course, some people succeed in becoming members of those basic political and cultural units that they as adults have chosen. But achieving full membership in a society other

than the one in which one was raised tends to be a rather slow and painful process. To be sure, the experience can also be exhilarating and beneficial to the self-experience of people and the development of their personalities. Having moved to a foreign country as long-term visitors or immigrants, people may well discover that the political and cultural setting of the society to which they moved makes it possible for them to develop aspects of themselves which they had not even thought of as being within the scope of their potential developments and which they might come to endorse.

28 For an account of the armed struggle against the apartheid regime and of terrorism in South Africa see Asmal, Asmal and Roberts, 1996, esp. pp. 41–4, 97–110, 120–5.

29 The biographical information is excerpted from William Finnegan's review of Breytenbach's *Return to Paradise* (1993) (in *New York Times Book Review*, 28 November 1993).

References

Ackerman, B.A. (1980), *Social Justice in the Liberal State*, Yale University Press, New Haven.

Aristotle (1984), *Politics*, Book III, 9, 1280b 10, tr. B. Jowett in J. Barnes (ed.), *The Complete Works of Aristotle*, Vol. II, Princeton University Press, Princeton, New Jersey.

Asmal, K., Asmal, L. and Roberts, R.S. (1996), *Reconciliation Through Truth. A Reckoning of Apartheid's Criminal Governance*, David Philip Publishers, Cape Town and Johannesburg.

Bahro, R. (1987), *Logik der Rettung*, Weitbrecht, Stuttgart and Vienna.

Barry, B. (1989), *Theories of Justice. A Treatise on Social Justice*, Vol. I, Harvester-Wheatsheaf, Hemel Hempstead.

Barry, B. (1995), *Justice as Impartiality. A Treatise on Social Justice*, Vol. II, Clarendon Press, Oxford.

Barry, B. (1996), 'Nationalism versus Liberalism' (contribution to a symposium on D. Miller's *On Nationality*, ed. B. O'Leary), *Nations and Nationalism*, 2, pp. 430–5.

Barry, B. (1998), 'International Society from a Cosmopolitan Perspective' in D.R. Mapel and T. Nardini (eds), *International Society. Diverse Ethical Perspectives*, Princeton University Press, Princeton, New Jersey.

Beitz, C.R. (1979), *Political Theory and International Relations*, Princeton University Press, Princeton, New Jersey.

Beitz, C.R. (1991), 'Sovereignty and Morality in International Affairs' in D. Held (ed.), *Political Theory Today*, Polity Press, Oxford.

Beitz, C.R. (1994), 'Cosmopolitan Liberalism and the States System' in C. Brown (ed.), *Political Restructuring in Europe: Ethical Perspectives*, Routledge, London.

Bentham, J. (1843), *The Works of Jeremy Bentham*, Vol. II, ed. J. Bowring (first published 1789), William Tait, Edingburgh.

Birnbacher, D. (1988), *Verantwortung für zukünftige Generationen*, Reclam, Stuttgart.

Bouterwek, F. (1794), *Miscallaneen oder Gedichte, Philosopheme, Erzählungen, Phantasien und Launen*, Vols I and II, Carl Ludwig Hartmann, Berlin.

Breytenbach, B. (1993), *Return to Paradise*, Harcourt Brace and Company, New York.

Clark, G. and Sohn, L.B. (1954), *World Peace through World War*, Harvard University Press, Cambridge, Massachusetts (revised 1984, World without War Publications, Chicago).

Cottingham, J. (1986), 'Partiality, Favouritism and Morality', *The Philosophical Quarterly*, 36, pp. 357–73.

Coulmas, P. (1990), *Weltbürger. Geschichte einer Menschheitssehnsucht*, Rowohlt, Reinbek bei Hamburg.

Diels, H. and Kranz, W. (eds), *Die Fragmente der Vorsokratiker*, Weidmannsche Verlagsbuchhandlung, Berlin.

Dworkin, R. (1981), 'What is Equality? Part 2: Equality of Resources', *Philosophy & Public Affairs*, 10, pp. 283–345.

Dworkin, R. (1993), 'Liberty, Equality, Community', ch. 6 of a presentation 'Untitled on Philosophy, Interpretation and Law', NYU Colloquium on *Law, Philosophy and Social Theory*, 14 October.

Elster, J. (1984), *Ulysses and the Sirens*, second edn, Cambridge University Press, Cambridge.

Elster, J. (1991), 'The Possibility of Rational Politics' in D. Held (ed.), *Political Theory Today*, Polity Press, Oxford.

Etzioni, A. (1968), *The Active Society. A Theory of Societal and Political Processes*, The Free Press, New York.

Fletcher, G.P. (1993), *Loyalty. An Essay on the Morality of Relationships*, Oxford University Press, New York and Oxford.

Gans, C. (1997), Review of D. Miller's *On Nationality* (1995), *European Journal of Philosophy*, 5, pp. 210–6.

Gewirth, A. (1988), 'Ethical Universalism and Particularism', *Journal of Philosophy*, 85, pp. 283–302.

Goodin, R.E. (1988), 'What Is So Special about Our Fellow Countrymen?', *Ethics*, 98, pp. 663–86.

Harris, H. (1927), 'The Greek Origins of the Idea of Cosmopolitanism', *The International Journal of Ethics*, 38, pp. 1–10.

Held, D. (1995), *Democracy and the Global Order: From the Modern State to Cosmopolitan Governance*, Polity Press, Cambridge.

Höffe, O. (1985), *Strategien der Humanität. Zur Ethik öffentlicher Entscheidungsprozesse*, Suhrkamp, Frankfurt.

Jackson, R.H. (1990), *Quasi-States: Sovereignty, International Relations, and the Third World*, Cambridge University Press, Cambridge.

Jaeger, W. (1936), *Paideia. Die Formung des griechischen Menschen*, Walter de Gruyter, Berlin and Leipzig.

Kant, I. (1968), *Kant. Werkausgabe*, Vols VII, XI, ed. Wilhelm Weischedel, Suhrkamp, Frankfurt.

Kant, I. (1970), *Kant's Political Writings*, ed. Hans Reiss, Cambridge University Press, Cambridge.

Korsgaard, C.M. (1993), 'The Reasons We Can Share: an Attack on the Distinction between Agent-Relative and Agent-Neutral Values', *Social Philosophy and Policy*, 10, pp. 24–51.

Krasner, S.D. (1988–9), 'Sovereignty: An Institutional Perspective', *Comparative Political Studies*, 21, pp. 66–94.

Kymlicka, W. (1989), *Liberalism, Community, and Culture*, Clarendon Press, Oxford.

Lichtenberg, J. (1981), 'National Boundaries and Moral Boundaries: A Cosmopolitan View' in P.G. Brown and H. Shue (eds), *Boundaries: National Autonomy and its Limits*, Rowman and Littlefield, Totowa, New Jersey.

Linklater, H. (1996), 'The Achievements of Critical Theory' in S. Smith, K. Booth and M. Zalewski (eds), *International Theory: Positivism and Beyond*, Cambridge University Press, Cambridge.

Linklater, H. (1998), *The Transformation of Political Community: Ethical Foundations of the Post-Westphalian Era*, Polity Press, Cambridge.

Lipset, R.G. and Lancaster, K. (1956–7), 'The General Theory of the Second-Best', *Review of Economic Studies*, 24, pp. 11–32.

MacIntyre, A. (1983), 'The Magic in the Pronoun "My"', (review of Bernard Williams, *Moral Luck*, 1981), *Ethics*, 94, pp. 113–25.

MacIntyre, A. (1984), 'Is Patriotism a Virtue?', *The Lindley Lecture*, 26 March 1984, University of Kansas Press, University of Kansas.

Margalit, A. (1983), 'Ideals and Second-Bests' in S. Fox (ed.), *Philosophy for Education*, Van-Lear Foundation, Jerusalim.

Margalit, A. and Raz, J. (1994), 'National Self-Determination' in J. Raz (ed.), *Ethics in the Public Domain*, Clarendon Press, Oxford.

Marmora, L. (1990), 'Ökologie als Leitbild der Nord-Süd-Beziehungen. Club of Rome – Brundtlandkommission – "Erdpolitik"', *Peripherie*, 39/40, pp. 100–26.

Meyer, L.H. (1997), 'More Than They Have a Right to: Future People and Our Future-Oriented Projects' in N. Fotion and J.C. Heller (eds), *Contingent Future Persons. On the Ethics of Deciding Who Will Live, or Not, in the Future*, Kluwer Academic Publishers, Dordrecht.

Mill, J.S. (1867), 'A Few Words on Non-Intervention', *Dissertations and Discussions*, Vol. III, Longmans, Green, London.

Miller, D. (1988), 'The Ethical Significance of Nationality', *Ethics*, 98, pp. 647–62.

Miller, D. (1989), *Market, State and Community. Theoretical Foundations of Market Socialism*, Clarendon Press, Oxford.

Miller, D. (1995), *On Nationality*, Clarendon Press, Oxford.

Miller, K.E. (1961), 'John Stuart Mill's Theory of International Relations', *Journal of the History of Ideas*, 22, pp. 493–514.

Nagel, T. (1991), *Equality and Partiality*, Oxford University Press, New York and Oxford.
Nathanson, S. (1989), 'In Defense of Moderate Patriotism', *Ethics*, 99, pp. 535–52.
Oldenquist, A. (1982), 'Loyalties', *The Journal of Philosophy*, 79, pp. 173–93.
O'Neill, O. (1994), 'Justice and Boundaries' in C. Brown (ed.), *Political Restructuring in Europe: Ethical Perspectives*, Routledge, London.
O'Neill, O. (1996), *Towards Justice and Virtue: A Constructive Account of Practical Reasoning*, Cambridge University Press, Cambridge.
Pogge, T. (1989), *Realizing Rawls*, Cornell University Press, Ithaca, New Yorks.
Pogge, T. (1992), 'Cosmopolitanism and Sovereignty', *Ethics*, 103, pp. 48–75.
Popper, K.R. (1957), *The Open Society and Its Enemies* (first published 1945), third and revised edition, Vols I and II, Routledge and Kegan Paul, London.
Rawls, J. (1989), 'Justice as Fairness: A Briefer Restatement', ms.
Rawls, J. (1993a), 'The Law of Peoples' in S. Shute and S. Hurley (eds), *On Human Rights*, Basic Books, New York.
Rawls, J. (1993b), *Political Liberalism*, Columbia University Press, New York.
Rawls, J. (1998), 'The Law of Peoples', ms.
Raz, J. (1986), *The Morality of Freedom*, Clarendon Press, Oxford.
Raz, J. (1989), 'Facing Up', *Southern California Law Review*, 62, pp. 1153–235.
Raz, J. (1994), 'Duties of Well-Being' in J. Raz, *Ethics in the Public Domain. Essays in the Morality of Law and Politics*, Clarendon Press, Oxford.
Scheffler, S. (1982), *The Rejection of Consequentialism. A Philosophical Investigation of the Considerations Underlying Rival Moral Conceptions*, Clarendon Press, Oxford.
Sen, A. (1984), 'Poor, Relatively Speaking' in A. Sen (ed.), *Resources, Values and Development*, Basil Blackwell, Oxford.
Shue, H. (1980), *Basic Rights. Subsistence, Affluence, and U.S. Foreign Policy*, Princeton University Press, Princeton, New Jersey.
Scharpf, F.W. (1988), 'Verhandlungssysteme, Verteilungskonflikte und Pathologien', ed. Max-Planck-Institut für Gesellschaftsforschung Köln, *Discussion Paper 88*, 1.
Simma, B. (1977), 'Menschenrechte und Souveranität nach westlichem Völkerrechtsverständnis', *Europäische Grundrechtszeitschrift*, 77, pp. 235–40.
Suganami, H. (1989), *The Domestic Analogy and World Order Proposals*, Cambridge University Press, Cambridge.
Walzer, M. (1977), *Just and Unjust Wars*, Basic Books, New York.
Weizsäcker, E.U. von (1989), *Erdpolitik. Ökologische Realpolitik an der Schwelle zum Jahrhundert der Umwelt*, Wissenschaftliche Buchgesellschaft, Darmstadt.
Wieland, C.M. (1788), 'Das Geheimnis des Kosmopoliter-Ordens' in C.M. Wieland, *Sämmtliche Werke*, Vol. XL, Georg Joachim Göschen, Leipzig.
Williams, B. (1981), 'Persons, Character and Morality' in B. Williams (ed.), *Moral Luck*, Cambridge University Press, Cambridge.
World Commission on Environment and Development (1987), *Our Common Future*, Oxford University Press, Oxford.

6 International Justice – Amongst Whom?

PETER JONES

For the most part, arguments about international distributive justice focus upon two issues. First, should we apply principles of distributive justice to the international world? Some theorists, such as Hayek, answer that we should not simply because they believe that we should not apply the idea of distributive justice to any political community. Others are happy to use the idea of distributive justice within state boundaries but unwilling to see it extended beyond those boundaries. So a first issue is whether we should find the very idea of international distributive justice acceptable. If we should, a second issue is what we should recognize as the principles of international distributive justice. There are many competing theories of intranational distributive justice and there is no reason to suppose that any fewer theories are available to us as potential principles of international distributive justice.

I shall say something on the first of these issues towards the end of this chapter. For the most part, however, I shall simply take for granted that we can and should apply the idea of distributive justice internationally. My interest relates more to the second issue – to the proper make-up of a theory of international justice. My concern, however, is with whom we should distribute amongst rather than with what the pattern of distribution should be. A distribution, just or unjust, must be a distribution amongst a number of parties. How, in the international case, should we conceive those parties?

The very adjective 'international' might be taken to imply an answer since it means 'between states' or 'between nations'. But in this paper I use 'international' without that specific meaning and as a synonym for 'transnational' or 'global', so that the phrase 'international justice' leaves open the question of whether we should think of that as justice amongst states or nations or individual persons or entities of some other sort.

I shall interpret 'distributive justice' in a similarly generous fashion. Taken strictly, that phrase might imply a theory that subjects the entire spread of holdings amongst humanity to a test of justice. I mean 'theories of international distributive justice' to include ambitious theories of that sort, but I also mean them to include more limited theories such as those that claim only that a certain minimum level of well-being should be secured for all. The critical issue for me is whom the distribution should be amongst, and that issue arises how ever radical or modest are the principles of justice that we bring to that distribution. Indeed, the question of who or what we should regard as the proper object of our concern arises even if we dismiss ideas of international justice and insist that the international distribution of resources gives rise only to questions of aid and 'imperfect duty'.

Within moral and political philosophy, the idea of international distributive justice seems to have found most favour amongst cosmopolitans, that is, amongst those who regard individual human beings as, ultimately, the proper objects of moral concern (e.g. Beitz, 1979, 1983; Richards, 1982; Pogge, 1989).[1] If we embrace the idea of distributive justice, and if we believe that state boundaries have no moral significance or only contingent moral significance, we shall see the idea of distributive justice as properly applied to humanity as a whole. There will be no good reason why distributive justice should be hemmed in by state boundaries so that it is something to be achieved within political communities but not across humanity at large. That is not to say that the cosmopolitan must be committed to international distributive justice, for he may reject the idea of distributive justice altogether. But, if he accepts that idea, he will be committed to applying it globally.

The cosmopolitan may, of course, have good reason to take account of the fact of the state's existence in the way he tries to achieve global distributive justice. Given that the human world is divided into states, he may have little option but to move towards his goal by securing distributive justice within and between political communities, rather than by proceeding as though humanity were constituted as a single worldwide community with no internal divisions of practical consequence. But, for the cosmopolitan, working within and between states will be no more than a political strategy, a modus operandi, forced upon him by the contingencies of the current world. Morally, he will see all of humanity as members of a single community and he will regard distributive justice as something to be achieved amongst all of them. Thus, while political boundaries may be of consequence for the way in which he tries to bring about his just world, they will have no place in his conception of what makes that a just world.

As well as accepting the existence of states as a fact of life with which they have to cope, cosmopolitans are usually ready to assign states an instrumental role in relation to global justice (e.g. Beitz, 1979, p. 153; Shue,

1988). They may regard all moral relations as, ultimately, relations between individuals, but that does not mean that they must restrict efforts to achieve global justice to the isolated and uncoordinated actions of individuals. That is not morally required, nor would it be practical. There have to be some mediating institutions that make it possible for individuals in different parts of the globe to stand in a just relation to one another. Those could be international or supranational institutions, but they could also be the governments of states. We might regard national governments as agents that are to act on behalf of those they govern and that should enter into arrangements with one another that make it possible for the individuals they represent to discharge their global obligations and to enjoy their global rights. The political machinery of states will then enable individuals to relate justly to one another on a global scale. Practically, resources will move from state to state but, morally, states will be merely conduits through which resources pass from individual to individual.

Does this model of international justice as justice amongst independent individuals capture all that we want to include in international distributive justice? One way in which it seems less than comprehensive is with respect to goods that individuals enjoy not independently but only in association with others. Consider debt relief. The beneficiary of debt relief is the society whose debts are relieved and it would seem that 'society' here has to mean the society in general and at large. It seems implausible to regard the subjects of debt relief as individuals, severally and separately, each of whom is entitled, as an independent individual, to a specific portion of the benefit that flows from debt relief.

Consider next the right to development. There is room for argument over how expansively we should understand 'development', over what sort of development is desirable, and even over whether development is the sort of thing to which there might be a right. But let us set those issues to one side and suppose that there is a right to development and that, by 'development', we understand a general improvement in the economic condition of a society. Who might hold that right? Again it seems implausible to suppose that it could be held by an individual entirely on his own and independently of anyone else. If there is a right to development, it would seem to be a right held by the political community that is to experience development. In other words, it would seem to be a group right rather than an individual right. The general point here is that, in so far as individuals can experience and enjoy an economic good only in association with others, we have to characterize the claimants to that good as groups rather than as independent individuals.[2]

Groups or Individuals?

Should we therefore allow that the parties to international distributive justice are sometimes, if not always, groups rather than individuals? There are several reasons why we might be reluctant to allow groups to displace individuals as the parties amongst whom we should secure global distributive justice.

One of these is a simple aversion to giving groups a moral status that is fundamental and ultimate. Certainly various forms of group membership and group activity are of great importance for most people's lives, but we can acknowledge that while still holding that, morally, groups have a significance that is derivative rather than ultimate: groups matter for what they contribute to the lives of individual persons. As Joseph Raz puts it (1995, p. 178), 'Cultural, and other, groups have a life of their own. But their moral claim to respect and to prosperity rests entirely on their vital importance to the prosperity of individual human beings'. It may be acceptable in law to give certain groups a standing that mimics the standing of individual persons, but in our moral thinking, it might be said, we should not ascribe to groups the sort of ultimate and irreducible status that we should ascribe to individual persons.

Secondly, reservations about giving groups an irreducible moral standing seem to apply with special force when we turn to international distributive justice. In moving from individuals to groups as the subjects of international justice, the group units to which we would move most readily are states. But is it really a concern for states *qua* states that drives our concern for international distributive justice? Certainly, economic inequalities can be extremely significant for the security and the independence of states. But, for the most part, what fires our concern for international distributive justice is not its bearing upon the standing of states but its impact upon the condition of the people who live within their borders. Distributive justice matters first and foremost for its impact upon the quality of ordinary people's lives and only secondarily, if at all, for its impact upon the 'state system'.

Thirdly, and again relatedly, we may fear that a shift to a group approach will deliver the wrong sort of distributive justice. If groups rather than individuals become the parties to a just arrangement, what will matter is how resources are distributed amongst groups rather than within them. We may therefore find ourselves endorsing an arrangement as just merely because the distribution of resources amongst groups fits a certain pattern and without reference to the pattern of resource-holdings within each group.

A shift from individuals to states as the subjects of justice is particularly liable to produce this attenuated conception of distributive justice. As Brian

Barry notes (1991, p. 207), 'the crucial characteristic of justice is that the obligation to make the transfers required by it does not depend upon the use made of them by the recipient'. If we couple that feature of justice with an acceptance of states as the proper subjects of justice, and if we accord states the autonomy that typically forms part of the modern idea of statehood, we must be content with a conception of international justice that ignores the way in which each state deploys its resources. The outside world should concern itself with whether a state has its just portion of resources but not with what each state does with its resources. A state-centric approach therefore 'permits countries to use resources that are justly theirs in wasteful ways, and it does not insist that a country that allows some to live in luxury while others have basic needs unfulfilled should lose income to which it is entitled as a matter of justice' (ibid., p. 208).

Barry himself is concerned to notice this feature of justice in opposition to those who insist that rich countries should attach strings to the resources they transfer to poor countries. On this issue, he points out, the values of humanity and justice carry different implications. If we conceive international transfers as matters of humanity, a donor society may reasonably lay down conditions designed to ensure that recipient societies use the resources transferred to them in ways that match the humanitarian aims of the donor society. If, on the other hand, we conceive international transfers as matters of justice, no such strings should be attached: '... if some share of resources is justly owed to a country, then the money is (even before it has actually been transferred) as much that country's as the rest of its income' (ibid., p. 207). Transfers simply adjust holdings amongst states so that each state ends up with the resources to which it is justly entitled and, assuming that we accord states equal rights of autonomy, no state has a right to interfere with the disposition of another state's justly held resources.

That reasoning seems sound enough, but it exposes an unhappy feature of the state-centric approach to international justice. Can the way in which resources are distributed between states matter so much and the way in which they are deployed within states matter so little? Suppose that the resources transferred from rich to poor states are purloined by already-privileged elites within poor states so that, as the gap diminishes between rich and poor states, the gap widens between rich and poor individuals within poor states. Have those transfers made the world a better place? Can the distribution of resources amongst states have moral significance if we comprehensively ignore the consequences of that distribution for the populations of states? It is hard to feel satisfied with a conception of distributive justice that refuses so completely to penetrate state boundaries.

Where, then, do we go from here? What I want to suggest is that the extent to which these concerns should deter us from adopting a group approach to international distributive justice depends very much upon how we conceptualize groups as parties to justice. I shall distinguish two ways of conceiving groups as moral claimants: the 'corporate' and the 'collective'.[3] These two conceptions locate in different places the moral standing that makes it possible for a group to be the bearer of just claims. To give added thrust to the distinction, I shall consider how each conception relates to groups as right-holders. The invocation of rights is not, I think, essential for my argument here and my distinction between the two conceptions of groups would retain its significance if we preferred to substitute a more general and less contentious term, such as 'claims', for rights.[4] But examining how we might characterize groups as right-holders throws the distinction into sharper relief.

Groups as Corporate Entities

The essential feature of what I shall describe as the corporate conception of groups is that it ascribes moral standing to groups as such. It does not regard the standing of a group as reducible to the standing of the several individuals who make up the group; for moral purposes, it conceives the group as a single integral entity. In so far as a group has rights, the corporate conception conceives those as rights held by the group as a unified entity rather than as rights held jointly by the separate and several individuals who make up the group. In other words, it conceives a group's rights as 'its' rights rather than 'their' rights.

Because it conceives groups as unified entities capable of bearing rights as unified entities, the corporate conception might be said to regard groups as 'individuals'. One group's claim against another is, morally, a claim of one 'group-individual' against another 'group-individual' rather than a claim of one set of individuals against another set of individuals. That is why, if we adopt the corporate conception, there is a strong temptation to characterize groups as 'persons'. Indeed, in law corporations are given the status of persons and the corporate conception of groups has been much associated with argument over whether, in our moral thinking, we should similarly characterize groups either as persons or as closely akin to persons in certain crucial respects. Should we, for example, attribute agency and responsibility to groups conceived as corporate entities? Even if he fights shy of applying the notion of personhood to groups, the corporate theorist needs some criteria by which he can distinguish the sorts of group to which we should ascribe a corporate identity, and the special moral status that goes with it, from groups of other sorts. That, too, has been a matter of dispute. Fortunately, none of these controversies need detain us here. What matters for the issue I am investigating is the simple idea that we should ascribe moral standing to groups *qua* groups – a standing that is directly analogous to the standing we ascribe to persons irrespective of whether we should regard groups as persons. We can leave on one side the issue of what sort of groups might be candidates for that standing.

Suppose now that we adopt political communities as the subjects of international distributive justice and we interpret those according to the corporate model. We might, in that case, characterize the subjects of justice as 'states' since those who conceive states as the morally relevant units of the international world are often willing to conceive them as corporate entities, at least in the limited sense which I give the adjective 'corporate' (cf. Nardin, 1983, p. 43). However, nothing turns on that usage; the crucial matter is how we conceive political communities as bearers of rights and duties whatever label we use for those communities.

If we conceive international distributive justice as justice amongst 'states', that is, amongst political communities conceived as corporate entities, we shall encounter all three of the objections that I described above. First, this way of understanding the subjects of justice necessarily entails attributing to political communities an irreducible moral standing as group entities, since it is that which distinguishes this conception of political communities as a corporate conception. We cannot disaggregate the claims of states into those of citizens. Secondly, and consequentially, states become the ultimate subjects of international distributive justice; we cannot pretend that 'states' are merely collective nouns for groups of individuals who, as individuals, are ultimately the subjects of justice and really the objects of our concern. Thirdly, a corporate conception of states forces a sharp outside/inside distinction upon us. In so far as states confront and relate to one another as corporate entities, they do so as 'individuals'; they must recognize and have regard for one another as individual entities and there will be no occasion for one state to look beyond another's entitlements *qua* state and concern itself with the way in which resources are distributed within that other state (cf. Hoffman, 1981, pp. 144–7; Amdur, 1977, pp. 456–7; Pogge, 1989, pp. 253–4).

Groups as Collectivities

How, then, might we conceive groups as claimants without running into these objections? The answer, I believe, resides in what I describe as the collective conception of groups. In contrast with the corporate conception, the collective conception locates moral standing in the individuals who make up the group rather than in the group as an independent moral entity. It ascribes no standing to a group that is not reducible to the standing of its individual members. Nevertheless its conception of a group as a moral claimant remains 'collective' in that it conceives the group's claim as a claim that its members present jointly rather than severally. Thus, while the standing needed for the group's claim to be a moral claim is provided, separately and severally, by the individuals who make up the group, the group's claims are joint claims and are ineradicably collective in nature.

If we apply this collective conception to the idea of group rights, what will distinguish these as group rights will be not that they are rights borne by a group that possesses a standing that is somehow independent of the standing of its members, but that they are rights held jointly rather than severally by the members of the group. If, for example, we ascribe a group of residents the right not to suffer atmospheric pollution from a nearby factory and if we conceive that right as a collective right, it will be a right that the residents possess jointly rather than independently, but not a right that implies that as a group they constitute an entity that is somehow morally separate from their individual selves.

Joseph Raz has stipulated the following as the conditions that must be satisfied if a group is to possess a collective right.

> First, it exists because an aspect of the interest of human beings justifies holding some person(s) to be subject to a duty. Second, the interests in question are the interests of individuals as members of a group in a public good and the right is a right to that public good because it serves their interests as members of the group. Thirdly, the interest of no single member of that group in that public good is sufficient by itself to justify holding another person to be subject to a duty (Raz, 1986, p. 208).

Thus suppose, for example, that a cultural minority possesses its own language and that the ability of its members to continue using their language is crucial to their well-being. Continued use of their language is, however, under threat from the majority society which wants to make its own language the only language that is recognized in the public domain. What is at issue, therefore, is whether the minority has a right that its language shall receive continued public recognition in spite of the wishes of the majority. If we take any single member of the minority, that individual's interest in the continued public recognition of his language may well not suffice to justify the expense and inconvenience that that will entail for the majority society. But if we aggregate the interests of all the members of the minority, that may well suffice to make the case for the minority's having that right and the majority's having the duties that it entails. In these circumstances, we can hold that the members of the minority have, as a group, a right that none of them has as an independent individual. That is why this sort of right is correctly described as a group right, a 'collective' right, even though its assertion entails giving no standing to the group that is not reducible to the standing of its members.

Raz (ibid., pp. 165–92, 207–9) is a proponent of the interest theory of rights and interests are central to the way in which he formulates the concept of a collective right. For Raz, a group possesses a collective right when the aggregated interests of its members are sufficiently weighty to justify others' having duties in respect of those interests, even though the interest of any single member taken on its own would not be enough to ground those duties. However, the notion that is central to the idea of a collective right (at least as I want to use that idea here) is not so much that of cumulative interests as that of joint possession. There are some goods that are public to a group such that, if they are to be available to any member of the group, they must be available to every member. Individuals can have rights as individuals to goods that they can enjoy individually; but there is something very odd about an individual's having, as an independent individual, a right to a good that bears upon other people's lives as much as it bears upon his own – particularly when the impact upon others stems from the very nature of the good rather from its incidental externalities.[5]

For example, there is nothing exceptional about attributing to an individual a right to vote, but there is something odd about attributing to an individual, as an individual, a right to democratic government where 'democratic government' describes the manner in which an entire society is to be governed. Can an individual really have, all on his own, a right that an entire society should be governed in a particular way? If a population has a right to be governed democratically, that is more readily intelligible as a collective right that the members of the population hold jointly than as an individual right that each of them holds separately (see further Jones, 1999b). A collective right is, then, a right of individuals to a shared good and a right that they hold jointly with, rather than independently of, their fellows.

Suppose, then, that we conceive the parties to international distributive justice as political communities interpreted according to the collective model. What difference does that make? First and obviously, conceiving a political community as a collective claimant does not entail ascribing it a moral status that is independent of the individuals who make up the community since, as I have explained, the collective conception does not require us to give moral standing to a collectivity *qua* collectivity. The standing that underwrites the collective claims of a community will be the standing of its individual members. A collective conception of groups and their rights is therefore immune from the protests of those who insist that, ultimately, only individuals can have moral standing. If 'state' is the word that most appropriately describes a political community conceived corporately, 'people' (as in 'a people') might best describe a political community conceived collectively.

Secondly and consequentially, a collective approach keeps faith with the conviction that international distributive justice matters for its impact upon the lives of ordinary people rather than for its impact upon states. The shared needs that generate claims of collective right are as much the needs of ordinary people as are individual needs. Moreover, because they regard individual persons as the units of standing, collective rights marry easily with individual rights. There is no incongruity in holding that individuals hold some economic rights as individual rights (e.g. the rights listed in Articles 22–27 of the UN's Universal Declaration of Human Rights) and other economic rights as collective rights (e.g. the 'right to development').

Thirdly, a collective approach to international distributive justice need not have the same respect for borders as a corporate approach. If a transfer of resources answers to the collective claim of a people and if, as in my earlier example, those resources are purloined by a privileged elite, 'outsiders' may reasonably complain. Their objection need not take the form of a paternalistic intervention designed to pre-empt a population's own judgement about how it should use its resources. Rather, their complaint can be simply that the transferred resources are not reaching those who are justly entitled to them. The objection to an elite's taking over the resources is not that that is unwise but that it is unjust. A population's collective right to resources is a joint entitlement to those resources; if the resources are deployed in a way that does not respect the jointness of the entitlement, they are deployed unjustly. So a collective conception of peoples as the parties to international distributive justice does not require us to limit our concerns to the way in which resources are distributed amongst states; it also justifies a concern with the way in which resources are deployed within states.

Applying this collective understanding of international distributive justice to the world may often be far from straightforward. For one thing, it would be unreasonable to insist that the goods to which a population has a collective claim must always be deployed in ways that benefit each and every member of the population absolutely equally.[6] For example, a society may use resources to improve its transport infrastructure; that is just the sort of use that is likely to be consonant with a population's having a collective entitlement to those resources. Even so, the benefits that flow from that improved infrastructure are unlikely to be spread absolutely evenly across the entire population; yet it would be unreasonable and unrealistic to cite that as evidence that the collective character of the population's entitlement had been violated. Judgements about what is consonant with a population's collective entitlement will have to focus upon the general character, purpose and tendency of economic measures and cannot be overly precise about the evenness with which the benefits of those measures are distributed amongst a population. That also means there may be scope for differences of judgement about how far policies and measures conform with the demands of collective justice.

Partly for that reason, we have also to confront the issue of 'national autonomy'. 'Peoples', like 'states', can be said to have an interest in being able to decide their own affairs; hence the routine ascription of rights of self-determination to peoples. That creates the possibility of a tension between a population's right of collective self-determination and our own view of the complex of just entitlements held by that population: faced with the issue of whether a particular deployment of resources is consistent with the collective nature of a population's entitlement, 'we' as outsiders and 'they' as insiders may reach different conclusions. If 'they' have a right of collective self-determination, 'we' would be wrong to prevent their exercising that right, even though the reservations we have about the use they make of their right may be justified. However, there remains a significant difference between (i) accepting an unjust condition because the population whose condition it is genuinely endorses that state of affairs and (ii) accepting an unjust condition merely because it falls within the boundaries of another state and without reference to whether the people, whose just claims are at stake, approve of their own condition. An approach that acknowledges popular self-determination as a collective right may require us to do the first; it does not require us to do the second.

A further complication concerns the identity of the groups that have collective rights. Up to now I have supposed that, for purposes of international distributive justice, these are 'peoples' understood as the populations of states and, given the way in which our world is organized politically, there is some justification for that. But the groups whose collective claims are international in reach need not coincide with politically defined units of population. For example, if we give priority to meeting basic needs and if some of those basic needs are collective in nature (e.g. a community's need for access to clean water), the group that bears the need-based collective right will be a group that encompasses only those who share in that basic need. In other words, the group that bears a collective right against the international community may be some of, rather than all of, a state's population. Most obviously, it may encompass only the poorer section of a country's population. That is another way in which a collective approach to international justice need not defer to state boundaries.

Groups and the Idea of International Distributive Justice

The distinction between corporate and collective conceptions of groups does, then, have a significant bearing upon how we might approach the subject of international distributive justice. Can we claim more for the distinction? If we adopt a collective rather than a corporate conception of political communities, should we regard more favourably the very idea of international distributive justice? The answer, I think, depends upon what we take to be at issue in deciding whether we should apply the idea of distributive justice globally.

One major objection to that idea appeals to the fact of international cultural diversity and runs as follows. Different societies possess different conceptions of justice; the global consensus necessary if the pursuit of international distributive justice is to be both practically feasible and morally acceptable is absent from our world. Any attempt to implement a conception of international distributive justice would entail some societies' imposing their cultural norms upon other societies and that would be morally intolerable. Rawls rejects a global application of his difference principle for just this reason; that principle, he reckons, is grounded in the political culture of liberal societies and its imposition upon nonliberal societies would constitute an act of international injustice – an injustice directly analogous to the injustice that would occur within a liberal society if some individuals used political power to impose their comprehensive doctrine upon other individuals (Rawls, 1993, esp. pp. 75–6).[7]

In his more recent work, Rawls describes the parties to international justice as 'peoples' rather than 'states', but his conception of peoples as moral claimants is clearly corporate rather than collective in character. His insistence that we should not transpose the liberal conception of the person to nonliberal societies rules out a collective conception of the rights of peoples (Rawls, 1993, pp. 65–7).[8] However, his appeal to cultural diversity against international distributive justice does not depend upon his corporate conception of political communities. It might also be made by a proponent of the collective conception.

Michael Walzer (1980) presents himself as a defender of the standing of 'states', but, unlike Rawls, his conception of political communities as moral claimants seems to be collective rather than corporate in nature. He attributes to states rights to territorial integrity and political sovereignty, but adds that these rights 'derive ultimately from the rights of individuals, and from them they take their force' and insists that we should not conceive states as 'organic wholes' or 'mystical unions' (Walzer, 1992, p. 53).[9] (There is a considerable irony in this contrast: Rawls, generally regarded as the leading liberal philosopher of our age, turns out to be an exponent of a corporate view that gives moral standing to political communities as corporate entities, while Walzer, generally viewed as a leading light of communitarianism, insists only upon a collective conception of political communities that relies upon the standing of the several individuals who make up those communities.) But Walzer is no less keen than Rawls to insist upon the fact of international cultural diversity and, for that reason, to reject an extension of principles of distributive justice beyond state boundaries. For Walzer, each political community has a collective obligation to respect the differences of other political communities and that, for him, rules out any conception of distributive justice that is global in scope (Walzer, 1980, pp. 226–9, 1983 and 1994). So international cultural diversity may persuade a collective theorist no less than a corporate theorist to rule out international distributive justice.

Another reason for rejecting the very idea of international distributive justice turns on the relation between a political community and the resources that fall within its territory. This relation is often conceived on analogy with an individual person and the things that that person owns: just as it would violate an individual's property rights to deprive him of something he owned and transfer it to someone else, so it would violate a political community's national property rights if it were obliged to transfer some of its resources to another country. Nozick (1974) uses a conception of individual property rights to object to intranational redistribution, and we might appeal to a similarly strong conception of national property rights to veto international redistribution. Indeed, some who reject Nozick's objections to redistribution within states seem to entertain Nozickian thoughts about the wrongness or the nonobligatory character of redistribution between states.

In contrast with the case of cultural diversity, the distinction between corporate and cultural conceptions of political community may have some bearing upon where one stands on this objection to international distributive justice. One source of international inequality upon which several theorists have fastened is the uneven distribution of natural resources across the globe. The natural resources that fall within a country's territory are, morally, a matter of pure chance and, if we allow countries to 'own' resources merely as they fall within their territories, we shall allow people's relative well-being to be dictated by chance. Rather than do that, we should treat the totality of natural resources as a global good to which everyone is equally entitled and whose benefits should be distributed fairly amongst all societies (see, for example, Beitz, 1979, pp. 136–43; Barry, 1991, pp. 196–200; Pogge, 1989, pp. 250–2, 264–5; Richards, 1982, pp. 287–93). If we take up this argument, it is not clear that it will be affected one way or the other by our conceiving political communities as either corporate or collective claimants. However, differences in the wealth of rich and poor countries often owe little to variations in the bounties of nature and very much to economic developments that have taken place over time. In large measure, rich populations are better off than poor populations because of the humanly developed economic circumstances they have inherited from the past. How, then, do the moral claims of a political community stand in relation to the human past and its legacies?

Corporate and collective conceptions of community may well deliver different answers to that question. Conceived corporately, a community has a moral identity that is not reducible to the identity of the several individuals who form its membership at any one time. It can therefore be conceived as a single entity with an identity that has endured over a long span of time. For example, rights to territory or land are often ascribed to groups such as nations and indigenous peoples and those rights are typically conceived as stretching back into the indefinite past and forward into the indefinite future. The possibility of those rights seems to depend upon a conception of groups as corporate entities that persist through time and that retain their identities as groups in spite of continuous turnovers in their populations. Thus, if we adopt a corporate conception of a community, there is no ready way in which we might divide it into two communities, one present, the other past, and ask how, morally, one stands in relation to the other.

If, however, we conceive a community as a collective claimant, that community will have no identity that is independent of the individuals who make it up at any particular moment. The claims of the community are simply the joint claims of its individual members and, as those members change, so will the community that bears a collective claim. If the individuals who make up generation X are different from those who make up generation Y, those two generations must be different collective claimants rather than the same collective claimant enduring through time. Consequently, on the collective model, it becomes possible to divide a community that we might otherwise conceive as an enduring entity into a series of temporally distinct collective claimants.

If we take up that possibility, we can conceive current political communities as standing in a contingent relation to the resources the past has made available to them. That, in turn, makes it possible to think of the legacies of the past (in which we should include knowledge, skills and technologies as well as material resources) as global resources that should be equally available to all and as suitable objects for just distribution amongst contemporary communities. In other words, a collective conception of community makes it easier to separate any particular present community from any particular past community and to treat the current distribution of the legacies of the past as no less arbitrary from a moral point of view than the distribution of natural resources. We then have a case for removing the consequences of that moral arbitrariness for the economic well-being of different communities of a sort that parallels the case that theorists such as David Richards and Brian Barry make in relation to individuals.[10]

I do not pretend that the collective conception alone can carry us all the way to this radical conclusion. It may be possible to insist upon a special relation between a current collectivity and the legacy of an historic community and, conversely, it may be possible to divorce states, corporately conceived, from strong claims of national entitlement that veto international redistribution. My claim is only that the contrast between enduring corporate entities and ephemeral collective claimants has some bearing upon whether it is legitimate, in the name of global distributive justice, to subject societies' relative enjoyments of the economic legacies of the past to assessment and adjustment.

Conclusion

The distinction between the corporate and collective conceptions of groups as moral claimants does, then, have considerable significance for our thinking on international distributive justice. It makes for different approaches to the issue of global justice and for different conceptions of what should count as global justice. It also has a bearing upon the issue of whether we should apply the idea of distributive justice to the international domain at all.

The distinction is likely to have other significances for our conception of just relations between groups that I have not explored in this paper. It is likely to be significant, for example, for claims that one group should compensate another for wrongs the first group visited upon the second at some time in the past. Suppose that a century ago group A wronged group B. If we adopt a corporate conception, A and B will be enduring entities and we can intelligibly hold that group A owes group B compensation, even though none of the individuals who currently belong to groups A and B were alive at the time of the wrong. If, however, we adopt a collective conception of groups as moral claimants, they will not have this sort of enduring identity and the identification of any current group with either the past wronging or the past wronged group will be more problematic.

Even if there is a morally relevant historical continuity between past and present groups of individuals, the corporate and collective conceptions will yield different understandings of what is going on when present action is taken to make good a past wrong. I have already explained that, on the corporate conception, we can simply think of group A compensating group B. If we adopt a collective conception, however, we shall need to distinguish four different groups: group A1 who, a century ago, wronged group B1, and groups A2 and B2 who are respectively their current heirs. An adjustment of holdings between groups A2 and B2 will be a matter of rectification rather than compensation. A2 has not wronged B2 and consequently a transfer of resources from A2 to B2 should not be described as A2's compensating B2. Rather, the transfer would be an act of rectification. Because A1 wronged B1, A2 now possesses holdings that should be held by B2. To put that right, we might, in the manner proposed by Nozick, imagine ourselves rewinding the film of history back to the point when the past wrong was committed, rectifying the wrong, and then running the film of history forward again to discover what would have been the conditions of A2 and B2 had the wrong not been committed (cf. Nozick, 1974, pp. 152–3, 230–1). The difference between their hypothetically corrected conditions and the current conditions of A2 and B2 will indicate the transfer that A2 needs to make to B2 to rectify the consequences of the past wrong. The collective conception need not therefore regard past group wrongs with indifference, but it will still differ from the corporate conception in its understanding of how past group wrongs relate to present group rights. That difference will be of practical consequence if the case for rectification between groups is more (or less) persuasive than the case for compensation.

Perhaps the most general significance of the contrast between the corporate and the collective conceptions is that it shows that insisting that, ultimately, only individual persons have moral standing does not entail shunning the claims of groups. Provided that, for moral purposes, we adopt a collective rather than a corporate conception of groups, we can embrace both the general idea of group claims and the more specific and urgent idea of group rights while still insisting that a group as such has no moral standing that is not ultimately reducible to the standing of its individual members. People have too frequently supposed that a commitment to individuals as the ultimate units of moral concern must entail a belief that what really matters for human beings are claims they can make, and goods they can enjoy, as independent individuals. In fact, that commitment entails nothing of the kind. We can insist that the ultimate units of morality must be individual persons while recognizing fully the collective nature of human existence and the collective character of much that matters most to human beings.[11]

Notes

1 By a cosmopolitan morality I understand a morality that (i) regards only individual persons (rather than, say, nations or states) as its ultimate subjects, that (ii) ranges over all human persons (rather than, say, only persons in one's own society), and that (iii) espouses principles that range over all humanity (rather than over only a limited set of individuals). Cf. Pogge, 1992, pp. 48–9. Someone's complete morality can, of course, be partly cosmopolitan and partly non-cosmopolitan. For example, it is not uncommon to find people holding that certain civil and political rights are universal to humanity, but that principles of distributive justice apply only amongst members of the same society.

2 For an argument that obligations to the world's starving usually make sense only as the group obligations of affluent nations or of humanity as a whole rather than the obligations of individuals, see McKinsey, 1981.

3 I examine the differences between these two forms of group right at greater length in Jones, 1999a.

4 David Miller (1995, p. 81), for example, suggests that, given the uncompromising character of rights, we do better to approach nations as groups that have 'claims' rather than 'rights'.

5 There are some cases, however, in which one might defend the idea of individual rights to goods that are public in nature. See Réaume, 1988.

6 Note too that, conceptually, the individual interests that aggregate together to make the case for a collective right need not be interests that are of equal moment for each member of the right-holding group.

7 Nardin (1983, esp. pp. 23–4, 109–12, 260–71) also appeals to the fact of international diversity in rejecting the attempt to include an idea of distributive justice within that of international justice. For critical comment on Rawls on this point, see Pogge, 1989, pp. 267–72.

8 Rawls (1972, pp. 378–9) spoke variously of 'states', 'nations', 'societies' and 'peoples' as the subjects of international justice. Another indicator of the corporate nature of Rawls's conception of peoples is his account of human rights. Although he wants to find a place for these within his political conception of international justice, he does that not by giving human individuals an independent status as individuals in the international domain, but by claiming that certain individual rights are recognized in the cultures of all peoples of good standing – liberal and nonliberal – and by going on to call those 'human' rights. In other words, in the international domain, individuals are to be ascribed certain rights not because they have independent moral standing as individual human beings, but only if and because they are accorded those rights by the peoples who constitute the fundamental moral units of international society. See Jones, 1996, pp. 183–204.

9 Walzer goes on to argue that states' rights are simply the 'collective form' of individual rights (1992, pp. 54–5). Elsewhere he writes, 'The real subject of my argument is not the state at all but the political community that (usually) underlies it. ... the idea of communal integrity derives its moral and political force from the rights of contemporary men and women to live as members of a historic community and to express their inherited culture through political forms worked out among themselves (the forms are never entirely worked out in a single generation)' (Walzer, 1980, pp. 210–11).

10 Richards (1982, pp. 287–93) argues that all persons should have fair access on a global scale to 'cultural' resources, by which he means historically evolved goods such as knowledge and technology, and that these resources, like natural resources, should be subject to a global difference principle. Similarly Barry (1991, pp. 199–200) argues that whether people find themselves heirs to goods such as 'productive capital, good systems of communication, orderly administration, well-developed systems of education' and the like, is as much an accident of birth as whether they find themselves members of societies that are rich or poor in natural resources.

11 This chapter was written during my tenure of a Nuffield Foundation Social Science Research Fellowship: I am very grateful to the Foundation for its support.

References

Amdur, R. (1977) 'Rawls' Theory of Justice: Domestic and International Perspectives', *World Politics*, 29, pp. 438–61.

Barry, B. (1991), 'Humanity and Justice in Global Perspective' in B. Barry (ed.), *Liberty and Justice: Essays in Political Theory 2*, Clarendon Press, Oxford.

Beitz, C.R. (1979), *Political Theory and International Relations*, Princeton University Press, Princeton, New Jersey.

Beitz, C.R. (1983), 'Cosmopolitan Ideals and National Sentiment', *Journal of Philosophy*, 80, pp. 591–600.

Hoffman, S. (1981), *Duties beyond Borders*, Syracuse University Press, Syracuse.

Jones, P. (1996), 'International Human Rights: Philosophical or Political?' in S. Caney, D. George and P. Jones (eds), *National Rights, International Obligations*, Westview, Boulder, Colorado.
Jones, P. (1999a, forthcoming), 'Group Rights and Group Oppression', *Journal of Political Philosophy*.
Jones, P. (1999b), 'Human Rights, Group Rights and Peoples' Rights', *Human Rights Quarterly*, 21, pp. 80–107.
McKinsey, M. (1981), 'Obligations to the Starving', *Nous*, 15, pp. 309–23.
Miller, D. (1995), *On Nationality*, Clarendon Press, Oxford.
Nardin, T. (1983), *Law, Morality and the Relations of States*, Princeton University Press, Princeton, New Jersey.
Nozick, R. (1974), *Anarchy, State and Utopia*, Blackwell, Oxford.
Pogge, T. (1989), *Realizing Rawls*, Cornell University Press, Ithaca.
Pogge, T. (1992), 'Cosmopolitanism and Sovereignty', *Ethics*, 103, pp. 48–75.
Rawls, J. (1993), ;The Law of Peoples' in S. Shute and S. Hurley (eds), *On Human Rights: the Oxford Amnesty Lectures 1993*, Basic Books, New York.
Raz, J. (1986), *The Morality of Freedom*, Clarendon Press, Oxford.
Raz, J. (1995), *Ethics in the Public Domain*, rev. edn, Clarendon Press, Oxford.
Réaume, D.G. (1988), 'Individuals, Groups, and Rights to Public Goods', *University of Toronto Law Journal*, 38, pp. 1–27.
Richards, D.A.J. (1982), 'International Distributive Justice' in J. Pennock and J. Chapman (eds), *Nomos XXIV: Ethics, Economics and the Law*, New York University Press, New York.
Shue, H. (1988), 'Mediating Duties', *Ethics*, 98, pp. 687–704.
Walzer, M. (1980), 'The Moral Standing of States: a Response to Four Critics', *Philosophy and Public Affairs*, 9, pp. 209–29.
Walzer, M. (1983), *Spheres of Justice*, Blackwell, Oxford.
Walzer, M. (1992), *Just and Unjust Wars*, 2nd edition, Basic Books, New York.
Walzer, M. (1994), *Thick and Thin: Moral Argument at Home and Abroad*, University of Notre Dame Press, Notre Dame, Indiana.

7 Global Equality of Opportunity and the Sovereignty of States

SIMON CANEY

Most people – including numerous political philosophers – do not endorse global principles of distributive justice. On the standard view, individuals owe obligations of distributive justice to those who are members of their state or their nation.[1] They also owe them to colleagues with whom they cooperate or to those with whom they have entered a contract. But they do not owe them to all human beings. On this conventional view, there are no global principles of distributive justice. In this chapter I seek to challenge this view. In particular, I aim to present a case for global principles of equality of opportunity (section I) and to meet several challenges to cosmopolitan principles of distributive justice. It is striking that many writers on ethics and world politics oppose global norms of distributive justice by invoking the sovereignty of states. In this paper I shall therefore examine four such arguments. The first – what I shall term the global government argument – maintains that global principles of distributive justice presuppose a world state and that the latter is objectionable because, unlike a state-based international order, it is tyrannical (section II). The second – what I shall call the state sovereignty argument – maintains that cosmopolitanism is inappropriate because it restricts the independence of wealthy states (section III). The third – what I shall call the self-government argument – maintains that cosmopolitanism is objectionable because it would require intervention into impoverished states (section IV). The fourth and final argument – the state responsibility argument – charges that, in virtue of their political independence, states are duty-bound to take care of their citizens, and that external agencies (i.e. other states or international organizations) are released from a duty to care for the interests of non-citizens (section V). None of these four challenges, I maintain, is persuasive.[2]

I Cosmopolitanism

Let me begin, therefore, by presenting an argument for a certain cosmopolitan conception of distributive justice. Why should we accept a cosmopolitan perspective? Different cosmopolitan thinkers have proposed different theories of justice to address this question. Nonetheless, despite employing different theoretical frameworks, most cosmopolitans tend to draw on a common line of reasoning. In particular, many leading cosmopolitan thinkers (for example, Brian Barry, Charles Beitz, Thomas Pogge, David Richards, Peter Singer and Hillel Steiner) affirm the following argument: we recognize that persons should not be disadvantaged because of their cultural identity. Accordingly we believe that persons should not be penalized because of their racial identity and/or their ethnic background. Similarly, we recognize that persons should not be worse off than others because of their social standing or their regional identity. Given this, however, it surely follows that persons should not be penalized because of their citizenship or nationality.[3] The latter are just as arbitrary as someone's race or ethnicity and since we think that a person's entitlements should not be affected by these we should, to be consistent, accept that a person's entitlements should not be affected by their nationality either. Principles of distributive justice should, therefore, take a cosmopolitan form and should not ascribe significance to someone's nationality.

What follows from this? I want to suggest that *one thing* that follows from it is that we should accept an ideal of global equality of opportunity (hereafter GEO). Given that our commitment to equality of opportunity is grounded in the thought that it is unfair for someone to be disadvantaged because of their cultural identity (i.e. ethnic identity, etc.) it follows that we should adopt global equality of opportunity. Otherwise some have fewer opportunities than others because of one feature of their cultural identity (e.g. their nationality). The rationale for equality ~~of opportunity~~ of opportunity thus implies that the latter should be globalized.

It is extremely important to stress that in defending GEO, I am not claiming that we should not adopt other more radical forms of cosmopolitan justice as well.[4] My strategy here is to start with a relatively uncontroversial principle, to show that we ought to apply it globally and to show that it requires radical redistribution and restructuring. Now, unlike some other principles of justice – like Rawls's difference principle, say – the ideal of equality of opportunity is relatively uncontroversial and is endorsed by a wide variety of different perspectives. Most people – whether they endorse 'desert' theories of justice or free market ideals or more egalitarian ideals like the difference principle –

accept the principle of equality of opportunity in the domestic context. As I have argued above, however, given the reasoning for this claim they should also adopt a global interpretation of equality of opportunity.[5] Bearing this in mind, we then need to know what this would involve in practice. This question has been addressed by Brian Barry and Hillel Steiner who both explore what it would mean to give everyone equal opportunities. Barry, for example, has affirmed the cosmopolitan argument given above and, appealing to an ideal of equality of opportunity, once defended a global system of equality of natural resources (see 1991, pp. 226 and 237–39 and also pp. 196–203; see further Beitz, 1979b, pp. 136–43, esp. 141). Similarly, Hillel Steiner (1994, pp. 235–36, 262–5 and 270; 1996, pp. 142–6; and 1999, pt II) has argued that everyone is entitled to an equal proportion of the earth's resources. Quite what specific measures are required by GEO I shall, however, leave to one side. All that is necessary for my argument is the claim that GEO would, in our current world, require considerable redistribution. In terms of health, resources, avoidance of poverty and control over their lives, it is quite clear that some enjoy far greater opportunities than others and accordingly that GEO justifies a radical change in the opportunities available to people throughout the world. Globalizing a fairly uncontroversial principle of justice would therefore require far reaching changes.

In short, then, my claim is that an analysis of the rationale underlying our commitment to equality of opportunity *and* our conviction that persons' cultural identities should not determine their entitlements provide strong support for GEO. Moreover, it is hard to deny that whatever GEO requires in detail, it would require a considerable redistribution of opportunities and powers throughout the world.

II The Global Government Argument

Clearly, however, many object to global principles of distributive justice. In the rest of this paper I shall concentrate on four challenges to GEO (and indeed to any ideal of cosmopolitan justice) all of which emphasize the importance of state sovereignty. According to the first challenge – the global government argument – the flaw with cosmopolitan ideals of distributive justice is that they need a world state. It is then argued that a world government would be oppressive and tyrannical. Bernard Boxill, for example, explicitly advances this criticism of the ideal of global equality of opportunity. He argues that GEO presupposes a world state and maintains that the latter is highly unattractive because it would not provide a right of emigration, a right which, he argues, is necessary to prevent tyranny.[6] Furthermore, others, like Danilo Zolo (1997), argue that the global government required by the cosmopolitan programme would necessarily be a form of imperialism.[7] The upshot of this argument is that we should adopt a framework of sovereign states and should, therefore, reject any cosmopolitan distributive ideals.

This argument against cosmopolitan ideals (and GEO in particular) suffers, however, from three problems. First, the assumption that cosmopolitan justice necessitates a world government should be questioned. As Charles Beitz and Thomas Pogge have pointed out, we should distinguish between cosmopolitan moral ideals (like global ideals of distributive justice) and proposals for a global political authority. Beitz, thus, makes a distinction between moral cosmopolitanism (which affirms a set of universal egalitarian moral tenets) and institutional cosmopolitanism (which affirms the need for a world state) (see Beitz, 1994, pp. 124–6; cf. 1979b, pp. 182–3). Similarly, Thomas Pogge (1994b, p. 90) distinguishes between moral cosmopolitanism and legal cosmopolitanism (which, like Beitz's institutional cosmopolitanism, refers to proposals for a world government). Indeed, Pogge (1988) explicitly criticizes the idea of a world state. What cosmopolitans aim for is a political framework that best furthers their ideal of a world in which people receive their entitlements as defined by a cosmopolitan theory of justice. Thus if, as the critics of world government allege, world government is repressive, then cosmopolitans like Beitz and Pogge are committed to rejecting it and adopting whatever institutional framework does better. Furthermore, it is worth stressing that world government is not necessary for the pursuit of global distributive ideals. It is erroneous to think that in the current world political structure (i.e. one without a world state) states cannot further the ideal of GEO. They can work both on their own and in cooperation with other states to ensure that people from different nations have more equal opportunities than is currently the case.[8]

Secondly, the argument fails to consider the alternatives to world government that cosmopolitans have proposed. In recent years, a number of cosmopolitan thinkers (including Daniele Archibugi, David Held, Richard Falk, Jurgen Habermas, Richard Linklater and Thomas Pogge) have outlined a variety of different institutional frameworks, which require reform of the current international framework but differ from a world state.[9] Common to most of these institutional proposals are plans to wrest power from states and to distribute some of it to lower levels and to distribute other decisions to supra-state institutions. Such forms of 'multilevel governance' clearly do not concentrate power in any one institution and, therefore, are not susceptible to the objection that they allocate undue amounts of power to a small elite.[10]

Finally, we should not be blind to the huge centralization of power that already exists under the current world system. The large amount of power wielded by multinational companies is well chronicled. Furthermore, the recent Multilateral Agreement on Investment is a testament to, and further source of support for, the power of multinational companies (MNCs) (Rowan, 1998). To complain that global political institutions would concentrate power is perhaps rather beside the point given that the centralization of power already exists. Indeed, given the large centralization of economic power in the hands of MNCs, there is a strong case for strengthening global political institutions that are accountable to the people, to combat such concentrations of economic might.

These three considerations suggest, then, that the adoption of global principles of equality of opportunity does not require a repressive world government.

III The State Sovereignty Argument

Even if we accept that global distributive justice does not necessitate a repressive world state, a critic might argue that it fails to accord enough room to states. That is, even if a cosmopolitan agrees that there should be an international framework consisting of states, some critics argue that cosmopolitanism sanctions interference in the independence of states. In the next two sections of this paper, I want to examine two versions of this argument. According to the first, namely the state sovereignty argument, cosmopolitan ideals of distributive justice justify the reallocation of wealth from prosperous states to the needy of the world and, as such, infringe the sovereignty of rich states. Global principles of distributive justice are, therefore, inappropriate because they curtail the freedom of wealthy states to govern as they would like by redistributing resources those states would otherwise use to members of other states.[11]

This argument, however, is flawed in several ways. First, we should recognize that global principles do not severely reduce the independence of prosperous states since they can be self-governing within the parameters defined by principles of justice. They can, thus, decide how to spend the money which is rightfully theirs: they just cannot spend money *which is not rightfully theirs*. All that the state sovereignty argument shows is that under a cosmopolitan scheme, states will not have unlimited freedom but it fails to show that this is to be regretted and it overlooks the large degree of freedom which states would enjoy under such an arrangement.

Secondly, we accept the legitimacy of these sorts of parameters when we think about other corporate bodies and social institutions. Thus we recognize that families or corporations or unions can be self-governing but that they should do so within the rules specified by a theory of justice. Given this, we need to know why we should not think that the independence of states should also be regulated by principles of justice. If non-state bodies should be regulated in this way why should states be granted immunity?[12]

Finally, the argument in question fails because it focuses on the loss of independence incurred by wealthy states but ignores the increase in independence acquired by impoverished states that would benefit from the cosmopolitan principles of justice. The point being made here is analogous to a point often made in discussions of domestic justice, and in particular the libertarian claim that taxation is wrong because it diminishes the freedom of those taxed. As many critics of this libertarian argument have pointed out, such taxation may limit the freedom of the taxed but it also enhances the freedom of the recipients of that money (see Cohen, 1988, pp. 293–4, 1991, pp. 167–70; Jones, 1982, pp. 217–18, esp. 222–3; Kymlicka, 1990, p. 147). The same point applies in the international realm. Global distributive schemes may limit the freedom of the advantaged but they similarly enhance the freedom of those who receive the benefits. A commitment to the self-determination of states does not therefore dictate a rejection of global principles of distributive justice.

Given these three points, therefore, we should reject the state sovereignty argument.

IV The Self-Government Argument

We should, however, consider a second argument against global justice which like the state sovereignty argument invokes the moral importance of the sovereignty of states. According to the self-government argument, the problem with cosmopolitan principles of distributive justice is that, in some circumstances, they require restricting the independence of those states containing impoverished citizens. Thus whereas the state sovereignty argument emphasized the independence of prosperous states, the self-government argument emphasizes the independence of impoverished states.

The self-government argument thus makes the following claims:

1 cosmopolitan principles of distributive justice may require intervention in states whose subjects are impoverished because external government is sometimes more efficient at meeting people's needs than are their own states;

2 state sovereignty is morally valuable;

therefore

C: cosmopolitanism fails to recognize the importance of self-government.

Such an argument is given by David Miller (1995, pp. 77–8). In addition, Chris Brown (1992, pp. 168–9 and 171) draws attention to this argument, arguing that it is an important challenge to cosmopolitanism that must be met.[13]

Now prior to evaluating this argument, we should record that Brown and Miller's version of this objection differs slightly. In particular, Miller emphasizes the importance of a *nation* being self-governing and hence values the independence of *nation*-states.[14] The objection raised by Brown, however, makes no explicit reference to national self-determination. Rather, his claim appears to be that statehood is valuable for a people (and that that holds whether the state in question is a nation-state or a multinational state).[15] For this reason, Brown's purely *statist* version of the argument has wider relevance than Miller's and would disqualify more cosmopolitan policies than would Miller's.[16] Now setting aside these differences let us consider the self-government argument. How persuasive is it as a critique of cosmopolitanism?

(a) One response a cosmopolitan might make is to challenge (1), by arguing that wealth and income are rightly due to states and not individuals. The claim that cosmopolitanism justifies intervention rests on the assumption that on a cosmopolitan account, resources are due to individuals and hence that cosmopolitans are committed to intervention when this proves to be the most effective way of ensuring that people receive their entitlements. So if a cosmopolitan simply denies that resources are due to individuals, the critique has no force. This move disallows the possibility of a conflict between the *entitlements of individuals* and *state sovereignty* by repudiating the former. And some cosmopolitans have indeed suggested that states are entitled to resources. Barry, for example, once appeared to endorse this position (see

Barry, 1991, pp. 203–8 and 239–40).[17] The problem, however, with this move is simply that it is unclear why resources are due to states themselves (as opposed to individuals). A more plausible position maintains that obligations are due to individuals and that resources should be distributed to states simply as a way of honouring duties to individuals. To deny this and to claim that the duties are borne to the state commits us to the highly suspect – and undefended – assumption that states have worth independently of any effect they have on humans.[18] Furthermore, the argument for GEO given in section I, entails that individuals are entitled to equal opportunities and hence claims that opportunities are due to people not states. It thus stands opposed to the claim that resources are due to states. The first response to the self-government argument is thus not very appealing and is not available to those committed to GEO.

(b) Cosmopolitans might, however, make a second response, focusing again on premise (1). This second response accepts that the duties are owed to individuals but it argues that (1) rests on the false empirical assumption that intervention will prove to be the most effective way of ensuring that people receive their entitlements. Interventions, it might be argued, are frequently based on inadequate information (Donnelly, 1993, p. 640). Furthermore, as interventions in Cambodia and Somalia attest they are also often poorly organized with no clear organizational structure (see Mayall, 1996). They are also poorly subsidized and may meet with resistance from some sections of the country being intervened in. Given this it follows that (1) is incorrect.[19] Cosmopolitans are therefore not committed to intervention and thus are not open to the charge of overriding state sovereignty.

Proponents of the self-government argument can, however, make a twofold reply to this challenge. First, as Brown points out, whilst intervention is sometimes ineffective there are surely some cases when intervention or external government will better further cosmopolitan objectives than would respecting sovereignty (Brown, 1992, pp. 168 and 189, fn 19). And in such cases, cosmopolitans should endorse intervention. Premise (1) is therefore correct: cosmopolitans are committed to overriding the sovereignty of impoverished states. Now a cosmopolitan might, at this point, respond by conceding this but then ask why we should accept the sovereignty of states – i.e. premise (2) – in circumstances where it leads to people having their needs unmet and experiencing poverty or famine. At this point, Brown and Miller can, however, introduce a second point, namely that there are some other goods – like being in control of one's life – which, by their nature, external agencies can not provide. Only through being a member of a self-governing state can one enjoy this good. This claim, we should note, does not make any controversial and dubious claims about states being valuable regardless of their effects on persons since the good to which it refers is claimed to be a good for the members of the self-governing state.

Now drawing on this point, Miller and Brown both argue that state sovereignty may be valuable even if a state is poor at providing certain goods (food, medicine, water, etc.) if it provides the good of self-determination. This, I think, is what Miller means when he argues that self-determination is 'on principle' valuable and is not valuable simply because rule by external agencies would be less efficient (Miller, 1995, p. 78, fn 31).[20] The point is made even more clearly by Brown who writes (1992, p. 168), 'while freedom from want is something that people place a high value on, it is not the only thing that is similarly valued. Self-government as an expression of autonomy is also highly valued'.[21] Now Brown and Miller, I believe, have drawn attention to an important value. As others like Berlin (1969, pp. 156–61) and Tamir (1993, pp. 71–4) have also stressed, we do think it important for a people to be self-governing (see also Caney, 1997, pp. 362–3 and 366). Thus drawing on this basis we can rephrase the self-government argument as follows:

1 cosmopolitan principles of distributive justice may require intervention in states whose subjects are impoverished because external government is sometimes more efficient at meeting people's needs than are their own states;

2 state sovereignty has value because it provides a good of self-government – a good external agencies can not provide;

therefore

C: cosmopolitanism fails to recognize the importance of self-government.

(c) Does this argument show that cosmopolitan ideals of distributive justice, like GEO, should be rejected? I think not, for three reasons.

First, premise (2) often does not apply. Obviously this argument has force only when it is accurate to say that the people are in some sense governing themselves. On a strict view, one might just restrict this to democratic states. On a more flexible view, one might say that this good applies when the government's policies are in harmony with the people's even if there is no democratic link. Berlin and Tamir, for example, do not claim that self-government requires democratic procedures (cf. Berlin, 1969, pp. 156–61; Tamir, 1993, pp. 71–4).[22] It is quite clear, however, that even if we accept this there are many non democratic states that do not govern in this way. In such circumstances the revised version of the self-government argument gives us no reason to reject cosmopolitanism.

Furthermore, even when it is accurate to describe a state as a self-governing people, the revised version of the self-government argument would only give us a reason to reject all global principles of distributive justice if we thought that the good of self-determination always took priority over other more basic material needs. Now it might be true in some situations that self-government is more important than aid, but it is implausible to claim that this good is so weighty that it invalidates the case for global justice in each and every case.[23]

Finally, we should note that cosmopolitans can accommodate the value emphasized by the revised version of the self-government argument. For cosmopolitans what matters is that people receive their just entitlements as specified by a cosmopolitan theory of justice and they can simply argue that among the 'goods' to be taken into account when assessing someone's entitlements is 'the good of self-determination'. This good should accordingly be factored into their overall account of people's entitlements.[24] From the point of view of global equality of opportunity, then, one (but only one) of the opportunities to be taken into account should be 'people's opportunity to live in a political system governed by themselves'. There is thus no fundamental conflict between the assumptions made by global theories of distributive justice and the values invoked by Brown and Miller. Cosmopolitans can, in other words, accept premise (2). Certain policies normally proposed by cosmopolitans might, perhaps, be rejected but the cosmopolitan framework rests in tact.

The self-government argument thus gives us no reason to reject a cosmopolitan account of distributive justice, in general, or GEO, in particular.

V The State Responsibility Argument

Now, having considered and rejected three state-based arguments against global principles of distributive justice, let us consider a fourth and final state-based argument, namely what I have called the state responsibility argument. This argument claims that:

1 as self-governing units, states bear the *main duty* for the standard of living

of their people (and external agencies are released from their duty to further the standard of living of the members of other states);

therefore

C: there is no case for global redistributions of wealth and cosmopolitanism should be rejected.

The thought underlying this argument is that if a unit is self-governing then it must take responsibility for its decisions and not rely on others (see, for example, Elfstrom, 1983, esp. pp. 712–14 and 722).

Many are sympathetic to the state responsibility argument, although they are often keen to qualify it. Peter Jones, for example, writes that '[i]f each political community claims the right to be self-determining, that may seem to entail that it, and it alone, bears the responsibility for providing for the well-being of its citizens' (Jones, 1994, p. 166; see also 1994, pp. 166–7 and 1990, pp. 48–9). Similarly, David Miller puts forward this argument in *On Nationality* (1995, pp. 75–7 and 108) and develops it at greater length in a paper on 'Justice and Global Inequality' (1999, pp. 193–7). Neither Jones nor Miller, however, adopt the crude version of the state responsibility argument given above. Jones, for example, adds several riders. He states in particular: (1) that if people are entitled by right to something then whether they receive their entitlements should not be completely vulnerable to the decisions made by their state; (2) that we tend to aid people whose dire situation is their own fault; and (3) that some people's lack of opportunities results not from their choices but from other factors (Jones, 1990, p. 49; see also Jones, 1994, p. 167). David Miller also supplements his account. For example, he does not repudiate all principles of global distributive justice and endorses five norms of global justice. These affirm that nation-states should (1) not harm others, (2) not exploit the weak, (3) comply with international treaties, (4) observe '[o]bligations of reciprocity' and (5) each possess a 'fair distribution of natural resources' (Miller, 1995, pp. 104–5).[25] Nonetheless, he maintains that the considerations adduced by the state responsibility argument weigh against 'egalitarian principles of [global] justice' (ibid., p. 108).

Now prior to analysing the force of these considerations, four preliminary points should be made. First, we should note with care the conclusion reached by the state responsibility argument. Here it is instructive to contrast it with the self-government argument. Whereas the latter emphasizes the *rights of states* and *forbids* aid to the impoverished on these grounds, the state responsibility argument emphasizes the *duties of states* (to their own) and *does not forbid* aid to the impoverished. Unlike the self-government argument which concludes that outside bodies *have a duty not to supply aid* to the impoverished members of other states, the state responsibility argument concludes that outside bodies *do not have a duty* (or *have less of a duty) to supply aid.* Aid, in other words, is not forbidden: it is just not required.

Second, we should observe that the state responsibility argument is most plausible as a claim about *justice*. That is, it is best construed as a claim to the effect that when an agent is self-governing he or she is not entitled, by justice, to claim aid. Given this, however, it is open for a cosmopolitan to defend aid on other grounds. Someone who thinks, for example, that wealth should be distributed to the impoverished throughout the world for 'humanitarian' reasons can accept that people are not entitled to assistance.[26] Now since my aim in this paper is to defend GEO as a principle of justice it is important to rebut the state responsibility argument. My point is only that others who defend global redistribution on other grounds are not vulnerable to this challenge.

Third, as with the self-government argument, we can distinguish between a nationalist and a non-nationalist version of the state responsibility argument. Miller's version maintains that *nations* that have acquired political independence have a duty to further the interests of their people (Miller, 1995, pp. 75–7 and 108). Jones's version, by contrast, does not make any reference to whether the state in question is a nation-state or a multinational state. Again, therefore, the non-nationalist version will have greater force against cosmopolitan principles of justice since it applies to a larger number of states (see again Barry, 1996, pp. 431–2). For this reason I shall focus on this non-nationalist version in the remainder of this chapter.

Finally, we should note that we can distinguish between a weak and a strong version of the state responsibility argument, where these are defined as follows. *Strong version of (1)*: as self-governing units, states bear the *sole duty* for the standard of living of their people (and external agencies have *no duty* to further the standard of living of the members of other states). *Weak version of (1)*: As self-governing units, states bear the *main duty* for the standard of living of their people (and external agencies *do not have the main duty* to further the standard of living of the members of other states).

Miller, we should note, clearly disavows the stronger version of (1). His claim is the weaker one that those external to a state are not the main duty-holders. And he explicitly claims that where a state has failed its own people, others might have a duty to supply the requisite aid. Thus, in a variation on the weak version, Miller writes that there might be 'a humanitarian obligation to, for example, send relief to famine victims in circumstances where relief was being withheld by their own government (whereas if the government *cannot* send relief, then there is a good case for saying that outside agencies have a duty of justice to supply it)' (Miller, 1995, p. 77, fn 30).[27] Others thus may have a duty to aid and whether this is a duty of justice depends on whether the government cannot assist its people or whether it can but chooses not to.

Having clarified the state responsibility argument, let us evaluate it. How plausible is it? And, does it undermine the cosmopolitan position? In the remainder of this section I want to suggest, *first* (a), that its core idea should be rejected and, *second* (b), that even if it is accepted, it needs to be supplemented with additional principles and the latter are quite consistent with cosmopolitan principles of justice.

(a) Let me begin with the first problem. To substantiate this claim, let me begin by addressing the assumptions underlying the argument, and in particular those underlying premise (1). The latter, I want to suggest, is plausible if we make two assumptions, namely:

i) that persons should be responsible for their ends; and

ii) that our conclusions about the responsibility of individuals can be applied to states (see, for example, Jones, 1990, p. 48 and 1994, p. 166).

Many liberal thinkers like Dworkin and Rawls affirm (i) (see, for example, Rawls, 1975, section VII; Dworkin, 1981, esp. section VIII). Furthermore, it is, I believe, a reasonable claim (although, as I argue later, it needs to be supplemented by other considerations). (ii), by contrast, is questionable. It is of paramount importance for the state responsibility argument that our conclusions about the responsibility of individuals can be applied to the responsibility of states. (ii) is, however, vulnerable in two ways. The first and most important point is that the very plural and diverse nature of most states makes it difficult to conceive of states as agents making decisions (McMahan, 1986, pp. 28–9). Rather they comprise diverse elements, divided by religion, class, interests, pursuits, region and (often) nationality. The policies adopted by states are thus never the choices of all the members of that state. Secondly, and as a corollary of this first point, (i) actually undermines the state responsibility argument. Implementing the state responsibility argument will mean that some will pay the price for the policies that others (their leaders) have adopted (see Green, 1996, p. 200; Jones, 1990, p. 49). (i) thus does not simply not support the state responsibility argument. It actually entails that the latter should be rejected. People are made to pay the price of choices they did not make.

Miller is, of course, sensitive to these sorts of concerns. He replies that it is appropriate to treat states as responsible agents if their decisions are democratic and if everyone's basic rights are respected (Miller, 1999, pp. 194–6). Such liberal democratic states may thus be treated as autonomous and responsible agents. Two replies can, however, be made to this argument. First, many states with impoverished people are not liberal democracies. Accordingly we cannot appeal to the state responsibility argument to show that the populations of such states are not entitled to aid. Secondly, it is worth recording that the revised version of the state responsibility argument does not address the second point. If we stick to the claim that people are responsible for their decisions this implies that we should reject the modified version which, whilst an improvement, would still result in some suffering because of policies they did not choose and which they might heartily reject. (ii) is thus implausible because it fails to show adequate respect for the decisions of individuals and flies in the face of the intuition that persons should take responsibility for their own decisions. Treating states as responsible agents is, thus, deeply unfair on individuals who are disadvantaged because of the state's decisions. This is especially so in non-democratic states but still applies in democratic states.

(b) Even if, however, this first problem can be met, the state responsibility argument does not invalidate a cosmopolitan perspective on global justice. A second problem with it as a critique of cosmopolitanism is that it is incomplete. In particular, those who defend (i) explicitly maintain that the norm of responsibility comes into play when the social structure is just. Rawls is a good case in point. Suppose that we overlook the first objection and analyse his account of how the norm of responsibility applies to individuals. He emphasizes that persons should take responsibility for their ends, but clearly he does not infer from this that there should not be any principles of distributive justice. On the contrary, he thinks that principles of distributive justice should regulate what he terms the 'basic structure' and fix the conditions within which agents should be responsible for their lives (see, for example, Rawls, 1993, pp. 189–90).[28] (i) on its own is therefore incomplete as an account of distributive justice. This crucial point is stressed by distinguished cosmopolitans like Barry and Steiner, both of whom affirm (i) but also affirm additional principles, principles which sanction global redistribution.[29] As Barry points out in his defence of cosmopolitanism against Miller's state responsibility argument, we do not think (i) invalidates all distributive principles in the domestic realm and so we should not think that it invalidates all distributive principles in the international realm.[30] The state responsibility argument must, therefore, be supplemented with an argument showing that cosmopolitan accounts of the nature of a just international structure (like, for example GEO) are incorrect.[31] Without such an argument the state responsibility argument is incomplete.

In short, then, the state responsibility argument is flawed as a critique of cosmopolitan justice on several counts. First, it wrongly homogenizes the members of a state and thus results in outcomes where some are disadvantaged because of policies they did not choose. Furthermore, even if we allow that liberal democratic states should take responsibility for their decisions, this gives us no reason to reject cosmopolitan programmes to aid members of non-democratic or non-liberal societies. Finally, even if we think that the people should pay the price for the decisions of their government, this is compatible with cosmopolitan schemes of distributive justice which regulate the basic structure.

VI Conclusion

The cosmopolitan claim defended in section I thus rests intact. Clearly, one might object to cosmopolitan principles of distributive justice on other grounds. My claim in this paper, however, is simply that our commitment to equality of opportunity provides strong support for a global ideal of equality of opportunity and that none of the four state-based challenges to that ideal (or to global justice in general) succeed.[32]

Notes

1 For a defence of special obligations to fellow nationals see Miller, 1995, chapter 3. For a discussion of his argument see Caney, 1999.

2 There are, I should emphasize, other arguments against global justice which also invoke state sovereignty. See, for example, Nardin, 1983.

3 See, for example, Barry, 1999, pp. 35–7; 1991, p. 226; and 1998, pp. 146–7. See also Beitz, 1979a, pp. 417–20; 1983, pp. 595–6; 1988, pp. 191–3; and 1994, pp. 124–5. For Pogge's affirmation of this line of reasoning see Pogge, 1989, p. 247; 1994a, p. 198; 1994b, pp. 89–90; and 1992a, pp. 88–90 and 92–5. This argument for cosmopolitanism is also given by Richards, 1982, especially pp. 278–82 and 289–93. For Singer, see 1979, pp. 14–23 and 171–2 and 1977, pp. 42–3. For Steiner, see 1994, p. 262 and 265. The same reasoning is also employed in two important recent defences of cosmopolitanism: see Jones,

forthcoming, especially pp. 17–18 (page numbers to draft version); and Richard Linklater, 1998. See finally Samuel Black's excellent discussion (1991) especially pp. 355–7.

4 A similar strategy is pursued by Charles Jones (forthcoming, chapter 1, section 4, 'The International Context', pp. 26–7). He defends a set of minimal rights and rightly points out that this should not forestall even more radical changes.

5 As Bernard Boxill (1987, pp. 143–4) points out in an article focused entirely on the ideal of global equality of opportunity, libertarians, Rawlsians and utilitarians should all be sympathetic to the ideal of global equality of opportunity.

6 See Boxill, 1987, pp. 155–60 (for the claim that GEO necessitates a world state) and pp. 160–6 (for the claim that a world state would be tyrannical). Boxill's important article also raises a number of other serious challenges to GEO. He argues, for instance, that equalizing opportunity requires a shared measure of opportunities and that this is absent in a culturally differentiated world (pp. 148–55).

7 The empirical claim that a world state would be despotic has been made by many distinguished thinkers, including Immanuel Kant. Cf. Kant, 1989, pp. 113–14.

8 For further discussion of this point see Caney, 1998.

9 See Archibugi, 1995; Falk, 1995, esp. chapter 7; Habermas, 1997, esp. pp. 127–35; Held, 1995; Linklater, 1998; Pogge, 1994b. Cf. also *The Report of the Commission on Global Governance*, 1995. It is only fair to note that Boxill's article appeared prior to all of these cosmopolitan schemes. We should also note that some cosmopolitans, including for example Kai Nielsen (1988, pp. 264–82), have endorsed the idea of a world state although he is keen to emphasize that it should be democratic and provide plenty of room for local autonomy.

10 The concept of 'multi-level governance' is frequently employed in discussions of the evolution of the European Union. See, for example, Marks, Hooghe and Blank, 1996. I am grateful to Tony Zito for drawing my attention to this article and to Ella Ritchie and Tony Zito for discussion.

11 A version of this argument is given by Black, 1991, pp. 360–2 and 373–7.

12 This point is made by Barry, 1991, p. 165. My discussion here is also indebted to Pogge, 1992b, pp. 93–4.

13 As Brown writes '[i]t may be that the principle of international autonomy ought to be abandoned – that those who value autonomy ought to be persuaded not to – but in order to arrive at this result this principle needs to be taken seriously' (1992, p. 171). See further Brown, 1993, p. 522.

14 Thus chapter 4 of *On Nationality* is devoted to defending national self-determination.

15 Thus his discussion in *International Relations Theory* (1992, pp. 168–9, 171) does not highlight, as Miller's does, the moral value of the sovereignty of *nation-states*. Furthermore, elsewhere he has explicitly stressed the non-nationalist character of his commitment to states: see Brown, 1994, pp. 173–5.

16 Brian Barry (1996, pp. 431–2) has argued that Miller's argument has little relevance to the real-world in which many, if not most, states are multinational and that Miller in practice treats states as if they are nation-states.

17 Barry's later work, however, clearly takes a more individualist position: see the references in footnote 18.

18 One central, and surely plausible, cosmopolitan tenet is that states possess value only to the extent that they serve people's interests. See Barry, forthcoming, pp. 31–6; 1998, passim but esp. pp. 144–7, 153 and 159–61; Beitz, 1988, pp. 191–3; 1994, *passim* but esp. pp. 124–6 and 130–5; Pogge, 1994b, pp. 89–90.

19 For this response to the self-government argument see Barry, 1996, pp. 432–3 and Green, 1996, p. 200. For a fuller discussion of why interventions are prone to be ineffective see Mason and Wheeler, 1996, pp. 100–6. See also Caney (forthcoming) for an analysis of four types of reason as to why humanitarian interventions might flounder.
20 See also Miller's discussion of what he terms 'communal autonomy' (1995, pp. 88–90).
21 As he adds (1992, p. 169) 'People clearly do not want to be malnourished, let alone to starve, but equally they seem to want to run their own affairs even in circumstances where loss of autonomy might improve their calorific intake. Any adequate account of rich-poor relations ought to take this into account'.
22 See relatedly Tamir's emphasis that self-determination and democracy are distinct (1993, pp. 57, 60–1, 69–72). Cf also McMahan's discussion of 'communal autonomy' (1986, pp. 31–5 especially pp. 34–5).
23 This point was made by Brian Barry during the discussion of his Austin Lecture at the 25th Annual Conference of the UK Association for Legal and Social Philosophy which was held at the University of Reading on 2–4 April 1998 and see chapter 1 of this volume.
24 For a similar point, cf Beitz, 1994, pp. 129–32 and 134 and Jones, 1996, pp. 83–4.
25 For a fuller discussion see Miller, 1995, pp. 104–8. The two phrases quoted come from ibid., p. 105.
26 Cf. here Brian Barry's distinction between justice and humanity (1991, pp. 182–210). See also Singer, 1972, pp. 229–43; 1977, pp. 36–53 and Cullity, 1994, pp. 99–127.
27 Miller also provides a subtle analysis of 4 different situations in which people's rights are violated and outlines different responses to each of these scenarios (1999, pp. 201–4).
28 For Rawls's discussion of the 'basic structure' see 1971, pp. 7–11 and 1993, pp. 257–88.
29 See Barry's affirmation of four principles of cosmopolitan justice (1998, pp. 147–9). See too Steiner, 1994, chapters 7 and 8 (esp. pp. 235–6, 265, 268 and 270–3).
30 Cf. his point that we give families autonomy but still accept the legitimacy of redistribution to their members: see 1999, p. 51.
31 Many cosmopolitans, we should note, emphasize that their aim is to provide an account of a just *international structure*. See, for example, Jones, forthcoming, passim but esp. pp. 16–17 and Pogge, 1989, part III; 1994a; 1994b.
32 I am grateful to members of the audience at the 25th Annual Conference of the UK Association for Legal and Social Philosophy for their helpful comments on an earlier version of this paper. Some of the material in this paper was also given at seminars at University College, Dublin, the University of Cork and Manchester University and I am also grateful to those present on those occasions for their instructive suggestions.

References

Archibugi, D. (1995), 'From the United Nations to Cosmopolitan Democracy' in D. Archibugi and D. Held (eds), *Cosmopolitan Democracy: An Agenda for a New World Order*, Polity, Cambridge.

Barry, B. (1991), *Liberty and Justice: Essays in Political Theory: Volume 2*, Clarendon Press, Oxford.

Barry, B. (1996), 'Nationalism versus Liberalism?', *Nation and Nationalism*, 2, pp. 430–5.

Barry, B. (1998), 'International Society from a Cosmopolitan Perspective' in D. Mapel and T. Nardin (eds), *International Society: Diverse Ethical Perspectives*, Princeton University Press, Princeton.

Barry, B. (1999), 'Statism and Nationalism: A Cosmopolitan Critique' in I. Shapiro and L. Brilmayer (eds), *NOMOS XLI: Global Justice*, New York University Press, New York.

Beitz, C. (1979a), 'Bounded Morality: Justice and the State in World Politics', *International Organization*, 33, 3, pp. 405–24.

Beitz, C. (1979b), *Political Theory and International Relations*, Princeton University Press, Princeton, New Jersey.

Beitz, C. (1983), 'Cosmopolitan Ideals and National Sentiment', *Journal of Philosophy*, LXXX, 10, pp. 591–600.

Beitz, C. (1988), 'Recent International Thought', *International Journal*, XLIII, Spring, pp. 183–204.

Beitz, C. (1994), 'Cosmopolitan Liberalism and the States System' in C. Brown (ed.), *Political Restructuring in Europe: Ethical Perspectives*, Routledge, London.

Berlin, I. (1969), 'Two Concepts of Liberty' in *Four Essays on Liberty*, Oxford University Press, Oxford.

Black, S. (1991), 'Individualism at an Impasse', *Canadian Journal of Philosophy*, 21, 3, pp. 347–77.

Boxill, B. (1987), 'Global Equality of Opportunity and National Integrity', *Social Philosophy and Policy*, 5, 1, pp. 143–68.

Brown, C. (1992), *International Relations Theory: New Normative Approaches*, Harvester Wheatsheaf, Hemel Hempstead.

Brown, C. (1993), 'International Affairs' in R. Goodin and P. Pettit (eds), *A Companion to Contemporary Political Philosophy*, Blackwell, Oxford.

Brown, C. (1994), 'The Ethics of Political Restructuring in Europe: The Perspective of Constitutive Theory' in C. Brown (ed.), *Political Restructuring in Europe: Ethical Perspectives*, Routledge, London.

Caney, S. (1997), 'Self-Government and Secession: The Case of Nations', *Journal of Political Philosophy*, 5, 4, pp. 123–38.

Caney, S. (1998), 'Cosmopolitanism, Realism and the National Interest' in G. Parry, A. Qureshi and H. Steiner (eds), *The Legal and Moral Aspects of Free Trade: Freedom and Trade, Volume III*, Routledge, London.

Caney, S. (1999), 'Nationality, Distributive Justice and the Use of Force', *Journal of Applied Philosophy*, 16, 2, pp. 123–38.

Caney, S. (forthcoming), 'Humanitarian Intervention and State Sovereignity' in A. Valls (ed.), *Ethics in International Affairs: Theories and Cases*, Rowman and Littlefield, Totowa, New Jersey.

Cohen, G.A. (1988), *History, Labour, and Freedom: Themes from Marx*, Clarendon Press, Oxford.

Cohen, G.A. (1991), 'Capitalism, Freedom, and the Proletariat' in D. Miller (ed.), *Liberty*, Oxford University Press, Oxford.

Cullity, G. (1994), 'International Aid and the Scope of Kindness', *Ethics*, 105, pp. 99–127.
Donnelly, D. (1993), 'Human Rights, Humanitarian Crisis, and Humanitarian Intervention', *International Journal*, XLVIII, pp. 607–40.
Dworkin, R. (1981), 'What is Equality? Part 1: Equality of Welfare', *Philosophy and Public Affairs*, 10, 3, pp. 185–246.
Elfstrom, G. (1983), 'On Dilemmas of Intervention', *Ethics*, 93, pp. 709–25.
Green, M. (1996), 'Review Essay: National Identity and Liberal Political Philosophy', *Ethics and International Affairs*, 10, pp. 191–201.
Falk, R. (1995), *On Humane Governance: Toward a New Global Politics*, Polity, Cambridge.
Habermas, J. (1997), 'Kant's Idea of Perpetual Peace, with the Benefit of Two Hundred Years' Hindsight' in J. Bohman and M. Lutz-Bachmann (eds), *Perpetual Peace: Essays on Kant's Cosmopolitan Ideal*, MIT Press, Cambridge, Massachusetts.
Held, D. (1995), *Democracy and the Global Order: From the Modern State to Cosmopolitan Governance*, Polity, Cambridge.
Jones, C. (1996), 'Revenge of the Philosophical Mole: Another Response to David Miller on Nationality', *Journal of Applied Philosophy*, 13, 1, pp. 73–86.
Jones, C. (forthcoming), *Global Justice: Defending Cosmopolitanism*, Oxford University Press, Oxford.
Jones, P. (1982), 'Freedom and the Redistribution of Resources', *Journal of Social Policy*, 11, 2, pp. 217–38.
Jones, P. (1990), 'Universal Principles and Particular Claims: From Welfare Rights to Welfare States' in A. Ware and R. Goodin (eds), *Needs and Welfare*, London, Sage.
Jones, P. (1994), *Rights*, Macmillan, Basingstoke.
Kant, I. (1989), 'Perpetual Peace: A Philosophical Sketch' in *Kant's Political Writings* (introduction and notes by H. Reiss (ed.); translated by H.B. Nisbet), Cambridge University Press, Cambridge.
Kymlicka, W. (1990), *Contemporary Political Philosophy: An Introduction*, Clarendon Press, Oxford.
Linklater, R. (1998), *The Transformation of Political Community: Ethical Foundations of the Post-Westphalian Era*, Polity, Cambridge.
Marks, G., Hooghe, L. and Blank, K. (1996), 'European Integration from the 1980s: State-Centric v. Multi-level Governance', *Journal of Common Market Studies*, 34, 3, pp. 341–78.
Mason, A. and Wheeler, N. (1996), 'Realist Objections to Humanitarian Intervention' in B. Holden (ed.), *The Ethical Dimensions of Global Change*, Macmillan, London.
Mayall, J. (1996) (ed.), *The New Interventionism 1991–1994: United Nations Experience in Cambodia, former Yugoslavia and Somalia*, Cambridge University Press, Cambridge.
McMahan, J. (1986), 'The Ethics of International Intervention' in A. Ellis (ed.), *Ethics and International Relations*, Manchester University Press, Manchester.

Miller, D. (1995), *On Nationality*, Clarendon Press, Oxford.
Miller, D. (1999), 'Justice and Global Inequality' in A. Hurrell and N. Woods (eds), *Inequality, Globalization, and World Politics*, Oxford University Press, Oxford.
Nardin, T. (1983), *Law, Morality and the Relations of States*, Princeton University Press, Princeton.
Nielsen, K. (1988), 'World Government, Security, and Global Justice' in S. Luper-Foy (ed.), *Problems of International Justice*, Westview Press, Boulder, Colorado.
Pogge, T. (1988), 'Moral Progress' in S. Luper-Foy (ed.), *Problems of International Justice*, Westview Press, Boulder, Colorado.
Pogge, T. (1989), *Realizing Rawls*, Cornell University Press, Ithaca and London.
Pogge, T. (1992a), 'Loopholes in Moralities', *Journal of Philosophy*, LXXXIX, 2, pp. 79–98.
Pogge, T. (1992b), 'An Institutional Approach to Humanitarian Intervention', *Public Affairs Quarterly*, 6, 1, pp. 89–103.
Pogge, T. (1994a), 'An Egalitarian Law of Peoples', *Philosophy and Public Affairs*, 23, 3, pp. 199–224.
Pogge, T. (1994b), 'Cosmopolitanism and Sovereignty' in C. Brown (ed.), *Political Restructuring in Europe: Ethical Perspectives*, Routledge, London.
Rawls, J. (1971), *A Theory of Justice*, Oxford University Press, Oxford.
Rawls, J. (1975), 'Fairness to Goodness', *Philosophical Review*, LXXXIV, pp. 536–54.
Rawls, J. (1993), *Political Liberalism*, Columbia University Press, New York.
Report of the Commission on Global Governance (1995), *Our Global Neighbourhood*, Oxford University Press, Oxford.
Richards, D. (1982), 'International Distributive Justice' in J.R. Pennock and J.W. Chapman (eds), *Ethics, Economics, and the Law: NOMOS XXIV*, New York University Press, New York and London.
Rowan, D. (1998), 'Meet the New World Government', *The Guardian*, 13 February, p. 15.
Singer, P. (1972), 'Famine, Affluence, and Morality', *Philosophy and Public Affairs*, 1, 3, pp. 229–43.
Singer, P. (1977), 'Reconsidering the Famine Relief Argument' in P.G. Brown and H. Shue (eds), *Food Policy: The Responsibility of the United States in the Life and Death Choices*, Collier Macmillan, London.
Singer, P. (1979), *Practical Ethics*, Cambridge University Press, Cambridge.
Steiner, H. (1994), *An Essay on Rights*, Blackwell, Oxford.
Steiner, H. (1996), 'Territorial Justice' in S. Caney, D. George and P. Jones (eds), *National Rights, International Obligations*, Westview Press, Oxford.
Steiner, H. (1999), 'Just Taxation and International Redistribution' in I. Shapiro and L. Brilmayer (eds), *NOMOS XLI: Global Justice*, New York University Press, New York.
Tamir, Y. (1993), *Liberal Nationalism*, Princeton University Press, Princeton.
Zolo, D. (1997), *Cosmopolis: Prospects for World Government* (translated by D. McKie), Polity, Cambridge.

8 Global Justice as Impartiality: Whither Claims to Equal Shares?[1]

ANDREAS FØLLESDAL

Introduction

A strong tradition within liberal contractualism holds that this normative view yields a strong case for distributive equality, both domestically and globally:

> considerations of justice apply at least wherever there is systematic economic interaction; for whenever there is regularised commerce there is an institution in Rawls' sense, i.e. a public system of rules defining rights and duties etc. Thus the Difference Principle would apply to the world economic system taken as a whole as well as to particular societies within it (Scanlon, 1973, pp. 106–7).

Nationality is just one further deep contingency (like genetic endowment, race, gender and social class), one more potential basis of institutional inequalities that are inescapable and present from birth. Within Rawls' conception, there is no reason to treat this case differently from the others. And so it would seem that we can justify our global institutional order only if we can show that the institutional inequalities it produces tend to optimize (against the backdrop of feasible alternative global regimes) the worst social position (Pogge, 1989, p. 247).

It seems obvious that an international difference principle applies to persons in the sense that it is the globally least advantaged representative person (or group of persons) whose position is to be maximized (Beitz, 1979, p. 152).

If Rawls' arguments are valid for domestic justice, why would not the same arguments compel the representatives of countries to choose a global difference principle to govern the relations between countries? I must confess that I can see no reason (Barry, 1989, p. 189 and 1973, pp. 128–32).

Such a tight link between contractualism and egalitarian principles of global justice may seem obvious, since the principles defended in John Rawls' theory of justice as fairness (Rawls, 1971) require equality of civil and political rights, and the difference principle takes equal shares as a base line, permitting deviations only insofar as the worst off representatives also benefit. Thus Brian Barry suggests that 'the Scanlonian construction leads directly to a very strong presumption in favour of equality here, since it invites us to ask why anybody should freely consent to being treated less well in respect of rights than anybody else in his society' (Barry, 1995, p. 70).

Barry has criticized Rawls' approach to international distributive justice since it fails to yield a global difference principle (Barry, 1989, pp. 183–9). Rawls is said to waver between two drastically different views of justice: 1) a view of justice as mutual advantage – reflecting the bargaining strengths of the parties; and 2) the contractualist view of justice as impartiality – seeking principles which cannot reasonably be rejected by anybody seeking agreement on fair grounds with one another.

This chapter presents and defends a different thesis, referred to as the moderate priority of compatriots, which stands in some contrast to the received opinion, that liberal contractualism justifies a general egalitarian baseline, robust across all distributive domains (Cohen, 1989).[2] Liberal contractualism, or justice as impartiality, of the kind associated with T.M. Scanlon and Brian Barry, can allow a world order of sovereign states which violates a global difference principle – as long as economic and financial regimes secure human needs and do not allow domination by rich states.

Section 1 suggests why the question 'Why equality?' is relevant within a contractualist perspective. Sections 2 and 3 sketch some reasons *against* inequality and *for* using equal shares of social primary goods as a baseline (Scanlon, 1988). Section 4 illustrates how these reasons fail to hold within a system of states enjoying sovereignty, since the impact of international institutional structures on affected parties is relevantly different from the domestic basic structure. Thus a baseline of unequal shares is not always objectionable or unfair, and the egalitarianism of justice as impartiality is not robust. Section 5 addresses Barry's criticism of Rawls' position. I conclude the paper by questioning, in section 6, the practical relevance of these conclusions for current world order, which is beyond a system of states.

The upshot of this argument is that justice as impartiality does not require a global difference principle, the validity of a domestic difference principle notwithstanding. Thus liberal contractualism can account for the distributive significance of state borders, without appeal to 'communitarian' premises of allegedly shared values or political beliefs among citizens. Instead, the grounds for moderate priority of compatriots rests on the normative significance of shared social institutions.

1 Why Equality?

'Equality of what?' is no doubt an important question in political philosophy – as admirably shown by Amartya Sen (1980), G.A. Cohen (1989) and others. However, a satisfactory theory must also answer the further question 'Why equality?' – a question which these authors apparently leave to the side. This question is particularly appropriate for liberal contractualism because of three challenges to the search for plausible principles for distributive justice of social institutions.

Firstly, liberal contractualism often draws on what we may think of as impact arguments to eliminate reasonable objection to rules, avoiding rules which require that some person must suffer a larger impact under them than anyone must suffer under some alternative rule (Scanlon, 1982 and 1975).[3] These impact arguments are made in terms of the stakes which affected parties have when comparing rules. The intuitive idea is that those who have most at stake dominate the ranking of alternative rules. However, I suggest that very few interests can satisfy the stringent measurability requirements of such comparisons of impacts. Objections to unequal shares of goods or impacts seem even more difficult to make, given the problems of comparing intervals of interest satisfaction.

This challenge is made more difficult by the two further considerations. Firstly, the plurality of conceptions of the good among citizens drastically reduces the scope of interests to which it is reasonable to appeal, particularly when arguing about social institutions maintained by force. Secondly, pluralism makes it less likely that parties will agree about the relative weight to be accorded changes in levels of goods or of interest satisfaction – contrary to a general claim for equality.

Thirdly, the phenomenon of adaptive interest formation reduces the set of relevant impacts on interests even further. Institutions have a fundamental impact on our expectations, rendering subjective preferences and satisfaction of existing life plans generally unsuitable as indicators of impacts on interests. This feature also renders it less plausible that inequalities generally must be lamented.

All of these features reduce the scope of goods and interests that are relevant for arguments about principles for institutional arrangements. I shall still suggest that 'social primary goods' provide indices which can satisfy these three conditions. The focus on individuals' social primary goods need not be regarded as based on an unwarranted and controversial assumption about the equal instrumental value of these goods for the satisfaction of everyone's highly divergent interests.[4]

Social primary goods play a useful role for the purposes of some normative theories, then, even though they are not directly correlated to individuals' condition, interest-satisfaction, or capabilities. Instead, they are suitable as an index in part because they lend themselves to expressing reasonable claims regarding how benefits of this kind are to be shared. Indeed, I shall suggest that there are grounds for claiming equal shares of precisely such goods.

2 Against Inequality

I first briefly discuss three grounds for lamenting specific kinds of inequalities, and then offer a more detailed account of a fourth argument in favour of equal shares of benefits.[5]

Preventing Misery

From the moral point of view, a set of institutions must be acceptable to all affected parties. If this normative commitment is to have any substantive content, it must be the case that acceptable institutions must engender and distribute benefits so as to meet the basic vital needs of all. To be sure, the current world order fails dismally on this point: those with nothing to sell in the market cannot buy food, and large economic inequalities can even prevent wage earners from acquiring food. Differences in relative political power perpetuate abysmal prenatal health care for the poor. To rephrase: we can properly object to large inequalities engendered by social institutions, based on the overriding importance of meeting basic needs. However, this objection does not amount to a general argument for equality. Instead, it is an argument against drastic inequality regarding certain specific goods, insofar as these inequalities engender misery.

Preventing Domination

In addition to satisfying basic needs, individuals have an interest in maintaining control over the social factors that shape their own lives – in particular if the alternative is that others wield such control over them. Large inequalities of wealth can prevent the less privileged from exercising control over their lives, and subject them to the bargaining power of the powerful in various spheres of life.

It is a reasonable objection to a social order if some individuals can drastically restrict the attractive options of others, prevent deliberation or otherwise leave them at the mercy of the powerful. Such distribution of control, e.g. in the form of income or employment opportunities, adds avoidable risk to those risks we already face through nature and luck. Such inequalities which engender domination fail to accord individuals proper respect as equals.

Such arguments from domination serve to restrict inequalities of certain goods and powers. These arguments are contingent on the impact of such inequalities for the distribution of control over individuals' lives, and apply against certain inequalities within state borders.

Equal Power for Fair Procedures

A further ground for equality also stems from our interest in controlling the social factors that shape our lives. Many social procedures and mechanisms require for their fairness a roughly equal distribution of procedural input levers. Some adversarial procedures illustrate this: if legal trials are regularly to identify the guilty, both parties must be represented by competent counsel. Similarly, political campaigns competing for voter attention must not be able to crowd out competitors in the media.

These procedural levers may include political power, social positions of power including access to political offices and to certain kinds of education, and income and wealth. Democratic institutions should disperse these levers of political influence broadly, and equally, among all parties to these procedures, insofar as relative shares of these levers often matter for the distribution of output benefits.

This argument for equality of procedural controls comes into play when relative shares of input levers is important for the output of the procedure. However, note that such arguments only apply when we have standards for determining what outputs the procedure should generate. To sum up, several arguments against certain kinds of inequality can be offered on the grounds that they violate individuals' claims to equal respect within domestic social institutions.

The Case for Equal Shares of Products of Cooperation

The final reason to consider is that individuals may claim equal shares when they have equal claims on those goods, e.g. when they have contributed equally to the production of the benefits, and when no-one can be said to have prior claims to the benefits – for instance when there is no prior agreement regarding distribution and each party's contribution cannot be determined.[6] On the other hand, it would not seem implausible for some to claim a larger share when they are entitled to it, exert more effort or contribute other special resources, or exercise legitimate control over needed resources, including talents. For instance, someone may legitimately have options which would offer larger benefits. They could then reasonably reject an equal share if that would be smaller than their best feasible, legitimate alternative – as long as it is sufficiently responsive to others' claims.

I submit that this argument is a specification of points made by authors otherwise as diverse as John Locke and Karl Marx in their respective discussions of the role of labour in creating property, and the claims arising to these goods.

John Locke's labour theory of value famously holds that 'Whatsoever then he removes out of the State that Nature hath provided, and left it in, he hath mixed his Labour with, and joyned to it something that is his own, and thereby makes it his Property' (Locke, 1963, para. 28). All have equal claims to goods in nature: 'His labour hath taken it out of the hands of Nature, where it was common, and belong'd equally to all her Children' (ibid., para 29). These equal claims of all to Nature are replaced by exclusive claims, under the famous proviso that 'there is enough, and as good left in common for others' (ibid., para 28). On this basis I suggest that when several jointly labour to produce goods, they have equal claims regarding these goods.

Marx combines his labour theory of value with a contribution principle – to each proportionally to his labour contribution (Marx, 1977). These premises allow him to define and (apparently) condemn exploitation understood as situations when a coalition of persons in the economy is endowed with less than its per capita share of alienable property (or share of the means of production) (Marx, 1967; Roemer, 1982; Elster, 1985, p. 216). Problems of heterogeneity of labour (skilled vs unskilled, the significance of natural talents) pose fundamental conceptual challenges to this argument, and the explanatory force is questionable (cf. Elster, 1985). I suggest that the conceptual challenges are less daunting in circumstances when the relative importance of different forms of labour cannot easily be ascertained, and that under such circumstances equal claims among those who contribute to the production of goods is a reasonable rule.

One area where this argument applies concerns how central social institutions should allocate benefits arising from cooperation. In addressing this question, few special claims have standing. In particular, the considerations of expectations, based on entitlement or effort, are not relevant to the topic of assessing sets of social institutions. Legitimate expectations, for instance on the basis of effort, justify claims within the institutions. However, when we seek to assess the sets of social institutions which create such incentives, legitimate expectations are irrelevant. Expectations are internal to social practices: the social institutions specify what is to count as each person's due reward, understood as their legitimate expectations. Different social institutions will have different distributive effects due to the incentives they set up and the expectations they engender and honour, but every just set of social institutions will honour the expectations engendered by its public rules.

Likewise, special effort cannot ground special claims to how sets of social institutions should distribute benefits. It is impossible to discern individuals' 'prior' or 'independent' tendency to effort by generally reliable methods which we would be prepared to implement in a set of social institutions. Again, within a set of institutions the situation is different: special efforts may well be rewarded, if the public rules stipulate effort as a basis for distribution. Adaptive interest formation and the incentives provided by social institutions affect individuals' willingness to exert themselves.

Intuitively appealing precepts like 'to each the fruits of their labour' fail to apply on similar grounds. In complex, interdependent societies like ours, the results of our actions are often the joint outcome of several individuals' efforts. We can only determine what counts as 'our' fruits in light of the existing institutions and the expectations they foster.

Other grounds for claims thus fail to hold regarding the issue of how fundamental social institutions should distribute jointly produced benefits. However, we must consider which goods these may be.

3 Social Primary Goods as Products of Cooperation

I shall suggest that the argument from cooperation holds for what John Rawls (1971) refers to as social primary goods among those who are coerced into maintaining the social institutions which constitute such goods. Among the benefits created by participation in social institutions are legal powers, some of which are social primary goods. These powers draw on a particular view of social institutions and how they can be said to exist only by the participation of others.

We may think of behaviour which is regulated according to public rules as social practices. For a social practice to exist there must be a set of rules, generally complied with and acted on by the participants in the practice, and this fact of general compliance must be common knowledge. We may talk of social institutions as the practices that are maintained by the use of legal powers. When a social institution is in place, sanctions enforce the public rules and hence provide public assurance of general compliance. Authoritative interpretations apply the rules to new or difficult cases.

The social institutions distribute important kinds of power among citizens, and thus have a large influence on their lives. The system of law, the educational system, markets, the health care system and other social institutions create and distribute opportunities for joint action. They reward certain abilities, permit certain conceptions of the good, reward certain kinds of effort, generate certain kinds of formal powers, and set side constraints on how the fruits of cooperation shall be distributed. These constraints and background conditions thus have pervasive effects on citizens' plans and lives, particularly due to the fact of adaptive interest formation. Institutions provide the backdrop against which individuals make plans and live their lives.

In the following, we consider three aspects of these social institutions which are important for the argument. They are artificial, in the sense that they are the creation of deliberate human action. They generate 'goods internal to the practices', namely legal powers which are created or constituted by the joint participation of all in upholding these institutions. I shall suggest that Rawls' social primary goods are legal powers.

Social Institutions are under Political Control

Social institutions are artificial, in Hobbes' and Hume's sense: they are created and maintained by deliberate human action (Hume, 1888, p. 528; Hobbes, 1968; cf. Baier, 1988). They are social artifices in Hume's sense. They are the result – often flawed – of human 'design and intention' (Hume, 1888, p. 475), and 'changeable by human law' (ibid., p. 528). That is, they could be otherwise through the intervention of political power. Thus alternative institutions could exist, with drastically different incentive effects and distributive consequences. Insofar as institutions are under political control, albeit imperfectly, principles of distributive justice apply for the comparative assessment of alternative institutional arrangements. However, normative theory on this issue is notoriously hard, given adaptive interest formation, pluralism of conceptions of the good, and the pervasive incentive effects of the institutions themselves.

Legal Powers: Products of Cooperation

Within domestic institutions, a wide variety of legal powers are constituted by the rules of social institutions. Political power, rights, and even income and wealth can be regarded as aspects of the rules which regulate social practices. As an example: money exists only within a social practice regulated by rules defining legal tender. Ownership, freedom of speech, and political rights are likewise aspects of social institutions.

Individuals enjoy such goods – such rights – only when there are rules generally complied with by the others who are subject to the rules. A claim of ownership is only true – and can only be made sense of – because the rules of ownership are publicly known and generally complied with by those participating in that practice. While their entitlements are theirs, they are entitlements only because others regulate their actions according to public rules.

I submit that the social institutions which constitute, specify and allocate such rights are products of cooperation, created by the participating individuals. A wide variety of legal powers are constituted by social institutions, i.e. by the general compliance with laws within a state, which all citizens uphold. Someone enjoys these powers and controls if and only if the participants in the practice generally recognize and act according to the rules specifying these rights. Individuals and associations can further their interests by means of these rights only when the duty-bearers do their part in the social institutions.

A right, on this view, is therefore a benefit of cooperation among a group of individuals: the right exists only when they participate in the social practice specified by that right. When we rely on our rights and legal powers to further our interests, we benefit indirectly from the participation of others in the social institutions.

Legal powers are thus goods produced by cooperation. When considering how institutions should distribute these goods, I therefore submit that all participants in social institutions must be granted an equal claim to the political and other legal powers that arise. 'Equal shares of products' is an appropriate standard.

This interpretation of social institutions supports an argument that citizens have equal claims on how social institutions should regulate the distribution of political power, income and wealth, because these powers are the products of cooperation. This grounds a claim on social institutions, that they should engender equal shares of these benefits.[7]

Social Primary Goods as Legal Powers

I furthermore suggest that we understand Rawls' list of primary social goods as a list of legal powers, which in turn are regarded as features of social institutions which exist only as goods internal to practices (cf. Rawls, 1988, p. 257: 'This list [of social primary goods] includes mainly features of institutions, that is, basic rights and liberties, institutional opportunities, and prerogatives of office and position, along with income and wealth').

This interpretation of social primary goods as legal powers suggests why not only strict limits on inequality, but equal shares of these goods, emerges as a reasonable claim.

Note that this argument holds among those who participate in producing the social primary goods – that is, among those who comply with the social institutions which define these legal powers. Thus some humans seem to fall outside the domain of those who can claim equal shares; particularly those with handicaps so severe that they cannot be said to act or restrain themselves in accordance with the social institutions. Liberal contractualism does not dismiss these individuals as beyond justice – liberal contractualism is, after all, not a case of justice as mutual advantage. Rather, liberal contractualism can hold that their misery should be alleviated to some extent, but this approach also seems prepared to accept that these persons can not reasonably object to receiving less than an equal share of these goods.

4 Domestic Equality, Global Inequality

I have presented three reasons against domestic inequalities of various kinds, and one reason for equal shares of certain goods. I suggest that similar claims against inequality and for equal shares do not apply with the same force when applied to global distribution among states.

Within a states system, governments enjoy broad formal powers of external sovereignty, as guaranteed by international institutions. There are few, if any, decision-making bodies above it, and states will generally not intervene forcibly or dictatorially in one another's internal affairs (Bull, 1977). Thus, the government – and in a democratic state, the citizens – are formally free from external agents to influence the social institutions which shape their lives. This is not to deny, of course, that the range of alternatives is often restricted by natural facts and the actions of other powerful agents. Still, I suggest that formal external sovereignty affects the relevance of arguments against inequality and for equality presented above.

A legitimate world order must clearly constrain global inequalities of income and wealth. Market shares, oligarchic transnational corporations, and structural adjustment policies affect a state's ability to determine its international and domestic policies. Citizens enjoy less control over outcomes when they have little purchasing power relative to foreigners in international markets. However, international inequalities in income do not determine the domestic distribution of control over non-material goods. Furthermore, domestic legislation can often insulate domestic political institutions from the impact of international economic inequality. For instance, legislation may prohibit foreign funding of political campaigns, and bar the immigration of foreigners who outbid domestic applicants to education and employment. Governments can regulate access to international markets. Hence state sovereignty can serve as a buffer to reduce the impact of international life income inequalities, preventing domination and avoiding unfair procedures.

So the claim to reduce international inequality of income and wealth is on the one hand bolstered by the concern to avoid misery and domination. On the other hand, the arguments from domination and unfair procedures do not appear sound across state borders, as long as states enjoy formal external sovereignty. Moreover, foreigners do not maintain the domestic social institutions of sovereign states. So they cannot claim that they participate in shared institutions to the same extent as compatriots do. Hence they are not equal contributors to the creation of social primary goods.

I conclude, then, that the moderate priority of compatriots is justified: in an ideal-type state system, the arguments against inequality and for equal shares do not apply with the same force as among compatriots.

5 On Barry's Reading of Rawls

This defence of the moderate priority of compatriots is consistent with the domestic egalitarianism of justice as fairness, and can be regarded as a friendly elaboration of some arguments in Rawls' theory. I have suggested that considerations of global justice do not require a global difference principle, but that justice nevertheless imposes certain requirements on the control over economic and financial regimes, both in order to meet human needs and to prevent domination by rich states. Thus, justice as fairness need not be committed to a global difference principle.

Let us now consider Brian Barry's acute observation that Rawls portrays the representatives of different states as refusing to acknowledge any obligations whatsoever regarding the international distribution of income. Brian Barry argues that Rawls wavers between two radically different views of justice. Rawls suggests that the appropriate way to think about issues of international relations is modelled as a particular version of the original position. He claims that the preferred principles for international relations would be those generally acknowledged in international law: self-determination, right of self-defence, *pact sunt servanda* and *jus in bello*. By that very standard, an updated list must include international economic obligations: international law now recognizes some international duties related to human rights. International law still does not satisfy the standards of justice requiring the satisfaction of basic needs. But treaty- and charter-based or customary international human rights law includes extensive secondary or residual international obligations of aid and assistance (cf. Sohn, 1982; Schachter, 1982; Alston, 1984; Alston and Quinn 1987).

But in 1971 Rawls did not even lament the apparent lack of principles for international economic distribution. How are we to understand this silence? Brian Barry claims that Rawls rules out any constraints on the international political economy in *A Theory of Justice*. Barry takes Rawls to reject such obligations for very complicated reasons (Barry, 1989, pp. 183–9).[8] Rawls is said to waver between two drastically different views of justice: 1) a view of justice as mutual advantage, reflecting the bargaining strengths of the parties; and 2) the contractualist view of justice as impartiality, seeking principles which cannot reasonably be rejected by anybody seeking agreement on fair grounds with another. Rawls does not follow either view consistently, says Barry: strong states should get away with more than equal power

> if the requirement of mutual advantage is that every state must stand to gain (not from behind a veil of ignorance, but really) from the set of rules defining the rights and duties of states, then we cannot expect that set of rules to have an egalitarian structure. It can be in the interests of the most powerful states only if it concedes a great deal more to them than to weaker states (ibid., p. 187).

Justice as impartiality, on the other hand, must support a global difference principle, or so Barry claims. If Rawls is really committed to this view,

> [t]he question for Rawls is why the representatives of different countries should be so strangely silent on the issue of international redistribution of income (ibid., p. 189).

Barry suggests that Rawls is silent because he is influenced by justice as mutual advantage. This influence should be discounted, says Barry – and holds that justice as fairness requires a global difference principle.

If my account of social primary goods is correct, justice as mutual advantage does not enter into Rawls' arguments at all.[9] However, I have argued above that justice as impartiality – the contractualist reading of justice as fairness – does not require a global difference principle. Even though equality is an appropriate baseline in special, important cases, such as the domestic distribution of goods within social institutions, this premise cannot be generalized on contractualist grounds to determine a just distribution of goods within various spheres.

In defence of Barry, one might object that this argument for equal shares of social primary goods does not explain why justice as fairness is completely silent regarding international distributive justice. The answer to this question emerges, I suggest, when we consider the context of Rawls' discussion of international justice in *A Theory of Justice*.

This discussion is part of his theory of conscientious refusal, which in turn is a development of his theory of political duty for non-ideal theory. Rawls is concerned with conscientious refusal against serving in wars claimed to be permitted by standards of international justice. These wars are in pursuit of national interest or self-determination, or held to be legitimate responses to violations against the principles of self-determination, the right of self-defence, *pacta sunt servanda* or *jus in bello*. Conscientious refusers argue that the particular act of war is not justified under international law. In the relevant section of *A Theory of Justice*, Rawls explains how these arguments are supported, and why they should be regarded as 'political' in a certain sense. For these purposes there is no need to discuss principles of international economic distribution. Wars might perhaps be justified by appeal to a (not yet legally recognized) right to international aid. Indeed, some writers have argued that industrialized states should redistribute their wealth precisely to avoid such wars (Brandt, 1980). However, proposed justifications of actual wars, and objections to them, have never referred to such principles. The silence in *A Theory of Justice* on this issue is thus no indication of a commitment to justice as mutual advantage, but rather due to the specific context of Rawls' discussion of international justice.

6 Application: Global and European

I have argued that there are few grounds for requiring regimes to ensure equal shares of benefits of cooperation among citizens of different sovereign states at the global level.

However, the practical significance of this conclusion remains unclear, because it is open to doubt whether the current world order can plausibly be regarded as a system of sovereign states in the sense relevant for arguments against inequality and for equality. The nature and level of institutionalized interdependence suggest that the arguments from avoiding misery, dependence and fair procedures hold across state borders. And international regimes suggest that many legal powers must be regarded as the products of international or global practices. Thus the defence of moderate priority for compatriots may not hold for the present world, where states are not sovereign in the relevant sense.

I close with an illustration. It would appear that Europeans cooperate under social institutions precisely so as to render claims to equal shares appropriate. Shared institutions, including a monetary union and freedom of movement for capital, workers, goods and services, allow for domination, while state sovereignty is drastically reduced. In light of these changes, I also submit that citizens of the EU must be said jointly to maintain the social institutions of all member states.

These characteristics of the EU have several normative implications. Welfare obligations go beyond national boundaries in Europe. Claims to equal shares of economic benefits at the European level are plausible, due to the interconnected institutions of European states. European markets cannot be allowed free reign without considering distributive aspects also. Markets – domestic, regional and global – are legitimate only within social structures that maintain background distributive justice over time. Domestic markets should not be allowed to run rampant, in ignorance of the long-term distributive impact of market transactions among those with tradable goods and services, and on those individuals who can offer nothing to the market.

Thus we should insist that arguments of solidarity, convergence and structural funds must be an integral part of attempts at creating an acceptable European market. Unacceptable inequality at the European level cannot always be resolved by internal redistribution within each state, so regulation and international transfers may be needed.

This chapter has sketched the case for the moderate priority of compatriots. It stands in some contrast to the received opinion, that liberal contractualism justifies a general egalitarian baseline, robust across all distributive domains. Thus liberal contractualism can account for the distributive significance of state borders, by focusing on the claims on goods 'internal to the practices' – without appeal to 'communitarian' premises of allegedly shared values or political beliefs among citizens. Instead, the grounds for moderate priority of compatriots rest on the normative significance of shared social institutions. We can shape the institutions which in turn shape us – and which shape the legitimate claims people have on one another.

Notes

1 First presented at UK Association for Legal and Social Philosophy 25th Annual Conference, on International Justice, Reading, April 1998. The paper was written under the auspices of ARENA – a programme of Advanced Research on the Europeanisation of the Nation-State, under the Research Council of Norway. This paper draws on my PhD dissertation (Føllesdal, 1991) and develops further themes found in Føllesdal, 1997.

2 Indeed, I would suggest that justice as fairness is not egalitarian in G.A. Cohen's sense (Cohen, 1989). Justice as fairness – and more generally justice as impartiality – do not hold that the aspect of which justice requires equal shares is an aspect of a person's condition in any fundamental way beyond the purpose of achieving agreement about distributive principles of justice.

3 Cf. 'The question to be asked is, is it unreasonable for someone to refuse to put up with the Losers' situation under A in order that someone else should be able to enjoy the benefits which he would have to give up under E?' (Scanlon, 1982, p. 123). And cf. Scanlon 1975, p. 660: 'We have various general concerns, of which health and amusement might be two. Associated with each of these there is a scale of the various levels or degrees to which the concern might be fulfilled at a given time. Various combinations of such levels represent different levels of well-being. The relation of urgency, then, will be a relation between various increments or decrements along one or more of these scales. I regard my comments in this section as expounding on Scanlon's approach.

4 *Pace* Cohen.

5 I here draw on Scanlon, 1988, and Temkin, 1988 and 1993.

6 Scanlon notes (1988, p. 12) that this argument is weak: 'the force of appeals ... depends on a prior claim that as participants in a cooperative scheme the individuals in question have equal claim to the fruits of this cooperation. This is an appealing moral idea, but a controversial one to serve as the starting point for an argument in support of a particular conception of justice'. My account in the following seeks to make the premise more acceptable.

7 Unless unequal shares of certain goods may benefit all, e.g. due to incentive effects, leaving open the institutional questions of whether the preferred institutions should involve high levels of redistribution and administrative bureaucracy.

8 Pogge is also puzzled by Rawls' silence, but does not draw such drastic theoretical conclusions as Barry. Cf. Pogge, 1989, p. 246.

9 Or at least not in determining reasonable outcomes in the way Barry suggests. We

nevertheless do assume that to be a member of a society is advantageous to everybody. If this premise is false for some, this might legitimately affect the content of principles of justice. But the bargaining power of some subset of individuals does not affect the principles. In game-theoretical terms: the lack of a core does not affect the distribution of pay-offs, and we would expect that adaptive preference formation under just institutions reduces the incentive for coalitions to demand larger shares – cf. Shubik, 1982, p. 145.

References

Alston, P. (1984), 'International Law and the Human Right to Food' in P. Alston and K. Tomasevski (eds), *The Right to Food*, Nijhoff, The Hague.

Alston, P. and Quinn, G. (1987), 'The Nature and Scope of States Parties' Obligations Under the International Covenant on Economic, Social and Cultural Rights', *Human Rights Quarterly*, 9, May, pp. 156–229.

Baier, A. (1988), 'Hume's Account of Social Artifice – its Origin and Originality', *Ethics*, 98, July, pp. 757–78.

Barry, B. (1973), *The Liberal Theory of Justice*, Clarendon Press, Oxford.

Barry, B. (1989), *Theories of Justice. A Treatise on Social Justice, Vol. 1*, University of California Press, Berkeley.

Barry, B. (1995), *Justice as Impartiality*, Oxford University Press, Oxford.

Beitz, C.R. (1979), *Political Theory and International Relations*, Princeton University Press, Princeton.

Brandt, W. (1980), *North – South: A Program for Survival. Report of the Independent Commission on International Development Issues*, Cambridge, MIT Press, Massachusetts.

Bull, H. (1977), *The Anarchical Society*, Columbia University Press, New York.

Cohen, G.A. (1989), 'On the Currency of Egalitarian Justice', *Ethics*, 99, pp. 906–44.

Elster, J. (1985), *Making Sense of Marx. Studies in Marxism and Social Theory*, Cambridge University Press, Cambridge.

Føllesdal, A. (1991), 'The Normative Significance of State Borders for International Distributive Justice', PhD dissertation, Harvard University. University Microfilms No. 9211679.

Føllesdal, A. (1997), 'Do Welfare Obligations End at the Boundaries of the Nation State?' in P. Koslowski and A. Føllesdal (eds), *Restructuring the Welfare State: Ethical issues of Social Policy in an International Perspective. Studies in Economic Ethics and Philosophy*, Springer-Verlag, Berlin.

Hume, D. (1888) [1739], *A Treatise on Human Nature*, eds L.A. Selby-Bigge and P.H. Nidditch, Clarendon Press, Oxford.

Hobbes, T. (1968) [1651], *Leviathan*, ed. and introduction by C.B. Macpherson, Penguin, Baltimore, Maryland.

Locke, J. (1963) [1690], *Two Treaties on Government*, revised and introduction by P. Laslett, New American Library, New York.
Marx, K. (1967) [1867], *Kapital I*, International Publishers, New York.
Marx, K. (1977) [1875], 'Critique of the Gotha Program' in *Karl Marx: Selected Writings*, ed. and compiled by D. McLellan, Oxford University Press, Oxford.
Pogge, T.W. (1989), *Realizing Rawls*, Cornell University Press, Ithaca.
Rawls, J. (1971), *A Theory of Justice*, Harvard University Press, Cambridge, Massachusetts.
Rawls, J. (1988), 'The Priority of Right and Ideas of the Good', *Philosophy and Public Affairs*, 17 (4), pp. 251–76.
Roemer, J. (1982), *A General Theory of Exploitation and Class*, Harvard University Press, Cambridge, Massachusetts.
Scanlon, T.M. (1974), 'John Rawls' Theory of Justice' in N. Daniels (ed.), *Reading Rawls*, Basic Books, New York.
Scanlon, T.M. (1975), 'Preference and Urgency', *Journal of Philosophy*, 72 (19), pp. 655–69.
Scanlon, T.M. (1982), 'Contractualism and Utilitarianism' in A.K. Sen and B. Williams (eds), *Utilitarianism and Beyond*, Cambridge University Press, Cambridge.
Scanlon, T.M. (1988), 'Notes on Equality' unpublished paper, Cambridge, Massachusetts.
Scanlon, T.M. (1991), 'The Moral Basis of Interpersonal Comparisons' in J. Elster and J. Roemer (eds), *Interpersonal Comparisons of Well-being*, Cambridge University Press, Cambridge.
Schachter, O. (1982), 'International Human Rights', *Recueil Des Cours*, 178 (5), pp. 327–51.
Sen, A.K. 1980 [1982], 'Equality of What?', reprinted from *The Tanner Lectures on Human Values Vol. I*, Cambridge, Cambridge University Press.
Shubik, M. (1982), *Game Theory in the Social Sciences: Concepts and Solutions*, MIT Press, Cambridge, Massachusetts.
Sohn, L.B. (1982), 'The New International Law: Protection of the Rights of Individuals Rather Than States', *American University Law Review*, 32, pp. 1–64.
Temkin, L.S. (1986), 'Inequality', *Philosophy and Public Affairs*, 15, Spring, pp. 99–121.
Temkin, L.S. (1993), *Inequality*, Oxford University Press, Oxford.

9 Contractualism and the Moral Significance of Human Well-being[1]

MATT MATRAVERS

1 Introduction

The publication in 1971 of John Rawls's *A Theory of Justice* heralded a period of optimism in Anglo-American analytic political philosophy and beyond. It not only restored the faith of some practitioners of the discipline that the often quoted death of political theory had been much exaggerated, but it also seemed to promise the possibility of a theory that was universal in scope. However, optimism, like technology, seems to have a short shelf-life these days. It quickly became a standard critique of Rawls that he had 'smuggled in' liberal premises to generate liberal conclusions and that the method of reflective equilibrium was nothing more than coherentism dressed up with a few cheap accessories. The fashion now is for increasingly limited and parochial theory or for some variation of anti-theory.

The argument of this chapter is that the promise of universalism stemmed from the engagement with what Rawls calls 'the fact of pluralism', but that it is precisely this starting point that vitiates the Rawlsian project and lends credibility to those who claim that the aspiration of political philosophers to generate a plausible universalist theory is doomed to failure. The next two sections provide brief introductions to the problem of justice as it is characterized by liberal theorists and the solution offered by justice as impartiality. The fourth section considers the relationship of the impartialist account of justice to moral theory more broadly defined. This is done in part by looking at the impartialist view of certain aspects of the criminal law, a topic taken up in section 5. Sections 6 and 7 examine possible impartialist accounts of injunctions such as that not to commit murder. Finally the chapter concludes with the claim that in order to be complete, justice as impartiality needs an account of the moral significance of human well-being, that this claim puts into doubt the attempt to distinguish rules of right from considerations of the good, and that this has serious implications for the way in which we should seek a universal account of justice.

2 The Problem of Justice

Amongst 'the circumstances of justice' that Rawls identifies as providing both the conditions for, and the problem of, justice is that whilst social cooperation is both feasible and desirable it does not yield sufficient benefits to meet all the demands of those who are engaged in the cooperative enterprise. Most importantly, people have what Rawls calls their own 'plans of life' or 'conceptions of the good' (Rawls, 1971, p. 127):

> These plans, or conceptions of the good, lead them to have different ends and purposes, and to make conflicting claims on the natural and social resources available. Moreover, although the interests advanced by these plans are not assumed to be interests in the self, they are the interests of a self that regards its conception of the good as worthy of recognition and that advances claims in its behalf as deserving satisfaction. … I also suppose that men suffer from various shortcomings of knowledge, thought, and judgment. … As a consequence individuals not only have different plans of life but there exists a diversity of philosophical and religious belief, and of political and social doctrines.

This diversity of philosophical and religious belief (and of related political and social claims) is what Rawls calls 'the fact of pluralism'. This is an unfortunate phrase. The term 'pluralism' is not meant to denote a particular position on the source(s) of value, as in the writing of someone like Isaiah Berlin. Rather, what is meant is nothing more than that there are profound differences in the answers people give to the question of what is the nature of the good life. Different people possess distinct beliefs concerning what it is that makes life worth living, what it is that is of value in a human life, what is the source of such value, and so on. Normally, people possess such 'conceptions of the good' as adherents or members of distinct ethical traditions; religious, humanist, utilitarian, Kantian or whatever. 'The fact' of such differences, however, is not meant merely to refer to the existence of a multiplicity of such traditions, but to the reasonableness of disagreement between conceptions of the good. Rawls claims that reason is insufficient to determine whether there are one or many sources of value and which, if any, conception of the good is the right one. Given that reason cannot demonstrate the superiority or inferiority of any one conception of the good to any other, the reasonableness of pluralism describes a situation in which there is *profound, reasonable*, and *seemingly irresolvable* disagreement between people about the nature of the good life for persons.

The problem of justice is that of finding rules that can govern cooperation and determine the distribution of the benefits and burdens that result from it given agents who profoundly but reasonably disagree in their conceptions of the good (and subsequently in their social and political beliefs). As Brian Barry has put it, in contrast to the traditional question of morality, 'how ought one to live?', the question of justice is 'how are we to live together, given that we have different ideas about how to live?' (Barry, 1995a, p. 77, emphasis suppressed).

3 Justice as Impartiality[2]

The impartialist answer is deceptively simple. If what is needed is to find rules of cooperation given the reasonableness of pluralism then such rules must be justified independently of any reference to the truth, falsity, or validity of any particular (or group of) reasonable conception(s) of the good. At the heart of impartialist theory is the aspiration to what Will Kymlicka has called 'justificatory neutrality'. This is the idea that 'the state does not justify its actions by reference to some public ranking of the intrinsic value of different ways of life, for there is no public ranking to refer to' (1989, p. 884). Another way of putting the same point is to say that the reasons that are appealed to in justifying the use of public power must be thin (that is, compatible with the demand of justificatory neutrality). So, in Rawls's original position the people are denied knowledge of their conceptions of the good in order to ensure that the two principles are fair. Their decision is informed only by a thin theory of the good and the metric of justice – primary social goods – is chosen precisely because it is rational to desire such goods no matter what else one desires. To a similar end proposed rules of justice that can be rejected as unreasonable in Brian Barry's variation of T.M. Scanlon's contractualism include those that appeal for justification to a particular conception of the good.

Typically impartialist theories of justice are restricted in three related ways: First, the principles of justice apply only to what Rawls calls 'the basic structure of society' (1971, p. 7) or are what Barry calls 'second-order' (1995a, p. 194). What this means is that impartial reasoning is restricted in its application to the problem of justice as it affects public institutions that govern the manner of distribution of such things as income, wealth and political rights (and to people only in relation to these things). It is not meant to be a guide to how to conduct one's personal life or a guide to how one ought to live in every aspect of one's life. Second, it follows from this that the principles that emerge from the application of impartialist reasoning are principles of justice not of morality as a whole. Quite how this distinction is to be drawn is discussed below, for the moment it is enough to say that questions of justice are those that concern the distribution of the benefits and burdens of social cooperation. Third, the principles of justice apply only to the distributive and not to the retributive sphere. These restrictions seem to follow from the characterization of the problem of justice as given above. Yet impartialist theorists correctly see themselves as engaged in an aspect of moral philosophy and even in Rawls's most avowedly political works he never distances himself from the claim that justice as fairness is a 'moral conception' (see, e.g., Rawls, 1985, p. 223 and 1993, pp. 11, 175).

The promise of universalism is implicit in the characterization of justice as addressing the reasonableness of pluralism. If rules of justice could be found that were at once justified and acceptable to people no matter what their conception of the good it would seem that normative political philosophy could once again aspire (in Brian Barry's words) to 'address ... the reason of every human being of sound mind' (1995a, pp. 3–4).

4 The Relationship of Justice and Morality

Impartialist theory is concerned that the account of justice that it offers is not meant to replace morality. Justice is part of morality but it is neither the whole of, nor a substitute for, it. This suggests that the relationship of questions of justice to accounts of morality is simply that amongst the range of moral propositions will be a class that concern questions of justice. The impartialist theorist identifies this subset of moral propositions by their subject matter; they concern the distribution of the benefits and burdens of social cooperation and apply to the basic structure of society. A theory of justice, then, aspires to give an account of the truth conditions of such propositions in a way that is compatible with the account of our reasoning about justice and our ordinary experience of justice. In addition, it aims to address the question of the agent's motivation to be just. Such an account *supplements* a given theory of morality by paying special attention to a particular class of moral sentences.

This seems perfectly reasonable. There is no reason to think that there cannot be distinct theories of piety, courage, or justice simply because all of these things have at one time or another been thought of as moral virtues. However, what makes the impartialist position more difficult is the claim that the account of justice must aspire to justificatory neutrality. This means that the straightforward understanding of the relationship of moral theory and theories of justice as described above is not right.

On an ordinary reading of the above it would seem that whereas a theory of morality would aspire to give an account of both the proposition that it is morally good (other things being equal) to help an elderly person across the road and that it is just to distribute the benefits and burdens of social cooperation in a given manner, a theory of justice concerns itself only with the latter.[3] However, the impartialist need for justificatory neutrality means that the types of reasons available to the agent in considering these two questions are not of the same kind, and may be incompatible. An agent may consider that it is morally right to help an elderly person across the road because the parable of the good Samaritan suggests that this is part of leading a life in emulation of the life of Christ (and this is the paradigm of a moral life). In such a case the agent may also have views about the just distribution of the benefits and burdens of social cooperation (views that appeal to reasons derived from a particular understanding of the Bible), but these are not reasons that are relevant when considering the question of justice. Rather, the agent is required to engage in different activities, reasoning from thick moral beliefs as a private individual (as a pursuer of a particular conception of the good), and from thin reasons as a citizen.[4]

It is this separation of the right from the good – of considerations of justice from other moral questions – that is the distinguishing feature, and distinctive contribution, of justice as impartiality, and it is the stability of the distinction between reasons of justice and what might for the moment be called other moral reasons that is the concern of this paper. In part this is a question of scope. For if it can be shown that there is a clear distinction between questions of justice and other moral questions then it would seem reasonable to maintain that there might be different sets of reasons appropriate to the different sets of questions. This is suggested by one reading of Rawls, especially in the works that followed *A Theory of Justice* as well as by the restrictions placed on impartialist theories mentioned above. A political conception of justice, Rawls (1993, p. 223) tells us,

> is framed to apply solely to the basic structure of society, its main political, social, and economic institutions as a unified scheme of social cooperation; ...

> it is presented independently of any wider comprehensive religious or philosophical doctrine; and ... it is elaborated in terms of fundamental political ideas viewed as implicit in the public political culture of a democratic society.[5]

The political conception is nevertheless a 'moral' one. Rawls writes that what he means by this is that the content of the conception of justice 'is given by certain ideals, principles and standards; and that these norms articulate certain values, in this case political values' (1993, fn. 11).

This is not the place to offer a full scale interpretation of *Political Liberalism*. A defensible reading (or so I believe) of what is relevant for this paper is that Rawls's political conception is moral in that it builds on the two 'moral powers' he attributes to persons: The capacity for a sense of justice and for a conception of the good (see Rawls, 1993, pp. 19, 103–10). In relying on this conception of the person (or at least, this conception of the citizen in democratic societies) he does not commit himself to a comprehensive moral view because of the limited scope of the conception of the person invoked. Thus, attributing to people a 'highest order interest' in their 'capacity to form, to revise, and rationally to pursue a conception of one's rational advantage or good' (ibid., p. 19) does not preclude Rawls arguing that such persons will also hold 'a determinate conception of the good' (ibid.). This may be 'comprehensive'. That is, it may include 'conceptions of what is of value in human life, and ideals of personal character, ... and much else that is to inform our conduct, and in the limit to our life as a whole' (ibid., p. 13). Thus, the political conception is political in its scope, in what it applies to, and in appealing only to a limited, non-comprehensive, moral ideal of persons as free and equal. A moral ideal that is itself to be thought of as capturing political values. That is, as relevant when thinking of oneself and others as participants in society conceived of as a cooperative venture for mutual advantage.

The plausibility of Rawls's theory need not detain the argument here, what is relevant for the moment is simply to get straight what impartialists understand to be the connections (or lack of them) between the reasons relevant to questions of justice and those relevant to other moral questions. Rawls's argument would seem to depend upon there being distinct, recognisable, political questions that are to be considered by people conceiving of themselves as citizens. This 'domain of the political' (Rawls, 1989) is defined by Rawls in a number of places as covering only 'society's main political, social, and economic institutions, and how they fit together ...' (Rawls, 1993, p. 11; see also pp. 223–30). Rawls is clear that this leaves a great deal out (ibid., p. 214):

> Many if not most political questions do not concern those fundamental matters, for example, much tax legislation and many laws regulating property; statutes protecting the environment and controlling pollution; establishing national parks ...; and laying aside funds for museums and the arts.

The position, then, on the relationship of Rawls's political, but still moral, conception of justice and more comprehensive moral theories does seem to be one of scope. Political questions, to which (impartial) public reason is addressed are only those to do with constitutional essentials and are approached from the perspective of the individual as citizen.

For Barry, for reasons to be discussed below, the scope of impartial justice is limited more pragmatically. Where people or groups disagree about matters that might deleteriously affect their ability to live in accordance with their conception of the good justice has a role. Thus restrictions on religious worship and homosexuality are matters of justice whereas a restriction on one's ability to ride a motorcycle legally without protective headgear is not (Barry, 1995a, p. 87). Moreover, as questions of justice can mostly only be addressed at a fairly abstract level impartialist theory is to be used in establishing basic constitutional provisions (see especially Barry, 1995a, ch. 4). Nevertheless, where Barry and Rawls agree is that when justice is being invoked it must be free from the taint of reasons that appeal to thick, comprehensive accounts of moral value. As noted above, it is in this way that impartial justice aspires to speak to the reason of all despite the diversity of views on the good prevalent in any given society.

In what follows the plausibility and stability of the distinction between the thin theory of justice and comprehensive moral theories (between the individual reasoning as a citizen and reasoning as a holder of a distinct comprehensive conception of the good) is tested. The method is to look at the use of public power in areas that do not (at least not uncontroversially) involve questions of *justice*. For example, the exercise of public power that is involved in the formulation and imposition of the criminal law.

Such an approach might seem misguided. If the areas to be examined are not in the domain of justice then it may seem that they can reveal little about theories of justice, especially theories that are carefully restricted in their scope. However, there are two reasons to think this approach appropriate. The first is that for both Rawls and Barry it is important that the use of public power be publicly justifiable (see, for example, Rawls, 1993, p. 137). Yet, public power is not merely (or, indeed, most often) exercised when questions of constitutional essentials are at stake. If a regime is to be legitimate, then, it must be that it can defend the use of public power in, say, the criminal law. This leads to the second reason for the approach that is taken below. Given that the use of public power must be publicly justified even in matters that are not, or at least not uncontroversially, matters of justice the nature of this justification must stand in some relation to the thin reasons invoked in considering constitutional essentials. There would seem to be three possibilities: (a) that all uses of public power can be described in the thin language of justice. A language that can then be applied directly; (b) that all uses of public power can be justified using normative resources that can be derived from the demands of justice, but without being restricted to the direct application of the language of justice; (c) that some uses of public power are to be justified in a different way from the way in which impartial reason justifies its use in cases of justice. However, if this is so then some account needs to be offered of the relationship of the two normative languages.

In what follows the argument proceeds largely without reference to any particular impartialist writer so it may be worth offering a preliminary summary of the problem. Impartial theories of justice depend upon separating the right from the good, reasons and questions of justice from other moral reasons and questions. This separation is necessary because the existence of reasonable disagreement about the good apparently precludes understanding justice in the traditional way; that is, as a moral virtue the content of which can be derived from a broader moral theory (including a theory of the good). The impartialist therefore attempts to establish the requirements of justice using a *procedure* framed by thin, public, political reasons. The idea that such a procedure can be established independently from thick considerations of the good gains plausibility from the restrictions on *scope* that impartialists place on their theories. The theory is meant only to apply in the domain of the political and thus appeals only to 'political' reasons. If successful the impartialist can fulfil an essential requirement for the liberal account of legitimacy: that the use of public power ought to be able to be publicly justified.

Yet if impartialist liberalism is committed to the public justifiability of the use of public power it is surely odd that impartialists have had so little to say about the criminal law, a central feature of the use of public power in contemporary societies. In the next four sections, various possible conceptions of the criminal law that are compatible with impartialism (in accordance with the three possibilities mentioned above) are considered. To anticipate the argument of the rest of the chapter slightly: the difficulty for the impartialist is that, although public, the criminal law (or some of its component laws) seems to contain an 'extra' normative element beyond justice, an element of wrongness. If the impartialist attempts to treat this in a reductionist manner by making it all a matter of justice, she is left with an implausible account of the criminal law. If she appeals to 'enriched' public reasons to account for the extra normative force of these public rules then the stability of the distinction of reasons of justice and other moral reasons is threatened. The difficulty is twofold: the domain of the political/public cannot be adequately theorized using only public reason (reasons of right) unless public reason is enriched. However, if it is so enriched then the distinction between public reason and other moral reasons is destabilized. Public reason threatens to collapse into its traditional place – a subset of moral reason – and this undermines the impartialist project. However, in the final section it is argued that this is not too threatening to the liberal conclusions of impartialist theory if the moral reasons that impartialism depends upon to make it plausible are liberal (and, most importantly, not derived from a *comprehensive* conception of the good). The outcome is a liberal, but not impartialist, theory.

5 Justice and the Criminal Law

Consider some fairly standard instances of the criminal law; prohibitions on assault, murder, burglary, and so on. Of course, the normative discussions that go on around such rules are, in part, discussions of justice. Indeed, the criminal law is probably the area most closely associated in ordinary language with issues of justice. However, for the most part insofar as justice is relevant it is to the implementation of the criminal law. It is unjust to treat one offender differently from a relevantly similar other; it is unjust knowingly to punish someone who did not commit a crime; and it is unjust to alter evidence or interfere with the ordinary running of a criminal trial. However, the claim that the laws against assault, murder, burglary, etc., are there to prevent injustice and that what is wrong with murderers is that they behave unjustly towards their victims twists ordinary language out of shape. The content of these laws expresses moral commitments that we have that are not ordinarily captured in the language of justice.

This would seem to be just what to expect from the impartialist restriction on the scope of justice.[6] The content of the criminal law seems to fall outside matters essential to the constitution even if the way in which that content is arrived at, and its formal shape,[7] do not. Nevertheless, the criminal law is an instance of the use of public power. What is more, it is often a paradigm case of the use of public power in upholding certain normative standards and values.

Of course, when the law speaks on matters of, say, whether one ought to drive on the left or right side of the road it can plausibly be seen as doing little more than solving a coordination problem. However, in prohibiting murder the law surely does more than this. It expresses both a belief in the moral value of human life and the threat of condemnation and punishment for those who violate that law.

The problem for the impartialist theorist is that in a society characterized by the reasonableness of pluralism there will be different views on the status and nature of the content of rules such as those prohibiting murder. Participants in most religions will regard this prohibition as capturing the wrongness of murder, where the nature of that wrongness is that it contravenes the law of (their) God, others might believe that the act of murder has some mind-independent property of wrongness that can be intuited by human beings using some special moral sense, others that there are mind-dependent but nevertheless objective moral facts and that 'murder is wrong' is one such, and so on. The question that arises is whether the public justification of the use of coercion by the state in pursuit of the maintaining and enforcing of such rules and in condemning and punishing those who transgress them can adequately characterize these types of rule whilst maintaining the commitment to impartiality when justifying the use of public power.

It might be thought that the question is being set up here in a manner so as to create difficulty for impartialist theory. The argument might be this: By seeming to *define* certain injunctive rules as having a moral content and by asking questions about what is *expressed* by such rules, the assumption is made that such rules do have and express a particular moral content independent of their being just or otherwise. Given that the impartialist wishes to avoid talk of morality and speak merely of justice this is unfair. If the impartialist cannot explain these rules as they are characterized above then this shows merely that the characterization is wrong not that the impartialist is in trouble.

However, this is not the position. Given that the impartialist allows that justice is not the whole of morality, that some criminal laws do express something and have to be justified somehow, and that such laws involve the exercise of public power, the impartialist must accept that there is a question as to the relationship of the use of power in these cases and the impartial restriction on public reason. The three possibilities for this relationship are mentioned above and each examined below.

6 All a Matter of Justice[8]

The first possible account of the relationship between questions of justice and what are called above other moral questions is to reduce the latter to the former. Applied to the discussion of this chapter: all uses of public power, including its use in the criminal law, concern matters of justice to be justified directly by the thin reasons of impartialist theory. One argument of this kind is found in the so-called fair play theory of punishment.[9] Fair play theorists of punishment treat the rule of law as a product of social cooperation. The benefit of the rule of law is made possible by each person restricting the pursuit of her self-interest in accordance with the demands of the law. These benefits and burdens are then to be distributed in accordance with a theory of distributive justice (a theory of the justified distribution of the benefits and burdens of social cooperation). Those who act in a manner unconstrained by the law and yet benefit from the peace and stability afforded by it free-ride on the system of cooperation. Punishment, according to fair play theory, corrects the unjust pattern of distribution created by the illegal act by penalizing the free-rider. As an account of punishment this theory has been severely criticized even by some of its early proponents.[10] Most damaging, and most relevant for the present discussion, is the claim that it 'distorts the essential character of crime' (Duff, 1996, p. 27). When someone murders or rapes he does not, or not only, free-ride on his victim (or on the general system of cooperation).

The fair play account would provide what is needed: a way to understand the use of public power in the criminal law such that it can appeal for justification, and can thus be made legitimate, by the account of justice. The thin language of impartial reason can be applied directly to this use of public power just as to its application to constitutional essentials. However, fair play theory as a complete theory of the criminal law (and of punishment) is implausible. Impartialists quite rightly distance themselves from it.[11] As they are careful to distinguish questions of justice from other moral questions they have no need or reason to adopt an implausible theory simply to make all moral matters issues of justice.

7 The Force of Pedigree

The idea that in a legitimate regime all uses of public power can be justified using normative resources that can be derived from the demands of justice, but without being restricted to the direct application of the language of justice is suggested by Rawls's references to the political conception of justice being limited to constitutional essentials. One purpose of a constitution is to establish decision procedures through which decisions can be taken on such issues as, to borrow from Rawls, taxation and national parks. It is not, or not obviously, a matter of justice whether a certain area is designated a national park, or an area of special scientific interest, or whatever. It *is* a matter of justice that should this decision be taken by, say, a local referendum then people should not be disqualified from voting on the basis of their skin colour. A just constitution ensures that the mechanisms for arriving at certain decisions are just. The force of those decisions is that they have been arrived at in the right way. The law has the force of its pedigree.[12]

The advantage of this argument is that it allows that the reasons invoked when a given policy is under discussion can be broader than the thin reasons of impartial justice. Yet the ultimate justification for the use of public power in implementing or maintaining the policy can appeal to the account of justice. Thus in a debate about whether to spend some public money on a war memorial or a public park the proponents can appeal to their own conceptions of the good; to arguments about the value of honouring the society's dead and to those for the importance of public amenities. When a decision is taken by a democratically instituted legislature (for example) neither side need alter its opinion about how the money ought to have been spent in order to accept that the decision is just. Subsequently, in defending the building of the park to those who would rather have had a war memorial it does not need to be said that what makes the use of public power just is that the park is a better outcome, or a means to the creation of greater value in the world. All that needs to be said is that the arguments were heard and the park won the day (see Barry, 1995a, pp. 145–52).

Of course, on such a model the legislature cannot enact laws that are inconsistent with the demands of justice. The force of pedigree cannot trump the demands of justice. Laws must then meet two requirements: they must be correctly instituted and not unjust in the sense of being incompatible with the claims of impartial reason. This second requirement is discussed below, but for the moment consider the application of this argument to the elements of the criminal law mentioned above.

It is, of course, true that the criminal law must be correctly instituted and that some of its force comes from its being so; from its being 'the law of the land'. However, this is insufficient to explain the full normative significance of the content of certain criminal laws. It is not true that when someone commits murder that what is wrong is that he has broken the law and that what is to be condemned is his unlawfulness. This is simply to repeat the mistake of fair play theory from a crude legal positivist perspective. Similarly, when defending the prohibition on murder it is not true that the complete account of the justified use of public power involved in such a prohibition is contained within the claim that the law was correctly instituted by a legitimate legislature. The prohibition of murder and the condemnation of murderers have a moral force that goes beyond that provided by pedigree.

The difficulty, as noted above, is that the nature of this moral force will be the subject of reasonable disagreement between members of the society who hold different conceptions of the good. An individual's belief about what makes murder wrong and whether, and if so how, murder being wrong should provide a reason not to do it will depend on the individual's view of the source and nature of moral value. This, of course, the impartialist takes to be the subject of reasonable disagreement. The difficulty, then, is explaining the moral force of certain parts of the criminal law whilst respecting the reasonableness of pluralism.

One way of avoiding the disagreement that underpins the reasonableness of pluralism is to leave aside deep questions of the nature of the wrong involved in, say, murder and concentrate instead on the surface of moral argument. It is a reasonable assumption that there will be widespread agreement that murder is wrong even in conditions of disagreement about why it is so. This opens up the possibility that the law expresses and gains normative force from this agreement. Everyone has reasons to believe that murder is wrong, but their reasons are different. The existence of the reasons is important and adds normative force to the prohibition on murder. The law against murder prohibits a wrong action, and those who murder can be condemned for doing wrong.

This would seem to be an accurate description of the current practices of law in pluralist countries. Moreover it seems to provide an account of the relationship of justice and other moral questions that involve the use of public power. To continue with the example, the law against murder has the force of having been correctly instituted and, when invoked, of being justly implemented, but it has additional normative force because it reflects a widespread moral conclusion.

As noted above, this account is probably close to the way in which the criminal law in pluralist societies actually works. However, it suffers from three defects. First, it is clear that even where there is surface agreement on certain moral conclusions this consensus is too much on the surface to be helpful in framing legislation. Agreement that deliberately and voluntarily killing another person 'with malice of forethought' is wrong is not the same as agreement about what constitutes voluntariness, killing, and forethought. Such agreement also does not extend to what difference it would make if the victim consented or requested to be killed, or if the attempt to kill failed.[13] These are matters on which the law must speak and, once again, each person's view on these things will be profoundly affected by the ethical tradition to which she belongs and by the conception of the good that she holds.

Second, although the existence of a shared belief in the wrongness of an act can add some normative force to the prohibition on murder it does not add enough, at least for those who think that the sanctions of the law have as (at least) one function the expressing of moral condemnation to an offender who is in principle capable of understanding why that condemnation should matter to him. The expressing to the offender that what he has done is wrong, but that the public authority holds no official view on why it is that what he has done is wrong leaves out something significant.

Third, and most importantly, there is surely something wrong with an argument that makes a significant part of the normative force of the law against murder contingent on there being agreement amongst the citizens that murder is wrong. As it stands, the argument is that once the law against murder is correctly instituted it gains additional normative force from the agreement that murder is wrong. However, it cannot be that the mere fact of agreement is sufficient to require that a law be correctly instituted, for there may be agreement that, for example, homosexuality is wrong. Yet a law against homosexuality would seem to be unjust and, as noted above, correctly instituted laws must, in addition to being so instituted, be compatible with the demands of justice. Moreover, it cannot be that the absence of agreement precludes a law having the required normative force, because it may be that, for example, there is no widespread agreement on what constitutes rape or on the degree of its wrongness. It may be a requirement of justice to have a law against rape (because of considerations of equal protection), but the absence of agreement as to the serious wrongness of rape would seem on this account to preclude that law having any additional normative force and this is absurd. The shared ideas of wrongness in a society (or their absence) must be subject to critical scrutiny. Moreover, the basis for the scrutiny must stand in some relation to the language of justice. Thus, it may be true that laws against homosexuality are unjust and that not having laws protecting people against rape would also be unjust, but it is also true that the reasons not to have criminal laws against homosexuality and to have such laws against rape are not *only* reasons of justice (at least as characterized so far). Although the argument that widespread agreement could supplement the normative force of rules that locate their primary justification in being correctly instituted appears to work for existing rules that are supported by such agreement, this is insufficient. Agreement is a contingent matter and sometimes reasons of wrongness are themselves sufficient to warrant the use of public power just as sometimes those reasons are the relevant ones, rather than reasons of justice, when criticizing some (proposal for the) use of public power. The relationship between the account(s) of the wrongness of acts such as murder and rape and the justification of the use of public power must be more secure.

8 Justice, Wrong, and Well-being

Recall: impartialists wish to separate the right from the good; reasons of justice from other moral reasons. By doing so they believe that they can offer an account of the legitimate use of public power: public power used in core constitutional matters is legitimate when it can be justified using public reason – reasons of justice – and thus when its use can be accepted by all reasonable citizens. In many sub-constitutional cases the justification of the use of public power can appeal to those justified decision making procedures established by the constitution. However, the case of certain instances of the criminal law appears to be different. The criminal law, at least in part, expresses normative judgements whose authority goes beyond that which is transmitted by just procedures. Such laws prohibit wrongdoing not, or not only, injustice. Thus Rawls carefully distinguishes between the domains of distributive and retributive justice. Whereas distributive justice involves fairness and reciprocity and whereas distributive inequalities are designed as 'a scheme of taxes and burdens designed to put a price on certain forms of conduct and in this way to guide men's conduct' for the greatest benefit of the least advantaged, 'the purpose of the criminal law is to uphold basic natural duties, those which forbid us to injure other persons in their life and limb, or to deprive them of their liberty or property' (all quotations from Rawls, 1971, pp. 314–15). The existence of this domain of natural duties, and of the use of public power in enforcing those duties, raises the question of how this domain and the reasons associated with it stand in relation to, on the one hand, public reasons of justice and, on the other, to non-public reasons attached to particular conceptions of the good. It has already been noted that there will be disagreement in the latter case about the nature and source of such natural duties even where there is agreement about their essential demands.

It might be thought that there is an obvious route for the impartialist to take here, one that need not be so circuitously arrived at. What is needed is a thin account of wrongness to accompany the thin account of justice. This should not be difficult for the impartialist theory of justice is founded in part on an account of people's interests. This account is used in a particular way when considering matters of justice, but can be used in other ways when looking at other questions. The interests of the person *qua* citizen underpin the account of justice. Interpreted differently her interests can justify the use of public power in pursuit of matters other than those essential to the constitution.

Consider, for example, the following argument. *Qua* citizen, the Rawlsian individual has a highest order interest in her capacity to choose, revise and to pursue a plan of life. Whatever this plan may be, Rawls alleges, she has an interest in her access to primary goods. That is, her access to primary *social* goods such as 'rights and liberties, powers and opportunities, income and wealth' as well as to primary *natural* goods such as 'health and vigor, intelligence and imagination'. Rawls's theory (notoriously[14]) concerns the fair distribution of primary social goods for such goods are 'at the disposition of society' whereas primary natural goods 'are not so directly under its control' (all quotations from Rawls, 1971, p. 62). Of course, a citizen's rights, including his right to life, are part of the package of primary social goods and, thus, a murderous attack is, in part, an injustice. A failure on the part of the murderer to respect a right that the victim can fairly claim. However, Rawls is explicit that this is not the whole story. Individuals have natural duties that include the duty not to harm or injure one another. Natural duties, Rawls argues, whilst part of the concept of right, 'obtain between all as equal moral persons' (ibid., p. 115). The thought is this: from an assumption of equal moral worth and a thin account of the person and of her interests two kinds of prohibitions and two normative languages arise. One revolves around fairness and justice, the other around harm and wrong. The relationship between them is that they both arise from, first, an account of interests and, second, the claim that the selves that possess those interests have equal moral standing.

The impartialist can claim a further connection and to complete the sketch of this argument it is worth considering this here. In both cases – that of justice and of wrong – the contractarian procedure is a useful one in unpacking the requirements of justice and of wrongness and for linking it to an account of motivation.[15] Notice, the language of contractarianism has to be understood in the context of the whole impartialist project. The requirements of wrongness, like those of justice, are expressed in a contract the function of which is to 'make vivid' the argument (ibid., p. 18). This *faux* contractarianism acts as a heuristic device through which the ideas of justice and wrongness can be examined. Thus, Rawls's natural duties are (he says) 'derived from a contractarian point of view' (ibid., p. 115), but all this means is that we can learn more about them by modelling the argument from interests and equality in an original position not (as he makes clear in the same paragraph) that the content of natural duties and their binding force is dependent on agreement in some presocial state of nature. Similarly, Brian Barry's Scanlonianism claims only an equivalence between the propositions that something is just and that it cannot be reasonably rejected (see Caney, 1998, p. 95 and Barry, 1998, pp. 214–15). Thus, we can learn more about what it is for something to be unjust by looking at why it could be reasonably rejected. It is not that the thing is unjust *because* it could be reasonably rejected. However, if the contract in Rawls and the Scanlonian formula in Barry are merely heuristic tools in deriving principles they play a more significant role in the account of motivation. For both, the fundamental motivation of the citizens of a well-ordered society is that given by Scanlon: It is the motivation to be able to justify one's actions to others (similarly motivated) on grounds that those others could not reasonably reject (see Barry, 1995a, §26; Rawls, 1993, p. 124).

The danger of *faux* contractarian arguments is that they can obscure the real source of the claims that are being made. This led to a great deal of misinterpretation of Rawls's intentions and thus to some misplaced criticism of *A Theory of Justice* in the 1970s and much the same is true of Barry's more recent work. The argument that to injure people, to do them harm, to kill or maim them, is wrong is grounded in the claims that people have (equal) moral value and are bearers of certain interests. Killing someone for pleasure possesses some 'wrong-making characteristic' (Rawls, 1993, p. 121) or is a 'wrong-making property' (Scanlon, 1982, p. 118; Barry endorses this in 1998, p. 214). For Rawls and Scanlon this property or characteristic has no motivational or justificatory force without the contractual device through which such properties or characteristics become reasons in moral argument and for action.[16] Nevertheless, the 'wrong-makingness' of the act of killing for pleasure, of course, stands independent of any hypothetical agreement or understanding of what it is to utter a moral proposition.

Here then would seem to be all that is needed. Not, of course, a full theory of the nature and content of wrong. Instead it is a thin theory; an attempt to posit certain restricted interests to which all can agree and that give rise to certain substantive moral claims. Note, this is not the theory of surface agreement discussed in section 7. It is not that all can agree that, say, murder is wrong, but not on the nature of that wrongness. Instead, all are asked to endorse a thin, but nevertheless still morally significant, conception of individual interests. The claim for social goods based on those interests is offered in the form of a claim of justice to a fair share of the social product. The claim that certain invasions of those interests are wrong, and that public power can legitimately be used to prohibit and condemn such invasions, is offered in the language of preventing wrong.

What links the accounts of wrong and of justice is a shared starting point – an account of the interests of persons who are to be considered the source of equal, valid, moral claims – and a shared mechanism by which these claims are understood and through which they come to enter moral and political discourse. The first of these links can be understood as a concern for the equal significance of persons' well-being. In matters of justice and of wrong it is unreasonable to ask of one agent that she do less well just so that another (or some group of others) might do better. As Scanlon puts it, 'an individual could reasonably reject a form of argument that gave his well-being no weight', but, similarly, it is 'unreasonable ... to reject a principle because it imposed a burden on you when every alternative principle would impose a much greater burden on others' (Scanlon, 1982, pp. 119, 111). Thus, in matters of wrong, a principle that allowed the violation of well-being just so that those who find pleasure in committing such violations is unreasonable and this reflects the wrong-making property of such actions.

If the above sketch could successfully be filled out then it would appear that the impartialist has an account of wrong, in addition to an account of justice, that has the necessary normative force. The criminal law can include a prohibition on murder because a principle allowing murder would give the well-being of some no weight. To murder is wrong precisely in virtue of this. Those whose well-being was disregarded could reasonably reject a principle allowing murder and the law can thus condemn murderers not because it happens that generally people think that murder is wrong, albeit for a variety of reasons reflecting their various perspectives, but because the murderer has acted in a way that could not be justified to others.

However, it will be remembered that our interest in the question of whether the impartialist could find a thin, non-comprehensive, account of the criminal law emerged from the impartialist claim to be able successfully to negotiate the reasonableness of pluralism by separating reasons of justice from other moral reasons. The promise of universality emerged from the aspiration of impartialist theory to justificatory neutrality and to examine whether the above account is successful in this respect requires an analysis of the relationship of the account of wrong and persons' thick conceptions of the good.

It is worth noting, but it will not be the subject of discussion, that there will be some people whose conceptions of the good are incompatible with the entire impartialist procedure from the ground up. What is meant by this is that some people may hold that certain others are inferior or of no moral standing. Others may reject the reasonableness of pluralism from the perspective of claiming to know the truth about the good and, in addition, reject the demand that, even where one believes that one knows the truth, one ought not to impose it on others. Such people no doubt raise questions and cause problems for the impartialist, but these are questions and problems that are raised even in the context of an account of justice. The situation may be made worse, but it is not of a different kind, given the inclusion of an account of wrong and thus there are no new or particular issues raised in this paper in relation to such people.

What particular issues, then, are raised by the expansion of the argument into the territory of wrong? The first thing to notice is that the account of right and wrong action is not separated from the account of justice.[17] This, of course, does not mean that the reasons relevant to questions of justice and those relevant to questions of wrongness are the same. However, it does mean that the reasons appealed to in the account of wrong are part, and the subject, of public reason. This means that where public power is invoked to prohibit some activity it may be on the basis that the activity is wrong, or that it is unjust, or both. Indeed, there is surely reason to think that in controversial cases it will more often be an appeal to harm and to wrong (rather than to unfairness) that will do the work. For example, a restriction on male homosexual practices might be proposed not on the unfair grounds of imposing a Christian conception of the good, but on grounds of offence or of public health. In such cases the argument will have to be one about whether the harm done to offended individuals, or the degree to which male homosexuality contributes to a harmful public health problem, outweighs the harm done to homosexuals through restricting their ability to express their sexuality. The language of conceptions of the good and reasonable pluralism although stressed by impartialist writers and their critics is often unhelpful in such cases. The idea that one has a *prima facie* claim to be free to express one's sexual preferences depends itself on a claim about the good, that the expression of one's sexual preference, or sexuality, is an important component of living the good life. It follows that the reasonableness of any proposal to restrict or allow homosexual practices can hardly be decided by considering which side has invoked a controversial claim about the good, rather the work must be done by the idea of harm. Thus, although the consideration of harm has been reached through examining impartialist accounts of elements of the criminal law, its role is central to impartialist theory.

Given the centrality of the idea of harm and of wrong, then, what challenge does this pose to the aspiration to justificatory neutrality? One problem should be apparent from the discussion of homosexuality above. The account of wrong depends on there being an agreed account of well-being. However, it cannot be that any claim is to be admitted here. The satisfaction of a given desire may well increase an agent's well-being, but that does not mean that this desire need be recognized by others as a legitimate reason in moral argument. An agent's desire for speed, for example, does not mean that that agent may reasonably reject a proposal to impose speed limits on public roads on the grounds that this will inhibit his well-being. What is needed is a restricted class of well-being claims that have moral weight. These Scanlon calls 'morally legitimate interests' (Scanlon, 1982, p. 119). Without this the Scanlonian formula is empty. However, the difficulty for the impartialist is whether a list of morally legitimate interests can be constructed without violating justificatory neutrality. The problem is compounded because within the class of morally legitimate interests will need to be a system of ranking. A decision on whether a given proposal may be reasonably rejected will need to appeal to the relative weights of different claims.

Constructing a weighted list of morally legitimate interests poses a challenge to any impartialist theory. The impartialist, of course, believes that there is an option that avoids the pitfalls of positing an objective list (which would depend too heavily on considerations of the good) and those of allowing that the list be constructed by local understandings (which would open the gates to relativism). This is the construction of a list that could be agreed to by all reasonable people whatever their conception the good. However, the increase in both the scope and the required detail of the impartialist account of justification means that both the content and the status of any such list will be too controversial to be subject to such agreement. The list of interests that all can agree to as morally legitimate is itself fairly narrow. The ranking of those interests will further restrict the points of agreement. Of course, the impartialist can claim that the construction of this list is itself a project to be engaged in using the idea that we wish to be able to justify our actions to others on grounds that they could not reasonably reject. So, each suggestion that something be added to the list must itself be tested. Thus, someone who wishes to add 'living in a homosexual free environment' will have to be able to justify this to others and this cannot reasonably be done. However, it is hard to see how this will result in the kind of list that is needed. All may agree that life and liberty are important, but beyond that there would seem to be scope for disagreement about what should be on the list and how what is on it should be ranked.

The enrichment of public reason with an account of morally legitimate interests and the extension of the impartialist account into the domain of wrong raises a related, but in many ways more significant issue. The original idea, it will be remembered, was that an individual believer in some conception of the good could continue to maintain his beliefs *qua* individual, but could also accept the legitimacy of justice *qua* citizen. The restrictions on the scope of justice made this demand seem not unreasonably strong. The use of public power in areas such as the criminal law raises the question of how this is to be justified. The answer cannot be found within a mere extension of distributive justice or within an account of just procedures. Rather, the idea of public reason itself needs to be enriched by an extension of the idea of morally legitimate interests and by inclusion of a public account of what it is for an action to be wrong. Insofar as the account of what it is for something to be wrong is itself a meta-ethical account it is in direct competition with many conceptions of the good that include meta-ethical claims. Scanlon's account of wrong is an *alternative* to a religious account not an addition. What the agent is being asked to endorse *qua* citizen is an alternative account of morally legitimate interests, of justice, and of right and wrong. The idea that this is something that can be endorsed without detriment to the claims that are made on the individual by her conception of the good, whatever her conception of the good, is far-fetched. The idea of an impartial justification of the use of public power must be given up.

Need the conclusion be that the idea of a universalist justification of the use of public power should be abandoned? There is no reason to think so. The temptation to believe that universality is dependent on impartiality should be resisted. The idea that a justification of the use of public power can be offered without damage to the claims of individual conceptions of the good is, or so it is argued above, mistaken. However, it is mistaken precisely because in formulating an account of morally legitimate interests from which the requirements of justice and of wrongness are to be derived one needs to posit what are reasonable and unreasonable moves in the argument. This cannot be done by trying to distinguish between moves that are dependent on conceptions of the good and those that are not. Instead it might be thought that appeal can be made to the best available reasons for believing one thing rather than another. In doing this one would be constructing a moral theory in which the requirements of justice and of wrongness take up their traditional places as subsets of this account. They may indeed together *constitute* the account of morality, for there is no reason to believe that a reconstructed moral theory would be comprehensive as that term is understood by impartialists. There are many virtues that are not moral virtues.

These final remarks suggest an alternative liberal theory and are, of course, radically underdeveloped. Their purpose is merely to suggest that the loss of impartiality does not mean that we have to endorse Barry's fear that the justified use of public power must await some conclusive proof that one conception of the good is rationally compelling or fall into post-modern playfulness or Walzerian relativism. Impartialists, or so this paper alleges, already appeal to the potency of reason, or at least they must do so if they are adequately to theorize the public domain. This should not concern us too much. Impartialists have always held that they use 'impartiality' as a term of art and that it is not meant to denote anything like the desire for neutrality so often attributed to liberals by their opponents (the kind of liberalism parodied by Robert Frost when he defined a liberal as someone who can't take his own side in an argument). The belief was that justificatory neutrality could deliver rules of justice that would enable liberals to regulate the activities of illiberal groups whilst maintaining a position of agnosticism on the validity, truthfulness or plausibility of the conceptions of the good held by these groups. What is in fact the case is that on the impartialist account many conceptions of the good will be excluded from the beginning because they incorporate views on the nature and equality of persons and subsequently on what is to count as a morally legitimate interest that are incompatible with those of liberalism. If this is true then we must either conclude that we can offer nothing much by way of justification for this and content ourselves with the hope that such liberal sentiments become more widespread or, as is suggested above, we must once again take up the task of trying to justify the conception of the person that we endorse. Universality comes with a cost: If one account of morality, justice and the person is the right one then it follows that the others are wrong.

Notes

1 I would like to thank my colleague, Susan Mendus, for very helpful comments and discussions on this paper.

2 Justice as impartiality is a term borrowed from Brian Barry (1989, 1995a). I take John Rawls's *A Theory of Justice* (1971) to be the exemplar of this approach and it is with this

work and Barry's own *Justice as Impartiality* (1995a) that I shall be mostly concerned. Rawls's more recent work diverges from the impartialist ideal in a number of significant ways (for a discussion of early and late Rawls see Barry, 1995b; Mulhall and Swift, 1996).

3 Consider, for example, a consequentialist who endorses 'utilitarianism as a public philosophy' (to borrow the title of Goodin's recent book (1995)) and some form of indirect utilitarianism as a guide to everyday conduct. The reasoning engaged in by the agent *qua* citizen and *qua* private individual might be very different but both would be explicable by reference to the same consequentialist meta-theory.

4 Another way of putting the same point would be to say that the relationship between the agent's conception of the good and commitment to justice is not necessarily that between a comprehensive moral account and a subset of that account. A comprehensive conception of the good is one which informs more or less every aspect of the agent's life. An agent with a 'liberal' comprehensive conception of the good (whatever that may be) might find the demands of justice compatible with her conception of the good (and thin reason continuous with that of her liberal conception). An agent with an orthodox religious comprehensive conception will be less likely to find such continuity. (Note, Rawls's claim in *Political Liberalism* (1993) that holders of reasonable comprehensive conceptions of the good will be able to act in accordance with the regulative priority of justice without inconsistency is often ambiguous between the claim that public reason is compatible with the reason of all reasonable comprehensive conceptions of the good and that it is continuous with all such accounts (each in their own way). The more sympathetic reading is surely the latter.)

5 It is worth pointing out that given a certain interpretation of the third feature (referring to ideas latent in the public political culture of a democratic society) these features of the political theory are shared by the original theory as presented in *A Theory of Justice*. On this 'defence of Rawls against Rawls' see Barry, 1995b, esp. §II.

6 In fact, for reasons to be discussed below, Barry thinks differently.

7 What I mean by 'formal shape' is that the criminal law is subject to restrictions and demands based on justice in addition to those that stem from an account of wrongness. For example, I take it that it is a requirement of justice that the criminal law offer 'equal protection' to all citizens.

8 The following three sections borrow from my discussion of moral reason and communicative accounts of punishment. See Matravers, 1999.

9 This account of the function of punishment can be found in Morris, 1968; Finnis, 1972; Murphy, 1973; von Hirsch, 1976; Sadurski, 1985 and 1989; Sher, 1987, ch. 5; Dagger, 1993. I have discussed it, and its relation to impartialist theory, in Matravers, 1998.

10 See Murphy, 1985, pp. 3–11; von Hirsch, 1990, esp. pp. 264–9 and 1993, pp. 7–8. For a good summary of many points of criticism see Duff, 1986, ch. 8.

11 See, for example, Barry, 1996, p. 329.

12 Assuming some account could be given of common law.

13 I am grateful to Antony Duff for this point. It is discussed also in Matravers, 1999, p. 115.

14 'Notoriously' because Rawls's use of primary social goods eliminates the possibility that it is just to distribute more resources to those who possess some natural characteristic that disadvantages them in the conversion of resources into welfare (for example the disabled).

15 'The requirements of wrongness' is (in slightly strange manner) meant to capture those rules that will arise from a theory of wrong. Thus, it is a requirement of wrongness that one not commit murder, just as respecting the liberty principle is a requirement of justice.

16 I am unclear whether this is what Barry believes. As noted above, he endorses the claim that killing for pleasure is a 'wrong-making property', but he seems then to go on to make the rejection of a rule allowing killing for pleasure dependent only on the desire of the hypothetical parties to his Scanlonian agreement (see Barry, 1998, pp. 214–15).

17 Brian Barry accepts this. He writes: 'The conception of justice with which I am working is a broad one which includes everything that Scanlon would include in the sphere of wrongness and a lot more besides' (Barry, 1998, p. 215). This does not affect the claims made earlier in this paper about the separation of the right and the good and the restrictions placed on the account of justice. Barry grants that there is a narrower concept of justice, the one employed earlier in this paper. He employs the broader sense of justice to cover all those things that could be subject to the Scanlonian formula. His inclusion of matters of right and wrong, of harm, etc., in the account of justice will, I think, surprise some readers of *Justice as Impartiality* and he does not go on to consider the degree to which this broader concept of justice restricts his impartialism.

References

Barry, B. (1989), *Theories of Justice. A Treatise on Social Justice*, Vol. I, Harvester-Wheatsheaf, Hemel Hempstead.

Barry, B. (1995a), *Justice as Impartiality. A Treatise on Social Justice*, Vol. II, Clarendon Press, Oxford.

Barry, B. (1995b), 'John Rawls and the Search for Stability', *Ethics*, 105, pp. 874–915.

Barry, B. (1996), 'A Commitment to Impartiality: Some Comments on the Comments', *Political Studies*, 44, pp. 328–42.

Barry, B. (1998), 'Something in the Disputation not Unpleasant' in P. Kelly (ed.), *Impartiality, Neutrality and Justice: Re-Reading Brian Barry's Justice as Impartiality*, Edinburgh University Press, Edinburgh.

Caney, S. (1998), 'Impartiality and Liberal Neutrality' in P. Kelly (ed.), *Impartiality, Neutrality and Justice: Re-Reading Brian Barry's Justice as Impartiality*, Edinburgh University Press, Edinburgh.

Dagger, R. (1993), 'Playing Fair with Punishment', *Ethics*, 103, pp. 726–52.

Duff, R.A. (1986), *Trials and Punishments*, Cambridge University Press, Cambridge.

Duff, R.A. (1996), 'Penal Communications: Recent Work in the Philosophy of Punishment', *Crime and Justice: A Review of Research*, 20, pp. 1–97.

Finnis, J. (1972), 'The Restoration of Retribution', *Analysis*, 32, pp. 131–5.

Goodin, R. (ed.) (1995), *Utilitarianism as a Public Philosophy*, Cambridge University Press, Cambridge.

Kymlicka, W. (1989), 'Liberal Individualism and Liberal Neutrality', *Ethics*, 99, pp. 883–905.

Kymlicka, W. (1991), 'The Social Contract Tradition' in P. Singer (ed.), *A Companion to Ethics*, Blackwell, Oxford.

Matravers, M. (1998), 'What's 'Wrong' with Contractualism?' in P. Kelly (ed.), *Impartiality, Neutrality and Justice: Re-Reading Brian Barry's Justice as Impartiality*, Edinburgh University Press, Edinburgh.

Matravers, M. (1999), '"What to Say?": The Communicative Element in Punishment and Moral Theory' in M. Matravers (ed.), *Punishment and Political Theory*, Hart Publishing, Oxford.

Morris, H. (1968), 'Persons and Punishment', *The Monist*, 52, pp. 475–501.

Mulhall, S. and Swift, A. (1996), *Liberals and Communitarians*, 2nd edn, Blackwell, Oxford.

Murphy, J.G. (1973), 'Marxism and Retribution', *Philosophy and Public Affairs*, 2, pp. 217–43.

Murphy, J.G. (1985), 'Retributivism, Moral Education, and the Liberal State', *Criminal Justice Ethics*, 4, pp. 3–11.

Rawls, J. (1971), *A Theory of Justice*, Harvard University Press, Cambridge, Massachusetts.

Rawls, J. (1985), 'Justice as Fairness: Political not Metaphysical', *Philosophy and Public Affairs*, 14, pp. 223–51.

Rawls, J. (1989), 'The Domain of the Political and Overlapping Consensus', *New York University Law Review*, 64, pp. 233–55.

Rawls, J. (1993), *Political Liberalism*, Columbia University Press, New York.

Sadurski, W. (1985), 'Distributive Justice and the Theory of Punishment', *Oxford Journal of Legal Studies*, 5, pp. 47–59.

Sadurski, W. (1989), 'Theory of Punishment, Social Justice, and Liberal Neutrality', *Law and Philosophy*, 7, pp. 351–73.

Scanlon, T.M. (1982), 'Contractualism and Utilitarianism' in A.K. Sen and B. Williams (eds), *Utilitarianism and Beyond*, Cambridge University Press, Cambridge.

Sher, G. (1987), Desert, Princeton University Press, Princeton.

von Hirsch, A. (1976), *Doing Justice: the Choice of Punishments*, Hill and Wang, New York.

von Hirsch, A. (1990), 'Proportionality in the Philosophy of Punishment: From "Why Punish?" to "How Much?", *Criminal Law Forum*, 1, pp. 259–90.

von Hirsch, A. (1993), *Censure and Sanctions*, Oxford University Press, Oxford.

SECTION 4
SOME ISSUES AND PROBLEMS OF INTERNATIONAL JUSTICE

10 International Social Justice, Global Warming and Global Democracy

BARRY HOLDEN

The idea of international social justice is inherently problematic. This has practical consequences since it multiplies the difficulties of dealing with international problems aggravated by issues of 'social justice'.[1] The need to respond to the threat of global warming is one such problem.[2] Attempts to combat global warming are complicated by, and made more difficult because, the important considerations of social justice they raise involve issues of *international* social justice. The argument of this paper is that some kind of global community would be a crucial help in surmounting these difficulties and that this could be brought into existence by the development of global democracy. The validity of the underlying case for global democracy is assumed – there is not the space to go into it here[3] – and there is a concluding suggestion that global democracy offers the best hope of actually generating a global community. However, the main aim of the present paper is simply to show how global democracy, *if* it were to develop, *could* help in dealing with the issues of international social justice that complicate responses to global warming. (It is worth remarking, however, that showing this could in turn bolster the case for global democracy.)

The structure of the argument is as follows. First, some of the inherent difficulties with international social justice are briefly rehearsed. Secondly, there is an indication of the nature and importance of the issues of international social justice involved in the global warming problem and how their resolution depends on overcoming the inherent difficulties with international social justice. Thirdly, there is an assessment of how the existence of some kind of global political community might help in overcoming these difficulties. And, fourthly, this leads on to a consideration of the role of global democracy in bringing about such a community.

1 Problems of International Social Justice

'Social justice' is in effect a modern term for the old idea of distributive justice. With Miller we can say that social justice concerns 'the distribution of benefits and burdens throughout a society' (Miller, 1976, p. 22). The inherent problems of the idea of international social justice concern the extent to which ideas of social justice may be inapplicable to the international realm where, it is held, there is no society or community.[4] It is typically contended that, since it is constituted by sovereign states, the international realm, rather than itself being a society or community, is composed of various distinct and *separate*, societies or communities – indeed separate and independent political communities.

Such problems are of course additional to those, both of form and content, associated with the very idea of social justice in the first place.[5] Even within a domestic society both what is meant by 'social justice', and what is to be adjudged socially just when the meaning is agreed, are highly controversial matters which cross cut the considerations concerning the particular nature of international social justice. However, we do not have the space to take these matters up here, and we shall concentrate specifically on some aspects of the idea of *international* social justice.

As already indicated a key problem regarding international social justice arises from the importance of the linkage between social justice and community. In part this is a terminological point, concerning the extent to which the term '*social* justice' can be properly applied only within a society. But underlying this, of course, is the more substantive question of the nature and validity of the grounds for any such restriction of application. This question raises issues about the nature of community and about the way in which it is membership of a community that makes socially just action[6] feasible by modifying and subsuming agents' narrow self interest. The (plausible) assumptions here are that: (a) there is typically a conflict between actions which are socially just and those which are self interested; and (b) agents normally act in a self-interested way. (True, the dictates of social justice and self interest clearly coincide in the case of the beneficiaries of the distribution of benefits and burdens but, equally clearly, they diverge in the case of the 'losers'.[7])

The crucial point then is that the international realm is *not* a community. But at issue is not just the 'passive' absence of community but also the 'active' presence of a system in which the pursuit of self interest, by sovereign states, is legitimated and intensified. When the focus moves on to the importance of a specifically political community – a community in which there is governmental power and authority – these points are strengthened and augmented. Within such a community pursuit of self interest by individual agents can be authoritatively restrained by an overall authority; outside it, in the international realm, it is precisely the lack of any such authority that is partly constitutive of the system – a system, moreover, in which the self interest of individual agents (states) is given an especial salience.

We shall discuss the dependence of social justice on community further in the third section, when we consider how a global community could validate international social justice; but some key points should be noted here.

The necessary linkage between the ideas of social justice and society is conceived in terms of the especial moral relationships amongst the members of a society. This can be seen as a matter of the connections between members engaged in a common venture, or, indeed, in 'a cooperative venture for mutual advantage' (Rawls, 1972, p. 4). Where the basic idea of a society is specifically strengthened into that of a community there can be other important considerations. Then, as in the communitarian perspective, the linkage can become part of the perceived integral connection between moral judgements or relationships – their nature and ambit – and a community and its culture. Here there is the notion of community and culture as being in a crucial way constitutive, and as delimiting the application, of moral ideas and relationships. This has both formal and substantive implications for social justice. Formally, considerations of social justice have the form of community-specific moral ideas and relationships, whilst the substantive implication is that agreed – and therefore effective – principles of social justice will exist only within a community.[8]

The ties of social justice to community are even stronger in the case of a political community.[9] As Janna Thompson (1998, p. 190) puts it '[c]ommunitarianism ... holds that the authority of principles of justice ... depends on an identity of individuals with their political society'. One manifestation of this is in the archetypical political community of the nation-state. Here the common culture and unifying institutions mean that 'its members identify with each other and are "committed to dividing, exchanging, and sharing social goods" amongst themselves' (Bellamy, 1998, p. 159, quoting Walzer, 1983, p. 31). This is partly a matter of feelings of social solidarity which 'create a sense of identification among a given group of people between whom it comes to be felt both legitimate and plausible that collectively binding decisions about the distribution of benefits and burdens should take place' (Bellamy and Castiglioni, 1998, p. 163). But it is also a matter of the nature of the state as such since 'formal obligations arise from being members of an institutionalized scheme of political cooperation as citizens of the same state' (ibid., p. 163). Or, as Miller (1995, p. 73) argues, where a nation coincides with a state,

> obligations of nationality are strengthened by being given expression in a formal scheme of political cooperation; and the scheme of cooperation can be based on loose rather than strict reciprocity, meaning that redistributive elements can be built in which go beyond what the rational self-interest of each participant would dictate.[10]

This is further reinforced by the fact that '[s]tates also possess a set of political mechanisms for [dividing and sharing social goods], that are capable of arranging and securing distributions according to the criteria agreed on by the group' (Bellamy, 1998, p. 159).

The function of 'securing' is, indeed, a central feature of the state, whose coercive authority overcomes collective action problems and makes it possible to contemplate and to carry out actions 'which go beyond what rational ... self-interest ... would dictate'. The international realm, by contrast, precisely lacks this feature. In a system of sovereign states, characterized by a validated pursuit of narrow national interests uncurbed by overall power and authority structures, there is neither the will nor the means to modify self-interested[11] actions. *Within* a state, by contrast, there are legitimate governmental structures for enforcement of action which is socially just rather than self interested. And this also means that there is less initial reluctance to engage in socially just action (which, in turn, complements the point about it being membership of a community that leads to such action being contemplated in the first place). Within a state, in other words, there is an absence of that Hobbesian prisoners' dilemma which validates and generates only actions of short term self interest.

In short, the above arguments maintain that ideas and principles of social justice are only applicable or realizable within a community or a political community, and hence not in the international realm. Now, one does not have to embrace a full-blown communitarian view to accept that indeed there is here a crucial difficulty for international social justice. Even if moral judgements and relationships – and therefore social justice – are not necessarily restricted to a community, there remain formidable obstacles in the way of contemplating and obtaining actions beyond what self interest would dictate without the unifying force of membership of a political community. But when in fact in the international realm there is not merely a lack of overall community and governance but also a legitimation and aggrandizement of (states') self interest, then the obstacles to social justice are clearly magnified. The generation of a global political community, through the development of global democracy, is thus arguably essential for that global application and operation of ideas and practices of social justice that responding to the global warming problem requires.

We shall turn to this argument in section 3, but it is first necessary to dispose of two possible objections to the view that the ideas and practices of social justice are not properly applicable to the existing international realm.

First, it might seem that social justice appears in a form of justice as fairness that *can* be applied to the states system. Not all interpretations of a state-centric international realm are characterized by thoroughgoing realism, and 'morality of states' theorists[12] accept that moral rules and judgements of a kind apply to the relations between states. Corrective justice is thus applicable to the extent that states are subject to the demands of justice in correcting wrongs – violations of the rules of the morality of states – they have committed. And the issues of fairness involved in correctly attributing blame and allocating remedial costs regarding such wrongs can look like, but really are not, issues of social justice. We shall see that this confusion is of significance in relation to global warming issues.

Secondly, there are those, like Hedley Bull (1977), who speak of an international society. However, this is a society *of states;* and the point remains that there is no conception here of a society as amounting to something other than, and subsuming, states. It remains the case in fact that the key idea of an international realm composed of separate, independent communities blocks the notion that an idea of social justice can be applied beyond those communities to the realm they inhabit. It remains true that '[s]ocial justice – in the sense of a concern not simply for the rules but for social outcomes, for the distribution of "goods" in a society – is not appropriate internationally' (Brown, 1998, p. 108).

It is, then, only if, and to the extent that, the state-centric view of the international realm can be challenged that the idea of social justice can properly be applied internationally. Indeed, as Brown, for example, points out the very notion of an 'international' realm is the real culprit here. Any coherent idea of social justice that can apply beyond national boundaries must be one of *global,* rather than international, social justice.

This notion that what is required is an idea of global social justice forms part of the view according to which 'international' social justice requires a global community. And we shall consider this view, and the importance of global democracy in generating some form of global community, in section 3. First, though, it is time to have a look at issues raised by the global warming problem.

2 Global Warming and International Social Justice.

We have considered generally the nature of, and the difficulties relating to, international social justice and we should now turn to the issues of international social justice that arise specifically in the case of the problem of global warming.

The first point to make concerns the importance of these issues. It is not just that failure to resolve, or to properly address, them is in itself morally undesirable; it is also that it will tend to sabotage attempts to deal with the problem of global warming. Paterson, for example, remarks that '[t]he general debate on global warming, as well as on other global environmental problems, is replete with assertions that agreements need to be equitable in order to produce effective responses to those problems' (Paterson, 1996, p. 182). An example he cites is Oran Young's statement that 'the availability of arrangements that all participants can accept as equitable ... is necessary for institutional bargaining to succeed' (ibid., p. 181, quoting Young, 1989, p. 368). Not only the claims of justice, then, but also success in combating global warming require that the perceived issues of social justice should be resolved, or at least successfully addressed.

But to what extent *are* these issues of social justice? The point is that despite a widespread perception of the difficulties with international social justice there does not seem to be a corresponding resistance to accepting that issues of social justice are involved in the problem of responding to global warming. Why is this? Is it perhaps because the global warming issues of justice look like, but are not really, issues of *social* justice?

A part of the answer to these questions is that to some extent the justice issues raised by the global warming problem are issues of corrective rather than distributive justice, but that the distinction becomes blurred. An important argument, and one frequently heard, is that some (rich, northern, 'First World') states are primarily responsible for global warming and that justice – corrective justice – demands that those states bear the costs of preventing, or attempting to mitigate, the harm it does to other states. However, this kind of argument overlaps or merges into a second, central in debates about responses to global warming, to effect that justice demands that there should be resource transfers from rich, northern states to poor, southern states.

> There is now a wide literature on global environmental problems, particularly global warming which emphasizes the need for the emerging regime to be based on principles of equity and justice. The predominant argument which emerges

concerns claims for large scale transfers from North to South as a necessary part of such a regime (Paterson, 1996, p. 181).

The legitimacy of the application of this second argument is apparently very widely accepted although it clearly involves principles of international distributive, and therefore social, justice. Our question is: how is this so, given the controversial status of such principles? One reason is the overlap just mentioned, resulting in a blurring of the distinction between questions of corrective justice – principles of which *are* clearly applicable to the international realm – and social justice. In other words the argument about justice requiring the costs of abating global warming to be borne by rich states because they caused it in the first place is liable to become blurred into an argument about social justice requiring rich states to bear (at least most of the) abatement costs because they are rich.

It is true that another reason for the apparent acceptance of arguments of social justice here is that the global warming issue is itself helping to modify that state-centric view of the world which outlaws conceptions of international social justice. (And we shall have occasion to return to this point about global warming possibly being part of the solution as well as posing the problem.) However, for now any such modification remains limited by the weight of traditional understandings of the international realm.

All this means that there is in a muddled sense a recognition that the problem of global warming raises issues of social justice, but at the same time, when it comes to the crunch, there is little real acceptance of their validity and there is a reluctance to treat them seriously. Whilst the notion that social justice issues are involved is given widespread lip service, the moral and practical imperatives of the state system remain dominant. It remains the case, then, that dealing with the issues of social justice involved in the global warming problem requires the resolution of the inherent problems of international social justice.

What, then, are these issues of social justice that are involved here? We shall briefly indicate the nature of the issues that are directly raised by efforts to respond to the global warming problem. It may well be, however, that these issues can only be properly understood against the background of, and as linked into, larger issues of the justice (or rather the injustice) of the distribution of wealth and power between the North and the South (Shue, 1992).

The issues, of course, primarily concern the distribution of the burdens of combating global warming. The distribution of the benefits is not a matter at issue, for two reasons. First, it can be held that all benefit equally – that the world as a whole is the beneficiary of the reduction of the harmful effects of global warming. Secondly, to the extent that there is a differential distribution of benefits this is a matter that is beyond human control (though there are relevant questions concerning the balancing of the allocation of burdens against the likely incidence of benefits). The distribution of burdens, though, is a matter of the distribution of the economic costs of the actions required to prevent and/or to mitigate the effects of further global warming. More specifically this involves questions such as which countries should take what (economically harmful) abatement measures – notably measures to secure decreases in carbon dioxide emissions – and who should pay what for developing new environmentally friendly energy technologies. Arguments from social justice involve such ideas as the rich countries of the North being able to afford the abatement measures and having the knowledge and economic resources to develop environmentally friendly technologies. To these are added the contention that it is unfair to expect the South to forgo the economic development that has already made the North rich. The result is a social justice argument to the effect that the rich countries have a duty to transfer resources to the poor countries to enable them to take the necessary abatement measure without unduly disadvantaging themselves. (As we have already noted this kind of argument can be linked into a general thesis concerning the social injustice of the North-South distribution of wealth.)

This is the basic international social justice argument relating to the global warming problem. However we should in passing note that in a full consideration various important issues would be taken up, amongst which would be the following. First, additional issues are involved in determining a just distribution of abatement measures, including questions about the fairness of different methods of categorizing such measures (see Paterson, 1996). Secondly, various important questions arise concerning the nature of the benefits and burdens of combating global warming. These include large issues, central in green political theory, about the relative benefits and burdens of industrialized and deindustrialized societies, as well as questions arising from uncertainties about the existence, nature, scale and timing of the harmful effects of global warming. This question of timing – of the length of time before harm actually occurs – raises a third issue, that of intergenerational justice. The simplifying assumption is made here that in the distribution of burdens it is simply the interests of the present inhabitants of the world that should be considered. However, it may well be the interests of future generations that will be harmed most by global warming and that therefore social justice involves a consideration of their claims too.[13] Fourth, in addition to questions about the validity of *international* social justice, there is of course the whole question of determining the 'right' answer to the substantive question of social justice involved in the basic argument indicated above. And this raises the issues central to the main body of literature on social justice (see Paterson, 1996 for a discussion of the linkages between the global warming issues and this body of literature).

We have not the space here to take up these issues, so let us return to the basic international social justice argument indicated just now. As we have already seen, since there is an overlap with the 'corrective justice argument' this kind of argument has had some effect. Possibly this 'dual grounding' gives some extra force to the case. Indeed, provision for transfers was written into the Rio Climate Convention. However, as subsequent difficulties at Kyoto and Buenos Aires exemplified, the case was not properly sustained. This surely indicates that under pressure the grounds come apart and considerations of international social justice become excluded as illegitimate. Hence they fail to bolster – let alone successfully press beyond – the claims of corrective justice against the assertion of (what are deemed) vital national interests. Again, the need to legitimate, and to thereby 'empower', the international social justice argument is demonstrated. So it is now time to turn to a consideration of how this might be achieved – how global democracy might bring about a validation of considerations of 'international' social justice by translating them into issues of 'global' social justice.

3 'International' Social Justice, Global Community and Global Democracy

In this section, then, we shall consider the argument that problems with international social justice can be resolved by global democracy bringing about a global community.

We shall need to consider how global democracy involves the development of a global community. But before we do this we need to say something about the notion of global democracy itself. (Terms such as 'cosmopolitan', 'supranational' or 'transnational democracy' are also sometimes employed; the extent to which these various terms are synonymous will be touched on below.)

For various reasons, including what are seen as the expanding processes of globalization and the international pre-eminence of democracy as a system of governance, there has recently been a growing interest in the idea of global democracy, as the subject matter of a number of recent books testify (for example, Archibugi and Held, 1995; Held, 1995; McGrew, 1997a; Archibugi, Held and Kohler, 1998). True, there is controversy here. Questions about the extent to which there are significant processes of globalization, and whether the international pre-eminence of democracy has been established, provoke ongoing debate. So, too, do questions about the nature, desirability and likely existence of global democracy (Holden, 2000). However, the growth of interest in the idea and the undoubted importance of the changes that are under way in the international realm, certainly warrant taking the subject of global democracy seriously.

What, then, is meant by the term 'global democracy'?[14] The meaning is somewhat fluid but we can say that the central notion is that of democracy existing at a level above or beyond the nation state. This can simply mean democracy that transcends states without specifying geographical reach or how many states, but it can also mean democracy that covers the globe, the world as one big democracy. The epithets 'supranational and 'transnational' may refer more readily to the former and 'global' and 'cosmopolitan' to the latter. This kind of idea involves some fundamental rethinking of the nature of democracy and its genesis has various bases and features. As I have said elsewhere:

> there is developing a theory of 'cosmopolitan democracy'. To sum this up one could say that the core idea of democracy, rule by the people, needs – and is starting to – be rethought because of changes in the world that may be rendering obsolete received notions of 'rule' and 'the people'. The traditional idea of democracy centres on the state. The state gives content to 'rule by the people'. It does this by specifying 'rule' as 'that which is done by the state', 'the people' as 'those who are citizens of the state' and accordingly rule by the people' as 'control of the state by its citizens'. Now changes are afoot that are undermining this account (Holden, 1996, pp. 138–9).

The key changes 'that are undermining this account' are those already alluded to under the rubric of 'globalization'. These include the diminishing power of states in the face of transnational forces, and the consequent loss of the ability of people to control what happens to them via democratic control of states.[15] If popular control – popular rule – is to be (re)established then it must be by means of popular control of mechanisms capable of governing transnational forces, i.e. transnational governmental organizations (international regimes and organizations).[16] Since the ambit of such organizations transcends national boundaries, so too must the units of popular control. In other words, the assemblages of people who are to exercise control must become transnational: hence transnational democracy. From a different perspective, and adapting May (1978), one could say about transnational democracy that there are many matters – such as the safety of nuclear power stations or factors determining, say, share prices and interest rates – that affect the interests of transnational assemblages of people; and where such matters are subject to acts of governance then democracy implies that those acts must correspond to the wishes with respect to those acts of those assemblages of people.

There are important matters regarding the nature and extent of any such assemblages;[17] and two in particular we should note here. First, there would be variations in extent from those that cross the borders of some (perhaps very few) states, to an assemblage of the whole world. We might link the former with 'transnational' and the latter with 'global' democracy (see above). Second, the extent to which such assemblages would be communities might seem to be crucial. This is a point which we take up below.

We argued earlier that the problems concerning international social justice arise from the international realm being constituted by separate communities rather than itself being a community. The argument to be developed below is that global democracy could help to resolve these problems to the extent that it could convert the international realm into a community. But why should global democracy have this effect? What is the nature of this link between global democracy and global community?

There are two main aspects. There is something of a distinction between the connections with a global community as such and with a global *political* community. These aspects do overlap but this distinction is helpful in considering the nature of the connections. Let us begin with the former.

The establishment of global democracy would contribute to the generation of a global community in at least three main ways. First, the very activity of democratic decision making itself fosters community, so that global democratic decision making would foster global community. True, this may be seen as putting the cart before the horse: since it is commonly held that the existence of democracy presupposes or requires the existence of community in the first place, it might seem that global community is needed for global democracy rather than vice versa. There is indeed something in this, although the traditional arguments about the prior requirement of community were applied to democracy as traditionally conceived and their application to global democracy is less clear. This issue is taken up below; but, be that as it may, the point to be made here is that it is also true that democracy can help generate community.

The actual process of democratic decision making – by involving all in mutual interaction focused on shared interests – does itself help to generate communal identity and structure.[18]

This overlaps into the second way in which the generation of a global community would be helped by global democracy. This concerns the cosmopolitan features of global democracy (sometimes indeed called 'cosmopolitan democracy'). A key impediment or objection to the development of a global community is the existence and importance of differing cultural communities in the various parts of the world. For many the lack of a world community is simply an aspect of this contingent fact of its division into such communities. However, it can be said there is more to it than this. It is held by 'communitarians' that there are fundamental reasons for this division and that it has great moral significance. Moreover, the differing particular cultures and value systems prevent or make undesirable the development of universal or global norms and ideas of the kind that must necessarily be integral to a global community.[19] Now, the cosmopolitan features of the global democracy project would challenge all this.[20] Furthermore, it is arguable that this challenge would be driven home by the project's validity – that it would have the legitimacy and potency to be successful. As indicated before the validity of the project cannot be established here, but it is worth noting that the overall strength of the case for global democracy includes the force of the justifications for democracy as such.

This again overlaps into a third kind of link between global democracy and global community, which likewise emphasizes the removal of obstacles to a global community. Here the focus is on sovereign states rather than (or often as embodiments of) cultural communities. Global democracy would be a solvent of the Westphalian states system which itself functions as a – perhaps the – primary obstacle to the development of a global community. Thus by its very nature global democracy would involve transcendence of state sovereignty and a diminution of states' importance. This could clear the way for a transcendence of national interests by a perception of the existence and importance of a global common good – a perception which is critical for (as well as in turn being reinforced by) any establishment of global community.

But what of the connection between global democracy and a global *political* community? Let us remember first that it is the importance of a political community that makes this connection significant. This importance is partly a matter of reinforcing community as such: a community is strengthened – perhaps even created – by being established as, or by becoming, a political community. (This is true even if the reverse is too – i.e. that a political community can also originate or take strength from a community as such.) But, as we noted earlier, the existence of a community in the form of a political community not only brings additional integrative features, supportive of the validity of ideas of social justice, but also, through its governmental dimension, makes socially just action feasible.

Let us consider, then, the nature of the connection between global democracy and the existence of a global political community. Essentially, it is a matter of democracy necessarily bringing political community with it. But there is a complication here. It might seem to be a matter of democracy simply *being* a political community: the existence of global democracy would then imply the existence of a global political community by virtue of democracy being by definition a form of political community. But this is to employ the traditional conception of democracy and it ignores a key point – central indeed to the very way in which global democracy contributes to global community – about the way theories of global democracy depart from traditional theories. This concerns the way they not only detach democracy from the archetypal political community of the state but seem generally to subvert traditional connections between popular decision making and orthodox territorial understandings of community. Indeed, as we saw, there is an important question about whether 'transnational assemblages' of people can be considered as communities.

All this is true, and important. Nonetheless, it also remains true that fundamental to the logic of identifying transnational assemblages is a specification of what those involved importantly have in common, in terms of a shared need to control decisions affecting their same specific interests (in this respect, arguably, they already have something of the nature of communities: see Holden (1996, p. 146) for further discussion). And it is by virtue of this that they could be established as units of popular control – as a type of political community. Indeed, one can say that by controlling the decisions affecting their interests these assemblages become self-governing 'communities of fate' (see McGrew, 1997b).

In the context of global warming the central interest is in an assemblage covering the whole world being a political community: the interest is in 'global' rather than simply 'transnational' democracy. And here there are two important additional considerations. First, the global warming problem is of great importance and is itself a – perhaps the – key factor in laying the basis for a 'global community of fate' of great importance. The interests of people all over the world are affected by the consequences of global warming, and there is a common need to control decisions concerning avoidance of these consequences. Here is a basis for a global democracy, which would be a form of global political community. Arguably, then, the need to deal with the global warming problem not only requires, but also helps to form, a global community. Second, there is a connection, and mutual reinforcement, between the idea of a global political community based on arguments such as these and traditional ideas of a global political community relating to a 'community of mankind' (for a recent discussion of this tradition in the history of political thought see Heater, 1996).

There is one further point to note, concerning the governmental aspect of a political community. International governance – some form of which would feature in a global political community – would help surmount those collective action difficulties which tend to obscure principles of international social justice and/or render actions in accord with them problematic. Now, global democracy would be important here not only because of its role in constituting a system which incorporates international governance but also by enhancing the effectiveness of such governance. There is not the space to take this up here but the reference is to traditional pro-democracy arguments emphasizing the role of legitimation, consent and the mobilization of popular support in making government effective.

4 Conclusion

It has been argued that global democracy could bring about a form of global community and thus help resolve the problems of international social justice that hamper attempts to combat global warming. But perhaps the argument can be pushed further than this. It may be that it is not just that a world community *could* be created by global democracy but, further, that there is some likelihood that it *will* be. Or, to put the point in a slightly different way, it may be that the only way there could be any likelihood of the necessary global community being brought into existence is by the development of global democracy. As we remarked earlier the question of the validity of the global democracy project is beyond the remit of this paper but, as we have also remarked, the contention that it is valid flows from, and can be supported by, important current work. After referring to 'David Held's work ... on new democratic forms which would operate at the global level' Chris Brown, for example, says '[i]t may be time for the issue of global institutional reform to shake off the stigma of utopianism' (Brown, 1998, p. 113).

It is, indeed, arguable that the current global democracy project has more likelihood of realization than any former project in the long tradition of thought about a global community, and that here there is some real possibility of much needed help in resolving the problems of international social justice that beset any attempts to deal with the threat of global warming.

Notes

1 Strictly speaking more circumlocutory phraseology should be used since of course one of the key issues (which is taken up below) is whether the concept of social justice *can* be properly applied to the international realm.

2 It will be assumed that there is, indeed, a problem. It is acknowledged that there is continuing debate about the reality or extent of a man-made global warming process, but this is beyond the scope of this paper. That there is now a consensus amongst most of the world's climate scientists that such a process does in fact exist will be taken as sufficient evidence of the existence of a problem. See, for example, Houghton, 1997.

3 The case for global democracy – arguments for its desirability and the possibility or probability of its development – can be found in Held, 1995; Archibugi and Held, 1995; McGrew, 1997; and Archibugi, Held and Köhler, 1998; the case is assessed in Holden, forthcoming. It might also be noted here that the importance of global democracy for the global warming problem is not confined to help with problems of international social justice; further dimensions are indicated in Holden, 1996 and I hope to take these up on another occasion.

4 Henceforth the term 'community' will usually be used to include cases where it might be more accurate to say 'society' or 'society or community' or 'society and/or community' (though on occasion 'society' will be used where it is the more appropriate term). This is partly a matter of convenience but it does also reflect some vagueness in the meaning of 'society' and the fact that it is to a society conceived as a community that the term social justice is often linked.

5 The question of the nature of social justice is, of course, a large one with a large literature, but a good overview is provided by Boucher and Kelly, 1998.

6 'Socially just action' is here used as shorthand to include both actions by individual agents in pursuit of socially just objectives and governmental policies designed to bring about such objectives. Now, it is true that the latter are simply a defining feature of a (political) community in a way the former are not (and that it is precisely the latter which can make the former feasible). However, substantive questions do still arise about what makes it feasible first to contemplate and then to enforce governmental policy in pursuit of social justice. And the answers here must show *how* membership of a community (as such not just one which is political) is important.

7 Use of the term 'losers' makes certain – plausible – assumptions about social justice requiring a departure from the current *status quo:* in other words distribution takes the form of redistribution, which involves action that is against the self interest of (some of) those who benefit from the current distribution of benefits and burdens.

8 By ruling out the universal – and hence the international – application of moral judgements this rules out international social justice (the relativism involved in this has been seen both as a vital ingredient and as a fatal defect). Consideration of this communitarian view of the

connection between community and particularity (especially the particularity of the genesis and application of moral judgements) raises interesting issues regarding the notion of a *global* community, which is presumably necessarily universal. There is not the space to go into these here but it could be argued, *inter alia,* that it is precisely the evident presence of moral issues and judgements generated from, and concerning, the world as a whole that might encourage the development of a global community. And the global warming problem clearly involves such issues and judgements.

9 A political community can be seen both as an especially important form of, and as strengthening, a community as such. This point is taken up in section 3 below.

10 Miller (1995, p. 73) is at this point specifically indicating the advantages of 'making the bounds of nationality and the bounds of the state coincide'. It should be remembered that here we are indeed specifically talking about nation-states; and it is, in fact, often assumed that states *are* typically *nation*-states. However, a feature of the contemporary world is the extent to which this is no longer (if it ever was) true. This does in fact pose an important difficulty for communitarian theories. It is also a disruptive influence on the states system and could therefore be regarded as a factor in strengthening development towards possible new global systems – global democracy included.

11 'Self-interested' here refers to the self interest of states. It is of course disputable – and a cosmopolitan would dispute – whether that which is in a state's particular interests is necessarily in the interests of its inhabitants. This is especially so in relation to the problem of global warming. This point overlaps with another to the effect that what is to be considered as being in a state's interests is in any case problematic, and that there is, arguably, a tendency to misleadingly equate a state's interests with its particular short term interests. An important consideration in the case of global warming is that, arguably, industrial policies often seen as in the short term interests of particular states may well be against their long term interests which, along with those of other states, will be harmed by the effects of global warming (and even if it can be argued that the interests of *states* will not be harmed those of their inhabitants will be).

12 See, for example, Beitz, 1979, Part One, Section 5.

13 This raises large issues that cannot be entered into here (although I hope to take some up on another occasion). For a recent illuminating treatment of some issues of intergenerational justice as they relate to the environment see Dobson, 1998.

14 This paragraph is based on part of my Introduction in Holden (forthcoming).

15 For the purposes of the argument which follows the validity of statements such as this will be assumed. True, as already indicated, there is controversy about the existence and/or importance of these changes (see, for example, Holden, forthcoming – especially the chapters by Hirst and Thompson, Perraton and Golub). However: a) there is an influential body of work – that of Held in particular – which insists that such changes are indeed happening and are important; b) the main point of the present chapter is to explore the implications of global democracy for international social justice and the global warming problem, *on the assumption* that such changes are happening, that they are important and that the development of global democracy occurs; and c) as will be suggested in the main text below the global warming problem may itself be adding to, or providing an important additional factor promoting, such changes.

16 That is, of course, to the extent that there are *any* mechanisms that can 'govern' here. The emphasis of globalization arguments is often on the extent to which transnational forces – particularly the operations of the global market – cannot be governed at all. However, it is

equally true that concern about globalization often leads to emphasis on transnational governmental organizations as the only possible regulatory mechanisms. This is not the place to enter into an assessment, and the validity of this latter stance will be assumed here. It should also be noted that the very idea that something can be done about global warming presumes there can be some kind of transnational – or at any rate intergovernmental – regulation of global matters. It should further be noted that whilst the existence of formal 'government' in the international realm may not be deemed likely there is a developing interest in the possibilities of international 'governance' (Rosenau, 1992).

17 I discuss this further in Holden, 1996; see also Saward, 1998, ch. 7 and forthcoming.

18 This may not seem true of all conceptions or theories of democracy; indeed some (including procedural, protective and multicultural) theories emphasize (democracy as a way of dealing with) separateness and conflict rather than overall community. Nonetheless: a) other equally important (including substantive, developmental and deliberative) theories do emphasize the community inducing features of democracy; b) it can be argued that these are more satisfactory theories; and in any case(c) *any* conception of democracy necessarily presumes some important interaction amongst all those involved in a democratic unit.

19 Of course this 'communitarian argument' forms part of the case against the validity of the notion of international justice in the first place. The overall point being made here is that establishing that which communitarianism denies (viz. the credibility of a global community) helps to undermine the 'case against' international social justice.

20 There is an overlap here with some further points about connections between global democracy and global political community that are taken up below. Cf. also the argument of Janna Thompson. After looking at how transnational democracy might help generate transnational commitments and thereby help validate ideas of international social justice, she considers communitarian objections. Communitarians insist that democracy is restricted to particular communities, but Thompson (1998, p. 194) concludes that the development of transnational democracy, and the accompanying awareness of global problems, would need to – and could – 'become a focus for community identity across borders'.

References

Archibugi, D. and Held, D. (eds) (1995), *Cosmopolitan Democracy*, Polity Press, Cambridge.

Archibugi, D., Held, D. and Kohler, M. (eds) (1998), *Re-imagining Political Community*, Polity Press, Cambridge.

Beitz, C.R. (1979), *Political Theory and International Relations*, Princeton University Press, Princeton.

Bellamy, R. (1998), 'Justice in the community: Walzer on pluralism, equality and democracy' in D. Boucher and P. Kelly (eds), *Social Justice from Hume to Walzer*, Routledge, London and New York.

Bellamy, R. and Castiglioni, D. (1998), 'Between Cosmopolis and Community: Three Models of Rights and Democracy within the European Union' in D. Archibugi, D. Held and M. Köhler (eds), *Re-imagining Political Community*, Polity Press, Cambridge.

Boucher, D. and Kelly, P. (eds) (1998) *Social Justice from Hume to Walzer*, Routledge, London and New York.

Brown, C. (1998), 'International Social Justice' in D. Boucher and P. Kelly (eds), *Social Justice from Hume to Walzer*, Routledge, London and New York.

Bull, H. (1977), *The Anarchical Society*, Macmillan, London.

Dobson, A. (1998), *Justice and the Environment*, Oxford University Press, Oxford and New York.

Heater, D. (1996), *World Citizenship and World Government*, Macmillan, Basingstoke.

Held, D. (1995), *Democracy and the Global Order*, Polity Press, Cambridge.

Holden, B. (1996), 'Democratic Theory and Global Warming' in B. Holden (ed.) (1996), *The Ethical Dimensions of Global Change*, Macmillan, Basingstoke.

Holden, B. (ed.) (2000), *Global Democracy: A Debate*, Routledge, London and New York.

Houghton, J. (1997), *Global Warming: The Complete Briefing*, 2nd edn, Cambridge University Press, Cambridge.

McGrew, A. (1997a), *The Transformation of Democracy*, Polity Press in association with The Open University Press, Cambridge and Milton Keynes.

McGrew, A. (1997b), 'Democracy beyond borders?: Globalization and the reconstruction of democratic theory and politics' in A. McGrew (ed.), *The Transformation of Democracy*, Polity Press in association with The Open University Press, Cambridge and Milton Keynes.

May, J.D. (1978), 'Defining Democracy: A Bid for Coherence and Consensus', *Political Studies*, 26, 1, pp. 1–14.

Miller, D. (1976), *Social Justice*, Clarendon Press, Oxford.

Miller, D. (1995), *On Nationality*, Clarendon Press, Oxford.

Paterson, M. (1996), 'International Justice and Global Warming' in B. Holden (ed.) (1996), *The Ethical Dimensions of Global Change*, Macmillan, Basingstoke.

Rawls, J. (1972), *A Theory of Justice*, Oxford University Press, Oxford.

Rosenau, J.N. (1992), 'Governance, Order and Change in World Politics', in J.N. Rosenau and E-O. Czempiel (eds), *Governance without Government: Order and Change in World Politics*, Cambridge University Press, Cambridge.

Saward, M. (1998), *The Terms of Democracy*, Polity Press, Cambridge.

Saward, M. (2000), 'A Critique of Held' in B. Holden (ed.), *Global Democracy: A Debate*, Routledge, London and New York.

Shue, H. (1992), 'The Unavoidability of Justice' in A. Hurrell and B. Kingsbury (eds), *The International Politics of the Environment*, Clarendon Press, Oxford.

Thompson, J. (1998), 'Community Identity and World Citizenship' in D. Archibugi, D. Held and M. Köhler (eds), *Re-imagining Political Community*, Polity Press, Cambridge.

Walzer, M. (1983), *Spheres of Justice*, Martin Robertson, Oxford.

Young, O.R. (1989), 'The Politics of International Regime Formation: Managing Natural Resources and the Environment', *International Organization*, 43, pp. 349–75.

11 Slaughtering a Few Sacred Cows: Do We Really Oppose International Intervention?[1]

AVNER DE-SHALIT

Introduction

The place occupied by political theory within public reflection on international relations has never been fully established.[2] Many still regard the international arena as a sphere in which morality has no sway. They further claim that since international relations involve relations between governments, and since every government owes greater obligations to its citizens than it does to other governments, then all we can expect from international relations are policies of 'might is right'.

On the other hand, there are those who believe that all we need when reflecting upon the morals of international relations is to apply principles that have already been applied within the state to the sphere of international relations. The rationale is as follows: in totalitarian regimes, politics is based on power and fear, whereas in the ideal regime the basis would be reason and morality. Somewhere in between, perhaps a little closer to the ideal regime, is democracy. The citizens in a democracy are concerned to see a balance between power, on the one hand, and reason and morality on the other. This is where political philosophy comes in: while accepting that power is part of the political game, we use political philosophy to criticize and control its arbitrary use.

According to this, the international arena resembles the intra-national arena in so far as a regime which is more or less resistant to the arbitrary use of power also lies between two poles: with the ideal type of regime on the one hand, and chaos on the other. The latter (chaos) is no different from the totalitarian regime, in that domination is sought through the exercise of power and fear. Political philosophy can thus be employed by those seeking a 'democratic' form of international relations. That is to say that the 'citizens' of the world could use political philosophy to oppose power and limit it.

I tend to agree with those who believe that there is a place for political philosophy within the international arena. But which political philosophy should we use? Should we simply apply principles to the international or interstate, or transnational contexts that have already been developed and put forward in the context of intrastate relations?[3] Or are we dealing with a whole new set of questions, and a need for new theories or, at least, a new rationale for similar principles?

I mean to argue that while, in principle, it is possible to extrapolate theories from the political theory of intrastate relations and apply them to the international arena (since the theories that determine moral principles are based on universal truth and can therefore be applied to all cases, including, of course, the international arena), we must nevertheless be cautious when moving from one sphere to the other.[4] The question of international intervention illustrates why this caution is needed. I would therefore like to argue the following:

a) that many of us oppose international intervention for the wrong reasons and that liberals, socialists and environmentalists should be willing to accept some forms of intervention;

b) that the circumstances that justify intervention do not exhaust the moral dilemmas at stake. Rather, we must ask ourselves the crucial question 'what form of intervention would be appropriate?' Only when we have answered this can we then ask 'What are the circumstances that justify intervention' (on condition, of course, that the intervention is carried out in the right form);

c) that in fact there are two attitudes towards (I am reluctant to say theories about) international intervention: the liberal and the socialist, both of which suggest criteria for an acceptable kind of intervention;

d) that analysis of these criteria shows the socialist theory to be more appealing.

Last but not least: intervention in this chapter refers to deliberative action by a state or coalition of states, whose purpose is to bring about political, legal, economic, or ideological changes in another state, changes which are often imposed on other states, or organizations or individuals within these states.[5]

Notice: a) that this definition does not necessarily relate to declared motives. A state may justify its intervention and present it as action taken in order to 'assist other states in the favourable resolution of pressing matters of humanitarian, regional security, or other interests' (von Lipsey, 1997, p. 4). This of course may be a cover-up for economic interests.

b) For the purpose of definition, we should distinguish intervention from voluntary exchange. Not every regular commercial exchange or bilateral agreement will necessarily be an intervention, even if greater advantages for one of the parties are involved. However, besides direct intervention (e.g. military acts, or a trade boycott), there is indirect intervention, which may very well be the consequence of voluntary exchange. Thus, manipulating public opinion through a scheme of academic grants should also be categorized as international intervention.

c) Intervention might aim at changing the formal structure of a state's institutions, and/or a particular policy. Many times economic sanctions (see below) are meant to change the latter rather than the former. States tend not to decide upon intervention in order to change the political structure of another state. However, intervention to stop harm to a certain minority or to change a certain policy is more frequent.

d) Intervention is much more than military invasion. 'The definition could be broadened by enlarging any or all of its conditions. For example, forms of coercion not involving threats of military force (like threats of economic sanctions or subversion) could be allowed into the definition' (Beitz, 1979, p. 72). (I elaborate on this point below.)

What are the Wrong Reasons for Opposing International Intervention?

The most common reason for opposing international intervention is indeed transferred from theory about relations within the state to international relations. The argument put forward is this: states, like persons, are autonomous entities.[6] Just as we oppose interference in an individual's self-governing and autonomy by a government, a group, or another individual, so we oppose intervention on an international level. The intervention of state A in the (internal) events of state B (whatever this means remains to be discussed) is criticized on the grounds that it interferes with and limits the sovereignty of B (or, as we shall see, B's autonomy), and should therefore be morally condemned.

Let us examine the argument that international intervention does harm to the sovereignty of a state. We should immediately note that this is a biased theory; it rules out any intervention which is meant to, and which can, help a particular government restore its own sovereignty. However, I have a problem with this argument for another reason: namely, that, in fact, there are two types of sovereignty in the international relations arena: internal and external sovereignty. The former derives from the original theory of sovereignty, which, of course, relates to intrastate relations. Sovereignty in this case is the ultimate political authority within a political system. It is possessed by the supreme source of authority. In other words, sovereignty belongs (or should belong) to the people. Thus, a parliament or a government are sovereign if the people agrees that these agencies conduct, legislate, and/or govern its daily life.

Thus, for a foreign action to harm this kind of sovereignty, an invasive act must be involved – there must be some power invading a territory and trying to take away the sovereignty of its citizenry.[7] Notice, however, that in practice not all acts of international intervention are invasive. If state A imposes high taxes on an import from state B but has no such policy regarding the import of goods from other states (for example, when economic pressure is applied for political reasons), then state A is clearly interfering in B's policies without committing an invasive act. Alternatively state A may implement such a policy for 'paternalistic' reasons: it may decide only to tax goods which it believes state B should not produce, and is seeking to impact on the economic policies of state B. Alternatively, state A may dictate economic policies in return for aid. For example, in the late 1970s the USA responded to Israel's request for arms by demanding that Israel open up its economic system, introduce competition, liberalize its financial laws and regulations, reduce taxes, and, in general, abandon its social-democratic policies in favour of a free market economy. These American demands did not prevent the people of Israel from being sovereign. Israel was manipulated, perhaps, to change its policies, but these policies were still decided in and by the people's political institutions: its parliament, its government, etc. So intervention does not necessarily harm internal sovereignty.[8]

This leads me to the second – i.e., the external – meaning of 'harming a state's sovereignty'. Here, sovereignty can only be applied to the international arena. Sovereignty in the international arena is understood to exist when legitimacy is formally and practically given to a certain government's policies by other states. Thus sovereignty in that sense implies that external bodies cannot enjoy any authoritative power (often this relates to power within another state's territory) (see Batty and Gray, 1966; Krasner, 1993, p. 142).

But at this point we run the risk of confusing sovereignty with autonomy and freedom of action. Indeed, sovereign parliaments and governments often act within constrained circumstances (see Maclean, 1996). In this scenario, the people (or, in fact, the government) are forced to change decisions about their policies due to external pressure, manipulation, etc. In the example above, the USA exploited the circumstances of Israel's urgent need for arms and imposed conditions that sought to change the country's ideological and social structure. Consequently, Israel became less autonomous. The parliament and the government still legislated, regulated and ruled, even though their options had been limited by the USA, to the extent that we could argue that they had no other choice but to choose what they did and legislate the way they did. So now we should understand the objection to international intervention as based on the claim that intervention limits the autonomy, rather than sovereignty of the other state.

But such a claim seems to me incredibly naïve and out of touch with contemporary reality. In a world which is a global village, in which people lose their jobs in London due to a collapse of the stock markets in Singapore or Bangkok, where poetry written in one country is translated into dozen of languages and has an impact far beyond its original culture, where one country's information sources are freely accessible to people in other states (the global electronic network), where due to technological innovation, investors and borrowers trade without borders, where immigration is in practice more or less free, despite laws which try to prohibit and limit it, where regional arrangements exist which guarantee a free flow of goods, money and labour, where production is transnationalized, and finally, where negotiations between the PLO and Israel are delayed because a Ms Lewinsky is claiming to have an affair with Mr Clinton, there is no reason to think in terms of (state) autonomy, terms which were dominant in the political and legal theory of the seventeenth, eighteenth and nineteenth centuries.[9]

At this point one could criticize my position by claiming that believing in individuals' autonomy may also be naïve, and even methodologically false. Would that imply that we should not respect individuals' autonomy? Well, it is true that even if one is, say, a communitarian, who believes that persons are constituted by their affiliations to 'community', one should still respect individuals' autonomy, as the basis for any moral theory. But I shall soon argue that this is not the case in the international arena, and that state autonomy is not necessarily desirable.

Let me summarize the argument so far. The common argument against intervention is that it harms a state's sovereignty. This can be understood as either internal or external sovereignty. If it is understood as harming internal sovereignty, it must assume that intervention is invasive, whereas in practice it is more often not invasive (and therefore cannot harm internal sovereignty). If, however, the claim is understood as harming external sovereignty, then the claim is not clear: it seems that in fact it should be understood as harming a state's autonomy. This, I have argued, is extremely naïve and irrelevant to the current complex world picture. Hence, those who extrapolate from the political theory of intrastate relations (respect for the autonomy of the individual) to international relations (opposing intervention out of respect for a state's autonomy) are making, what I consider, a far-fetched philosophical move.

Circumstances vs Forms of Intervention

If my argument bears up so far, then at least the most common justification for opposing intervention – namely that it endangers sovereignty or autonomy – would provide the wrong basis for this position. I will be offering other reasons for opposing intervention, but for now, I wish to argue that there are good reasons for liberals, socialists and environmentalists not to adopt the automatic stance of opposing international intervention.

Liberals have two good reasons for not opposing international intervention. First, they believe in the wide open market, which is international and global in nature. Liberals relate to the actors in the international arena primarily according to their economic functions – as either producers, traders, consumers – and only then (if at all) according to their nationality. International intervention, then, may require justification not because it is inter- (rather than intra-) national, but because it interferes with the free market. According to this, the market should be open, and the exchange of goods should take place freely, without any interruption. Capital and information should flow easily and quickly from one place to another without political intervention. However, for the same reason international intervention can sometimes be justified.

What if one side becomes a monopoly? This could prevent the market from being open and free, and thereby interfere with the rights of the 'economic units', be they producers, traders, or consumers.[10] Thus international intervention is seen by liberals as a means of guaranteeing that there is no monopoly. The obvious example is the war against Iraq in 1991. There were fears in the international business community and among certain oil producers (e.g. Saudi-Arabia) that by occupying Kuwait, Iraq would hold a monopoly in oil production.[11] The USA therefore spearheaded a military intervention, intended to prevent oil prices from rising and to block an Iraqi monopoly.

Notice that there is no need for intervention to actually take place. A party (e.g. Iraq) will think twice about trying to form a monopoly, since the option of international intervention (not necessarily military; economic intervention would suffice) exists as a very real deterrent.

At this point I would like to draw attention to the almost paradoxical fact that a state can initiate a monopoly in the international arena and thereby harm the free market which is comprised of individuals and firms. But firms cannot decide upon policies, and therefore another state needs to step in, in order to prevent the emergence of the monopoly. The situation may be further complicated due to the nature of hegemony. Political and military power sometimes accompany the state's economic and commercial power and thus produce a hegemony. There is a danger, then, that the very states capable of intervening to secure the free market and the absence of monopolies, will decide to become monopolies themselves. This is sometimes described by neo-Gramscians as 'hegemonic leadership'. A state is able to institutionalize its economic and military dominance through a complex web of relationships and control mechanisms that are also beneficial to elite groups in secondary states (Camilleri and Falk, 1992, pp. 89–90). And yet, liberals nevertheless regard intervention as a guarantee against monopolies, because often the hegemonic powers need a free and flourishing market, that will create rich consumers, and therefore these powers will tend not to create monopolies. So, the theory goes, the hegemonic party performs three specific functions in a liberal economic order: it 'offers an outlet for surplus production; acts as a lender of last resort, thereby maintaining stability; and generates the outflow of capital and credit needed to maintain capital accumulation on a global scale' (ibid., p. 90; see also Kindelberger, 1981). Of course, this type of hegemony is a kind of intervention, which, again, would be justified by liberals.

The second reason liberals should not rule out intervention automatically, is because of their support for human rights, and because international intervention is sometimes a realistic way of securing these rights. Here I have in mind intervention by non-governmental organizations (NGOs) rather than by governments. For example, the actions of such NGOs as 'Doctors Without Borders', 'Amnesty International', or 'Human Rights Watch', are designed to safeguard the human rights of citizens in countries where rights are often abused. Liberals regard these organizations as 'metaphorical funnels through which diplomatic, humanitarian and reconstruction aid may be directed toward the root causes of conflict, and later provide forms around which state structures can be recast' (von Lipsey, 1997, p. 53). Liberals also claim that these organizations are listened to, and their criticism is respected, partly because they are perceived as professional, but also because, unlike states, they lack political interests.[12]

Socialists also have two good reasons not to oppose international intervention automatically. First, they have never been very pleased with nationality and have always suspected the state. It would seem odd if proponents of cross-national class solidarity were to take a stance in defence of the nation or state. Thus arguments against intervention on the basis of the harm it would do to nationality should not appeal to socialists. The second reason is that socialists are sensitive to international and cross-national justice and to the protection of vulnerable groups such as minorities and the working class, whatever their nationality. Socialists have never accepted that political state boundaries should hinder the pursuit of justice. A good example would be the case of Rwanda. Following a plane crash on 6 April 1994, in which the presidents of Rwanda and Burundi died, violent clashes erupted between the Hutu and the Tutsi tribes. Within three months 500,000 people were dead. The world seemed silent, mainly because the USA had suffered an earlier abortive, attempt to intervene in Africa, namely in Somalia. Eventually, many weeks too late, the UN Secretary General, Mr Boutrous-Ghali initiated an international intervention in Rwanda, backed and supported by leftists and socialists all over the world.

There is a third group which may not automatically oppose intervention. I have in mind the environmentalists. It is clear that a strong environmental protection policy may lead to international intervention in the sense of limiting a state's autonomy (see Hurrell and Kingsbury, 1992, p. 7). It is widely acknowledged that since most forms of pollution not only affect the place they are produced but also cause damage to neighbouring communities and countries as well, there is no other way of reducing pollution than by international agreements. Unfortunately, most of these agreements are never honoured. Environmental goods are public goods, and it takes only one free rider to spoil an agreement. Thus environmentalists often argue that behind all this talk of state sovereignty and opposition to intervention, lie economic interests, which contribute to the deterioration of the state of the environment and the economic domination of the affluent North over the poor South. Therefore, they recommend some form of enforcement in order to save the planet. Of course, this does not have to be a military intervention – it can take the form of sanctions, popular boycotts, diplomatic pressure, and so on.[13]

As an example of how intervention can help and what happens when no intervention takes place because it is out of the question, consider the following case. France dumps sodium chloride into the river Rhine,[14] most of which comes from French Alsace. River pollution is mainly felt in Germany and Holland. These two countries pressure France to install a system for reducing the discharge of sodium chloride. France agrees, and demands that most of the cost is covered by Germany and Holland, to which these two states agree. The reason the victims rather than the polluters paid for the new system was that they had no other choice. The relations between the three states would make intervention – even popular boycott – unthinkable. Environmentalists have thus been arguing that for such cases to be avoided, there must be a morally justifiable, widely accepted and readily available non-military mechanism of international intervention.

Now, let me refer to an example of international intervention: when the democratic world imposed sanctions on South Africa, to pressure its regime to abandon apartheid. It was quite widely believed among liberals and socialists that the world was responsible for taking some action against this system. It was not clear, however, whether the boycott on South African products was harming the ruling white elite or the black and coloured masses. In other words, this was a question of the form of the intervention. The controversy arose because not enough attention had been paid to the question of the form. Too much attention had been paid to the circumstances that did or did not call for international intervention. But it would be wrong to think that circumstances alone can constitute the justification for intervention. First, circumstances are only vaguely defined. For example, it is widely, but mistakenly, believed, that in practice, international intervention would be legitimate in the case of totalitarian regimes. But in 1986 the international court in The Hague ruled that no state has the right to use the excuse of humanitarian intervention in order to justify a move into a place if this would not be welcome, and if it is accompanied by force.[15] This, of course, raises questions: who decides what counts as welcome? Who is asked? Consequently the UN decided to define the proper circumstances for intervention as self-defence only. This, of course, opened the gate for a broad interpretation of self-defence. For example, the UN has the power to rule that a situation that arises in a certain place constitutes a threat to regional peace, and to call for intervention on that basis.[16] Again, this implies that talking about the right circumstances for intervention is not fruitful. Rather we should concentrate on the question of 'what would be the right form of international intervention?'

Liberal and Socialist Attitudes to Intervention

There are three possible forms of intervention: the first is economic and takes place mainly in the market; the second is ideological and takes place mainly in civil society; the third is military, which takes place within the sphere of the state. I will now summarize two attitudes to these three forms of intervention: the liberal and the socialist. I shall then relate these forms to another crucial parameter characterizing the form of intervention: whether it is exploitative or not.

The first form then, is economic. The means employed are financial and other economic actions, and the agents are individuals and companies. So long as these actions do not result in monopolies, the liberal does not consider it intervention, but legitimate market activities. The socialist , however, would tend to resent this type of activity. And yet, the reason put forward by socialists is not that such acts interfere with anyone's business, but rather that the motives for these acts might be immoral. The socialist draws a distinction between on the one hand, trade which is reciprocal and yields mutual advantage, and trade, often between the North and the South, which aims at changing custôms, systems of beliefs, or social and political structures. Sometimes the change is intended to guarantee a market for products produced by the intervening country. A good example would be the export of cigarettes from the USA to Third World countries. The Americans exploit the fact that while in the USA every packet of cigarettes has a warning sign on it, and advertisement is regulated, in Third world countries no limitations are imposed on the cigarettes trade at all. Hence there is a large export of cigarettes from the USA to Third World countries. To liberals this may appear a purely legitimate and innocent trade activity. Socialists however often perceive such economic activities as intervention, since trading activities of this nature are meant to alter norms and behaviour in Third World populations. Indeed, many people in the Third World became addicted to cigarettes due to the appealing image of an 'American product'. Thus habits and customs were manipulated to guarantee a customers market for the American tobacco industry. (Cigarettes, by the way, have been the cause of more deaths than most types of weapon.)

The second form of intervention is so well hidden that it is often ignored by many people. I call it 'ideological' since it seeks to change a particular society's political and economic ideology by entering into voluntary agreements which take place in civil society. The agreements are between governments, but often involve academic and research institutions. The intervening country invites and subsidizes students from other countries to study at its best universities, and in return these students contract to return home and work in higher education, research and social activities, where they are expected to foster cultural and political relations between the two states. As a by- product, most of these students adopt and internalize the main norms of the state in which they study. When they return home they become advocates of these norms, and act to bring about gradual change in the ideology of the elite in their country. France and Britain did this in the late nineteenth century and first half of the twentieth century; the USA leads these efforts in the contemporary world. Another form of such intervention involves sending NGOs with certain ideological missions to other countries, or else providing support for NGOs that accept the ideological framework of the intervening country. For instance, the USA encourages and subsidizes the activities of liberal organizations in Africa, Asia and the Middle East; the Scandinavians support peace organizations in the Middle East, and so on.

Now this type of intervention may seem proper and moral, especially to liberals. They regard it as part of the free market of ideas, which should flourish everywhere. However, socialists would accept this kind of intervention only if the acts involved were indeed to the advantage of the party being 'helped'. Benefit in this case is often defined as helping the citizens of another county to become independent, as liberating them from the need for help. So some forms of cultural exchange only serve to maintain a system whereby the party receiving the assistance continues to depend on foreign guidance and help, and are therefore rejected by the socialists. Other acts genuinely seek to liberate those receiving the assistance from their dependency on guidance and help, and are therefore welcome.[17]

The third form of intervention is military. It is often carried out by states and their armies, though sometimes by the UN. This is straightforward since both liberals and socialists usually resent this manner of intervention, unless gross injustice to a third party, can only be corrected through this intervention. Now, the liberal would justify his or her objection to such intervention on the grounds that it violates the rights of the individual and/or the property rights a state has over its natural resources. The socialist also objects to such intervention, but often dismisses the argument of property rights. According to the socialist, the property rights standpoint ignores first that natural resources were never distributed or redistributed according to any criteria of justice. Saudi-Arabia is rich in oil and Mexico enjoys attractive sea shores due to luck, which should not, according to many socialists, affect the enjoyment of such goods (Cohen, 1988). Moreover, the liberal ignores the fact that in practice, it is not the state (and hence not the people) that owns these natural resources, but rather private ownership (as in a privatized system) or, more often, official state ownership, which in practice means that the upper classes have easier access to these resources. If this is the case, the socialist would argue, then state property rights over natural resources cannot be a genuine reason to resent military intervention.

On what grounds, then, would a socialist object to military intervention? S/he would do so if – and therefore because – this intervention is meant to protect the economic interests of the intervening party and/or its allies. This leads me to my next argument, namely that the key parameter with regard to the form of intervention is not necessarily whether it is economic, ideological, or militaristic, but rather whether it is exploitative or not.

Before I discuss this, I would like to summarize my argument so far: international intervention has three main configurations: economic, ideological and military. Whereas liberals tend to object to military intervention and do not regard the trade acts in the sphere of civil society and economy as intervention, the socialist tends to be less critical of military intervention if the case involves righting some kind of gross injustice, and, at the same time, tends to be more critical of ideological and economic intervention. I side with the socialist position because it distinguishes more successfully between different forms of intervention. Notice, however, that the distinction is not based on circumstances, but on the form. Let us then return to the issue of exploitation.

Intervention and Exploitation

When people discuss the right circumstances for international intervention they often relate to the state whose affairs are being influenced. The most well known example is Kant's Perpetual Peace, where he asserts that a precondition for respecting a state's autonomy and the principle of nonintervention is that this state is republican – or in contemporary terms, it has a just constitution. Charles Beitz (1979, p. 90) also distinguishes between states whose internal affairs are conducted according to just principles and states 'that are unjust according to the appropriate principles of justice'. This seems to me, however, rather arbitrary: how do we decide whether these principles are just or not? Does a completely free market tie in with these principles? The USA often defines socialist regimes as blatantly unjust: should it therefore be allowed to intervene in such states? In most cases, if we are to justify or oppose intervention according to the situation in the state whose affairs are being influenced, it will probably be the case that the intervening party will blame this state as being unjust while the state itself will claim that it is just.

I have therefore argued that justifying intervention should be related to the intervention's form rather than to the circumstances of intervention, and therefore I suggest examining the body (often state) that intervenes rather than the state whose affairs are meant to be influenced. My claim is that a socialist theory of international intervention is more sensitive to exploitative forms of intervention. According to socialists, international intervention is to be opposed if it exploits the persons of another society.

At this point one has to distinguish between exploiting circumstances and exploiting persons (Wolff, 1985, pp. 24–41). A can exploit certain circumstances to force (or coerce) B to do Y. This, however, does not imply that B is exploited. A does not necessarily benefit from doing this, and therefore one cannot conclude that A exploits B. Exploitation entails A benefiting from an exchange which involves treating B without equal concern in a process of bargaining.[18] Exploiting circumstances, therefore, may be a legitimate act in a process of bargaining. But benefiting from an ill treatment (without equal concern) of other people is what makes an act exploitative and therefore morally condemnable.[19]

I now want to examine two international agreements as examples for two processes of intervention, one which is legitimate because it is not exploitative, the other indeed is exploitative and therefore is to be opposed. The first agreement is the Trade in Ivory agreement.[20] This agreement is not exploitative. On the contrary: it liberates and protects Third World populations. Ivory trade from the African elephant was a business, worth an estimated $5 billion annually. Most of the products were sold in highly industrialized countries, mainly Japan. However, African people did not earn most of the income. Instead traders and those dealing with illegal import in the industrialized countries earned it. As a matter of fact, several African countries — Botswana, South Africa and Zimbabwe — did manage to create an internal order in which killing of elephants and trade was moderate and controlled. These countries' people benefited from a greater portion of the final prices of ivory products. However, a trade agreement was necessary because as long as Japan and other industrial countries allowed free sale of ivory products, demand was high, and incentives for the killing of the African elephant were rising. Japan reacted to international public criticism (mostly from NGOs) by withdrawing its previous reservations to CITES (Convention on International Trade in Endangered Species) by the year 1994. Once Japan passed a tough law punishing traders, world prices for raw ivory plunged by 90 per cent, thereby reducing incentives for killing the elephants and for illegal trade. When the poaching was stopped, the elephant population stabilized and later rose, until those Africans who were living on ivory trade could renew their business without threat of losing their source of income. While working on this agreement, Japan's internal affairs were influenced, by a process of economic and ideological intervention: economic sanctions were proposed by NGOs as threats, the culture of using ivory products for ceremonies and health care was criticized, mostly by NGOs and officials of several states. However, no exploitation of any person was involved.

The second case is the on going attempt to construct a global warming agreement, in particular with regard to the greenhouse effect. Of course, all nations are effected by greenhouse warming. Indeed, some nations might be effected more severely, but the fact that scientists have not been able to be precise about who is going to suffer more, makes all nations more or less equally vulnerable to the increase in emissions of carbon dioxide and other such gases. The USA is the heaviest polluter when it comes to emissions of carbon dioxide. For example, data released by the World Resource Institute about the cumulative emissions of carbon dioxide from fossil fuels for the last forty years shows that the USA polluted 15 times as much as India did. And yet, since this pollution is not local but rather global — what is at stake here is the build up of carbon dioxide in the atmosphere — the USA does not suffer from the results of its policies more than India, or any other country, for that matter. The USA exploits these circumstances. The world needs the USA to agree to any agreement; without the USA's cooperation any such agreement will be useless. Thus the USA has been pushing towards an additional agreement, according to which the USA would agree to reducing carbon dioxide emissions to a level of 7 per cent below the level in the year 1990, on condition that the world agrees to a completely free trade in polluting rights. Third World countries are ready to accept an agreement on trade in polluting rights, as long as this trade is limited. The USA forces them to change their attitude. This is an economic intervention in the policies of many states and in their attitudes to environmental protection. Moreover, I claim, the USA's position, is an exploitative intervention in the affairs of other states. Why?

It seems that other countries will have no other option but to agree to the USA's terms. This could be seen as an innocent process of bargaining. However, notice that once the world agrees to a completely free trade, American firms will buy pollution rights from firms in other countries: since the trade will be completely free (according to the USA's terms), Third World governments will not be allowed to control this trade and prevent firms from selling all their polluting rights to US firms. The prices US firms will pay will be low in US terms. They will allow the Americans to produce more and more, while the Third World will have to import more and more products from the USA. Third World people will be more dependent – economically, and therefore politically – on the USA without being autonomous. Moreover, this sort of pollution is not local: all states will continue to be equally vulnerable to the buildup of carbon dioxide in the atmosphere. Thus the USA will not lose anything: it will continue to produce as much as it has produced. It will have to pay for the right to do so. But it will not pay a lot: since the market will be free, buying goods (pollution rights) in the Third World will be cheap in American terms. At the same time the USA will benefit, because Third World countries will stop producing these goods, and will have to purchase them from the USA. This seems to me an exploitative sort of intervention.

If we return to the theoretical discussion above, Third World people are not treated with equal concern: their longing for autonomous lives is not respected; rather they are means for American firms to become even richer. The problem, from the Third World point of view, is that they simply must reach an agreement – any agreement – in order to stop the growing risk of suffering from extreme climatic changes. Out of this fear they have no other choice but to agree to the USA's terms: by this the USA intervenes in their internal affairs, controls and changes their economies. It is for this reason that I regard this emerging agreement — discussed in these days in Buenos Aires — as an exploitative agreement that has to be morally condemned.

Notes

1 I would like to thank the participants of the Association for Legal and Social Philosophy conference for fruitful comments.
2 For a good introduction to this question, see Barry, 1991.
3 Transnational matters do not necessarily involve nations, but, for example, individuals or firms from different states or nations.
4 Notice that I am not putting forward the argument raised by Walzer, 1994, or an Hegelian argument about two systems of moral reasoning (see Brown, 1966; Caney, 1966). On the contrary, I accept what Mazsini teaches us, that a nation that forgets its obligations to other nations is doomed to deteriorate and lose its national features.
5 Notice that I do not accept that the state whose affairs are designed to be influenced must be a sovereign state. I discuss these below. I also do not accept what is usually part of the definition of intervention, namely that the agent aiming to influence the affairs of a certain state is a state, and that this agent must be external to the state whose affairs are influenced.

Indeed, intervention can be carried out by an internal agent, although this does complicate the legal and political situation.

6 One does not have to regard the state as an organic whole, in the way Hegel did, in order to conceive it as an autonomous entity.

7 The examples I have in mind are Israel invading Lebanon in 1982 and declaring that the Christians' leader, Bashir Jumail, is the new president, or Syria invading Lebanon in the late 1980s, nominating its allies as parliament members and ministers.

8 John Stuart Mill, among others, objected to international intervention on the basis that it harmed internal sovereignty, and that just as persons should be left alone to make their own mistakes, so should states. However, Mill failed to acknowledge that when a state was making mistakes it was the individuals — often from the least advantaged sections of society – who suffered. Mill's move from morality between persons to morality between states was too hasty. See also Michael Walzer's claim that members of political communities should find their own way to their own freedom (Walzer, 1992, p. 87)– a liberal argument which may have very conservative consequences, since many peoples may be left alone to find their own freedom for many many years.

9 Notice the difference between this argument and the one put forward by Charles Beitz (1979, pp. 67–92). Beitz claims that autonomy provides an inadequate foundation for the principle of nonintervention, whereas I claim that we should not think in terms of states' autonomy any way.

10 According to Hillel Steiner (1984) this monopoly yields exploitation. I discuss this theory in my 'Transnational and international exploitation', 1998.

11 Notice that in order to form a monopoly an agent does not need to be the sole producer.

12 It should be noted that this attitude towards organizations assumes a very narrow conception of politics. These organizations do compete one against the other, for financial resources, media coverage, access to decision-making centres, and they are even often involved in party politics. They therefore do have political interests many times.

13 Of course, not every diplomatic pressure constitutes 'intervention'. Negotiations and diplomatic talks can result in agreements which are voluntarily taken by both sides, without any manipulation.

14 For a detailed description see Camilleri, 1992, p. 186.

15 This was decided with relation to the USA-Nicaragua affair.

16 On these grounds the UN authorized its forces to enter Bosnia.

17 The economist Schumacher referred to these two approaches in his *Small is Beautiful* (1973).

18 I elaborate on this in de-Shalit, 1998.

19 In the above article I explain why this definition is consistent with both the Marxian and the liberal theories of exploitation. For the former see Wood, 1995; Roemer, 1982; Cohen, 1995. For the latter see Steiner, 1984.

20 Details are from Porter and Welsh Brown, 1995.

References

Barry, B. (1991), *Liberty and Justice: Essays in Political Theory: Volume 2*, Clarendon Press, Oxford.

Batty, H. and Gray, T. (1966), 'Environmental rights and national sovereignty' in S. Caney, D. George, and P. Jones (eds), *National Rights, International Obligations*, Westview Press, Boulder, Colorado.
Beitz C. (1979), *Political Theory and International Relations*, Princeton University Press, Princeton.
Brown, C. (1966), 'Cultural pluralism, universal principles and international relations theory' in S. Caney, D. George, and P. Jones (eds), *National Rights, International Obligations*, Westview Press, Boulder, Colorado.
Camilleri, J.A., and Falk, J. (1992), *The End of Sovereignty?*, Edwar Elgar, Cheltenham.
Caney, S. (1966), 'Individuals, nations and obligations' in S. Caney, D. George, and P. Jones (eds), *National Rights, International Obligations*, Westview Press, Boulder, Colorado.
Cohen, G.A. (1988), *History, Labour and Freedom*, Oxford University Press, Oxford.
Cohen, G.A. (1995), *Self-Ownership, Freedom and Equality*, Cambridge University Press, Cambridge.
de-Shalit, A. (1998), 'Transnational and International Exploitation', *Political Studies*, Vol. 4, pp. 693–709.
Hurrell, A. and Kingsbury, B. (1992), *The International Politics of the Environment*, Clarendon Press, Oxford.
Kindelberger, C. (1981), 'Dominance and Leadership in the International Economy', *International Studies Quarterly*, 25, pp. 242–54.
Krasner, I.S.D. (1993), 'Sovereignty, Regimes and Human Rights' in V. Rittberger and P. Meyer (eds), *Regime Theory and International Relations*, Clarendon Press, Oxford.
Maclean, I. (1996), *The Oxford Dictionary of Politics*.
Porter, G. and Welsh Brown, J. (1995), *Global Environmental Politics*, Westview Press, Boulder, Colorado.
Roemer, J. (1982), 'Property Relations vs. Surplus Value in Marxian Exploitation', *Philosophy and Public Affairs*, Vol. 11, pp. 281–313.
Schumacher, E.F. (1973), *Small is Beautiful: A Study of Economics as if People Mattered*, Vintage, London.
Steiner, H. (1984), 'A Theory of Exploitation', *Ethics*, Vol. 94.
von Lipsey, R. (1997), *Breaking the Cycle*, St. Martin's Press, New York.
Walzer, M. (1992), *Just and Unjust Wars*, 2nd edn, Basic Books, New York.
Walzer, M. (1994), *Thick and Thin: Moral Argument at Home and Abroad*, University of Notre Dame Press, Notre Dame, Indiana.
Wolff, J. (1985), 'Exploitation', MA thesis, University College London.
Wood, A. (1995), 'Exploitation', *Social Theory and Practice*, Vol. 21, pp. 150–65.

12 Justice and Fairness in the Battle Against Acid Rain[1]

CECILIA ALBIN

In recent years, environmental negotiations have assumed a prominent place in international affairs. The first concerted international effort to address environmental issues was the United Nations Conference on the Human Environment held in Stockholm in 1972, which also recognized their connection to questions of economic development. This landmark conference was followed by multilateral talks over marine and air pollution, ozone depletion, hazardous wastes and North-South trade and aid, among other matters. Until the fall of the Berlin Wall and the end of the Cold War, however, such negotiations unrelated to the superpower competition remained in the diplomatic backwaters. The relatively low priority and limited attention they attracted from the major powers, and the prevailing East-West hostilities, made negotiations outside the areas of 'high politics' ill equipped to produce breakthroughs.

The phenomenal increase in the number and range of environmental talks in the last decade stems partly from the improvement in East-West relations, and the expanded notions of national interests and international security which this change has stimulated. One aspect of this redefinition is the recognition that the protection of many environmental resources is integral to national and international welfare, and requires transboundary cooperation at unprecedented levels.[2] The result of another hallmark event, the 1992 United Nations Conference on Environment and Development (UNCED) in Rio de Janeiro, was the development of principles, goals, and procedures for both new and continued negotiations over threats such as ozone layer depletion, climate change, air and water pollution, the loss of biodiversity, desertification, deforestation, and hazardous wastes.[3]

Environmental talks are often conducted in the shadow of general principles, legal or ethical, pertaining to the problem at hand. These may be enshrined in multilateral framework agreements, which then provide a broad normative context within which specific measures are negotiated over a period of time. The 1979 Convention on Long Range Transboundary Air Pollution (LRTAP), under which several protocols on acid rain emission controls have been drafted, is founded on principles such as 'good neighbourliness' and 'no harm', 'polluter pays', the equitable utilization of shared resources, and the duties of cooperation, exchange of information and consultation. Another feature is the presence of dual and conflicting time frames. In the long term environmental negotiations promise significant benefits, particularly to future generations. In the shorter term, however, they are of a 'win-lose' nature as they must distribute financial and other burdens among existing parties whose gains from reaching an agreement can vary considerably.[4]

A major hurdle in reducing transboundary environmental threats is how to tackle fundamental questions of justice and fairness. These concern the exploitation and preservation of scarce or finite environmental resources which are essential to human well-being, the international allocation of the high costs of protective measures coupled with inequalities between countries and, many would argue, obligations of present generations to future ones. Poor states hold that they should not have to compromise on their own welfare or economic development in order to bear the cost of resolving environmental problems, especially those caused mainly by rich industrialized nations such as climate change and ozone depletion. They maintain furthermore that all countries, regardless of their financial or technological assets, should have equal access to the 'global commons' (resources held in common by or affecting the international community as a whole). Such conceptions of justice and fairness have influenced negotiations over some issues including ozone depletion, the protection of the world's seas and oceans, and international trade in toxic wastes. Many industrialized countries exporting their hazardous wastes to poor countries for cheap disposal once sought global regulations based on the principle of Prior Informed Consent (PIC). This would permit trade if the recipient agreed to import the waste before it was sent. Developing countries, by contrast, viewed any regulation as the legalization of an unjust practice and insisted on an outright ban of the practice (Clapp, 1994). The 1988 Basel Convention adopted the PIC principle with additional conditions, but by 1994 the UN Environment Programme had established a global ban on international trade in toxic wastes.

The European acid rain talks provide a fascinating case study of how conceptions of justice and fairness can influence international negotiations, and how they interact with factors such as political 'pragmatism', domestic politics and interests, and scientific considerations. Like climate change and many other environmental issues, it raises clear-cut questions about obligations and cost-sharing because of differences in responsibility between polluting and victim countries, in sensitivity to the problem and gains to be had from regulatory agreements, and in economic and technological ability to implement protective measures. Leading proposals based on economic and environmental efficiency criteria have required some of the poorest European countries with the least resources to undertake the greatest and most costly measures, to the benefit of rich countries with more to gain from abatement (see Klaassen, Amann, and Schöpp, 1992).[5] Unlike the climate change case, there is now a solid record of the acid rain talks conducted under the LRTAP Convention within the United Nations Economic Commission for Europe (UN-ECE) which span over two decades. They have resulted in decisive emission reductions over time, and in the development of effective mechanisms to monitor and tackle air pollution which may be used in other threatened regions such as South Asia. While European acid rain abatement clearly could not have succeeded as well as it has without addressing some conceptions of justice and fairness, questions about the distribution of the cost burden remain with respect to new needed measures.

Overview of the Acid Rain Case

The basic distributive issues in negotiations over air pollution concern who should undertake emission cuts (given inequalities in past, current and future projected emission levels) and at whose cost (given differences in resources, responsibility for the problem, and in gains to be had from regulations), and by how much emissions should be reduced and by when (given at once the high costs of abatement and the devastating effects of pollution on some countries). How, then, have European governments tackled these issues? What notions of justice and fairness have actually influenced the process to date and why? How have conflicting conceptions been tackled? Do issues of justice and fairness appear to have had a bearing on the results and the 'success' of the negotiations?

We will discover that the European acid rain talks have raised difficult issues of justice and fairness ever since their inception in the mid-1970s. The parties accepted early on the overall structure, process and procedures of the talks under the UN-ECE, which are well-established. The controversial issues have largely involved the outcome – the distribution of the burdens and benefits arising from acid rain abatement.[6] We will see that the political and scientific context of the negotiations has influenced the extent to which considerations of justice or fairness have been taken into account. East-West hostilities and mistrust, along with scientific uncertainty and conflicting arguments about the benefits to be had from costly abatement measures, long pervaded the discussions and left little room for ethical concerns. As one negotiator recalls: 'In the past, we had to work one against the other, at least that was the feeling' (Kakebeeke, 1997). The end of the Cold War, coupled with improved scientific evidence of the causes and harmful effects of transboundary air pollution, changed this situation. Starting with the deliberations over a second sulphur protocol in 1991, the talks have become less political and more 'problem-solving' in nature. They have also been grounded in agreed scientific and environmental criteria, allowing certain conceptions of justice and fairness to play a greater role.

A fundamental basis and engine of negotiations over acid rain and other environmental issues is the principle of 'no harm'. It holds that states must avoid harming the environment of other countries and, when they fail to do so, remedy the damage caused. Improved scientific evidence has strengthened the role played by this principle over time, and has helped to drive forward the process of reaching agreement on emission controls. Apart from this norm, arguments about justice and fairness were generally not taken seriously and had no real impact on the European acid rain talks during the first decade. Political, tactical and scientific considerations explain the heavy reliance on the principle of equal percentage reductions during this time, when the first sulphur protocol was negotiated. By contrast, since the latter part of the 1980s several, partly conflicting notions of outcome fairness and justice, and 'horse-trading' among these and other concerns, have guided the talks.

An influential notion in the acid rain talks, as in those over ozone depletion (the 1987 Montreal Protocol on the Depletion of the Ozone Layer) and climate change (the 1992 Climate Change Convention), has been the differentiation of obligations given inequalities in circumstances and resources among countries. One expression of this in the second sulphur protocol (the Oslo Protocol of 1994) is the use of the 'critical loads' criterion.[7] It alleviated bitter conflicts over how to credit countries which had already undertaken abatement measures and faced more costly options for further emission cuts. The differentiation of emission targets and deadlines with a view to economic ability is another important feature of this protocol. Taking account of divergences among countries has been critical to the progress in acid rain abatement since the end of the 1980s. Indeed, negotiators have come to view responsiveness to such considerations as vital to effective cooperation on environmental protection.

One major fairness issue, which arose especially in the drafting of the 1994 Protocol, remains unresolved. The most environmentally effective and cost-efficient abatement measures tend to impose heavy burdens on poor polluting states, with relatively few resources and gains to be had from combating acid rain. Calls for financial and technological transfers to these states have not been acted upon in the official talks to date. By contrast, such resource transfers have been an important part of other environmental agreements and their success, including the 1987 Montreal Protocol. It is too early to assess whether this will have a major impact on the fulfilment of commitments made under the second sulphur protocol. Without such 'cost-sharing' in the future, however, the need to continue to compromise on environmentally required acid rain emission targets in order to accommodate poorer countries appears unavoidable.

Getting the European Acid Rain Talks Underway: The Role of Scientific Evidence and the Principle of 'No Harm'

'Acid rain' has come to refer to transboundary air pollution generally. Several kinds of air pollutants can travel over long distances in the atmosphere, before they are deposited on the earth's surface. The chief ones are sulphur dioxide (SO_2), nitrogen oxides (NOx), volatile organic compounds (VOCs) and ammonia (NH_3). Scientific understanding has deepened dramatically about such emissions: their sources (notably coal and oil fired power and heating stations, combustion plants, machines, and road and off-road vehicles), their transport across national boundaries, and their damage to forests, freshwater, agricultural crops, ecosystems, buildings, and human health. Acid rain today remains a serious environmental problem. One issue is the steady deterioration in the condition of European forests. A 1994 survey showed that between 20 per cent and 60 per cent of the sample trees in eighteen European countries, and over 26 per cent of the total sample, were defoliated or discoloured. The most severely affected areas are found in Central and Eastern Europe (CEE).[8] In Bulgaria, acid rain emissions have had adverse effects in parts of the country inhabited by over 40 per cent of its population.[9] Scandinavian lakes and fish populations also continue to suffer considerable damage.

The commencement of negotiations over European air pollution was triggered by Scandinavian countries, particularly Sweden which argued that foreign sources of SO_2 emissions were responsible for the acidification of its lakes. The 1972 UN Conference on the Human Environment greeted these

Swedish assertions with scepticism, but adopted unanimously the principle of 'no harm' among other norms. An investigation by the Organization for Economic Cooperation and Development (OECD) verified soon thereafter that imported sulphur was indeed causing the problems reported in Scandinavia. Another turning point was the 1975 Helsinki Conference on Security and Co-operation, at which the Soviet Union (USSR) proposed the environment as a relatively apolitical area for pursuing the East-West dialogue (Sokolovsky, 1997). Sweden and Norway managed to secure air pollution as the focus of these discussions (McCormick, 1989). The OECD lacked the appropriate membership, as well as legal mechanisms for ensuring the implementation of agreements. The UN-ECE, representing Western and Eastern Europe as well as North America, therefore became the organizer and forum of the talks that got underway in 1977.

The first achievement in the negotiations was the UN-ECE Convention on Long-Range Transboundary Air Pollution. Signed by 34 countries and the European Community (EC) in 1979, it entered into force in 1983. It contained none of the commitments to actual reductions in SO_2 or NO_x emissions on which Sweden and Norway had insisted. The opposition was too fierce from a coalition of acid rain exporters, led by the UK and the Federal Republic of Germany (FRG) which relied on coal-fired power stations. The Convention established vague obligations to limit and, 'as far as possible', gradually reduce and prevent transboundary air pollution. Yet, together with EC environmental legislation, it has provided the main institutional frameworks and principles for subsequent negotiations over specific emission cuts. The ECE was given the administrative and secretarial responsibilities for implementing the Convention (Article 11). The organization has also become influential in the actual bargaining process. It has several of its senior advisors on the Executive Body, the Convention's main organ, and plays a role in working groups and meetings in which protocols are negotiated.[10]

So far five protocols relating to the Convention have been concluded: the 1984 Protocol on financing the European Programme for Monitoring and Evaluation of Transboundary Air Pollution (EMEP), the 1985 Helsinki Protocol on the reduction of SO_2 emissions, the 1988 Sofia Protocol on the control of NOx emissions, the 1991 Geneva Protocol on the control of VOC emissions, and the 1994 Oslo Protocol on further SO_2 emission reductions.[11] Negotiations over new protocols concerning heavy metals, persistent organic pollutants (POPs), and NOx and related substances, are in progress at the time of this writing. We will focus on the talks leading to the Helsinki Protocol and the Oslo Protocol.

The Early Days: Equal Percentage Reductions as a Facilitating Principle

Soon after the signing of the LRTAP Convention, the Scandinavian countries continued their efforts to secure actual cuts in SO_2 emissions. They won an unexpected powerful ally in 1982 at the Stockholm Conference on the Acidification of the Environment. The FRG, until then a major exporter of SO_2 emissions and opposed to reductions, on this occasion turned into a vigorous proponent of abatement. The possible risk of getting the German Green Party into a pivotal position in Bonn after the 1982 election, and the discovery that acid rain was damaging German forests extensively, triggered the sudden change of heart.

At the first session of the Executive Body of the LRTAP Convention in June 1983, two blocs of countries confronted each other. Sweden, Norway, Denmark and Finland proposed a 30 per cent equal percentage reduction in the SO_2 emission levels of 1980 by 1993, with one important exception: Credit would be given to those countries which had recently reduced their SO_2 emissions.[12] The FRG, Switzerland and Austria added that the best available technology (BAT) which was economically feasible should be used to achieve these cuts. This stricter proposal also targeted SO_2 emissions from mobile and smaller sources, and referred to the possibility of NOx emission reductions (Chossudovsky, 1988). The USA, the UK, France, the USSR and several East European countries formed a second bloc which objected to any substantial emission cuts. The UK and the USA for their part argued that more research was first needed to increase scientific understanding of the causal relationship between domestic SO_2 emissions and acid deposition abroad. This strong opposition meant that once again only a vague agreement was reached on the need to 'decrease effectively' SO_2 emissions.

Disappointed by the inaction, the ministers of nine West European states and Canada assembled in Ottawa in March 1984 and formed the '30 per cent Club'. They thereby committed themselves to unilateral cuts of at least 30 per cent in their 1980 levels of SO_2 emissions over a ten-year period. Another eight West and East European states joined the Club three months later. The influence of the USSR secured the inclusion also of the CEE countries. This was significant given the nature of the acid rain problem, and the requirement of at least 16 ratifications for the protocol to enter into force. The creation and expansion of the 30 per cent Club put pressure on other countries to follow suit, and set the stage for the talks leading to the 1985 Helsinki Protocol.

Across-the-board 30 per cent cuts in SO_2 emissions (by 1993 based on

1980 emission levels) emerged once again as the acceptable formula to most participating countries in these talks.[13] Scientific knowledge was most advanced about ways to combat air pollution caused by SO_2 emissions, and the parties therefore agreed to focus on this pollutant. The majority of states also endorsed the choice of 1980 as the baseline year, which had been widely accepted for some time. Most national emission levels had peaked around this time, and monitoring and data concerning emissions prior to 1980 were unsatisfactory. However, a dispute arose over the arguments of the USA and the UK that an earlier base year be selected, so as to credit them for SO_2 emission reductions undertaken in the 1970s. The two countries held that the choice of 1980 was unfair, placing a heavier burden on them by disregarding earlier reductions and requesting them to undertake the same percentage cuts as other states (Nitze, 1997). Initially the Dutch delegation made a similar argument about being entitled to credit for pre-1980 reductions. It then accepted the proposal of a 30 per cent cut in 1980 emission levels, having calculated that the Netherlands would be able to honour it (Kakebeeke, 1997). Other parties considered the British and American abatement measures prior to 1980 insufficient and rejected their request for an earlier base year, which would have required insignificant or no further reductions of them.

East European negotiators objected to the suggested uniform obligations, and attempted unsuccessfully to promote a multi-tiered protocol. Under this proposal, countries not yet able to undertake a 30 per cent reduction by a fixed date would be offered the alternative of a lower reduction target, a freeze in SO_2 emissions, or an extended deadline (Levy, 1993). Having eventually accepted the equal percentage approach, the USSR pressured other Eastern bloc states also to accept a 30 per cent emission cut. Some did, knowing that they lacked the necessary national abatement programs to achieve the goal (Zurek, 1997). The USSR also managed to secure the inclusion of the option to reduce transboundary fluxes. Moscow held that regulating national emissions which were unharmful to other countries and thus did not violate any international norm was unfair, and outside the scope of the LRTAP Convention which targets transboundary air pollution only. This option permitted the USSR to fulfil its own obligations under the protocol quite cheaply: it moved its emission sources eastward and thereby reduced transboundary fluxes. The concession was essential to secure Soviet adherence to the protocol.

The final protocol required member states to reduce national annual SO_2 emissions or their transboundary fluxes by at least 30 per cent compared to emission levels in 1980, no later than 1993. Parties were also urged to consider further cuts beyond this requirement 'when environmental conditions warrant'.[14] Twenty-one states signed the protocol at Helsinki in July 1985, including polluters such as France, Italy and the USSR which had previously rejected emission controls. It entered into force in September 1987. Nine of the thirty parties to the LRTAP Convention chose not to adhere, most of them for reasons involving arguments about justice or fairness. Most notable was the failure of the UK, West Europe's greatest SO_2 emitter, and the USA, the world's greatest SO_2 emitter, to sign. Both countries held once again that the terms of the protocol were arbitrary and unfair, and that existing scientific evidence was insufficient to justify the costs involved. The USA insisted that the substantial emission cuts which it had undertaken prior to 1980 should be taken into account. The UK Minister of State at the Department of the Environment stressed that the 30 per cent reduction and the chosen baseline year had no particular legitimacy over other, at least equally justifiable standards. If the protocol had demanded a 40 per cent reduction based on the year of peak emissions, for example, the UK would already have fulfilled its obligations.[15]

By the target year of 1993, all parties to the Helsinki Protocol had reduced their national SO_2 emissions by at least 30 per cent. Taken together they had reduced the 1990 levels of SO_2 emissions by 48 per cent. East European countries reached their targets largely because of their severe economic situation in the early 1990s. Twelve parties to the protocol had achieved cuts of at least 50 per cent.[16] Having resisted a formal commitment to the 30 per cent goal, the UK and Poland reported that their emissions too had in fact decreased by at least this percentage. Decline in domestic economic activity is an important reason behind the Polish achievement. The British government ceased denying in 1986 that SO_2 emissions, including those from UK power stations, were causing transboundary damage and that scientific knowledge about the damage justified substantial abatement measures. This new recognition diminished the relevance of British arguments about credit for pre-1980 emission cuts. Nonetheless, Britain,the USA and Poland have not become parties to the protocol and remain among the greatest producers of SO_2 emissions.

Explaining the Helsinki Protocol Negotiations

Matters involving controversial fairness issues triggered the most difficult phases in the talks leading to the Helsinki Protocol. These disputes over specific emission limits, choice of baseline year, and time for implementation ultimately concerned the question of whether abatement requirements should take account of differences among countries, such as divergences in past clean-up efforts, access to modern abatement technology, and in capacity to afford protective measures. The negotiations never resolved these disagreements satisfactorily in the eyes of several polluting countries, which eventually chose not to sign the protocol. The USA and the UK certainly used fairness arguments tactically to serve domestic interests and to justify their positions, but genuine perceptions of unfair treatment also contributed to their decision not to sign (Björkbom, 1997b; Nitze, 1997).

The principle of uniform reductions clearly influenced the course and outcome of the talks significantly, and an alternative approach was never seriously considered. At first it may seem to have played such a pivotal role as a standard of justice or fairness. The distributive principle of equality is rooted in Western political thought and is applied frequently in international negotiations, understood as equal benefits or burdens regardless of differences in resources, contributions or other circumstances. It appears to have had some intrinsic appeal also in this case. Relying on this notion '... would at least give the impression that all [countries] had to make the same effort at the same time' and accept the same burden (Kakebeeke, 1997). In the European acid rain talks, however, the widespread use and acceptance of this principle had little to do with the parties' conceptions of fairness. Several countries, among them the Soviet Union, Poland, and other CEE states, made clear that they considered the approach an unfair, inadequate and unscientific way of tackling the acid rain problem. It failed to reflect the real inequalities among countries in emission levels, contributions to transboundary ecological damage, and in economic resources (Sokolovsky, 1997; Zurek, 1997).

Why then did so many countries accept a sulphur protocol based on 'equal' obligations? How did the 30 per cent figure become such a significant standard for evaluating national abatement efforts? Importers of acid rain, notably Sweden, Finland, Norway and Canada, proposed equal percentage cuts as early as in the mid-1970s. When the LRTAP Convention came into force in 1983, the Scandinavian countries proposed the negotiation of a protocol calling for at least 30 per cent cuts in SO_2 emissions. The 30 per cent figure was introduced on a trial basis, '... to start the ball rolling towards a target, which hopefully could be defined and defended on scientific grounds later on' (Björkbom, 1997c). In the Helsinki Protocol talks specifically, it was expected to facilitate substantial emission cuts at a time when pollution levels were alarmingly high and the Convention had yet to result in any actual reductions.

This figure was judged to entail the strongest possible measures which states would not find too demanding economically or otherwise, and which they therefore could support. For example, existing abatement technology in a number of key countries was estimated to make a 30 per cent reduction feasible (Klaassen, 1996). The clarity of the concept and application of uniform obligations were also significant advantages, given existing scientific uncertainties and the tense Cold War climate. These calculations proved their value with the creation of the 30 per cent Club in 1984. The normative pressure which the Club and the 30 per cent norm could exercise on reluctant states secured a rapid growth in its membership.

The high degree of scientific uncertainty at the time also explains the broad acceptance of uniform obligations and equal percentage cuts in the Helsinki Protocol talks. Very little was known about critical loads, the relative contribution of a given country's emissions to acid deposition in other states, and the depth of emission cuts which would be required (and from whom and by when) to reach particular environmental goals. While also exploiting this insufficient knowledge as an excuse for inaction, the USA and the UK were thus right to claim in the negotiations that the principle of uniform cuts and a 30 per cent reduction lacked scientific justification and that the environmental benefits of undertaking the costly measures were unclear. However, an agreement based on differentiated obligations (larger cuts and burdens for some states, and lighter or no burdens for others) would have called even more for a precise and solid justification, probably involving scientific evidence which was not readily available (Churchill, 1997). Uniform reductions thus emerged once again as the politically most realistic and, under the circumstances, reasonable approach to the majority of participating countries. It was a means to secure a common basis for action without the need for prolonged discussion of science or past abatement efforts.

The East-West political tensions were present throughout the talks leading to the Helsinki Protocol. Mutual mistrust and suspicion were expressed in East European countries not making data on their emissions available when this could disclose information about sensitive activities, and in the West not accepting some statistics released by the Eastern bloc (McCormick, 1989). The politicized climate helps to explain the positions and behaviour of many parties, and the narrow scope for discussing arguments about fairness and environmentally-based approaches seriously in the negotiations. Cold War pressures, particularly from the USSR, certainly influenced many East European countries to sign the Helsinki Protocol. These states may in fact never have intended to implement it, and may in any event not have been able to do so in the absence of the economic recession which later occurred (Kakebeeke, 1997). In sum, the talks took place in a competitive environment which favoured a relatively simple approach such as uniform reductions to ensure some progress.

The political and economic interests of countries influenced the Helsinki Protocol talks significantly. While cost-benefit calculations led most to accept 30 per cent reductions, they also caused a few states to refuse to sign the protocol. The USA had under its 1970 Clean Air Act already committed itself to SO_2 emission cuts and was not prepared to move further (Nitze, 1997; Park, 1987). Moreover, it was far more engaged in the dispute over air pollution with Canada and may not have signed the Protocol even if it had considered the terms fair. The UK, an exporter of acid rain with relatively little to gain from the protocol, was also reluctant to commit itself to new measures for domestic reasons. At the time it was considering privatizing the electricity sector, and the country's future energy requirements were uncertain (Waldgrave, 1985). By contrast, among victims such as the Scandinavian countries and the FRG, domestic pressures for effective action were strong and influential. Apart from the promise of a healthier environment, Sweden and the FRG were keen to develop a lucrative export industry of clean technology. These economic interests stood in sharp contrast to those of CEE countries, which depended on imported technology to meet new emission reduction requirements. In sum, however, most states saw the protocol as either compatible with their existing national abatement plans or as well within their capacity to honour (Björkbom, 1997b).

These political, scientific and tactical considerations explain how the principle of equal percentage cuts came to influence an important international negotiation, all while ignoring and in some cases violating certain conceptions of fairness. Many countries easily met and outperformed their Helsinki Protocol obligations because of already existing national abatement plans. Some analysts argue that the SO_2 emission cuts achieved from 1985 and onwards would have occurred even without this international agreement. However, it is clear that the protocol put legal constraints on the future emission levels of signatory states, strengthened the LRTAP Convention considerably, and stimulated continued negotiations on further air pollution regulation. Experience would soon vindicate the proposition that '... once the first step in a regulated and managed process of multilateral co-operation is taken, the inner logic of the need to go further tends to assert itself inexorably' (Chossudovsky, 1988).

The 30 per cent reduction standard succeeded in maintaining momentum in the talks and in facilitating agreement by virtue of its simplicity. But in due course the drawbacks of simplicity became apparent with respect to fairness, environmental effectiveness and economic efficiency. There are in fact no objective criteria for selecting a required percentage reduction, a reference year (on basis of which cuts or ceilings will be calculated), or a target year (by which the requirements must be achieved) (Haigh, 1989). Any such percentages, years and ceilings are bound to be arbitrary, notably in how past reductions and present emission levels are treated.

More generally, the equal percentage approach cannot recognize differences in responsibility for the acid rain problem, in resources available to reduce it, and in gains to be had from abatement measures. The actual distribution of the collective costs and benefits resulting from reducing national emission levels by an identical percentage will therefore be very unequal across countries. Many heavily polluting states required to undertake the greatest cuts in real terms are least able to afford abatement strategies.[17] In addition, they often prioritize other more imminent needs. Such factors reduce the number of states willing to accept agreements based on uniform obligations. This approach also ignores differences in the sensitivity of various ecosystems, and targets the total level of national emissions rather than transboundary emissions. It does not distribute reduction requirements among countries in such a way as to attack the pollution problem most effectively on a regional scale.

Negotiators learnt from these early experiences, and used more sophisticated formulas in producing the next generation of protocols on acid rain (Jagusiewicz, 1997a). The question became not whether but how to take account of the circumstances of countries so as to bolster their ability and will to comply with international regulations. This new approach thus recognized the fairness issues which had not been resolved in the 1985 Protocol, and their importance to the effectiveness of acid rain agreements. It surfaced in the talks leading to the 1988 Sofia Protocol on NOx emissions. A Working Group on NOx was charged in November 1986 with drafting a new protocol within a year's time. In fact, the arduous negotiations came to last for two more years. Unlike the Helsinki experience they sought to strike a compromise between conflicting positions on fair and acceptable abatement strategies, particularly regarding whether requirements should take account of countries' past emission reductions or their technological and financial resources. High-level negotiators describe this process as 'horse-trading' and 'incremental concession-making' so typical of international bargaining (Kakebeeke, 1997; Nitze, 1997). The NOx Protocol adopted in October 1988 in Sofia, Bulgaria, required parties to reduce their annual national levels of NOx emissions or transboundary fluxes so that these, by end of 1994, would not exceed their levels in 1987 or any previous selected year. In case a country chose a year prior to 1987 as its baseline year, as the USA did to receive credit for its earlier abatement efforts, the annual national emission levels between 1987 and 1996 should on average not exceed the 1987 level. Parties were also required to control emissions from major stationary sources and new mobile sources.

The Sofia experience is distinct in marking a turn towards differentiating obligations. The NOx Protocol's flexibility regarding choice of baseline year already allowed for some differentiation and thereby bolstered its fairness in the eyes of certain parties. It also ruled that future negotiations should establish new targets for combating air pollution based on 'critical loads' and BAT. The first-mentioned criterion allocates abatement obligations in relation to the vulnerability of each country's ecosystem(s) to acid deposition, to maximize their environmental impact and value on a regional scale. It was the first time that this scientific criterion was incorporated into an international agreement, and reflected the reality that uniform reductions had become viewed as ineffective and unfair. Two additional principles were adopted in subsequent discussions within the ECE as the basis for new protocols on SO_2 and NOx: the relative costs of reducing emissions in different countries, and the relative contribution of a country's emissions to acid deposition in other countries ('source-receptor relationships').[18] In 1991 21 parties signed the Geneva Protocol concerning the Control of Emissions of Volatile Organic Compounds or their Transboundary Fluxes. Like the Sofia Protocol, it allowed for a measure of differentiated obligations by permitting countries to choose among three alternative targets and presented itself as an initial step towards later regulations based on critical loads.[19]

Negotiating a Second Sulphur Protocol

The 1985 Helsinki Protocol and its shortcomings triggered in due course renewed talks on the reduction of SO_2 emissions. It stipulated no further action after the achievement of the 30 per cent emission cuts by 1993, and despite these measures undertaken European emission levels remained too high to avoid environmental damage. In 1991 the Executive Body asked the Working Group on Abatement Strategies to formulate provisions for a new sulphur protocol, based on a scientifically sound and politically fair approach.

Specialized working groups and task forces had by then done extensive preparatory work in two important areas: the use of the criterion of critical loads in the formal negotiations, and the possible inclusion of a 'burden-sharing' scheme in the new protocol. It was agreed that a second sulphur protocol should be based on the use and recommendations of scientific models, notably the Regional Acidification Information and Simulation (RAINS) model developed at the International Institute for Applied Systems Analysis in Austria. The overwhelming view among parties was that this model, incorporating the critical loads criterion, would be less arbitrary in requiring emission cuts based on empirical knowledge about environmental harm (Kakebeeke, 1997; Williams, 1997).

It was recognized that poor states would have to undertake some of the greatest abatement measures. This is not only because they are among the worst polluters. The emphasis on cost-effectiveness in the RAINS model requires reduction measures to be taken where they are the cheapest, namely in predominantly poor countries in the UN-ECE region. As a result some CEE countries would have to spend up to 5 per cent of their GNP on abatement costs without generally making any comparable gains, environmental or other, on a national scale.[20] Concerns about reducing this seemingly unfair impact and maximizing participation in new abatement plans induced discussions about possible 'cost-sharing' schemes. The Dutch first raised the idea in 1989 on behalf of the poorer European countries. They became a strong supporter of cost-sharing, along with Russia and Poland (Klaassen, 1997). The UN-ECE Task Force on Economic Aspects of Abatement Strategies then studied various cost-sharing mechanisms including an acidification fund, a tradable emission permits system, and joint implementation of emission cuts by two or more countries. Much time was spent considering different principles for allocating financial support which a cost-sharing fund might use, and institutional requirements to operate it. Under one proposal countries would contribute to or receive monies from a fund based on GDP, GDP per capita, national abatement costs, and/or relative gains from participation in the venture.[21] The Task Force established that the relevant basis for any allocation rule was incremental cost; that is, the amount by which a country's cost of achieving multilateral targets exceeded the cost of its national abatement plans.[22]

However, in the substantive negotiations which began within the Working Group on Strategies in August 1991, there was hardly any discussion of cost-sharing schemes other than joint implementation of emission cuts. The Chair steered the talks away from the matter, convinced that any East European insistence on direct financial or technological compensation would result in confrontation with Western states and make a new protocol impossible. West European governments accepted that some burden-sharing was necessary, but argued that existing voluntary aid channels and bilateral agreements should be used rather than a formal obligatory scheme (Björkbom, 1997b). One stated reason was that CEE abatement costs could be smaller than the estimates of the RAINS model (Keiser, 1997).

The official negotiations developed in two overlapping phases. The first consisted of discussions on collective environmental goals for the ECE region as a whole that a new protocol should promote or achieve, based on the RAINS model criteria (e.g., critical loads, source-receptor relationships and relative abatement costs). The second stage involved bargaining over the different SO_2 emission cuts and deadlines required of individual countries to meet these regional objectives, taking into account also technological capacities, economic costs, equity concerns and social factors not included in the RAINS model. At the outset, the RAINS and other computer models were used to generate information about different scenarios according to the desired level of environmental protection and financial cost. Parties recognized that the critical loads concept would be used only as a guideline, and that the actual achievement of critical loads was a long-term objective. They agreed that, in a second stage, they had to negotiate 'target loads' which also account for other factors. It was accepted that critical loads cannot be achieved at present, even if BAT was used (Wuester, 1997c). A level of acid deposition causing no damage to any part of Europe's ecosystems would moreover require prohibitive financial expenditures, which would fall unevenly on states in the absence of a cost-sharing scheme.

The actual negotiations on a second sulphur protocol therefore came to focus, firstly, on establishing an acceptable degree of 'gap closure' between the critical loads level and existing rates of sulphur deposition. It was agreed that critical loads would be calculated to protect all but the most vulnerable 5 per cent of Europe's ecosystems. This measurement of critical loads was seen as an inevitable compromise, given that protection of the most sensitive 5 per cent of the ecosystems would entail exceptionally high costs (Levy, 1995).[23] In the talks during 1993, most parties felt that new emission targets should reduce by 60 per cent the gap between critical loads (calculated to protect 95 per cent of the ecosystems) and the 1990 emission levels. In early 1994, as various states started to object to the reduction requirements or deadlines they had been allocated, the collective goal shifted to a 50 per cent gap closure. Agreement was eventually reached on the goal of a 60 per cent gap closure and incorporated into the new protocol.[24]

The most protracted talks concerned what specific SO_2 emission cuts and deadlines would be required of individual states, to reach the target gap closure at the regional level. Indeed, disagreement over reductions and deadlines for implementation meant that the new protocol could not be completed by late 1993 as originally intended. Sweden, Germany, the Netherlands and Austria favoured high reduction targets with early deadlines. By contrast, Southern European countries (Greece, Italy, Spain, Portugal) and Ireland, which have no significant problem with acid rain, were concerned about the costs of abatement. Also preoccupied with economic considerations but much affected by acid deposition, the CEE countries were willing to support reductions. The UK insisted on a later deadline for itself (the year 2010 instead of 2005 or 2000). The British delegation argued that its abatement measures would otherwise be too costly and even wasteful, in requiring new pollution control technology on plants scheduled to be closed in due course (Murlis, 1995). The USA and Canada occupied an ambiguous position in the talks. They fell outside the geographic scope and mandate of regional models such as RAINS. Furthermore, while supporting sulphur emission controls in principle, they were already bound by their own bilateral acid rain agreement and hesitant to accept further commitments.[25]

There was a consensus in the first part of 1993 that Western countries should reach their reduction targets to bring about a 60 per cent gap closure by 2000, while East European states would have until 2005 to do so. However, in August 1993 it became clear that the proposed measures of all states would not achieve the 60 per cent gap closure. A review of the suggested national emission cuts followed. In the next month several countries objected to the requirements and deadlines which had been allocated to them. A group of countries seeking lower targets (the UK, Belgium, Denmark, France, Ireland, Spain) confronted a coalition of other states advocating higher targets (e.g. Sweden, Norway, Germany, the Netherlands, Austria). Eventually ten states agreed to measures already set out in their domestic abatement plans, nine states committed themselves to greater emission cuts than demanded by their domestic plans, and two (Portugal and Greece) would do less than they had originally foreseen (Klaassen, 1996). Disappointed by the outcome, Executive Body Chairman Jan Thompson noted at a session in December 1993 that a 60 per cent gap closure was unlikely to be met before 2015.

Also debated was the possible inclusion in the protocol of a provision for 'joint implementation' (JI) of abatement obligations. Although possible to view as a form of cost-sharing, JI was discussed in the talks to improve cost-effectiveness on a regional scale. The agreed emission ceilings had already been calculated based on cost-effectiveness, using the RAINS model. The main role for JI would therefore be to enhance the economic efficiency of reduction allocations among countries in case the RAINS estimates were not optimal, or new technologies shifted cost advantages (Wuester, 1997e). JI would allow parties to reach their own targets by paying for emission cuts in another country with lower abatement costs. Particularly states which have implemented substantial controls in the past may find that they could reduce emissions to the same extent at much lower cost in countries with few abatement measures already in place (e.g., in the CEE). However, the idea raised problems concerning environmental effectiveness and fairness which became a focus of the talks. Firstly, for Europe as a whole, JI deals could undermine the effectiveness of emission cuts. A change in the location of acid rain emission reductions as a result of JI bargains would affect the location of their environmental impact, and the degree of their impact due to the varying sensitivities of different ecosystems. The range of factors harmed by acid rain also make it technically difficult to compare the effects of sulphur emissions and emissions cuts from different sources (Bailey et al., 1996). Secondly, when two parties with different abatement costs are allowed to implement their obligations jointly to their mutual benefit, it may have negative environmental effects on third parties.

As a result, disagreement emerged in the negotiations over whether and on what conditions JI schemes should be permitted. Dependent on oil for its energy needs, Norway foresaw difficulties to fulfil its obligations under a new sulphur protocol without JI. By use of such a provision, the government could avoid taxing the oil industry and maintain its abundant oil supply. The majority of countries, by contrast, were critical. The Netherlands strongly opposed JI, arguing that the RAINS model had already optimized cost-effectiveness. Germany held that it conflicted with the BAT concept that states should do all they can technologically to cut emissions, and almost blocked the inclusion of a JI provision in the protocol (Sliggers, 1997). France insisted on strict conditions. For example, JI could be restricted to neighbouring countries to prevent major changes in the location and impact of emission cuts. The parties eventually decided that the issue required more work before a detailed agreement could be reached. This strategy secured Norway's signature.

The Protocol on Further Reduction of Sulfur Emissions, replacing the 1985 Helsinki Protocol, was adopted in Oslo in June 1994 and signed by 28 parties. The USA was not one among these, viewing the critical loads criterion as being in conflict with its 1990 Clean Air Act.[26] Nonetheless, the new protocol did nonetheless bring several new countries into the process of multilateral abatement. It aims to reduce the gap between critical loads and the 1980 levels of SO_2 emissions by 60 per cent, using three target years (2000, 2005 and 2010). This is designed as a first step towards reaching critical loads. The individual emission cuts required vary enormously. Wealthier states must reduce their 1980 emission levels by between 74 per cent and 83 per cent by the year 2000 (the UK by 50 per cent in 2000 and by 80 per cent in 2010). Poor states may implement smaller reductions and also take more time. Hungary, Bulgaria, Croatia and the Russian Federation are expected to cut their emissions by between 22 per cent and 60 per cent by 2010.[27] The national targets agreed in some cases did not follow the 60 per cent gap closure scenarios. The protocol also contains requirements with respect to emission limits for major power plants, the sulphur content of gas oil, the exchange of technology and the use of BAT. It states furthermore that reduction requirements may be implemented jointly, with the agreement of the parties to the protocol and in accordance with rules and conditions which the Executive Body will adopt. Another novelty is the creation of a relatively strong implementation regime. There are no provisions for cost-sharing. Poor countries may receive loans and grants through regular European and international aid channels, and through bilateral agreements on technology or financial transfers.

After the signing of the protocol, work was undertaken to further define the concept and possible consequences of joint implementation. It focused on the development of a scheme which would avoid erosion of environmental effectiveness (critical loads) and negative effects on third parties, and on ways of processing proposals for JI deals from individual countries. In 1996 government delegates accepted a set of JI provisions which were submitted to the Executive Body.[28] The Task Force on Economic Aspects of Abatement Strategies also continued work on possible cost-sharing mechanisms after the adoption of the protocol. But since 1997 the issue is no longer part of its mandate, arguably because its proposals were not 'practical' enough to settle a question which is as political as it is technical and economic (Björkbom, 1998). The process of ratifying the Oslo Protocol has moreover been very slow, especially among the CEE countries. By the end of 1997, 11 signatory parties had proceeded with ratification.[29] The 16 ratifications needed for the protocol to enter into force are expected in 1998. Nonetheless, it represents a new breed of international environmental agreement. It has broken new ground by establishing emission targets based on critical loads, emphasizing the importance of equitable distribution of abatement costs, and by introducing relatively strong compliance provisions. It now serves as a model in negotiations aimed at producing new protocols.

Searching for Greater Effectiveness and Fairness

The political context surrounding the drafting of the second Sulfur Protocol was dramatically different from that of previous talks. The end of the Cold War, the improvement in East-West relations, and the greater scientific knowledge now available allowed the negotiations to become more 'problem-solving' in nature than had hitherto been the case. Although the economic decline and transition process in East Europe raised sensitive issues of burden-sharing and financial help, the Western and CEE countries cooperated well in moving the process of air pollution abatement forward. Former East bloc countries were eager to integrate into the rest of Europe. The fact that these states sought to use their participation in environmental negotiations to gain accession to the European Union was an important factor making the 1994 Oslo Protocol possible (Björkbom, 1997b).

This new context also permitted sharper focus on the issues at hand, and left more scope for considerations of justice and fairness to play a role. High-level negotiators point out that conceptions of justice and fairness were at the heart of the process and more important in the negotiation of the 1994 Protocol than had previously been the case (Kakebeeke, 1997). These conceptions, in part conflicting, concerned the use of the RAINS model, burden-sharing, differentiation of obligations based on economic ability, and joint implementation of emission cuts. In all areas except burden-sharing, they influenced the talks and the outcome significantly.

The parties held that the RAINS model would improve the fairness, scientific basis and effectiveness of the new protocol. Allocating emission cuts based on criteria such as what the environment can endure, and countries' relative contributions to ecological harm and abatement costs, was regarded as far less arbitrary than earlier approaches (Zurek, 1997; Williams, 1997). The effects-based approach using RAINS naturally tends to require greater reductions of heavily polluting states, save states with high abatement costs from having to undertake extensive measures, and reward control measures undertaken previously. It also yields long-lasting requirements rather than time-limited uniform emission limits. While using them primarily on scientific grounds, the parties thus believed that the critical loads concept and the RAINS model also incorporated important principles of fairness.

In differentiating obligations based on scientific and economic efficiency criteria, the RAINS model simultaneously raised another question. In practice it places a heavy burden on poor polluting states with relatively little to gain from acid rain abatement. This situation prompted the debate on the burden sharing issue which, according to the Secretary to the Working Group on Strategies, raised the most essential issues of justice and fairness in the process leading to the 1994 Protocol (Wuester, 1997e). The Netherlands held that a form of cost-sharing or financial aid to help poor states required to make large cuts in SO_2 emissions was a matter of fairness as well as necessity. Although contradicting the generally accepted 'polluter pays' principle, the argument was that assistance was justified when countries were unable to meet their obligation to pay themselves.[30] This would help to ensure their participation in new ambitious abatement plans to the benefit of all. But many Western countries, which would be the financial donors, opposed the idea: They held that they had no duty to finance cuts in acid deposition which originates within CEE countries. The fact that a formal cost-sharing scheme was never discussed seriously in the formal talks or included in the protocol reflects, in yet other eyes, a marginalization of poor countries in the negotiation process (Levy, 1995).

East European countries, especially Russia, asked for Western financial and technological aid with abatement and presented it clearly as a matter of justice and fairness. But they never insisted on the adoption of a formal burden-sharing scheme, nor attempted to link their cooperation to receiving aid. Although faced with difficult economic and political conditions at home and with costly requirements under a new protocol, they were accommodating on the issue. Their eagerness to assert environmental responsibility and financial independence in efforts to gain entry into the EU, and a realization that most Western countries would never accept formal cost-sharing, probably explain this behaviour (Sprinz, 1997). There were also unclarity about the benefits of cost-sharing for one sole pollutant, and technical difficulties with designing a viable scheme.

The abandonment of the idea of formal cost-sharing paved the way for another conception of justice to influence the negotiations: that of differentiating obligations with a view to economic ability rather than the RAINS criteria alone. The parties agreed to this principle early on, exactly because they considered it to be essential for fairness (Keiser, 1997). Later deadlines for fulfilling reduction obligations and, in some cases, lower targets were granted to CEE countries in transition and other poorer states. Only when a few well-to-do countries such as the UK, France and Belgium requested favourable 'differentiation' for themselves to save costs did a debate occur. Although compromising the RAINS recommendations, this approach was deemed to be a more feasible way to compensate for inequalities in resources and abatement costs than formal burden-sharing. It could be seen as an informal cost-sharing device which struck a balance between several conflicting principles which had arisen in the talks, including 'no harm', polluter-pays, formal burden-sharing based on economic ability and need, and those underlying the RAINS model. A formal cost-sharing mechanism may have reduced the need to renegotiate and relax the original targets and deadlines. Existing aid channels may not be as effective, as they tie much financial help to conditions of the donor agencies or countries. However, the chair of the talks argues that the CEE countries' 'flexibility' on the issue of formal burden-sharing made the successful conclusion of the 1994 Protocol possible.

The reasons for delays in ratifying and implementing the protocol are unclear. Russia and Bulgaria have pointed to their desperate economic situations and high abatement costs, but otherwise few parties have provided explanations. The 1994 Protocol, compared to previous ones, requires more demanding measures of many countries than they had previously planned, including changes in energy policies. More time is therefore required to adapt domestic policies to the new commitments. Expert assessments vary as to whether the absence of a formal cost-sharing scheme will affect the compliance by CEE countries. Several negotiators involved, including those from the Czech Republic and Poland, argue that economic factors will not be decisive (Jilek and Sochor, 1997; Zurek, 1997). Other observers hold that the fairness issues relating to burden-sharing were never truly resolved in the drafting of the new protocol and that this is likely to reduce its effectiveness. It may explain why so few CEE countries have ratified it to date (Wuester, 1997d; Sokolovksy, 1997). Questions as to whether the protocol's implementation regime will be effective certainly stems from doubts about the ability of CEE states to meet their obligations. A formal cost-sharing scheme linked to the protocol might have facilitated ratification in some cases.

Ethical considerations played a key role in the talks over joint implementation. The domestic interests of various countries first pulled the matter in different directions, but government delegates eventually agreed in 1996 on important principles of procedural and substantial justice in settling the issue.[31] While the text of the protocol is brief on the topic, the rules for JI eventually adopted by the Executive Body will certainly incorporate the principles of no harm to third parties and strong protection of third party interests, and critical loads (Wuester, 1997e). The drawback is that these restrictions will limit the chances for improving the cost-effectiveness of emission cuts and may encourage separate implementation instead.

There are several similarities between the talks leading to the 1994 Protocol and previous acid rain negotiations. The domestic politics and perceived self-interests of many countries influenced their bargaining positions and alignments, including on controversial issues such as the depth of emission cuts, formal cost-sharing and joint implementation. Political 'pragmatism' and practical necessity were influential if not decisive factors when parties agreed to act upon particular conceptions of justice or fairness (such as granting later deadlines and lower emission targets to economically weak countries), and when they neglected others (such as formal cost-sharing and the polluter-pays principle). Several, partly conflicting conceptions of justice and fairness were nonetheless influential. These conceptions help to explain why the RAINS recommendations had to be renegotiated and why the second Sulfur Protocol could not simply endorse environmentally or economically 'optimal' abatement strategies. The 1994 Protocol is the first to call for an improvement in calculations of internationally optimized allocations of emission cuts, taking into account an equitable distribution of abatement costs (Article 6).

Looking to the Future

The question 'What would be a just and fair solution?' has not primarily driven the acid rain talks. The over-arching concern has been to improve European environmental conditions, at an acceptable cost to the region as a whole and to individual parties. As in other international negotiations, the principal factors driving the behaviour of participating states have been perceived national interests (economic and other) and domestic considerations (e.g., energy and transportation policy, damage from acid deposition, access to clean technology). Such self-interests and individual circumstances have in turn influenced what countries, for both genuine and tactical reasons, have taken and argued to be just and fair, and what ethical conceptions they have acted upon. While the parties have invoked principles serving their own interests in the talks, their arguments have at the same time often been seen as legitimate from a more impartial viewpoint. Moreover, the goal of improving environmental protection at acceptable cost has required countries to be responsive to ethical issues and conceptions other than their own.

The European acid rain case illustrates well that the engine running international negotiations does not consist solely of the promotion of individual interests and the maximization of individual gains in a narrow sense. Firstly, the principle of 'no harm' has provided the foundation for negotiations over transboundary air pollution from the outset. Secondly, the shared concern about protecting Europe's ecosystems has raised influential questions concerning the allocation of the benefits and financial burdens of acid rain abatement. In response, as the previous discussion shows, governments have modified their positions in order to accommodate certain ethical issues. Clearly, pragmatic considerations of how to move the negotiations to a successful outcome often determined whether a particular issue or conception of justice was taken seriously. For example, it is doubtful that the 1994 Protocol could ever have materialized without resort to the principle of differentiated obligations. But there are also examples of arguments about justice or fairness being ignored at the price of losing important signatures and eroding effectiveness (as in the talks leading to the 1985 Helsinki Protocol), and of ethical issues influencing the negotiations because of their perceived moral weight (as in the talks on rules for joint implementation of abatement obligations).

Shared norms, such as those of 'no harm' and differentiated obligations based on economic and ecological considerations, have facilitated the process of achieving new collective abatement measures. Opposing notions of justice and fairness have, however, been as common and caused arduous episodes in the European acid rain talks. This does not merely reflect countries' different interests, which undoubtedly inform their choice of principle. It is also an expression of the fact that many negotiating situations are plagued by moral ambiguity. There are frequently several conflicting principles recognized as important in providing guidelines for a solution; in this case, those of 'no harm', polluter-pays and critical loads versus burden-sharing and differentiated obligations based on economic ability. The effects-based approach using RAINS illustrates well that what may be fair and effective at one level can be seen as grossly unfair and unreasonable in other respects. As a result parties usually make competing ethical claims, all of which may merit consideration. On occasion agreement was still possible to reach despite (or, some would argue, because of) the subjugation of some notions of fairness. But what more often permitted a successful outcome was the recognition that conflicting ideas about justice or fairness had to be balanced and reconciled in order to win the acceptance of those concerned. Such 'horse-trading' is as much a reflection of the moral complexity surrounding international negotiations, as an exercise in political pragmatism.

The UN-ECE Working Group on Strategies is at present negotiating parallel new protocols on heavy metals, persistent organic pollutants (POPs), and NOx and related substances. This move away from discussing a single pollutant one at a time is likely to increase effectiveness by stressing that different pollutants affect each other and that more than one pollutant usually causes a particular environmental problem (Björkbom, 1997b). There is also a new effort to try to allow individual countries to choose which pollutant(s) would be most economical or otherwise acceptable for them to reduce, given their circumstances. This element of choice, if introduced, is likely to enhance the perceived fairness of abatement measures (Kakebeeke, 1997). It may, however, compromise effectiveness as reducing different pollutants have different environmental effects.

Disagreement remains over the significance of resource transfers to poor polluting countries. Some observers argue that burden-sharing is still an unresolved fairness issue which may undermine continued progress in the European acid rain talks (Keiser, 1997; Klaassen, 1997). Others hold that it is now largely irrelevant: Both West and East European countries will have to undertake costly emission cuts under new protocols, and the transition process of CEE economies has reached an advanced stage (Wuester, 1997b; Björkbom, 1998). Nonetheless, without cost-sharing, there appears to be no escape from the need to renegotiate and relax scientifically established emission targets and deadlines for poorer countries also in the future. What could avoid such an erosion of effectiveness is a burden-sharing mechanism, possibly based on costs to achieve collective targets above national abatement expenditures or 'incremental costs'.

Conceptions of justice and fairness became influential in the European acid rain negotiations over time, partly because of their perceived significance for effective abatement. These circumstances are likely to subsist: scientific evidence concerning the damaging effects of air pollution, monumental abatement costs coupled with inequalities in national resources and in gains to be had from emission cuts, contradictions between the nature of effective measures at the regional and national levels, and the early experiences of ignoring ethical issues by use of uniform obligations. In the search for agreement on new stricter (and even more expensive) measures and in the review of existing protocols, the demands both for fairness in the distribution of the cost burden and for cost-effectiveness will undoubtedly persist. Formulas balancing environmental, economic and technological considerations with ethical concerns will be essential. In the future battle against air pollution in regions as diverse as Europe, North America and Southeast Asia, and indeed environmental degradation in other areas, two decades of acid rain negotiations under the UN-ECE have much to say and much to teach about the unavoidability of justice.

Notes

1 This chapter is based on a chapter in a forthcoming book by the same author, entitled *Just and Fair? International Negotiation Today.* It is a product of a research project, 'Improving the Effectiveness of International Negotiation: The Role of Justice and Fairness', funded by the United States Institute of Peace, Washington, DC (Grant Number USIP-109-96F). I am grateful to Ambassador Lars Björkbom for giving much valuable information and clarification and for commenting in detail on an earlier draft.

2 A considerable literature discusses the concept of 'environmental security'. See Tuchman Mathews, 1989; Ullman, 1983; The Report of the Commission on Global Governance, 1995; Homer-Dixon, 1994; Rowlands, 1991.

3 Analyses of the Rio Conference and the broader UNCED process can be found in Grubb et al., 1993 and Spector, Sjöstedt and Zartman, 1994. Susskind (1994) assesses the achievements and shortcomings of global environmental treaties both within and outside the UNCED process.

4 Negotiations over new or unallocated environmental resources which promise near-term benefits, such as those over the Law of the Sea and Antarctica, are increasingly rare. This and other obstacles in international environmental negotiations are discussed in Albin, 1991.

5 In this discussion the European acid rain negotiations refer to those conducted within the UN-ECE. Another important forum for such talks is the European Union (previously the European Community).

6 There have been disagreements over other matters. East European states did not recognize the European Community as a separate negotiating party when the acid rain talks first got started within the UN-ECE. More recently, some countries have argued that a fair process requires greater openness and transparency in the scientific modelling work supporting the negotiations. The data and values used to calculate optimal abatement strategies with integrated computer assessment models, such as the Regional Acidification Information and Simulation (RAINS) model discussed below, should be exposed to greater scrutiny (Williams, 1997). However, unlike climate change and several other environmental cases, such disputes over rules of procedures and parties have not marked the UN-ECE acid rain talks significantly.

7 'Critical loads' is a measurement of susceptibility to ecological damage from acid rain. It refers to deposition levels for sulphur as well as nitrogen below which significant harmful effects on specified sensitive elements of the environment (including forests, freshwater and fish) do not occur according to present knowledge.

8 'The State of Transboundary Air Pollution', 1996. It should be noted that air pollution is one of several probable causes of the observed damage to forests.

9 'Strategies and Policies for Air Pollution Abatement', 1995. American and European research has pointed to linkages between air pollution and human diseases and deaths. A major British study published in 1997 found that air pollution caused by road traffic fumes triggers

an increase in heart attacks.

Overviews of the problem and politics of European acid rain can be found in Park, 1987; Schneider, 1991; Alcamo, Shaw, and Hordijk, 1990; Boehmer-Christiansen and Skea, 1991; Carroll, 1988; Fraenkel, 1989.

10 Until late 1991, ad hoc working groups negotiated protocols under the LRTAP Convention. The Executive Body (EB) created in November 1991 a permanent negotiating body responsible to itself – the Working Group on Strategies. By decision of the EB, this working group is now in charge of negotiating and implementing new protocols.

11 Lars Björkbom, a key participant in all the talks under the LRTAP Convention to date, points out that the drafting of the protocols was perceived and presented as an extension of the LRTAP Convention. In fact, however, they are freestanding in the sense that the Convention does not foresee the negotiation of protocols or other specific instruments on acid rain abatement (Björkbom, 1997b).

The texts of the LRTAP Convention and the protocols can be found in *1979 Convention on Long-Range Transboundary Air Pollution and its Protocols*, 1996.

12 The LRTAP Convention states that acid rain abatement policies should take into account efforts already made at the national, as well as international, levels (Article 3).

13 'Positions and Strategies of the Different Contracting Parties to the Convention on Long-Range Transboundary Air Pollution Concerning the Reduction of Sulphur Emissions or their Transboundary Fluxes', 1985. Chossudovsky (1988) provides a more detailed account of the negotiations leading to the Helsinki Protocol than is possible to include in this paper.

14 The Helsinki Protocol of 8 July 1985, Article 3, in *1979 Convention on Long-Range Transboundary Air Pollution and its Protocols*, 1996.

15 Speech by William Waldgrave, UK Minister of State at the Department of Environment, to the German Foreign Policy Society, Hamburg, 1985, quoted in Lammers (1991).

16 'Strategies and Policies for Air Pollution Abatement', 1995, Tables 1 (p. 4) and 17 (p. 137).

17 Under national reduction plans of the early 1990s, Poland would undertake a 37 per cent reduction of its SO_2 emissions (3210 kton in 1990) at the cost of 0.31 per cent of its gross domestic product (GDP) annually, and Ukraine a 56 per cent reduction in its SO_2 emissions (2,782 kton in 1990) for 0.44 per cent of its GDP, by the year 2000 compared to 1980. By contrast, rich countries with very low SO_2 emission levels, such as Switzerland (62 kton in 1990) and Norway (54 kton in 1990), would be able to undertake cuts of about 50 per cent by 2000 compared to 1980, at the cost of 0.01 per cent and 0.09 per cent of their GDPs, respectively (Klaassen, Amann and Schöpp, 1992).

18 'The Critical Load Concept and the Role of Best Available Technology and Other Approaches', 1991.

19 The 1991 Geneva Protocol concerning the Control of Emissions of Volatile Organic Compounds or their Transboundary Fluxes, in *1979 Convention on Long-Range Transboundary Air Pollution and its Protocols*, 1996.

20 The 5 per cent figure comes from Sliggers (1997). In one scenario using the RAINS model, the objective was to reduce sulphur deposition to the 50 percentile critical sulphur deposition levels at a minimal cost to Europe as a whole. About 3 per cent of European ecosystems would then be exposed to deposition above the critical sulphur deposition values when taking account of current national reduction plans, compared to 18 per cent with the latter alone. Some countries would have to cut their emissions by over 90 per cent compared to levels in 1980, and would experience a multifold increase in abatement costs (e.g., an increase by 560 per cent for Poland). Other countries would have no or a negligible cost increase, or could even increase their emissions (Klaassen, Amann, and Schöpp, 1992;

Amann et al., 1992).

21 'Economic Principles for Allocating the Costs of Reducing Sulphur Emissions in Europe', 1989. See also Sliggers and Klaassen, 1992 and Bergman, Cesar, and Klaassen, 1992.

22 'Progress Report by the Chairman of the Task Force on Economic Aspects of Abatement Strategies', 1997.

23 According to calculations using the RAINS model, it would cost the same to protect the 96th through the 98th percentiles as the entire first 95 percentiles. The last 2 per cent cannot be protected at any cost (*Energy Economist*, November 1993, referred to in Levy, 1995).

24 *Acid News*, No. 4, October 1993; *Acid News*, No. 1, February 1994.

25 *Acid News*, No. 4, October 1993.

26 *Acid News*, No. 1, February 1994, p. 13. US policy is based on the human health-related effects of pollutants, while European policy emphasizes environmental effects.

27 Annex II to 'Protocol to the 1979 Convention on Long-Range Transboundary Air Pollution on Further Reduction of Sulphur Emissions and decision on the Structure and Functions of the Implementation Committee, as well as Procedures for its Review of Compliance', 1994.

28 'Joint Implementation under the Oslo Protocol', 1995. In late November 1996, the Executive Body approved an amendment to the 1994 Oslo Protocol regarding by-products [EB.AIR/WG.6/R.34]. It has, of course, no legal value until the protocol has entered into force.

29 The 11 countries are Canada, the Czech Republic, Denmark, France, Liechtenstein, Luxembourg, Netherlands, Norway, Spain, Sweden, and the UK. Five more countries – Austria, Belgium, Germany, Slovenia, and Switzerland – have indicated that they have almost completed their legal procedures for ratification (Wuester, 1997e).

30 The polluter-pays principle holds that those responsible for environmental damage should pay for that damage through compensation and clean-up efforts or the adoption of abatement measures ('Progress Report by the Chairman of the Task Force on Economic Aspects of Abatement Strategies', 1997). The OECD has noted an exception to this principle when the polluters concerned are economies in transition to a new form of organization, such as a market economy.

31 'Joint Implementation under the Oslo Protocol', 1995.

References

Personal Interviews

Lars Björkbom, Chair of the Working Group on Strategies (the Negotiating Committee) under the 1979 UN-ECE LRTAP Convention, previously Head of the Swedish delegation to the negotiations under this Convention, and participant in the negotiations of all the protocols under the Convention, on 10 July 1997 (1997a) and 15 July 1997 (1997b), and in writing on 10 November 1997 (1997d), 28 November 1997 (1997e) and 8 January 1998 (1998).

Robin Churchill, Reader in Law at Cardiff Law School, University of Wales, and co-leader of research project on 'Effectiveness of Legal Agreements to Protect Global Commons', on 21 July 1997.

Andrzej Jagusiewicz, Polish staff member of the UN-ECE, Geneva, and member of the Polish delegation to the negotiations leading to the 1988 Sofia Protocol, on 17 September 1997 (1997a) and 11 November 1997 (1997b).

Pavel Jilek, Deputy Director of the Air Protection Department, Ministry of the Environment, Czech Republic and Czech delegate to the Working Group on Strategies under the LRTAP Convention, and *Vladimir Sochor*, Czech delegate to the UN-ECE Task Force on Economic Aspects of Abatement Strategies (joint answers provided in writing), on 16 September 1997.

William Kakebeeke, Special Advisor, Ministry of the Environment, the Netherlands; member of the Dutch delegation (from 1977 until 1994) to the negotiations leading to the 1979 UN-ECE LRTAP Convention and the subsequent negotiations under this Convention; Vice Chairman of the negotiations leading to the 1988 Sofia Protocol, on 25 July 1997.

Volkert Keiser, Directorate-General for the Environment (Air and Energy Directorate, Air Quality and Acidification), the Netherlands; head of the Dutch delegation in the UN-ECE Executive Body and the Working Group on Abatement Strategies since 1992, on 1 October 1997 (in writing).

Ger Klaassen, staff member of the Transboundary Air Pollution Project at the International Institute for Applied Systems Analysis, Austria, during the negotiations of the 1994 Second Sulfur Protocol, and involved in the Group of Economic Experts in developing economic models for this protocol, on 22 July 1997. (His statements reflect his own personal opinion, and not the official position of the European Commission by whom he is now employed.)

Mark Levy, Visiting Lecturer, Williams College, Massachusetts, on 14 July 1997.

William Nitze, Assistant Administrator for the Office of International Activities, Environmental Protection Agency, Washington, DC; member (and at times Chair) of the US delegation to the negotiations under the 1979 UN-ECE LRTAP Convention from 1987 until 1990, on 18 July 1997.

Lars Nordberg, Deputy Director, Environment and Human Settlements Division, United Nations Economic Commission for Europe (the Secretariat), Geneva, on 18 June 1997.

Johan Sliggers, expert on air pollution in the Air and Energy Department, Ministry of Housing, Spatial Planning and Environment, The Hague, Netherlands and involved in the talks leading to the 1994 Second Sulfur Protocol and in the present negotiations over heavy metals, NOx and VOCs as a member of the Dutch delegation, on 1 August 1997.

Valentin Sokolovsky, Head of the Soviet/Russian delegation (from 1978 until 1991) to the negotiations leading to the 1979 UN-ECE LRTAP Convention and the subsequent negotiations under this Convention, on 27 August 1997 (in writing). Participated in the European acid rain talks in other capacities (e.g., as Head of the UN-ECE Working Group on Abatement Strategies from 1989 to 1991) and is since 1992 an adviser to the Minister of the Russian State Committee on the Protection of the Environment and Natural Resources.

Detlef Sprinz, Senior Fellow at the Potsdam Institute for Climate Impact Research, Germany and observer of the UN/ECE negotiations leading to the 1994 Second Sulfur Protocol, on 25 July 1997.

Janusz Zurek, Head of the Department of Environmental Policy, Institute of Environmental Protection, Warsaw, and member of the Polish delegation to the negotiations leading to the Helsinki, Sofia and Oslo (Second Sulfur) Protocols under the 1979 UN-ECE LRTAP Convention, on 8 October 1997 (in writing).

M. Williams, Member of the UK delegation to the negotiations under the 1979 UN-ECE LRTAP Convention since 1993, on 31 July 1997.

Henning Wuester, Secretary to the Working Group on Strategies under the 1979 UN-ECE LRTAP Convention (since the beginning of the negotiations of the 1994 Second Sulfur Protocol), United Nations Economic Commission for Europe, Geneva, on 24 June 1997 (1997a), 18 July 1997 (1997b), and in writing on 10 November 1997 (1997c), 11 December 1997 (1997d) and 12 December 1997 (1997e).

Primary Documents

1979 Convention on Long-Range Transboundary Air Pollution and its Protocols, Economic Commission for Europe, United Nations, Geneva, October 1996 [ECE/EB.AIR/50].

'Cost sharing for the abatement of acidification in Europe: The key to a protocol', draft paper prepared by J. Sliggers and G. Klaassen for the session of the UN/ECE Task Force on Economic Aspects of Abatement Strategies, Geneva, 3–4 December 1992.

'The critical load concept and the role of best available technology and other approaches', report of the Working Group on Abatement Strategies, September 1991, Economic Commission for Europe, United Nations, Geneva [EB.AIR/WG.5/R.24/Rev.1].

'The critical loads and levels approach and its application in preparation of the new Sulfur Protocol', report by the Bureau of the Working Group on Effects for a special session in Oslo, 13–14 June 1994. Executive Body for the Convention on Long-Range Transboundary Air Pollution, Economic Commission for Europe, United Nations, Geneva, 3 May 1994 [EB.AIR/R.85].

'Economic principles for allocating the costs of reducing sulphur emissions in Europe', report submitted by the delegation of the Netherlands for the fifth session of the Group of Economic Experts on Air Pollution, Executive Body for the Convention on Long-range Transboundary Air Pollution. Economic Commission for Europe, United Nations, Geneva, 26–28 June 1989 [EB.AIR/GE.2/R.26, 19 May 1989].

'International Strategies to Combat Air Pollution Reviewed by the Executive Body at its Third Session, Helsinki, 8–12 July', press release, 12 July 1985, Economic Commission for Europe, United Nations, Geneva [ECE/ENV/7].

'Joint Implementation under the Oslo Protocol', report by the Chairman of the open-ended group of experts, Working Group on Strategies (16th session, 19–23 February 1996), Economic Commission for Europe, United Nations, Geneva, 23 November 1995 [EB.AIR/WG.5/R.57].

'Positions and Strategies of the Different Contracting Parties to the Convention on Long-Range Transboundary Air Pollution Concerning the Reduction of Sulphur Emissions or their Transboundary Fluxes', Economic Commission for Europe, United Nations, Geneva, 6 August 1985 [ECE/EB. AIR/7].

'Progress Report by the Chairman of the Task Force (Prof. David Pearce) on Economic Aspects of Abatement Strategies' of 9 January 1997 to the Working Group on Strategies, section IV on 'burden sharing', Economic Commission for Europe, United Nations, Geneva [EB.AIR/WG.5/R.70].

'Protocol to the 1979 Convention on Long-range Transboundary Air Pollution concerning the control of emissions of nitrogen oxides or their transboundary fluxes', first revised edition, United Nations, New York and Geneva, May 1995 (ECE/EB.AIR/21/Rev.1).

'Protocol to the 1979 Convention on Long-Range Transboundary Air Pollution on Further Reduction of Sulphur Emissions and decision on the Structure and Functions of the Implementation Committee, as well as Procedures for its Review of Compliance', Economic Commission for Europe, United Nations, Geneva, 1994 [ECE/EB.AIR/40].

'Recommendations of the Council on Guiding Principles Concerning International Economic Aspects of Environmental Policies', Document C(72) 128, 6 June 1972, Organization for Economic Cooperation and Development, Paris, France.

Records of ECE Senior Advisers on Environmental and Water Problems, Working Party on Air Pollution Problems, 19th and 20th Sessions, 10 April 1990–22 May 1991, Economic Commission for Europe, United Nations, Geneva [ENVWA/WP.1/R.23&24+Add.1; 25-32].

'The State of Transboundary Air Pollution', report prepared within the framework of the Convention on Long-range Transboundary Air Pollution. Air Pollution Studies, No. 12, Economic Commission for Europe, United Nations, Geneva, 1996 [ECE/EB.AIR/47].

'Strategies and Policies for Air Pollution Abatement', 1994 major review prepared under the Convention on Long-range Transboundary Air Pollution, Economic Commission for Europe, United Nations, Geneva, July 1995 [ECE/EB.AIR/44].

'Strategies for reducing sulfur dioxide emissions in Europe based on critical sulfur deposition values', background paper prepared by G. Klaassen, G. Amann and W. Schöpp for the UN/ECE Task Force on Integrated Assessment Modelling, 30 November–2 December 1992 in Geneva, draft, November 1992, International Institute for Applied Systems Analysis, Laxenburg, Austria.

'Tackling Air Pollution from Lawnmowers to Jumbo Jets', ECE Press Release, 28 November 1996, by Lars Nordberg, Deputy Director, Environment and Human Settlements Division, Economic Commission for Europe, United Nations, Geneva.

Books and Articles

Acid News, No. 2, April 1993; No. 4, October 1993; No. 1, February 1994.

Albin, C. (1995) ' The Global Security Challenge to Negotiation: Towards the New Agenda' in C. Albin (ed.), *Negotiation and Global Security. New Approaches to Contemporary Issues,* special issue of *The American Behavioral Scientist*, May 1995.

Alcamo, J., Shaw, R. and Hordijk, L. (eds) (1990), *The RAINS Model of Acidification. Science and Strategies in Europe,* Kluwer Academic Publishers, Dordrecht, The Netherlands.

Amann, M. et al. (1992) 'Strategies for reducing sulfur dioxide emissions in Europe', background paper prepared for the UN/ECE Task Force on Integrated Assessment Modelling, 3–5 June 1992, Bilthoven, the Netherlands. Laxenburg, Austria: International Institute for Applied Systems Analysis, 27 July 1992.

Bailey, P., Gough, C. and Millock, K. (1996) 'Prospects for the Joint Implementation of Sulphur Emission Reductions in Europe', *Energy Policy*, Vol. 24, No. 6, pp. 507–16.

Bergman, L., Cesar, H. and Klaassen, G. (1992), 'Efficiency in transboundary pollution abatement: a scheme for sharing the costs of reducing sulphur emissions in Europe' in J.J. Krabbe and W.J.M. Heyman (eds), *National Income and Nature: externalities, growth and steady state*, Kluwer Academic Publishers, Dordrecht, Boston and London.

Björkbom, L. (1997c), 'Protection of natural ecosystems from transboundary air pollution in Europe', paper for SCOPE UK meeting on effective use of the sciences in sustainable land management at the Royal Society, 21 February 1997.

Boehmer-Christiansen, S. and Skea, J. (1991), *Acid politics: Environmental and Energy Policies in Britain and Germany*, Belhaven Press, London.

Carroll, J. (ed.) (1988), *International Environmental Diplomacy*, Cambridge University Press, Cambridge.

Chossudovsky, E. (1988), '*"East-West" Diplomacy for Environment in the United Nations: The High-Level Meeting within the Framework of the ECE on the Protection of the Environment, A Case Study,* United Nations Institute for Training and Research (UNITAR), New York.

Churchill, R.R., Kütting, G. and Warren, L.M. (1995), 'The 1994 UN ECE Sulphur Protocol', *Journal of Environmental Law*, Vol. 7, No. 2, pp. 169–97.

Clapp, J. (1994), 'Dumping on the Poor', Occasional Paper No. 5, Global Security Programme, University of Cambridge, Cambridge, August.

'Developments in the Law. International Environmental Law' (1991), *Harvard Law Review*, Vol. 104, pp. 1487–639.

Faure, G.O. and Rubin, J.Z. (1983), 'Organizing Concepts and Questions' in G. Sjöstedt (ed.), *International Environmental Negotiation*, Sage Publications, Newbury Park and London.

Fraenkel, A. (1989), 'The Convention on Long Range Transboundary Air Pollution: Meeting the Challenge of International Co-operation', *Harvard International Law Journal*, Vol. 30, pp. 447–77.

Grubb, M. et al. (1993), *The Earth Summit Agreements. A Guide and Assessment*, The Royal Institute of International Affairs and Earthscan Publications, London.

Haigh, N. (1989), 'New tools for European air pollution control', *International Environmental Affairs*, 1, pp. 26–37.

Homer-Dixon, T.F. (1994), 'Environmental Scarcities and Violent Conflict', *International Security*, Summer, pp. 5–40.

Hutton, J. and Halkos, G. (1995), 'Optimal Acid Rain Abatement Policy for Europe', *Energy Economics*, Vol. 17, No. 4, pp. 259–75.

Klaassen, G. (1996), *Acid Rain and Environmental Degradation: The economics of emission trading*, Edward Elgar Publishing, Cheltenham.

Klaassen, G., Amann, M. and Schöpp, W. (1992), 'Strategies for reducing sulfur dioxide emissions in Europe based on critical sulfur deposition values', background paper prepared for the UN-ECE Task Force on Integrated Assessment Modelling, 30 November–2 December, Geneva, Switzerland (draft, November 1992), International Institute for Applied Systems Analysis Laxenburg, Austria.

Lammers, J. (1991) 'The European Approach to Acid Rain' in D.B. Magraw (ed.), *International Law and Pollution*, University of Pennsylvania Press, Philadelphia.

Levy, M. (1993), 'European Acid Rain: The Power of Tote-Board Diplomacy' in P. Haas, R. Keohane and M. Levy (eds), *Institutions for the Earth: Sources of Effective International Environmental Protection*, MIT Press, Cambridge, Massachusetts.

Levy, M. (1995), 'International Co-operation to Combat Acid Rain', *Green Globe Yearbook*, 1995.

Mason, R. (1995), 'Joint Implementation and the Second Sulfur Protocol', *Review of European Community and International Environmental Law*, Vol. 4 (4), December, pp. 296–303.

McCormick, J. (1989), *Acid Earth. The Global Threat of Acid Pollution*, Earthscan Publications, London.

Murlis, J. (1995), 'Critical Loads: the Policy Background' in R.W. Battarbee (ed.), *Acid Rain and its Impact: The Critical Loads Debate*, Ensis Publishing, London.

Park, C. (1987) *Acid Rain. Rhetoric and Reality*, Methuen & Co., London and New York.

Report of the Commission on Global Governance (1995), *Our Global Neighbourhood*, Oxford University Press, Oxford.

Rosencranz, A. (1988), 'The Acid Rain Controversy in Europe and North America: a Political Analysis' in J.E. Carroll (ed.), *International Environmental Diplomacy*, Cambridge, Cambridge University Press.

Rowlands, I. (1991), 'The Security Challenges of Global Environmental Change', *Washington Quarterly*, Winter.

Schneider, T. (ed.) (1991), *Acidification Research: Evaluation and Policy Applications*, Proceedings of an International Conference, 14–18 October, Maastricht, The Netherlands.

Sliggers, J. and Klaassen, G. (1994), 'Cost sharing for the abatement of acidification in Europe: the missing link in the sulphur protocol', *European Environment*, Vol. 4, Part 1, pp. 5–11.

Spector, B., Sjöstedt, G. and Zartman, I.W. (1994), *Negotiating International Regimes. Lessons Learned from the United Nations Conference on Environment and Development (UNCED)*, Graham & Trotman Ltd, London.

Sprinz, D. and Vaahtoranta, T. (1994), 'The interest-based explanation of international environmental policy', *International Organization*, Vol. 48, No. 1, Winter, pp. 77–105.

Susskind, L. (1994), *Environmental Diplomacy. Negotiating More Effective Global Agreements*, Oxford University Press, Oxford and New York.

Sweet, J. (1993), 'Who's Afraid of Acid Rain?', *Energy Economist* (*Financial Times*), November, pp. 15–19.

Tuchman Mathews, J. (1989), 'Redefining Security', *Foreign Affairs*, Spring, pp. 162–77.

Ullman, R.H. (1995), 'Redefining Security', *International Affairs*, Summer, pp. 129–53.

Wuester, H. (1992) 'The Convention on Long-range Transboundary Air Pollution: its Achievements and its Potential' in T. Schneider (ed.), *Acidification Research: Evaluation and Policy Applications*, Proceedings of an International Conference, 14–18 October, Maastricht, Elsevier Science Publishers, The Netherlands, Amsterdam.

13 Restoring Justice in the Aftermath of Conflict: Bridging the Gap between Theory and Practice[1]

RAMA MANI

Political Considerations

Building a Just Peace: Why it Matters

From 1990 to 1995, five and a half million people lost their lives in a total of 93 wars involving 70 states (Smith, 1997, p. 13).[2] The majority of political conflicts today are internal, and occur predominantly in developing countries. The challenge faced in the poor and battered societies which succeed in emerging from internal conflict is that of consolidating incipient peace and avoiding a relapse into chaos and violence. Angola, Afghanistan and Cambodia are bitter reminders of the price of building peace on flimsy foundations.

A glance at recently-concluded conflicts points to the central role played by justice in the transition to peace. As expressed by Nobel Peace Prize laureate Rigoberta Menchu in the context of the Guatemalan peace agreement, 'Peace without justice is only a symbolic peace'.[3] Justice is both the clarion call to conflict and its first casualty: injustice, real or perceived, is often the cause of conflict and its inevitable consequence. Justice is also the primary requirement and demand of populations emerging from conflict in most cases. If people cannot have their faith in law and justice restored after the turmoil and brutalities of conflict, they will have little confidence in the peace process, which may falter as a consequence.

Each country emerging from conflict presents a *sui generis* situation, with its particular history, culture and development informing its post-conflict challenges. What post-conflict societies as dissimilar as Cambodia and Mozambique, or El Salvador and Rwanda, do have in common is that they are all engaged in the process of building peace between erstwhile enemies, and they are doing so, most often, at a time when the link between peace and justice – however tenuous previously – has been brutally severed by conflict.

This study provides a theoretical perspective, not case studies; however, its analysis is mindful of and pertinent to a number of developing countries which have emerged recently from conflict, including El Salvador, Guatemala, Haiti, Mozambique, Namibia, Rwanda, South Africa, and Cambodia.[4] Although theoretical in its orientation, this study is political in intention: faced with the difficulties besetting peacebuilders in their endeavours to address complex justice claims in the aftermath of conflict, it is the attempt of a political scientist to turn to legal and political philosophy for guidance, coherence and clarity in conceptualizing this task.

Post-Conflict Peacebuilding

The concept of peacebuilding owes its origin to Johann Galtung who drew the distinction between peacemaking, peacekeeping and peacebuilding – all three now commonplace terms in United Nations (UN) vocabulary and practice. For Galtung, peacebuilding followed peacemaking and peacekeeping and consisted in the practical implementation of peaceful social change through socioeconomic reconstruction and development (Galtung, 1976; see Ramsbotham, 1997, p. 3).

In its current guise, the concept was popularized by UN Secretary-General Boutros Boutros-Ghali, who described post-conflict peacebuilding as, 'actions to identify and support structures which will tend to strengthen and solidify peace in order to avoid a relapse into conflict' (Boutros-Ghali, 1992, p. 11). According to UN documents, the central objective of peacebuilding in the UN view is avoiding a relapse into conflict, and the preferred mechanism for achieving this aim is identifying the root causes of conflict and eliminating them through structural reform and development (Boutros-Ghali, 1994, esp. pp. 265–78; 1997, Part II).

Reflecting the distinction made in peace research between negative peace, that is, the mere cessation of hostilities, and positive peace, that is, the removal of structural and cultural roots of violence, scholars have identified two distinct but correlated objectives of peacebuilding. The first is the negative objective of avoiding a relapse into conflict, which is emphasized by the UN, and the second is the positive objective of consolidating peace by creating conditions conducive to reconciliation, reconstruction and recovery (Ramsbotham, 1997, pp. 5–6).[5] Scholars also imbue peacebuilding with interpersonal elements, such as changing conflictual attitudes, and view peacebuilding as the attempt to address the structural, cultural *and* relational roots underlying conflicts. Peacebuilding, then, is 'a comprehensive term that encompasses the full array of stages and approaches needed to transform conflict towards sustainable, peaceful relations and outcomes' (Lederach, 1994, p. 14, cited in Ramsbotham, 1997, p. 4). Oliver Ramsbotham (1997, pp. 9–10) emphasizes the three interlinked deficit areas which positive peacebuilding aims to address: political/constitutional incapacity; economic/social debilitation and psychosocial trauma.[6]

In practical terms, peacebuilding operations in the last decade in the full range of countries emerging from conflict have included an array of short and long-term tasks: supervising ceasefires; demobilizing, disarming and reintegrating combatants; monitoring human rights; establishing a new police force and military; holding elections, and supporting economic and institutional reconstruction.[7] The actors involved in peacebuilding include a large number of UN departments and agencies, particularly the Department for Political Affairs and the UN Development Programme; the World Bank and other international financial institutions; regional organizations; development banks, bilateral aid agencies, and international non-governmental organizations.

Both aspects of the twinned goals of peacebuilding, consolidating peace in the positive sense and avoiding a recurrence of conflict in the negative sense, underline the importance of addressing justice in the course of peacebuilding. Succinctly, if justice is not addressed, it will be difficult to consolidate peace, as the process will lack credibility and popular trust; if injustice continues to prevail, it may re-ignite conflict, as unmet grievances continue to fester. Recent studies of post-conflict peacebuilding by academics and 'practitioners'[8] corroborate the importance of addressing the issues of justice and restoring the justice system in the peacebuilding process (see, for example, Ramsbotham, 1997; Overseas Development Council, 1996, esp. pp. 7, 12–14; UN High Commissioner for Refugees and International Peace Academy, 1996, esp. pp. 34–39). What is first necessary is to clarify what specific claims justice makes on societies emerging from internal conflict.

The Scope of Post-Conflict Justice: Legal, Rectificatory and Distributive Dimensions

Recent events in South Africa, Bosnia and Rwanda have focused public attention on the question of the application of justice for crimes perpetrated during conflict. Although this issue is critically important, it represents only one dimension of the complex demands of justice that arise in the context of transition, particularly from internal conflict. The contention here is that an integrated and multidimensional analysis of justice claims is needed to better understand and respond to the challenge of building a just and lasting peace after conflict. Accordingly, three distinct but interdependent dimensions of justice are identified here which are usually pertinent and pressing in the aftermath of conflict: legal justice, rectificatory justice, and distributive justice.[9]

Legal justice, or *the rule of law* as it is referred to here often suffers during conflict: the entire justice system may be delegitimized (as in South Africa), debilitated (as in Haiti) or destroyed (as in Rwanda), and needs to be reformed or rebuilt. There are several compelling rationales for restoring the rule of law after conflict, both as an immediate priority and as a long-term goal. Restoring the rule of law is a first indication to combatants and a war-weary population of a return to order and stability. At a minimum, a rule of law regime assures citizens that their government is formally subject to the law, and not above it; it signals that all citizens, regardless of their affiliation and background, are equal before the law. By providing a forum for the nonviolent resolution of disputes through an impartial and independent judiciary, the rule of law is an essential element in preventing and deterring future conflict.[10]

Rectificatory justice refers to the ways in which societies deal with injustices committed during conflict, which typically include gross violations of human rights, war crimes and crimes against humanity, including genocide and apartheid.[11] Post-conflict and other transitional societies have adopted a variety of approaches in dealing with past abuses, including truth commissions, trials and prosecutions, compensation and symbolic gestures such as commemorations and memorials.[12] Although each society's approach necessarily varies according to its needs, capacities, culture, history, political realities and constraints, it is now commonly acknowledged that some official process of reckoning with past abuses is necessary to allow survivors, perpetrators and society at large to come to terms with the past and begin constructing a lasting peace.

There are at least three clear rationales – the psychosocial, the political and the legal – for addressing rectificatory justice after conflict. The psychosocial rationale emerges from the need for psychosocial healing on the part of survivors, perpetrators and society at large, to serve as the basis for societal reconciliation and the consolidation of peace. The political rationale revolves around the need to combat impunity, to deter future abuses, to establish the legitimacy and credibility of the new regime, to stabilize peace and to further democracy and the rule of law.[13]

The legal rationale operates in at least three ways. The first is state responsibility (Brownlie, 1990, pp. 432–76). Under international treaty and customary law, the responsibility of states to provide redress for the abuses and crimes typically committed during conflict is clearly established. Importantly, these responsibilities apply even when the offences were committed under a prior government, and even to states which are not themselves parties to the treaties, but are under their purview due to international customary law (Roht-Arriaza, 19 ; Orentlicher, 1995). The second emanates from the rights of victims to compensation and redress, which are specified in human rights covenants and other relevant treaties, and establish clear obligations on states (Van Boven, 1993, reproduced in Kritz, 1995, pp. 511–50; Lutz, 1995). Thirdly, international law and the specific treaties strictly circumscribe the mitigating circumstances under which derogations might be permissible, and rule out derogation entirely for certain fundamental rights.[14] Therefore, even in the constrained and tense aftermath of conflict, states are legally bound to respect their international obligations, and may not claim exemption.

Distributive justice is concerned here with how a society deals with the inequitable distribution of and access to resources and power that may have caused or exacerbated conflict. It effectively entails addressing the root causes of conflict, which often lie in real or perceived socioeconomic and/or political injustice. Peacebuilding definitions and rhetoric seem to emphasize this aspect. Nevertheless, perhaps with the exception of the Guatemalan peace agreements, the attention to distributive justice remains largely rhetorical, and little has been done in practice to address it through the sort of structural changes proposed in the definitions of peacebuilding above. The pressing rationale for addressing distributive justice is preventive and deterrent: identifying and eliminating – or at least alleviating – those root causes of conflict located in unequal distributions of resources and power could play an important role both in securing negative peace, by avoiding a return to violence by disenchanted groups, and in deepening positive peace, by laying the basis for a more just, equitable and peaceful society.

While they are not exhaustive of all the justice claims that might arise in these circumstances, the three themes identified here capture the essential demands of justice after conflict, although all three may not be equally salient in all cases. They correspond to the three areas of deficits in post-conflict societies referred to earlier, which peacebuilding aims to restore. Rebuilding the rule of law is an essential component of political/constitutional reconstruction; distributive justice is the *leitmotif* of socioeconomic programmes undertaken in post-conflict reconstruction; rectificatory justice is the central component in psychosocial rehabilitation. However, the dynamic linkages between the three dimensions have not been consciously recognized in existing literature or practice, and with the exception of rectificatory justice, they are not necessarily viewed as issues of justice.

Although distinct, these three dimensions of justice are usually interdependent and mutually reinforcing in the post-conflict context. Reestablishing the rule of law is necessary not simply for social order but also to restore rectificatory and distributive justice. Abuses cannot be rectified and resources cannot be redistributed unless the normative and institutional framework of a rule of law regime are in place, for example a constitution guaranteeing human rights and equal treatment, a police force to arrest violators and prisons to incarcerate them. Likewise, the process of restoring rectificatory and distributive justice tests and strengthens the principles and institutions of the rule of law, such as the equality of all citizens before the law, the guarantee of humane treatment to prisoners and the right to fair trial.

It is the interdependence and mutual reinforcement between the three dimensions of justice that make it desirable and perhaps even necessary to address all three simultaneously in the aftermath of conflict.[15] The time-frame for each dimension may differ: rectificatory justice is a relatively short-term order, and generally is undertaken shortly after the end of conflict; restoring the rule of law and instituting distributive justice measures are longer-term objectives, which ideally must be initiated immediately after conflict, but may not be achieved fully for a long time.

The process of redressing each dimension of justice will generate political dilemmas and encounter obstacles as it comes into conflict with the other exigencies of post-conflict reconstruction and peace building. A common dilemma faced is that between change and stability. There is a legitimate fear in many post-conflict societies that seeking to restore justice and the rule of law will unravel a fledgling peace by provoking retaliation from the *status quo ante*, as witnessed in several Latin American transitions in the 1980s. There is the fear that the pursuit of justice will undermine rather than further reconciliation, by reopening old wounds and animosities. A further dilemma is whether to apply universal standards and principles of international law, or to adopt a nationally-defined, culturally-specific approach. The examination of these practical difficulties falls outside the scope of this analysis, but they are mentioned to highlight the dilemmas involved in building a just peace, and to underline the necessity for philosophical consideration of the interlinked claims of justice and their tenuous relationship with peace in post-conflict societies.

Theoretical Considerations

The first section established why justice plays such a central role in the aftermath of conflict, and identified the three distinct but interrelated justice claims which typically arise in these circumstances. This section examines how theories of justice might facilitate the task of peacebuilders in post-conflict societies by addressing their concerns more directly in each of the three areas of justice delineated above.

The Rule of Law: Minimalist or Maximalist Conceptions?

'The rule of law' has been portrayed variously as a political ideal and a legal institution; as the centrepiece of any viable political system, and as inimical to democracy; as a current reality and a distant aspiration.[16] Its place in intellectual discourse can be traced back as far as Aristotle (1981), with his injunction that the rule of law was preferable to the rule of man. Despite its recent resurgence in academic debate and international practice, and its popularity with aid donors especially in post-communist and post-conflict states, confusion persists about its meaning and scope among scholars and practitioners alike. This conceptual confusion is the central problem in applying philosophical approaches and theories of the rule of law to the task of restoring legal justice and the rule of law in post-conflict societies.

The controversy is partly attributable to the dichotomy in legal philosophy between the traditions of positive law and natural law.[17] Legal positivists stress what the law is, rather than what it should be. For positivists it is the source and formal criteria rather than the content which is determinant, and if law fulfils established criteria of legality, even a bad law is still a law.[18] In sharp contrast, in a tradition going back to Thomas Aquinas' stipulation that 'a Law, properly speaking, regards first and foremost the order to the common good',[19] natural lawyers insist that 'what the law is depends in some way on what the law must be' (Dworkin, 1993, p. 239). Law, for naturalists, has a necessary correlation to morality.

This difference in legal opinion is reflected in two opposing conceptions of the rule of law, which might best be described as 'minimalist' and 'maximalist'.[20] Other scholars have noted similar distinctions: Dworkin (1987, pp. 9–32) distinguishes between the 'rule book' conception and the 'rights' conception which approximates the minimalist-maximalist differentiation made here,[21] while Shklar (1987, pp. 1–16) distinguishes between Aristotle's and Montesquieu's conceptions of the Rule of Law.[22]

The *minimalist* view divests the rule of law of any substantive moral content, and draws its definition from the historical origin and role of the concept. Whether traced back to the writings of Aristotle and Plato, or to the signing of the *Magna Carta*, the concept of the rule of law was devised as a means of protection from the arbitrariness of rule by man and from the abuse of power by the state. Its main purpose was 'to subject human conduct to rules, thereby affording predictability in legal relationships and in the interactions that occur within the frame of law' (Flathman, 1994, p. 303). One minimalist conception takes the rule of law to mean literally what it says, that people should obey the law and be ruled by it, and that law, therefore, should serve to guide the behaviour of people.[23] More typically, the rule of law in a minimalist perspective implies a government which is subject to and operates within the law, and which guarantees the protection of the individual from the state. The *Rechtstaat* (state of law) could be seen as one model of the minimalist view.[24] The minimalist view and its functions were well summarized by Hayek (1944, cited in Raz, 1979, p. 210):

> Stripped of all its technicalities this means that government in all its actions is bound by rules fixed and announced beforehand – rules which make it possible to foresee with fair certainty how the authority will use its coercive powers in given circumstances, and to plan one's individual affairs on the basis of that knowledge.

This certitude affords a certain degree of freedom to citizens if they stay within the bounds of established rules.[25]

> … A *predictable action* of the state, i.e. *its measurable interference, even if oppressive, is to be preferred to immeasurable intervention* (unpredictable, arbitrary action), *even if at one time benevolent*, as such immeasurable state of affairs creates insecurity (Neumann, 1986, p. 32: italics original).

As the minimalist view makes no reference to the substantive content of the rules but only to their form and procedure, the rule of law in this conception could be consistent with a wide variety of political systems besides liberal democracy, such as a theocracy or monarchy which follow certain regular procedures in order to rule efficiently. Minimalist proponents themselves concede that the rule of law could coexist with gross human rights violations, and discriminatory laws such as apartheid (Raz, 1979, p. 221). Minimalists, and positivist lawyers generally, are not unconcerned with substantive justice and values like human rights, but regard them as distinct ideals which are independent of the rule of law.[26]

The *maximalist* view is closer to the natural law position and sees the rule of law as a *chapeau* encompassing structural, procedural and substantive elements. In the maximalist view, the rule of law is more than mere rule *by* law, and requires more than a mechanistic series of structures and procedures for its realization. For maximalists it is not possible to separate substantive justice from formal justice, as minimalists would insist: laws are about justice. Typically maximalists would reject the *Rechtstaat* model of the rule of law for this reason.

The idea that the rule of law might mean more than its institutions and the predictability they provide, and include values as well was popularized by nineteenth century jurist A.V. Dicey (1959, pp. 202–3).

> The 'rule of law' ... has three meanings. It means, in the first place, the absolute supremacy or predominance of regular law as opposed to the influence of arbitrary power; ... [second] equality before the law; ... [third] the laws of the constitution are ... the consequence of the rights of individuals.[27]

A forceful contemporary articulation of the maximalist view is provided by the Organisation for Security and Cooperation in Europe (OSCE):

> [The participating states] consider that the rule of law does not merely mean formal legality which assures regularity and consistency in the achievement and enforcement of democratic order, but justice based on the recognition and full acceptance of the supreme value of the human personality and guaranteed by institutions providing a framework for its fullest expression.[28]

Maximalist proponents concede that the 'rights' conception is more complex and susceptible to failure than the more straightforward and clear-cut minimalist or rule book conception. They also concede that it is more politically controversial and philosophically contestable than the rule book conception (Dworkin, 1987, esp. pp. 12–13). They would hold that the rule of law is not necessarily a Western concept specific to liberal democracy or a common law system; rather they would regard it as potentially universal and universally applicable.[29]

Despite this dichotomy, there is significant common ground between the two positions. In effect, the maximalist position would accept the minimalist position as a necessary starting point for the rule of law, but would find it incomplete. Both positions require laws to conform to principles of the rule of law or legality. These principles require that laws be general; promulgated;

clear and open; noncontradictory; prospective; constant and relatively stable; possible; and that official action be congruent with declared rule.[30] Both might agree that courts should be easily accessible, and principles of natural justice should be observed, such as open and fair hearing, absence of bias and due process, to ensure the impartial and regular functioning of the legal order (Raz, 1979, pp. 216–18; Rawls, 1971, pp. 238–9).[31] The difference between the two positions, then, concerns not the formal composition of the rule of law but its fundamental ethos; whether the substantive and moral content of the law is and should be a determining feature of the rule of law, or is peripheral or exterior to it. It is this contention that carries over to and influences the operationalization of the rule of law in post-conflict societies.[32]

Operationalizing the Rule of Law in Post-conflict Societies

In order to operationalize the rule of law, it is necessary to consider the particular needs of the post-conflict society in question, the nature of its prior and remaining legal system, and the overall political and socioeconomic context of its recent emergence from conflict. In almost every case, there is an understandable urgency felt by national governments and the international community in the post-conflict context to restore security and stability after the destabilization of conflict, and to build negative peace to avoid a relapse into conflict. 'A young democracy without a rule of law may soon degenerate into a people ruled by warlords and tribalism. A fragile government without an independent and adequately resourced judiciary may soon perish … a lasting peace is not achievable unless it carries with it the imperative of law' (Plunkett, 1998, p. 63). On the other side, however, is a population of victims and survivors stripped of justice, rights and human dignity during conflict, who resolutely demand that justice be restored before they can place their faith in the possibility of peace. They want not just law and order but a legal order that guarantees them justice, and safeguards their rights and dignity as equal human beings. In this context, where the need for law and order hangs as heavily in the balance as the demand for legal justice and a just peace, which of the two conceptions of the rule of law is more appropriate and tenable?

The minimalist view has the decided advantage of being clear in what it is and is not about. The clear boundaries it draws between what comprises the rule of law and what is extraneous to it provides an easier basis for implementation in situations like post-conflict ones. After the chaos and uncertainty, the subversion or violation of the law by government and/or rebel forces during conflict, the minimalist guarantee – of a government formally subject to the law; an independent, nonpartisan judiciary for dispute resolution; functioning law enforcement agencies – is undoubtedly necessary. However, the question it raises is whether this conception is sufficient in the aftermath of conflict.

The maximalist view has the inconvenience of being less clearly delineated, politically contentious, and given to expansive reach. Indeed, one of the reasons the current popularity of the rule of law has been criticized is because of its proclivity to incorporate other political ideals, while minimalists would insist that the rule of law is only one of many values possessed by law, and must be kept distinct from other ideals like equality or democracy (Raz, 1979, esp. pp. 210–12). The overlap and confusion between the language and practice of human rights on the one hand and the rule of law on the other, poses another problem, for, despite their correlation in the maximalist conception, human rights and the rule of law are two distinct ideals which cannot simply be coalesced into each other.[33]

More significantly, adopting a maximalist approach would necessitate a deeper understanding of the complex and sometimes unfamiliar legal practices prevalent in many non-Western post-conflict societies, such as legal pluralism and the coexistence of customary law alongside modern state-law.[34] Integrating these disparate elements, in the difficult circumstances following conflict, to form a coherent rule of law acceptable both to the local population and to international norms, is far from straightforward and poses a major challenge to legal philosophers and practitioners. Some scholars have criticized the rule of law for its association with the liberal democratic ideal which emphasizes individualism and liberty to the detriment of communal and locally based values.[35] International practitioners too have noted their own singular inability to adequately understand and incorporate the local culture and legal system, and the input of the local population in their rule of law programmes.[36]

Nevertheless, despite these challenges, the maximalist conception is eminently worth pursuing in the post-conflict context, not least for its relentless assertion that law must be about justice.

> It is not merely that justice is one admirable quality that good laws possess: rather justice is the very purpose of law. Consequently, a law that does not secure justice fails to achieve its *telos* and in that sense does indeed fail as *law* (Gaus, 1994, p. 349).

In light of the popular demand and need for justice to serve as the foundation for peacebuilding as expressed in the majority of conflict-to-peace transitions, it may be unsustainable and even meaningless to restore the rule of law without grounding it in justice and human rights. Indeed, some of the societies in question did have a minimalist rule of law regime, such as apartheid South Africa. The South African legal regime was considered illegitimate by the majority of its population as well as by the international community, because, in Nelson Mandela's words, the law applied was 'immoral, unjust and intolerable'.[37] It is not the outward institutions and structures that will inspire public trust in legal justice and popular engagement in the reconciliation process, but the substance of the laws, and the state's commitment to uphold them and guarantee legal justice and human dignity. If the emphasis in legal reform is given to form over substance or to order over the claims of justice, it may succeed, at least temporarily, in warding off renewed conflict, but it would provide an insubstantial foundation for consolidating a lasting peace: in focusing on short-term negative peace, it may short-circuit positive peace.[38]

Rectificatory Justice: Moving from Punishment to Reparative Justice

The central problem in applying theoretical conceptions of rectificatory justice to practice in post-conflict societies is the difficulty in actually locating a body of relevant philosophical literature on the subject. The concept of rectificatory justice has attracted scant scholarly attention since Aristotle's *Nicomachean Ethics,* and the term itself was discarded from philosophical discourse. Finnis describes how Thomas Aquinas, 'purporting to interpret Aristotle faithfully, silently shifted the meaning of Aristotle's second class of particular justice, and invented a new term for it: "commutative justice"' (Finnis, 1980, p. 179). This new term was taken to cover 'the whole field in which ... the problem is to determine what dealings are proper between persons (including groups)' (ibid.). However, commutative justice so defined is too unspecified to be relevant or applicable to the context of post-conflict societies. The interest here is in Aristotle's original term, rectificatory justice, which aims to have 'a rectifying function in private transactions', and could be used to rectify violations committed during conflicts, such as those listed earlier (Aristotle, 1981, p. 117).

While rectificatory justice fell into disuse, the concept of punishment became prominent as the primary form of corrective or retributive justice. Various accounts of punishment, retributive,[39] utilitarian[40] and hybrid theories, have been proposed. They have been rigorously examined elsewhere and will not be repeated here.[41] Fundamentally however, it must be asked whether traditional theories of punishment provide a sufficient and adequate response to the claims of rectificatory justice today, especially to the specific demands in post-conflict settings. Punishment theories generally address offenders: they typically neglect the two other parties affected by the offence and ensuing rectificatory justice measures – victims and affected communities or societies.[42] This neglect is serious in post-conflict societies, as it is not isolated crimes and criminals that are in question here, but wider patterns of massive and systematic violations, which often victimize not only their targeted victims and survivors, but the entire community or society as well. 'Brutality brings about a culture of fear and insecurity that pervades the community at large' (Malamud-Goti, 19 (Roht-Arriaza), p. 165),[43] as experienced in Mozambique, Rwanda and Cambodia, to name but three cases (see, e.g., Nordstrom, 1992, pp. 27–43). The processes and effects of victimization have been documented and studied since the Holocaust. They reveal the loss of autonomy, self-worth and self-control of victims, and underline victims' need to regain autonomy, dignity and reintegration in community (Danieli, 1995, pp. 572–82; Becker, 1995, pp. 572–82).[44] Punishment is not equipped to take account of any of these needs, and therefore is an inadequate form of rectificatory justice for post-conflict societies.

An additional dilemma in the context of post-conflict societies is that abuses and violations are often excessive and egregious and give rise to demands – legal, political and popular – for rectificatory justice; simultaneously, there is a paramount need to reintegrate both survivors and offenders into normal social life, and promote societal reconciliation to form the foundation for a lasting peace. Traditional punishment measures, which sideline victims and deepen hostility and alienation between offenders and victims by their adversarial nature, are not conducive to either reconciliation or reintegration (see Wright, 1996, esp. chs 5 and 6; also see Cragg, 1992, pp. 106–11 and 172–4). Despite the institution of national and international tribunals for the Rwandan genocide, the reluctance of Tutsi survivors to provide testimony in court for fear of Hutu reprisal, and the fear of Hutus that they may at any moment be accused by Tutsi neighbours of complicity in genocide, illustrates the point.[45]

Despite international legal stipulations urging redress, the reality is that punishment and even trials are very rarely carried out in practice in post-conflict societies, due to severe political obstacles, infrastructural weaknesses and/or financial constraints. In Cambodia, the Peace Agreements made euphemistic mention of the genocide committed by the Khmer Rouge, and issued no call for legal remedy, in order to avoid offending the political sensitivities of all factions involved and avert a possible relapse into conflict (see, e.g., Findlay, 1995, esp. p. 10). In El Salvador, the UN Truth Commission identified by name the main perpetrators of human rights abuses, but stopped short of calling for prosecution and punishment, because it found the judiciary too impaired to provide the accused with fair trials. Moreover, the ARENA government, the Supreme Court and military, who rejected the Commission's report, would have bitterly opposed trials: tellingly, the government declared an amnesty just before the report's release to preclude the possibility of prosecution (Johnstone, 1995, pp. 34–45). In Ethiopia, despite political will to punish, five years after the detention of about 2,000 suspected war criminals associated with the Menghistu regime, only a handful have been tried to date while the others remain incarcerated without trial, due to logistical and other failings.[46]

Consequently, prosecution and criminal punishment are rarely a realistic option or an adequate response in post-conflict societies for a variety of reasons. What is required is a conceptualization of rectificatory justice which incorporates the needs of victims, perpetrators and society, and strives to balance the sometimes contradictory imperatives of formal justice on the one hand and societal reconciliation, political accommodation and material capacity on the other.

Conceptualizing and Operationalizing Reparative Justice

Given the needs of post-conflict societies and the absence of a theoretical framework to address these needs, a new concept of *reparative justice* is proposed here as a more appropriate response to rectificatory justice claims in post-conflict societies. The concept of reparation has a long tradition both in law and in social psychology. Literature on reparation outside these fields is fairly limited, so the concept leaves itself open for construction and adaptation to the specific needs of post-conflict countries.

The legal and psychological descriptions of the term offer a starting point for this construction. The objective of reparation in legal terms is as follows:

> reparation must, as far as possible, wipe out all the consequences of the illegal act and re-establish the situation which would, in all probability, have existed if that act had not been committed.[47]

In law, reparation includes:

> all measures which a plaintiff may expect to be taken by a defendant state: payment of compensation (or restitution), an apology, the punishment of the

> individual responsible, the taking of steps to prevent a recurrence of the breach of duty, and any other forms of satisfaction (Brownlie, 1990, p. 458).

Psychologists describe reparation as follows:

> The term *reparation* has a double meaning. First, it is a psychoanalytical concept, developed by Melanie Klein (Klein & Riviere, 1937/1987), that is used to explain the intrapsychic process of repair. But it is also a legal term used, for example, in connection with economic compensation after a war. This double meaning is significant because repair in the psychoanalytic sense must occur at both the individual and social levels, but it can only take place fully if it is linked to reparation in the legal sense – that is with truth and justice for the victim and compensation when it is helpful (Becker et al., 1995, pp. 583–591).

These basic characterizations of reparation in law and psychology reveal the two significant advantages of a conceptualization of reparative instead of rectificatory justice. First, reparation comprehends the two distinct kinds of injustice suffered by the victim, and seeks to redress both: the legal injustice – such as injury, loss of life, employment or property, and the moral or psychological injustice – victimization, trauma, loss of dignity.[48] Secondly, and as a consequence, it envisages the possibility of both material and non material remedies, including formal legal measures as well as informal or symbolic ones. Material damages may be paid back in cash, but may also include reclaiming or restituting property, education, housing, health care and employment. Non-material reparation may include several measures such as the disclosure of truth and public recognition of the wrong doing (Van Boven et al., 1995, p. 502). Therefore, reparative justice is both *sensitive* to the nature of the offence and its impact on the victim and society and *flexible* in devising a suitable response or combination of responses to it. Importantly, reparation does not exclude punishment, as alluded to in the legal definition above. Indeed, trial and punishment will remain a putative part of the response to past abuses in many cases, not least due to the stipulations of international law, and the symbolic and political goal of combating impunity.[49] However, punishment seen within the framework of reparative justice might take non-criminal and noncustodial forms more appropriate to the needs and capacities of post-conflict societies, such as community service.[50] Reparative justice offers a framework for combining measures, both formal and informal, to address the varied requirements of each post-conflict situation.

Reparative justice conceived in this manner seems particularly suited to post-conflict societies, as the central aim of reparation is to overcome the alienation caused by the offence and to rebuild the basis of trust for renewed cooperation (Cragg, 1992, p. 171). Reparative justice seeks to accommodate the needs of offenders, victims and the wider society, as well as the government or authorities.

> From the point of view of the authorities, reparations represent an acknowledgement on the part of the offender that he is not above the law. From the point of view of the public [and victim], reparations imply a desire and willingness to live within the law, by accepting responsibility for wrongdoing and undertaking to correct it. And from the point of view of the offender, reparations provide a basis for rebuilding trust that may have been undermined by the offence, thereby creating the conditions for reassuming a normal place in society (ibid.).

There are strong conceptual bases and pragmatic reasons, therefore, for developing the concept of reparative justice, and for elaborating its requisite principles in a manner that is analytically and descriptively suited to post-conflict requirements of rectificatory justice.

Reparative justice already has its manifestations in concrete legal and social practices, and offers a repertoire of measures and mechanisms that might be adopted or adapted to suit the needs of particular societies. The main forms of reparation acknowledged in international legal practice are restitution, compensation, indemnity, satisfaction and declaratory judgement.[51] In addition to the non-material reparation measures alluded to above, the common forms of social reparation witnessed in the context of transitional and post-traumatic societies have included commemoration, symbolic redress, education and establishing the truth.[52] Official truth commissions with varying mandates have functioned in El Salvador, Haiti, Guatemala and South Africa; informal mechanisms have included traditional healing in rural Mozambique; an ecclesiastical initiative, 'the Recovery of Historical Memory' (REHMI) in Guatemala; and commemorative museums at the sites of genocide in Rwanda. Often, as suggested above, official mechanisms have been combined with informal measures to respond to the multiple and crosscutting needs of reparative justice.

The conceptualization of reparative justice proposed here is preliminary, and will require further elaboration before it can be operationalized easily in post-conflict societies. For example, while the aim of reparation is to 'wipe out all the consequences', this is difficult to do for crimes like genocide, systematic rape, or mass violation of human rights. Nor is it easy to calculate an appropriate compensation, monetary or non-material, for deep emotional damage and victimization, which defy measurement. The problem is compounded when victims are entire groups or society at large, or when injustice and violence have been physical as well as structural and systemic, such as forced removal of black populations in South Africa, or the denial of indigenous rights in Guatemala.[53]

Despite these theoretical and practical difficulties, the concept of reparative justice merits serious further consideration. Even in this incipient form, it offers a promising, encompassing, flexible and sensitive framework for accommodating the diverse needs of victims, offenders and societies, and for building both negative and positive peace without abnegating justice.

Distributive Justice in Post-Conflict Societies

Although the issue of distributive justice has occupied the attention of philosophers for centuries and produced a prolific literature, it is difficult to identify conceptions of distributive justice that might be applicable to the particular exigencies and conditions of post-conflict societies. The rich literature on distributive justice over the last 25 years, since John Rawls' catalytic *A Theory of Justice* (1971/1973), has been generated essentially in Western liberal-democratic milieux. Despite the universal liberal leanings of a good number of these approaches, these theories are far removed from the realities of injustice afflicting post-conflict societies.

What the majority of societies emerging today from conflict share in common is low income and low levels of development, further set back by conflict; they usually are marked by deep inequality of resources and power, which often was a cause of conflict. By way of example, Haiti is the poorest country in the Americas, with a GNP per capita of $220. In El Salvador, since 1900 productive land has been concentrated in the hands of an oligarchy of fourteen families (Johnstone, 1995, p. 11). In Guatemala, the top 20 per cent of households earn 63 per cent of household income, while the bottom 20 per cent earn a mere 2 per cent of it. South Africa's bottom 20 per cent have a 3 per cent share of income, compared to 63 per cent for the top 20 per cent (World Bank, 1996, 1997). In both South Africa and Namibia, apartheid law discriminated against the majority black population to keep them poor and powerless. Unless a proposed theory of distributive justice can speak to the realities of distributive injustice faced in post-conflict societies such as these, to the levels of deprivation and the degrees of inequality – and to the expectations of change held by the populations emerging from conflict – they will lack credibility.

The predicament faced in applying existing theories of distributive justice to such societies has been well described by one British scholar:

> Although justice is agreed to be a universal ideal, whenever it is elaborated for use in social practice or examined at length theoretically, it appears as a concept constituted by a limited context. And since the literature results largely from experience and theory developed in Western societies, nearly all discussion is to a great extent specifically related to Western forms of social order (Woodman, 1996, p. 153).

Recent works in distributive justice have proposed theories based on one or more of the following: contractual arrangements; desert; self-interest; mutual advantage, and the contribution principle which justifies differential returns to individuals based on the differing value of their respective contributions to society (see, e.g. Rawls, 1971; Barry, 1989; Sadurski, 1985, Campbell, 1988).

While parts of individual theories might be relevant to post-conflict societies,[54] the assumptions and starting points of these theories are difficult to conceptualize, even hypothetically, in impoverished, unequal post-conflict societies such as those described briefly above. The assumptions of rough equality between individuals and the exercise of rational free choice underlying these theories make them unfeasible for meaningful application to societies where equality and free choice usually have been stripped from the majority of individuals, and may apply at best to an elite minority. In post-conflict societies, therefore, the contract tradition premised on equality and rational free choice is not applicable; desert and the contribution principle are unsatisfactory as they may favour the extant patterns of skewed distribution based on grossly unequal status and opportunities which underlay or even gave rise to conflict in these societies; mutual advantage is unsuitable for individuals who have been treated unequally for decades.

By way of example, one might consider Rawls' difference principle, which is regarded by some philosophers as a possible basis for an egalitarian principle of redistribution with international applicability (see, e.g. Beitz, 1985). However, it has been observed that Rawls' principles are individualistic and grounded in liberty, and, therefore, inappropriate for African and other non-Western societies, where membership of a closely-woven social group may be preferred to individual liberty, or where opting out of such membership and its concomitant obligations may not be a choice.[55] If a theoretical position begins with assumptions which are far removed from the starting point of the actual population in each post-conflict society in question, if it defeats the imagination and neglects the experiences of the local population, as portrayed above, it is unlikely to form the basis for a credible and viable framework for distributive justice in that society.[56]

It may be more useful to look at approaches to distributive justice from the point of view of the dichotomy between *teleological* or goal based, and *deontological* or duty based[57] theories of justice.

The main teleological approach to justice is utilitarianism, which 'recommends a choice of actions on the basis of consequences, and an assessment of consequences in terms of welfare' (Sen and Williams, 1982, pp. 3–4). Utilitarians are willing to sacrifice individual justice if it serves collective societal utility. Utilitarianism has been sharply criticized by other philosophical traditions,[58] and the sharpest criticism is that it is an aggregative theory. Deontologists have grave doubts about the validity of a collective and aggregative theory for what they see as the essentially individualist value of justice.[59] Deontologists criticize utilitarians for stripping individuals of their dignity by treating them as means and not as ends in regarding them merely as units in a calculus.

Notwithstanding the philosophical validity of these critiques, the contribution of the utilitarian analysis of distributive justice cannot be entirely ignored from the point of view of this study of post-conflict justice. Admittedly, the emphasis on individuals and their equal worth in non-utilitarian theories is of critical importance not only for theories of justice but also on the ground, where the loss of dignity and self-worth experienced by victimized populations can best be met by a theory of justice which reaffirms equal worth and individual dignity. Nevertheless, aggregate societal well-being cannot be excluded from the framework. After the emotional and socioeconomic devastation that usually accompany conflict, the sacrifice of collective social well-being for individual benefit – as it is often a choice between the two, due to limited resources – is a luxury post-conflict societies may aspire to, but can ill afford in the short-term. The majority of *required* distributive justice measures in post-conflict societies, such as land redistribution in El Salvador and Guatemala, may offend the sensitivities and entitlements of the privileged minority, and in that sense violate individual justice *strictu sensu*. However, such redistribution may serve overall societal benefit and, moreover, may provide perhaps the only way to eliminate the roots of conflict and consolidate lasting peace. Such 'utilitarian' decisions may also be politically expedient and economically necessary to meet the legitimate expectations of citizens who have struggled through war and now anticipate peace dividends. It may be useful, therefore, to revisit utilitarianism and integrate some utilitarian considerations in the overall constructions of distributive justice theories suited to post-conflict societies.[60] As Rawls (1971/73, p. 30) himself conceded, 'All ethical doctrines worth our attention take consequences into account in judging rightness. One which did not would simply be irrational, crazy'.

Deontological theories of justice are typically divided between rights approaches and duty approaches. Often, the two are presented as alternatives to each other. Rights have often been associated with libertarian views of distributive justice, where the concern is to preserve the entitlements of (usually privileged) individuals from any encroachment, particularly by the state.[61] The libertarian conception is irrelevant to this discussion, not least because the 'central demand of libertarian justice whether national or international is: do not redistribute' (O'Neill, 1986, p. 289), which is obviously inappropriate in post-conflict societies.

Several kinds of rights are distinguished in political philosophy: prosthetic and conservative rights, legal and moral rights, claim rights and ideal rights. In post-conflict societies the concern is limited to the universal human rights enshrined in the International Bill of Human Rights,[62] and more specifically, in the context of distributive justice, to economic, social and cultural rights which are pertinent to distributive inequalities.[63] However, even human rights have proven controversial. Some philosophers accept the category of political rights which they describe as negative rights, in that they purportedly require no 'positive' action by states to enforce those rights but only 'negative' or preventive action to prevent their encroachment. However, these philosophers resist the idea of social and economic rights, which they describe as positive rights, in that they require positive intervention and action by the state and other actors. Their main conceptual difficulty with positive rights is the problem of assigning agency, in contrast to negative rights, where agency seems easier to assign, typically to governments. They describe positive rights as manifesto rights: as no identifiable agent can be allocated to the corresponding obligations raised by these rights, they create imperfect obligations, and the right 'disappears' (O'Neill, 1986).

This distinction between negative and positive rights is misleading: negative rights also require positive, resource-consuming action by states, such as the maintenance of a police force, a judiciary and a penal system to guarantee and protect these rights.[64] Therefore, there is a 'positive' component even in so-called negative rights. If this is the case, there is no valid justification for prioritizing negative rights over positive ones, particularly in impoverished post-conflict countries. In the case of both positive rights, as encoded in the International Covenant on Economic, Social and Cultural Rights (CESCR), and negative rights, as codified in the Covenant on Civil and Political Rights

(CCPR), the manifest agent is the government which ratifies the treaty (United Nations, 1988). The reason positive rights are thought to create imperfect obligations is that it is recognized that governments in poor countries may simply lack the resources and capacity – the agency – to fulfil their obligations. Indeed, the CESCR does provide for developing countries to meet their obligations gradually and incrementally, recognizing these difficulties. However, if both negative rights and positive rights require resources, capacity and positive action, then the governments in poor countries will be (and often are) equally incapable of meeting either set of obligations, in which case the distinction between perfect and imperfect obligations falls through. In poor post-conflict countries, negative rights are as difficult to fulfil as are positive rights, due to multifarious demands on the state's limited resources. It is only by putting both socioeconomic and political rights on the same footing and by assisting impoverished and embattled governments to meet both that the rights approach to distributive justice will have meaning in post-conflict contexts. The indivisibility and interdependence of political and socioeconomic rights was reiterated forcefully at the 1993 World Conference on Human Rights, and the right to development was reaffirmed.[65] International legal opinion concurs that both sets of rights enjoy the same legal status and validity (Alston and Steiner, 1996, p. 268). Despite these assertions, socioeconomic rights, which are usually what is at issue in distributive injustice particularly in post-conflict societies, have often been marginalized as much by academics as by practising human rights organizations and non-governmental actors, in preference for political rights (ibid., p. 269). However, providing the basic needs for survival and a decent living through the provision of economic rights is the minimum prerequisite to exercise the political right to life and liberty so cherished by liberals.[66] Unless this is recognized and an integrated framework of indivisible economic and political rights is put forward, the rights approach will have little applicability to post-conflict societies.

As expressed by Kant (1927, p. 58), 'Both the love of man and respect for his rights are duties, but the former is only conditional, while the latter is unconditioned and inevitably obligatory'. A Kantian framework for a duty approach to distributive justice has been proposed among others by Onora O'Neill (1986). Given the current inadequacy of the rights approach in addressing economic and social rights, the duty approach might provide a valuable complement by encouraging governments and other external actors to respond to distributive justice claims based on duty. However, the duty approach as proposed by O'Neill suffers from a weakness, as the duties she argues for lack even the limited acceptability and enforceability that rights have come to acquire. O'Neill provides an unconvincing account of why governments might feel obliged to act spontaneously based on duty when they have difficulty respecting even their international legal obligations. Duties are portrayed by O'Neill as overcoming the imperfect obligation problem encountered by positive rights. However, her argument neglects the fact that duties too, however convincingly demonstrated in philosophical argument, lack 'teeth' if they are not encoded and enforced through domestic law or international treaty. Human rights, both political and socioeconomic, are already established in political and legal discourse and have been rapidly expanded and codified in the last 50 years (see United Nations, 1988 and 1997; see also Alston and Steiner. 1996). Although the duty and obligation approach has gained considerable ethical and political appeal in recent years, perhaps born of a certain distaste associated with the demand for rights without reference to the corresponding responsibilities of rights claimants (see, e.g. Commission on Global Governance, 1995, ch. 2), the translation of duties into (legally enforceable) action is not imminent. Moreover, whereas duty/obligation language may not be as visible as rights language in international legal and political practice, it is a fundamental part of international law, which states, 'responsibility is the necessary corollary of a right'.[67] Even the utilitarian Bentham stated that to have a right is to be the beneficiary of someone else's duty.[68] Rather than pitting one against the other, rights and duties are more effective when treated as complements, as they carry greater weight collectively in providing a deontological impulsion for action.[69] The deontological approach has promise for application to post-conflict societies' distributive justice claims, but for the present, it is inadequate in its response to economic rights and in its combination of duties with rights.

Operationalizing Distributive Justice in Post-Conflict Societies: The Problem of Inequality

Perhaps the central reason why existing approaches to distributive justice are unsatisfactory for the purposes of post-conflict societies is their inadequate attention to the concept of inequality. Although inequality seems a logical starting point for theories of distributive justice,[70] it occupies a relatively minor part in contemporary theories. Egalitarianism remains popular among many liberal scholars, but it has increasingly little to do with equality *per se*, and rarely proposes economic equality or redistribution (as communism nominally aspired to do). Some modern day egalitarians favour treating people as equals, rather than treating people equally (Dworkin, 1981a; 1981b; 1987, pp. 206–13). Some believe that acceptable equality can result from rigorous provision of equal opportunity.[71] Others find justifiable bases for unequal treatment such as desert or the contribution principles, and accept that unjustifiable inequalities must be rejected as unjust.[72] Such approaches might be acceptable and even appropriate in Western societies where social and economic inequalities, although widening, are not yet unacceptable; they are inadequate and untenable in post-conflict societies, where grievances about inequalities of distribution often provoke conflict.

An interesting innovation is the notion of complex equality, presented by Walzer, who suggests that 'equality is a complex relationship between persons ... it is not an identity of possessions', and, therefore, requires not a single distributive principle but 'a diversity of distributive criteria that mirrors the diversity of social goods' (Walzer, 1983, pp. 18–19). His argument caters to the differing values and meanings diverse societies seem to attribute to different goods, and, as such, is a novel and attractive idea. It is criticized by 'cosmopolitan' thinkers, who oppose his 'communitarian' approach, and it may seem to radical egalitarians to provide an excuse for entrenching the status quo ante – a particular danger in post-conflict societies.[73] Nevertheless, Walzer's theory is welcome for its suggestion that it is necessary and possible to find innovative approaches to address inequality within theories of distributive justice.

In practice, post-conflict societies face a dilemma. As described above, the fragile governments in these deeply unequal societies emerging from conflict face a strong popular demand from an expectant population for distributive justice, which is usually expressed in terms of greater equity. Yet, on the other hand, they face political, moral and economic constraints to doing so. Politically, they may be hamstrung by the opposition of the established economic elite to any redistribution that might reduce their privileges. Morally, they are faced with the prevalent liberal-democratic ideal in the international – mainly Western – community of individual rights and liberty which frowns on any perceived inhibition of personal freedom and entitlements. But most decisively perhaps, they are confronted by the prevalent economic misperception, particularly among international financial institutions (IFIs) that greater equity is detrimental to economic growth, despite emerging evidence to the contrary.[74] As these fragile post-conflict governments are often deeply dependent on IFIs for financial assistance during the transition, they are obliged to follow the neo-liberal economic policies handed down which target economic stabilization and growth, to the neglect of political, socioeconomic and ethical demands for redistributive justice and at the cost of greater equity (Willett, 1998; Boyce and Pastor, 1997). This has been the fate of many post-conflict countries including Cambodia, El Salvador, Haiti and Mozambique (Boyce and Pastor, 1997; Maguire, 1996, pp. 72–82).[75] 'Long-run economic policy after a civil war must promote not only economic adjustment, but also a process of political adjustment: the consolidation of peace. In such a context, distributional equity cannot be relegated to a lower priority than economic growth ... partly because inequity is often a cause of domestic conflict' (Boyce and Pastor, 1997, p. 304).

There is an urgent need for reinvigorated theories of egalitarianism which address the marked inequalities common to post-conflict societies. Sen's forceful argument that equality can be efficient, and Dworkin's case that equality is not detrimental to liberty lend respectability and acceptability to the concept of equality (Sen, 1992; Dworkin, 1996). What is now needed is theories which speak out with conviction in favour of greater socioeconomic equity as a prerequisite both for economic growth and for political equality; both for short-term negative peace and for lasting positive peace.

Conclusion: Bridging the Gap: Integrating Theory and Practice

Peacebuilders are in urgent need of fresh insight, contending principles, comparative studies, and, perhaps most importantly, philosophical depth and precision, as they grapple with the overwhelming, complex and overlapping demands of justice in poor and battered societies emerging from conflict. Fresh and contemporary theories of justice could introduce a wealth of ideas, conceptions and analytical devices with the potential to be immensely useful to peacebuilders in this task. However in their current state these philosophical resources are, for the most part, remote and inaccessible to practitioners on the ground, as they are often rooted in the Western liberal-democratic tradition, and tend to focus on problems particular to these societies. Existing philosophical approaches need to be appropriately expanded or adapted to make them useful to practitioners grappling with human realities; in turn, the rigour and validity of theories generated in the West could be tested against these 'nonstandard' situations.

In closing, three general observations arising from the discussion so far are highlighted. The first concerns the relatively new field of *International Justice*. In a sharp departure from traditional approaches, which limited the field of application of theories of justice to the community or state, scholars of international justice deliberately extended theories and principles of justice beyond national borders to address contemporary international problems. One area of concern was an enquiry into the obligations of the rich towards the poor in developing countries (see esp. Beitz et al., 1985; O'Neill, 1991; Hoffman, 1981). Several emerging global issues such as the environment and inter-generational equity have been included in its scrutiny.[76] Although post-conflict justice claims have so far not been analysed to the knowledge of this author, the field of international justice provides fertile soil for rigorous ethical and philosophical enquiry in this area.[77]

The second observation concerns the debate between *cosmopolitan and communitarian* approaches, which, although more germane to international relations theory, is highly pertinent to the discussion of justice here. The issues raised in all three dimensions of justice begs the important and as-yet-unanswered question of whether there exists a single universal set of values and ideas about justice which may be applied uniformly across different societies and cultures, including post-conflict developing countries (cosmopolitanism), or whether the values and ideas informing justice are and must be articulated within and by each community based on its specific realities and needs (communitarianism). While it is generally argued by liberal theorists that there is necessarily only one universally acceptable set of values about justice, several contemporary theorists like Alasdair MacIntyre, Walzer, and even Rawls present a communitarian vision, where the whole or part of a given society's conception is determined and articulated internally based on its specific cultural and societal needs.[78]

This debate is particularly apposite to the discussion of post-conflict societies. While a definitive response cannot possibly be arrived at here, the discussion so far suggests that if ideas and institutions about such a fundamental and personal value as justice are imposed externally without an internal resonance, they will flounder despite all assertions of their universalist credentials; if these concepts are articulated internally, there must be some universal standard against which to evaluate them, to ensure that they do not entrench unjust principles or discriminate against weak groups under the guise of respect for traditional cultural values.[79]

A third observation is closely related to both points made above. A fundamental flaw and weakness of contemporary approaches to justice is the absence or lack of access to *non-Western perspectives*. While justice has long been vaunted as a universal value expressed through all ages in all cultures, the fact remains that philosophical narratives of non-Western traditions are rare and infrequently solicited.[80] References to non-Western ideas of justice are occasional and drawn from anthropology and religion rather than contemporary philosophical debate and discourse. The exposition of all three dimensions of justice has underlined how rooted in Western traditions, cultures and legal systems contemporary theories of justice are, whether they be about the rule of law, rectificatory justice or distributive justice. Modern developments and applications of justice theories are also responses to specific issues of justice arising in Western societies, such as questions of natural versus positive law, the defects of penal systems, or quandaries concerning minimum pay, wage differentials or reverse discrimination policies.

Increasingly, the claims of justice demanding the attention of philosophers will emerge in developing non-Western societies, the post-conflict scenarios explored here being a case in point. This raises two challenges: views from and exchanges with philosophers from the non-Western world, including the concerned societies, need to be elicited sincerely and made part of contemporary mainstream discourse on justice, in order genuinely to broaden and universalize the debate; second, Western scholars should broaden their perspective and take on these emerging non-Western dilemmas of justice in their purview as legitimate subjects of interest.

Justice is perhaps the most deeply and richly investigated value in the long and carefully-documented tradition of Western philosophical thought. Yet a wide gulf has grown between theories of justice, devised mostly in the Western world and the realities of injustice, experienced often in the non-Western developing world. This gap is particularly apparent in the recent emergence on the international agenda of post-conflict societies embarking on the arduous task of peacebuilding. There is much that both practitioners on the ground and philosophers far removed could and need to learn from each other; it also shows that there is scope for the gap to be narrowed. If philosophical theory could be brought closer to real-life experience, philosophers and practitioners could become allies in the urgent challenge faced around the globe today of building a just and lasting peace in societies recently ravaged by conflict.

Notes

1 I am grateful to Prof. Geoffrey Hawthorn, Prof. Anthony Duff and Dr Jim Whitman for their extensive feedback, and to Ms Toni Erskine and Prof. Mahmood Mamdani for their valuable comments on earlier drafts of this chapter.

2 See also Wallensteen and Sollenberg, 1996 for a detailed analysis and list of armed conflicts.

3 *The Guardian*, 26 December 1996. Her comment was made following the Guatemalan government's passage of the National Reconciliation Law which effectively amnestied

human rights abusers, and contradicted the spirit of the peace agreement signed by the government in the same month.

4 As has often been pointed out, the 'post' in post-conflict is often a misnomer, as conflict often continues in different forms, sometimes, quite openly. Cambodia and Rwanda are borderline cases of peacebuilding by the description used here, as violence and confrontation is quite open, whereas we are concerned here with countries where, though peacebuilding between rival forces is arduous, the peace has been maintained for some duration, and there is no imminent threat of a return to open conflict. For these reasons, and because the focus here is on developing countries, cases like Former-Yugoslavia, Afghanistan and Angola are not referred to.

5 This paper provides an excellent and thoughtful synthesis of academic and UN/pragmatic reflection on peacebuilding.

6 His full conceptual framework is provided in p. 22.

7 This list of peacebuilding activities is only indicative and is far from exhaustive. It is drawn from the UN texts above, esp. the *Supplement*, 1995, p. 11.

8 Throughout this chapter 'practitioners' and 'peacebuilders' refer to all actors involved on the ground in peacebuilding, both national and international, as listed above.

9 The three dimensions named here correspond to Aristotle's categorization in Ostwald, 1986. For Aristotle, justice comprised what was 'lawful' and what was 'fair'. The former he called complete, universal or general justice, and is also often translated as legal justice, and the latter, he described as partial, particular or special justice. He subdivided partial justice into two kinds, rectificatory and distributive justice. His characterizations of legal, rectificatory and distributive justice fit quite well with the depiction here. NB: it is not being suggested that Aristotle's formulations for achieving justice are applicable here – they are not (for example, slavery and the subordination of women did not offend his sense of distributive justice). It is simply that Aristotle's categorization corresponds to the justice claims of post-conflict societies identified here.

10 These rationales are additional to the arguable *duty* of governments to provide their citizens with the administration of justice, and their international treaty obligations, e.g. human rights covenants, which imply this.

11 The vast majority, perhaps 80 per cent, of casualties in internal wars are civilians; women and children are disproportionately victimized; rape is often used as a weapon of war; children are forcefully recruited as soldiers. Often there may also be systemic violence, such as forced removal from homes (as in South Africa) or displacement, which are rarely addressed even in those societies which undertake to restore rectificatory justice like South Africa. The violations witnessed in internal conflict are not so unlike Aristotle's categories of 'clandestine' and 'forced' involuntary transactions. Ostwald, 1986, p. 117.

12 Rectificatory justice has been a constant theme in the history of conflict particularly since 1945, viz. the Nuremberg and Tokyo trials established after World War II, and successive attempts by new democratizing governments to deal with abuses committed by prior regimes in Southern Europe, Latin America, and more recently, Central and Eastern Europe. For a comprehensive treatment see Kritz, 1995.

13 For some debates on the political rationales, see Kritz, 1995; Huntingdon, 1995. pp. 65–81; O'Donnell and Schmitter, 1995, pp. 57–64; Zalaquett, 1995, pp. 203–16.

14 Article 4 of the Covenant on Civil and Political Rights discusses derogations during emergencies. Art 4(2) states that no derogation is possible for the right to life, protection from torture and degrading punishment and slavery.

15 This interdependence and integrity of the three dimensions has also been noted by theorists who take a holistic view of society. 'There are three sorts of relationship: that of the parts to the whole, that of the whole to the parts, and that of one part to another. Legal justice pertains to the first, since it relates citizens to the State, distributive justice pertains to the second sort, since it relates the State to the citizens. Commutative justice pertains to the third, relating one private citizen to another' (Merkelbach, 1938, p. 253, cited in Finnis, 1980, p. 185).

16 Hutchinson and Monahan, 1987, provide a range of views supportive and critical of the Rule of Law: their own article, 'Democracy and the Rule of Law', describes it as inimical to democracy; Judith Shklar criticizes its intellectual vacuity but sees it as an essential element of constitutional government in 'Political Theory and the Rule of Law'; Duncan Kennedy, a leading proponent of the Critical Legal Studies movement, challenges the real existence or authority of knowledge about the Rule of Law in his 'Towards a Critical Phenomenology of Judging'. Joseph Raz describes the rule of law as an *ideal* towards which one might aspire (1979, p. 223), whereas for Lon Fuller the principles of the rule of law are *essential* for law's existence (1969).

17 In recent decades several other schools of legal theory have arisen to contest the traditional duopoly of natural law and legal positivism, such as critical legal studies, legal realism, sociological jurisprudence.

18 Legal positivists would clarify that they do not disregard morality, but simply place it afterwards. In their view, naturalists, who deny that bad law is still law, are in fact denying or ignoring the moral questions raised by bad law, which, they would claim, positive law is better equipped to confront. See Hart, 1992, ch. IX.

19 St Thomas Aquinas, *Summa Theologica*, Treatise on Law (written 1267–74), in Porter, 1989, p. 157. For a concise exposition of the major legal theories, see e.g. 'The Nature of Law: Theories' in Golding, 1975.

20 This discussion draws on Mani, 1997.

21 Minimalist and maximalist are the author's own terms to depict this dichotomy, and are not drawn from legal literature. Certain scholars are described as maximalist or minimalist if their work seems to cast them roughly on one or other side of this conceptual divide, e.g. Dworkin would be referred to here as a maximalist, and Raz as a minimalist.

22 Shklar depicts the former as larger but affecting fewer people, and the latter as narrower but affecting the majority of people.

23 For this view see Raz, 1979, pp. 210–28. Raz seeks to demolish the myth of the 'overriding importance' of the rule of law, and its association with myriad other political ideas.

24 One development of rule of law theory in its minimalist vein was the concept of the *Rechtstaat* or the state of law, popularized in nineteenth-century continental Europe. Though an important concept, it is not possible to develop it here for reasons of space. See e.g. Neumann, 1986, ch. 12. The concept of the *Rechtstaat* gave primacy to administrative control in its bid to eliminate arbitrariness. A state following iniquitous laws could, nevertheless be a state of law. For this reason several eminent rule of law proponents, including Dicey, Oakeshott, Hayek, Fuller and Lowi, reject *Rechtstaat* as an inadequate and distorted expression of rule of law doctrine. See Flathman, 1994 and Gaus, 1994.

25 The relationship of the rule of law to freedom is expressed by Franz Neumann (1986, pp. 31–5), and Raz (1979, pp. 220–1).

26 Dworkin, who himself defends the rights conception, concedes this point, 1987, p. 11. See also Hart, 1992.

27 Although this work has been criticized for its parochialism and idealization of English law and history, it greatly influenced and catalysed thinking on the concept.
28 'Document of the Copenhagen Meeting of the Conference on the Human Dimension of the CSCE', Copenhagen, 5–29 June 1990, point 2, p. 3. NB: the OSCE was then called the Conference on Security and Cooperation in Europe.
29 Maximalists observe that the rule of law has been championed this century in disparate and far-flung countries like Canada, India and Zambia (albeit all parts of the erstwhile British empire) (Walker, 1988, pp. 1–3).
30 These eight points, described as the 'inner morality of law' are outlined by Lon Fuller (1969). Some scholars refer to these eight points as the principles of the rule of law.
31 Raz and Rawls both use Fuller's eight points as a basis for their own elaborations of the principles of the rule of law.
32 It should be noted that contemporary legal theories such as sociological jurisprudence, legal realism and critical legal studies have contributed a third, and radically different, perspective on the nature of law and the rule of law. These theories point out that judicial discretion and uncertainty are prevalent even in the most sophisticated legal system. Consequently, in practice, the rule of law does not necessarily guarantee predictability and certainty as claimed in theory. For this reason, contemporary legal theory opposes formal definitions and struggles for more realistic and elastic definitions of the rule of law (Mani, 1997, p. 4; Kennedy, 1987).
33 On this relationship see Mani, 1998a.
34 Space does not allow a deeper discussion of the difficulties in contending with customary law and legal pluralism. See Mani, 1998b.
35 Rawls, for example, uses the rule of law ideal to bolster his championship of liberty (1971, pp. 239–43). For this criticism of the liberal rule of law and its undermining of local communal life, see Sandel, 1987.
36 This view is echoed by many international legal and human rights practitioners. See Mani, 1997.
37 Mandela's speech to Court in 1962, cited in Asmal, Asmal and Roberts, 1996, p. 54.
38 This argument is fleshed out in Mani, 1998b.
39 The retributive view was well laid out by Immanuel Kant, in whose words, 'the penal law is a categorical imperative'. See Kant, 1991, pp. 154–5.
40 The utilitarian theory of punishment was first laid out by Bentham, 1948. See Tunick, 1992, pp. 67–84 for a discussion of Bentham's views.
41 For discussions and comparisons of the three types of theories, see esp. Hart, 1968; Lacey, 1988, ch. 2; Duff, 1986, chs 6 and 7; Cragg, 1992, chs 1–3.
42 Many modern theorists and penal practitioners have attempted to correct this imbalance, and incorporate victims. See esp. Duff, 1992, pp. 43–68, who suggests that punishment can be both backward and forward looking, and proposes an ideal theory of punishment based on communication and repentance.
43 Malamud-Goti's observation of state repression in Latin America is equally true during internal conflict.
44 Cross cultural studies reveal similarities across disparate situations, despite the different circumstances, effects and needs in each case, e.g. survivors of Nazi, Cambodian and Rwandan genocide, victims of Southern European, Latin American and Central American state repression and torture.
45 On the trials, see Lawyers Committee for Human Rights, 1997.

46 Interview, Todd Howland, international legal consultant to Chief Prosecutor's Office, Ethiopia (Boston, 27 September 1997).
47 *Chorzow Factory Case (Indemnity) (Merits), Germany v. Poland* (1928), in Harris, 1991, p. 491.
48 The familiar legal practice of damage illustrates this duality: the offender is liable to repay two kinds of damage or hurt caused to the victim: moral damage or hurt caused to the victim by the offence, and monetary damage or loss incurred as a result, e.g. loss of actual or anticipated salary due to incapacitation.
49 The (hopefully) imminent establishment of an International Criminal Court is of optimum relevance here.
50 Community service and other noncustodial punishments have often been proposed in Western penal systems, (e.g. Cragg, 1992; Duff, 1992). Of relevance here is the innovative development of the idea of 'restorative justice' in some industrialized penal systems, which could be borrowed from. One practical example is Victim/Offender Reconciliation Programmes (VORP) which bring victim and offender directly in contact and utilize techniques of mediation and conflict resolution to reconcile them with each other. See Cragg, 1992, p. 193; Wright, 1996, pp. 138–40. Although the aims and approaches are somewhat similar, it is preferable to separate the penal practice of restorative justice from the concept of reparative justice proposed here for the specific context of post-conflict societies.
51 Restitution and compensation are perhaps the most common in legal practice: 'Restitution in kind is designed to re-establish the situation which would have existed if the wrongful act or omission had not taken place, by performance of the obligation which the State failed to discharge: revocation of the unlawful act, return of property wrongfully removed or abstention from further wrongful conduct. Compensation is 'reparation in the narrow sense of payment of money as a valuation of the wrong done' (Van Bowen, 1995, pp. 506–7).
52 On these measures see Danieli, 1995; Albon, 1995, p. 43; Zalaquett, 1995, pp. 225–6; Benomar, 1995, pp. 32–41, Priscilla Hayner, 1996 and 1995.
53 Cragg, 1992, p. 172, points to some general difficulties of reparation, without reference to post-conflict cases.
54 For example, the compensation principle proposed by Brian Barry (1991) in 'Chance, Choice and Justice' might be usefully adapted.
55 Woodman makes this observation in his critique/appraisal of Rawls' theory from an African perspective, 1996, pp.153-4.
56 Rawls (1996) himself clarified that he was basing his case on a liberal democratic society, such as USA. He would perhaps be the first to acknowledge that his theory is not easily transferable to impoverished post-conflict societies.
57 Scholars who draw this distinction in theories of justice include O'Neill, e.g., 1986; Rawls, e.g. 1971/73; Miller, e.g., 1976. Of course this is not the only categorization of justice theories: there are perhaps as many alternative typologies as theorists offering them.
58 Both O'Neill (1986, chs 4–5) and Rawls (1971/73, pp. 22–33, 180–92) present their theories as explicit and conscious alternatives to the various forms of utilitarianism. O'Neill and Miller (1976, pp. 31–40) describe various kinds of utilitarianism: act, rule, cardinal, ordinal etc.
59 See O'Neill, 1986 and Rawls, 1971/73 for more extensive critiques of utilitarianism such as the difficulty of establishing units of accountability. These are not elaborated here, as they are not directly relevant to this discussion.

60 See Sen and Williams, 1982, for a balanced assessment of utilitarianism's use and value today.
61 Nozick, 1974, defends this view.
62 The Bill includes the Universal Declaration on Human Rights as well as the two covenants mentioned below. See United Nations, 1988, pp. 1–42.
63 The violation of key political and civil rights was covered under rectificatory justice, examined earlier.
64 Many scholars have made this argument, including Sadurski, 1985, ch. 6.
65 See Vienna Declaration and Programme of Action, adopted by the World Conference on Human Rights on 25 June 1993, UN-Doc.A/CONF.157/23 of 12 July 1993, point 5.
66 On basic needs and economic rights see Beitz, 1981. Also useful, though focused on political rights, is Dworkin, 1977.
67 That is, that each right carries with it an obligation on an agent to fulfil that right. Brownlie, 1990, p. 434, citing Judge Huber in a report on *The Spanish Zone of Morocco Claims*.
68 E.g. Hart and Lyons, discussed in Miller, 1976, pp. 62–5.
69 The capabilities approach proposed by Sen and Nussbaum (1993) offers a way to integrate rights and duties in both the philosophic and economic realm, and might be worth pursuing in this context.
70 For example, Aristotle stated that distributive justice lay in 'the distribution of honours, of material goods, or of anything else that can be divided among those who share in a political system', 'For in these matters it is possible for a man to have a share equal or unequal to that of his neighbour' (Aristotle, 1981, p. 117).
71 Viz. Rawls' (1987) second principle of equal opportunity.
72 An illuminating comparative discussion of approaches to justice and equality and of the contribution principle is Taylor's 'The Nature and Scope of Distributive Justice' (1986).
73 After all, Walzer used his theory to explain and perhaps even exonerate the caste system in India, which even this author, a 'high-caste Brahmin' by birth, would oppose.
74 An incisive defence of greater equity and critique of IFIs' policies may be found in Boyce and Pastor, 1997, pp. 287–314.
75 The devastating human impact of introducing free market policies too soon after conflict was noted by Daniel Premont (Director, UN Centre for Human Rights, Cambodia, 1994–96), personal interview, Geneva, 29 June 1998.
76 Notably, Brian Barry (1989, 1991) has made invaluable contributions to this field.
77 The theorists who perhaps have gone the furthest in applying distributive justice principles from a Western perspective to the problems of developing countries include Beitz, 1985, O'Neill (1986) and Nussbaum, 1995.
78 Alasdair MacIntyre presents a communitarian picture, e.g., 1988. Walzer is typically described as a communitarian, despite his cosmopolitan shades. Rawls too, though cosmopolitan in many ways, argues in effect that conceptions of justice are specific to political communities.
79 Martha Nussbaum (1998 and 1995) presents an articulation of universal values which could respond to and accommodate the communitarian challenge *and* be acceptable in non-Western developing countries.
80 Woodman, 1996, makes this point forcefully.

References

Albon, M. (1995), 'Project on Justice in Times of Transition' in N. Kritz (ed.), *Transitional Justice*, Vols. 1, 2 and 3, US Institute of Peace, Washington, DC.

Alston, P. and Steiner, H. (1996), *International Human Rights in Context*, Oxford University Press, Oxford.

Aristotle (1981), *The Politics*, Book III, revised edn, Penguin, Harmondsworth.

Asmal, K., Asmal, L. and Roberts, S. (1996) *Reconciliation through Truth: A Reckoning of Apartheid's Criminal Governance*, David Phillip Publishers, Claremont.

Barry, B. (1989), *A Treatise on Social Justice, Volume 1: Theories of Justice*, Harvester-Wheatsheaf, London.

Barry, B. (11991), *Liberty and Justice: Essays in Political Theory*, Clarendon Press, Oxford.

Becker, D. et.al. (1995), 'Therapy with Victims of Political Repression in Chile: The Challenge of Social Reparation' in N. Kritz (ed.), *Transitional Justice*, Vols. 1, 2 and 3, US Institute of Peace, Washington, DC.

Beitz, C. (1981), 'Economic Rights and Distributive Justice in Developing Societies', *World Politics*, 33, 3, pp. 321–46.

Beitz, C. (1985), 'Justice and International Relations' in C. Beitz et al. (eds), *International Ethics*, Princeton University Press, Oxford.

Beitz et al. (eds) (1985), *International Ethics*, Princeton University Press, Oxford.

Benomar, J. (1995), 'Justice after Transition' in N. Kritz (ed.), *Transitional Justice*, Vols 1, 2 and 3, US Institute of Peace, Washington, DC.

Bentham, J. (1948) [1789], *An Introduction to the Principles of Morals and Legislation*, Hafner Press, New York.

Boutros-Ghali, B. (1992), *An Agenda for Peace*, United Nations, New York.

Boutros-Ghali, B. (1994), *Building Peace and Development*, United Nations, New York.

Boutros-Ghali, B. (1995), *Supplement to An Agenda for Peace*, Position Paper of the Secretary General on the Occasion of the 50th Anniversary of the United Nations (A/50/60-S/1995/1), United Nations, New York.

Boyce, J. and Pastor Jr, M. (1997), 'Macroeconomic policy and Peace Building in El Salvador' in K. Kumar (ed.), *Rebuilding Societies After Civil War*, Lynne Rienner, London.

Brownlie, I. (1990), *Principles of Public International Law*, fourth edn, Oxford University Press, Oxford.

Campbell, T. (1988), *Justice*, Macmillan, Houndsmill.

Commission on Global Governance (1995), *Our Global Neighbourhood*, Oxford University Press, Oxford.

Cragg, W. (1992), *The Practice of Punishment: Towards a theory of restorative justice*, Routledge, London.

Danieli, Y. (1995), 'Preliminary Reflections from a Psychological Perspective' in N. Kritz (ed.), *Transitional Justice*, Vol. 1, US Institute of Peace, Washington, DC.

Dicey, A.V. (1959) [1885], *An Introduction to the Study of the Law of the Constitution*, Basingstoke, Macmillan.
Duff, R.A. (1986), *Trials and Punishments*, Cambridge University Press, Cambridge.
Duff, R.A. (1992), 'Alternatives to Punishment – or Alternative Punishment?' in W. Cragg (ed.), *Retributivism and its Critics*, Franz Steiner Verlag, Stuttgart.
Dworkin, R. (1977), *Taking Rights Seriously*, Duckworth, London.
Dworkin, R. (1981a), 'What is Equality? Part I: Equality of Welfare', *Philosophy and International Affairs*, 10, 3, pp. 185–246.
Dworkin, R. (1981b), 'Part II: Equality of Resources', *Philosophy and International Affairs*, 10, 4, pp. 283–345.
Dworkin, R. (1987), *A Matter of Principle*, Harvard University Press, London.
Dworkin, R. (1993), '"Natural" Law Revisited' in P. Smith (ed.), *The Nature and Process of Law*, Oxford University Press, Oxford.
Dworkin, R. (1996), 'Do Liberty and Equality Conflict?' in P. Barker (ed.), *Living as Equals*, Oxford University Press, Oxford.
Findlay, T. (1995), *Cambodia: the Legacy and Lessons of UNTAC*, Oxford University Press and SIPRI, Oxford.
Finnis, J. (1980), *Natural Law and Natural Rights*, Clarendon Press, Oxford.
Flathman, R. (1994), 'Liberalism and the Suspect Enterprise of Political Insitutionalization: The Case of the Rule of Law' in I. Shapiro (ed.), *The Rule of Law* [*NOMOS XXXVI*], New York University Press, London.
Fuller, L. (1969), *The Morality of Law*, second edn, Yale University Press, London.
Galtung, J. (1976), 'Three Approaches to Peace: Peacekeeping, Peacemaking and Peacebuilding' in *Peace, War and Defence. Essays in Peace Research*, Vol. 2, Christian Ejlers, Copenhagen.
Gaus, G. (1994), 'Public Reason and the Rule of Law' in I. Shapiro (ed.), *The Rule of Law* [*NOMOS XXXVI*], New York University Press, London.
Gaus, G. (1994), 'Public Reason and the Rule of Law' in I. Shapiro (ed.), *The Rule of Law* [*NOMOS XXXVI*], New York University Press, London.
Golding, M. (1975), *The Philosophy of Law*, Prentice Hall, London.
Hart, H.L.A. (1968), *Punishment and Responsibility*, Clarendon Press, Oxford.
Hart, H.L.A. (1992), *The Concept of Law*, Clarendon Press, Oxford.
Harris, D.J. (1991), *Cases and Materials on International Law*, fourth edn, Sweet & Maxwell, London.
Hayek, F. von (1944), *The Road to Serfdom*, London.
Hayner, P. (1996), 'Commissioning the Truth: further research questions', *Third World Quarterly*, 17, 9, pp. 19–29.
Hayner, P. (1995), 'Fifteen Truth Commissions: A Comparative Study' in N. Kritz (ed.), *Transitional Justice*, Vols 1, 2 and 3, US Institute of Peace, Washington, DC.
Hoffman, S. (1981), *Duties Beyond Borders*, Syracuse University Press, Syracuse.
Huntingdon, S. 'The Third Wave: Democratization in the Late Twentieth Century' in N. Kritz (ed.), *Transitional Justice*, Vols. 1, 2 and 3, US Institute of Peace, Washington, DC.

Hutchinson, A. and Monahan, P. (eds) (1987), *The Rule of Law: Ideal or Ideology?*, Carswell, Toronto.

Johnstone, I. (1995), *Rights and Reconciliation: UN Strategies in El Salvador*, Lynne Rienner, London.

Kant, I. (1927), *Perpetual Peace*, tr. Helen O'Brien, Sweet and Maxwell, London.

Kant, I. (1991), 'The Right to Punishment and the Right to Pardon', *Metaphysics of Morals* in Hans Reiss (ed.), *Kant: Political Writings*, Cambridge University Press, Cambridge.

Kritz, N. (ed.) (1995), *Transitional Justice Transitional Justice*, Vols. 1, 2 and 3, US Institute of Peace, Washington, DC.

Lacey, N. (1988), *State Punishment: Political Principles and Community Values*, Routledge, London.

Lawyers Committee for Human Rights (1997), 'Prosecuting Genocide in Rwanda: the ICTR and National Trials', New York, July.

Lederach, J.P. (1994), *Building Peace: Sustainable Reconciliation in Divided Societies*, United Nations University Press, Tokyo.

Lutz, E. (1995), 'After the Elections: Compensating Victims of Human Rights Abuses', reproduced in N. Kritz (ed.), *Transitional Justice*, Vols. 1, 2 and 3, US Institute of Peace, Washington, DC.

MacIntyre, A. (1988), *Whose Justice? Which Rationality?*, Duckworth, London.

Maguire, R. et al. (1996), *Haiti Held Hostage: International Responses to the Quest for Nationhood, 1986–1996*, Thomas J. Watson Jr. Institute for International Studies, Providence.

Mani, R. (1997), 'Promoting the Rule of Law in Post-Conflict Societies', report of a seminar organised by the author under the auspices of the Common Security Forum, at Harvard University, 26 September, Common Security Forum, CHE, Kings College, Cambridge.

Mani, R. (1998a), 'Conflict Resolution, Justice and the Law: Rebuilding the Rule of Law in the Aftermath of Complex Political Emergencies', *International Peacekeeping*, 5, 3, pp. 12–13.

Mani, R. (1998b), 'The Rule of Law or the Rule of Might? Restoring Legal Justice in the Aftermath of Conflict', presented to the panel on Post-Conflict Regeneration at the Third Pan-European International Relations Conference and Joint Meeting with the International Studies Association, Vienna 16–19 September.

Merkelbach, B.-H. (1938), *Summa Theologiae Moralis*, Paris.

Miller, D. (1976), *Social Justice*, Clarendon Press, Oxford.

Neumann, F. (1986), *The Rule of Law: Political Theory and the Legal System in Modern Society*, Berg Publishers, Leamington Spa.

Nordstrom, C. (1992), 'The Dirty War: Civilian Experiences of Conflict in Mozambique and Sri Lanka' in K. Rupesinghe (ed.), *Internal Conflict and Governance*, Macmillan, Basingstoke.

Nozick, R. (1974), *Anarchy State and Utopia*, Basic Books, New York.

Nussbaum, M. (1995), *Women, Culture and Development – A Study of Human Capabilities*, Clarendon Press, Oxford.
Nussbaum, M. (1998), 'In Defence of Universal Values', lecture, Seeley Lectures, Cambridge University, March.
Nussbaum, M. and Sen, A. (1993), *The Quality of Life*, Clarendon Press, Oxford.
Ostwald M. (tr. and ed.) (1986), *Nicomachean Ethics*, Macmillan, London.
O'Donnell, G. and Schmitter, P. (1995), 'Transitions from Authoritarian Rule: Tentative Conclusions about Uncertain Democracies' in N. Kritz (ed.), *Transitional Justice*, Vols. 1, 2 and 3, US Institute of Peace, Washington, DC.
O'Neill, O. (1986), *Faces of Hunger: An Essay on Poverty, Justice and Development*, Allen and Unwin, London.
O'Neill, O. (1991), 'Transnational Justice' in D. Held (ed.), *Political Theory Today*, Polity Press, Cambridge.
Orentlicher, D. (1995), 'Settling Accounts: The Duty to Prosecute Human Rights Violations of a Prior Regime' in N. Kritz (ed.), *Transitional Justice*, Vols. 1, 2 and 3, US Institute of Peace, Washington, DC.
Overseas Development Council (1996), 'Making Peace Work: Lessons for the International Development Community', Conference Report, Washington, DC, 9 May.
Plunkett, M. (1998), 'Reestablishing Law and Order in Peace-Maintenance', *Global Governance*, 4, 1, pp. 61–80.
Porter, J. (ed.) (19), *Classics in Political Philosophy*, Prentice Hall, London.
Ramsbotham, O. (1997), 'Clausewitz in Reverse: The End of a Ten Year Experiment? Reflections on the UN's Post-Settlement Peacebuilding "Standard Operating Procedure", 1988–1998', paper presented at the Annual Conference of the British International Studies Association, Leeds, 17 December; to be published in Ramsbotham, O. and Woodhouse, T. (eds) (1999), *Conflict Resolution*, Frank Cass, Ilford.
Rawls, J. (1971/73), *A Theory of Justice*, Oxford University Press, Oxford.
Rawls, J. (1996), *Political Liberalism*, second edn, Columbia University Press, New York.
Raz, J. (1979), *The Authority of Law: Essays on Law and Morality*, Clarendon Press, Oxford.
Roht-Arriaza, N. (ed.) (1995), *Impunity and Human Rights in International Law and Practice*, Oxford University Press, Oxford.
Sadurski, W. (1985), *Giving Desert its Due: Social Justice and Legal Theory*, Reidel Publishing Company, Lancaster.
Sandel, M. (1987), 'The Political Theory of the Procedural Republic' in A. Hutchinson and P. Monahan (eds), *The Rule of Law: Ideal or Ideology*?, Carswell, Toronto.
Sen, A. (1992), *Inequality Reexamined*, Clarendon Press, Oxford.
Sen, A. and Williams, B. (eds) (1982), *Utilitarianism and Beyond*, Cambridge University Press, Cambridge.
Smith, D. (1997), *The State of War and Peace Atlas*, Penguin, London.

Taylor, C. (1986), 'The Nature and Scope of Distributive Justice' in F. Lucash (ed.), *Justice and Equality, Here and Now*, Cornell University Press, Cornell.

Tunick, M. (1992), *Punishment: Theory and Practice*, University of California Press, Oxford.

United Nations (1988), *Human Rights: A compilation of International Instruments*, United Nations, New York.

United Nations (1997), *Volume II, Regional Instruments*, United Nations, Geneva.

UN High Commissioner for Refugees and International Peace Academy (1996), 'Healing the Wounds: Refugees, Reconstruction and Reconciliation', Conference Report, Princeton University, 30 June–1 July.

Van Boven, T. (1993), 'Study Concerning the Right to Restitution, Compensation and Rehabilitation for Victims of Gross Violations of Human Rights and Fundamental Freedoms', Final Report, UN Doc, no. E/CN.4/Sub.2/1993/8, July, reproduced in N. Kritz (ed.), *Transitional Justice*, Vols 1, 2 and 3, US Institute of Peace, Washington, DC.

Van Boven, T. et al. (1995), 'Seminar on the Right to Restitution, Compensation and Rehabilitation for Victims of Gross Violations of Human Rights and Fundamental Freedoms: Summary and Conclusions.' in N. Kritz (ed.), *Transitional Justice*, Vols 1, 2 and 3, US Institute of Peace, Washington, DC.

Walker, G. de Q. (1988), *The Rule of Law: Foundation of Constitutional Democracy*, Melbourne University Press, Carlton, Victoria.

Wallensteen, P. and Sollenberg, M. (1996, 'The End of International War? Armed Conflict 1989-95', *Journal of Peace Research*, 33, 3, pp. 353–70.

Walzer, M. (1983), *Spheres of Justice: A Defence of Pluralism and Equality*, Blackwell, Oxford.

Willett, S. (1998), 'Globalisation, International Financial Institutions and Political Instability', presented to the panel on Post-Conflict Regeneration at the Third Pan-European International Relations Conference and Joint Meeting with the International Studies Association, Vienna 16–19 September.

Woodman, G. (1996), 'Legal Pluralism and the Search for Justice', *Journal of African Law*, 40, 2, pp. 152–67.

World Bank (1996), *Social Indicators of Development, 1996*, World Bank, Washington, DC.

World Bank (1997), *World Indicators of Development 1997*, World Bank, Washington, DC.

Wright, M. (1996), *Justice for Victims and Offenders: A Restorative Response to Crime*, Waterside Press, Winchester.

Zalaquett, J. (1995), 'Balancing Ethical Imperatives and Political Constraints: the Dilemma of New Democracies Confronting Past Human Rights Violations' in N. Kritz (ed.), *Transitional Justice*, Vols. 1, 2 and 3, US Institute of Peace, Washington, DC.

List of Contributors

Cecilia Albin is Lecturer in Politics at the University of Reading. Her research interests and publications are in the areas of international negotiation, conflict resolution, the Middle East, and post-Cold War security issues. She is the editor of *Negotiation and Global Security: New Approaches to Contemporary Issues*, and is currently writing a book on the role of justice and fairness in international bargaining.

Brian Barry is Arnold A. Saltzman Professor in the Departments of Philosophy and Political Science at Columbia University, New York. Until September, 1998, he was Professor of Political Science at the London School of Economics. He is the author of a number of books including *Theories of Justice* (1989) and *Justice as Impartiality* (1995). *Culture and Equality: an Egalitarian Critique of Multiculturalism* will be published in 2000.

Chris Brown is Professor of International Relations at the London School of Economics. He is the author of several books and numerous articles on international political theory. In 1977 and 1998 he was Chair of the British International Studies Association and is currently Honorary President of BISA.

Simon Caney is Lecturer in the Department of Politics, University of Newcastle. He has published in philosophy and politics journals on contemporary liberal political philosophy, human rights, international justice and nationality. He is currently completing a work on global political theory. He is the co-editor (with Peter Jones and David George) of *National Rights, International Obligations* (Westview, 1996).

Tony Coates is Lecturer in Politics at the University of Reading. His main teaching and research interests are in the fields of political theory and international ethics. He is the author of *The Ethics of War* (Manchester 1997).

Avner de-Shalit is Senior Lecturer at the Hebrew University of Jerusalem and an Associate Fellow at the Oxford Centre for Environment, Ethics and

Society, Mansfield College, Oxford. He is the author of *Why Posterity Matters* (Routledge, 1990) and *The Environment: Between Theory and Practice* (Oxford University Press, forthcoming). He is co-editor of *Communitarianism and Individualism* and *Liberalism and its Practice.*

Andreas Føllesdal is Senior Researcher at ARENA – a research programme on the Europeanization of the nation state, under the auspices of the Research Council of Norway – and Professor of Philosophy at the University of Oslo. His publications are in the fields of European political theory and applied and social ethics. Recent publications include 'Democracy, Legitimacy and Majority Rule in the EU', 'Subsidiarity', 'Sustainable Development, State Sovereignty and International Justice', 'Third Country Nationals as Euro-citizens – the Case Defended', 'Minority Rights: a Liberal Contractualist Case', *Restructuring the Welfare State* and *Democracy and European Union.*

Michael Freeman teaches Political Theory in the Department of Government at the University, where he is also Deputy Director of the Human Rights Centre. He has published numerous articles on human rights, minority rights, ethnic conflict and nationalism. He is currently writing a book on human rights.

Barry Holden is Senior Lecturer in Politics at the University of Reading. He teaches mainly in the field of political philosophy and international ethics, and has research interests in democratic theory and global environmental problems. He is the author of *The Nature of Democracy* and *Understanding Liberal Democracy* and the editor of – and a contributor to – *The Ethical Dimensions of Global Change.*

Peter Jones is Professor of Political Philosophy at the University of Newcastle. He has written on a variety of subjects in contemporary political philosophy, including rights, toleration, democracy, the nature of liberalism and welfare policy. His recent work has focused on strategies for dealing with diversities of belief and culture.

Rama Mani served as the Senior External Relations Officer to the Commission on Global Governance in Geneva from 1992 to 1995. She has also worked for non-governmental and private organizations in India, Algeria and France. She is about to complete a doctoral thesis on peacemaking at the University of Cambridge.

Matt Matravers is Lecturer in the Department of Politics at the University of York. He recently edited *Punishment and Political Theory* (Hart Publishing, 1999). He is the author of a number of papers on justice and punishment and, with Brian Barry, of the entries on Justice and International Justice in the *Encyclopedia of Philosophy* (Routledge, 1999). He is currently completing a book, *Justice and Punishment*, to be published by Oxford University Press in 2000).

Lukas H. Meyer teaches Political Theory and Political Philosophy at the University of Bremen, where he is *Wissenschaftlicher Assistent* at the Institute of Intercultural and International Studies. He has published articles on public international law and intergenerational justice. His current research centres on historical justice.

For Product Safety Concerns and Information please contact our EU representative GPSR@taylorandfrancis.com Taylor & Francis Verlag GmbH, Kaufingerstraße 24, 80331 München, Germany

Batch number: 10726013

Printed by Printforce, the Netherlands